TECHNOLOGY AND NAVAL COMBAT IN THE TWENTIETH CENTURY AND BEYOND

CASS SERIES: NAVAL POLICY AND HISTORY
ISSN 1366-9478

Series Editor: Geoffrey Till

This series consists primarily of original manuscripts by research scholars in the general area of naval policy and history, without national or chronological limitations. It will from time to time also include collections of important articles as well as reprints of classic works.

TECHNOLOGY AND NAVAL COMBAT

IN THE TWENTIETH CENTURY AND BEYOND

Edited by

PHILLIPS PAYSON O'BRIEN

University of Glasgow

FRANK CASS
LONDON • PORTLAND, OR

First published in 2001 in Great Britain by
FRANK CASS PUBLISHERS
Crown House, 47 Chase Side
London, N14 5BP

and in the United States of America by
FRANK CASS PUBLISHERS
c/o ISBS, 5824 N.E. Hassalo Street
Portland, Oregon, 97213-3644

Website: www.frankcass.com

British Library Cataloguing in Publication Data

Technology and naval combat in the twentieth century and
  beyond. – (Cass series. Naval policy and history; 13)
  1. Naval art and science – Technological innovataions –
  History – 20th century
  I. O'Brien, Phillips Payson, 1963–
  359'.00904

ISBN 0-7146-5125-7 (cloth)
ISSN 1366-9478

Library of Congress Cataloging-in-Publication Data

Technology and naval combat in the twentieth century and beyond / edited
by Phillips O'Brien
    p. cm. – (Cass series – naval policy and history; 13)
    Includes bibliographical references and index.
    ISBN 0-7146-5125-7 (cloth)
    1. Naval art and science–Technological innovations–History–20th
century. 2. Naval art and science–Technological
innovations–History–21st century. I. O'Brien, Phillips Payson,
1963–. II. Series.
    V53.T43 2001
    359'.00904 – dc21

                                                          00-069447

Typeset in 10.25/12 Sabon by Cambridge Photosetting Services
Printed in Great Britain by
MPG Books Ltd, Victoria Square, Bodmin, Cornwall

Contents

Introduction

Phillips Payson O'Brien

The twentieth century was the most technologically dynamic period in naval history, but this will come as no surprise to anyone with even a passing interest in seapower. At the beginning of the century the most technologically advanced fleets in the world were dominated by coal-burning, steel-sided capital ships. The Royal Navy's battleship *Albemarle*, laid down in January 1900, displaced about 14,000 tons, was armed with four 12-inch and 12 6-inch guns, and could reach a maximum speed of around 20 knots per hour. Naval combat between similar vessels would occur at a distance of thousands of metres. At the end of the century the most powerful surface ships of the most technologically advanced fleet, the US *Nimitz*-class carriers, were so powerful that, had a crew member of the *Albemarle* ever come across one, he would have considered it magical. The latest generation of *Nimitz* carriers displace almost 100,000 tons, are nuclear powered and nuclear armed, and carry a complement of more than 80 aircraft capable of engaging an enemy hundreds of miles away.

In many ways, therefore, the history of naval power in the twentieth century was a history of the control and application of naval technology. The various major powers that have striven either to maintain their relative position in world seapower, or to supplant their more established rivals, have usually seen technological superiority as the key to their endeavours. The different chapters in this volume, by some of the most respected and experienced naval historians writing today, tell of this struggle.

This technological race was not, however, a contest of equals. The major naval powers approached their tasks from different perspectives and with very different strengths and weaknesses. Some, such as the Italian Navy described in the chapter by Brian Sullivan and the Japanese Navy, described by David Evans and Mark Peattie, were trying to compensate for their massive, relative economic weakness through technological superiority. In the case of the Italian Navy before the First World War, we see the superb ship designer Benedetto Brin designing some of the most innovative and thought-provoking vessels of the period. In many ways he foretold the arrival of Admiral John (Jacky) Fisher's battlecruiser concept through his plans for lightly armoured, heavily armed, fast capital ships. Yet, the gap in relative economic strength was simply too large for the Italians to surmount, no matter how sophisticated their warship plans turned out to be. The picture is ultimately one of frustration, with the Italian Navy, even under the control of Mussolini and the Fascists, severely handicapped in its attempts to create a truly balanced naval force.

The picture given of the Japanese Navy by Evans and Peattie is, on the surface, far more successful. Knowing that it would be practically impossible for a country with Japan's economy to compete numerically with the greatest naval powers, such as Britain before the First World War and the United States before the Second, the Japanese Navy opted deliberately for a policy of stressing quality over quantity. It is in many ways the story of significant success. In the 1880s the Japanese Navy was a motley collection of foreign-built vessels. During the ensuing years the Japanese established a home-grown capacity to build technologically up-to-date warships. The Japanese Navy 'came of age' in its steady growth towards its famous '8–8' fleet (eight battleships and eight battlecruisers). The naval arms control process that governed major power strength between the Washington Conference of 1921–22, and the second London Naval Conference of 1935–36, provided a temporary hiccup to Japanese naval growth. The Imperial Japanese Navy's desire to have a fleet 70 per cent as strong as Britain or America was shelved, for capital ships, by the famous 5–5–3 ratio. Still, the Japanese pressed on with their plans to match British and, primarily, US strength by possessing qualitatively superior vessels. When the arms control process ended, this desire reached its apotheosis with the construction of the *Yamato* and *Musashi*, the two largest and most heavily armed battleships ever built.

Yet, while the Japanese experience seems vastly different from the Italian experience, its ultimate result was rather similar. Neither nation was able to compensate for the fact that their economies were not a match for powers of the first rank. Even the excellent and technologically advanced Japanese fleet was brutally crushed by US economic power during the Second World War. Without at least a competitive economic base, it seems, a nation cannot compete in a prolonged war involving naval technology.

The Japanese and Italian experiences, however, were extreme. Their overall economic weakness was quite marked, whereas other powers who attempted to challenge the naval status quo at different times in the twentieth century – France, the USSR and Germany – were relatively stronger. The French case differed the least. In Paul Halpern's chapter we have a significant economic power, though one obviously weaker than its main counterparts, trying to build a competitive fleet while at the same time controlling costs. This was one of the main supports behind the *Jeune École*, the famous and seemingly misguided French naval movement that stressed large numbers of torpedo boats over more expensive capital ships. It remains a salient lesson to those eager to back any new technological development. Years of experimentation produced a fleet incapable of fulfilling a number of the nation's basic naval needs. It was only after returning to the production of large-scale traditional capital ships, with some excellent design features, that the French Navy began to reassert itself in European terms.

The French, however, remained in an unenviable position. Economically stronger than the Italians, they were still considerably outpaced in industrial terms by the leading European economic powers: Britain and Germany. It was only when Germany challenged Britain that a situation existed whereby a power of equal if not superior industrial and technological resources challenged the dominant seapower of its time. The German challenge to the supremacy of the Royal Navy, particularly before the First World War but also later, under the leadership of Adolf Hitler, is perhaps the best-known example of an arms race at sea.

Michael Epkenhans, examining the years leading up to the First World War, and Werner Rahn, focusing on the interwar years, provide a fascinating picture of a nation with enviable economic strengths providing a somewhat cautious and conservative challenge to the status quo. Before the First World War, Germany had passed Britain in industrial production and had become a world leader in such technologically vital areas as electrification and machine-tool construction. However, under the direction of the famous Admiral Tirpitz, egged on spasmodically by the equally well-known Kaiser Wilhelm II, the Germans opted for a methodical challenge to British supremacy. Tirpitz's obsessive preparations for the one great capital ship battle that he assumed would determine the next major war at sea, led to the creation of the world's second strongest dreadnought battle fleet. At the same time, however, the German Navy seemed inculcated by a certain technological conservatism. Even after some very promising beginnings in naval air and, crucially, submarine development, the German Navy clung, or perhaps was forced to cling, to Tirpitz's notion of a decisive capital ship duel at sea.

The interwar years provide an interesting contrast. Under the strictures of the Versailles Treaty, the German Navy was strictly limited, both in terms of overall numbers and in terms of ship size. In particular, the size limitation of any individual vessel to 10,000 tons forced the German Navy to abandon the doctrines of Tirpitz and adopt more radical trade-warfare thinking which reached a point of technological sophistication with the construction of the famous 'pocket' battleships. These relatively small vessels could never have confronted enemy capital ships in open combat, but they were in many ways considerably superior, especially in cruising radius and striking power, to all other 10,000-ton vessels then built or being built. Yet, when finally freed from the restrictions imposed by

Versailles, the German Navy reverted to its traditional pre-First World War pattern of battleship construction. Even after the experiences of the First World War, when German submarines were by far the most effective naval weapon against Great Britain, the Germans opted for the large capital ship construction programme known as Plan Z. Once again, the Germans had opted for a slow, drawn-out challenge to Britain's supremacy in European waters, a challenge that had no time to develop because of Hitler's decision to invade Poland.

During the Cold War the next great challenger for naval supremacy arrived – the USSR. After the collapse of communism in Europe with the concurrent exposure of the Soviet Union's economic inefficiencies, it has become somewhat difficult to remember just how serious the USSR's naval challenge was viewed at the time. Yet, as Evan Mawdsley shows, in terms of ship construction, the Soviet Navy was remarkably successful in the short period of its prominence. Between 1946 and 1991 almost 400 major surface units and 664 submarines were constructed, while a naval air arm consisting of thousands of units was deployed. In technological terms this fleet was quite advanced, consisting of nuclear-powered vessels, and including such famous weapons programmes as the 'backfire' bomber. Yet, for all these successes the Soviet challenge was to prove about as effective as the Japanese challenge before the Second World War. In many cases the ships built were unnecessary, constructed more to present the image of a USSR able of competing with the United States instead of realistically providing for a Soviet Navy capable of effectively challenging the US fleet.

The collapse of the Soviet Union brings back the earlier point that a naval challenge can only be effective if the challenger's overall economic strength is at least comparable with the power being stalked. It is somewhat ironic that the one thing that all of the naval challengers in the twentieth century had in common was that their efforts failed. Indeed, in the cases of Italy, Japan, France and the USSR the question could rightly be asked whether their efforts were far more counter-productive to their nation's well-being, both in economic and international terms. Only the Germans stood any reasonable chance of supplanting the dominant power of the time, but they opted for such a long-drawn-out process that in two instances their efforts were negated by war before they had any chance of coming to fruition.

This collapse of these naval challenges might seem to imply that the dominant naval powers of the twentieth century, first Great Britain and then the United States, followed more far-sighted and technologically pro-ficient plans than the lesser fleets. The picture of the British fleet during the period of its dominance, given by Nicholas Lambert for the years before 1914 and Jon Sumida for the interwar period, is somewhat uneven. Before the First World War the Royal Navy, led by Admiral Fisher, was fond of technological 'plunging'. Revolutionary designs such as the dreadnought class battleships and battlecruisers were first built by the British, who seemed determined to use all technological advances to maintain their naval supremacy. The interwar picture seems, on the surface, considerably less dynamic. The British Admiralty in these years has often been criticised for being too timid in its defence of supremacy. Yet, as Dr Sumida so aptly reminds us, British naval performance in the Second World War was in many ways considerably more impressive than during the First. Even after the devastating German capture of the Norwegian and French coastlines, with the concurrent loss of all of Britain's effective naval allies, the Royal Navy was able to maintain a significant measure of sea control. A German sea invasion was pre-empted and enough shipping was able to get in and out of the British Isles to keep the nation functioning as a major power until the United States entered the war. During the First World War, with France and Italy as naval allies and the German Navy limited to a small number of bases along a short stretch of coastline, the Royal Navy had proved less resilient.

After the Second World War, when Great Britain quite clearly lost its naval position to America, we have an equally complex picture. Eric Grove shows where those who dwell on Britain's supposed catastrophic decline have gone too far. The Royal Navy, in fact, remained somewhat politically astute, especially under the leadership of Lord Mountbatten. While the Soviet Union was building far larger classes of vessel and even the French were opting for such prominent items as attack carriers, the British Navy remained a highly professional, if smaller, force. Yet now, with the collapse of the USSR and the decision of the British government to build two large strike carriers, the Royal Navy is poised to return to its clear position as second naval power in the world.

While in the twentieth century Britain slid from naval dominance to a position in the second rank, the United States rose dramatically. Only a decade or so before 1900 one would have seen a US fleet barely larger than that of Belgium's. Now the US Navy is dominant in an historically unprecedented fashion. The US fleet is not only stronger than the rest of the world's forces combined, it could probably sink all of those other fleets at relatively little cost to itself. This rise, which is now based on a combination of size and technological superiority, was not always smooth. Before the Second World War the US Navy had to contend with political marginalization and it was only the war itself that finally catapulted the Americans into clear superiority over the Royal Navy.

During the Cold War, as George Baer points out, it was technological superiority that kept the US fleet firmly on course. With the advent of nuclear weaponry and long-range air power, questions arose about the survivability of major naval assets. The major American naval leaders who thrived in these years were the ones who were able to marry their favoured platforms to the dominant technologies, from Rickover's famed nuclear subs to the United States' continuing support for the largest and most powerful carriers afloat. Yet, as Baer points out, technology, combined with a shifting global balance of power, has forced the US Navy to reinvent itself. After the Second World War this process was contentious, whereas, in a somewhat hopeful note, the collapse of Soviet power has been met with a more thoughtful and coordinated response.

What then of the immediate future? For the US Navy, as Norman Friedman points out, success in the future will depend upon a combination of the development of delivery platforms with surveillance technology. Looking back on recent developments, the development of anti-ship missile technology, combined with the ability to track Soviet vessels on the high seas, has significantly changed the threat posed by the US fleet. Non-carrier surface vessels armed with anti-ship missile technology helped diversify a threat that had seemingly been focused in carrier air power, while the ability to track passively Soviet vessels allowed for a better concentration against enemy forces. In the future it is the development of such technologies, presumably including space platforms, that will allow the US Navy to continue in its dominant global role as a power-projection force.

For the Royal Navy, as Geoffrey Till explains, the future is equally complex, but the resources involved are so much smaller that the British might have to rethink some basic assumptions. Should the Royal Navy try to be a smaller, but effective version of the US Navy or should it aim to combine with other European powers in developing a new role? In an extremely interesting shift, however, Till describes how the Royal Navy's view of its role in the outside world has, even after the so-called 'Revolution in Military Affairs', reverted to an almost eighteenth- or nineteenth-century perspective. Instead of preparing for decisive action in home waters, in the manner of an Admiral Fisher, the Royal Navy and leading British politicians are opting for a policy stressing global power projection and 'showing the flag'. The key to this policy shift, needless to say, is the proper allocation of resources. Whether or not the two strike carriers now planned for construction are actually funded will go a long way towards demonstrating whether these plans are serious or not.

This question of funding, as David Andrews points out, will be key beyond the next few decades as well. The New Defence Nexus, brought about by the end of the Cold War, posits that ever-declining defence resources will be combined, over time, with a less clearly defined role for naval forces. The growth of new technologies leaves open the possibility that radical new designs such as trimarans, will take the place of traditional mono-hulls. Yet, all such changes will be partly dependent on their concurrent role within the domestic economy. For instance, naval vessel configuration might very well march hand-in-hand with merchant vessel technology.

This reliance is obviously crucial. If the different chapters in this book have but one combined lesson, it is that navies are ultimately both an excellent indicator and a creation of a nation's overall economic and technological strength. The sheer technological complexity of warships means that they cannot be 'faked'. Nations trying to leap beyond their economic capacities in the twentieth century – Italy, France, Japan and the USSR among them – always failed. Indeed, one of the striking facts of the naval balance in the twentieth century was how little things changed. In 1907 the Royal Navy was dominant, with the US fleet just moving into second position. Now the US navy is dominant, with the British about to move into second position. Any challenge to this balance, be it from the Chinese or some other power, will have to walk hand-in-hand with that nation's overall technological development.

PART I

PREPARING FOR THE FIRST WORLD WAR

1

Italian Warship Construction and Maritime Strategy, 1873–1915

Brian R. Sullivan

In the half-century after national unification, Italian warship designs and naval theories reflected great ingenuity but lack of capital and raw materials, geography and technological backwardness constrained the Royal Italian Navy (Regia Marina). None the less, in the period *c*. 1862–89, Italian sea-power theorists developed many concepts later attributed to Alfred Thayer Mahan. They argued that national security, prosperity and influence depended on seapower. After the Suez Canal opened, greatly increasing Mediterranean sea traffic, this seemed obvious to educated Italians.

The theorists drew their concepts from Italian experience for application to national maritime strategy. Domenico Bonamico, in particular, argued that enclosed seas like the Mediterranean imposed different conditions on navies operating therein than did oceans. If Italy fought France or Britain, even a victory that gained Italy control of the Mediterranean still would not necessarily grant it access to the oceans beyond. This reality – not French possession of Corsica and British control of Malta, as Mahan argued – meant that the benefits the American insisted would accrue to nations conducting successful naval offensives could not be acquired in Italy's case.[1]

The Italian peninsula had a vulnerable 3,000-mile coastline. The country's frontiers joined those of France and Austria-Hungary, both with powerful armies. Unlike Britain, a navy alone could not defend Italy. The Alps did provide significant protection against invasion, but the Italians still needed a large army to defend the Po Valley, as well as a powerful fleet to protect their shores. For the 'least of the great powers', geography challenged its army but imposed a defensive strategy on its navy.[2] Italian theorists stressed capital-ship primacy. Before *Jeune École* advocates advanced the idea in the 1880s of fleets based on torpedo boats and cruisers, such notions circulated in the Regia Marina. But Italian naval leaders rejected arguments that technology was making light craft superior to battleships. Proponents of smaller ships continued to press their case. Still, battleship enthusiasts dominated the navy.[3]

Among these was Admiral Simone de Saint Bon, navy minister from 1873 to 1876. Study of the American Civil War had convinced Saint Bon that basic naval power lay not in the number of a country's battleships but in the capacity of its shipyards and steel mills. Recognizing the naval architect Benedetto Brin as both a genius and a man of similar views, the admiral appointed him as inspector general of naval engineering, the Regia Marina's chief designer. Both knew their service faced restricted funding for the foreseeable future. The navy had fallen into disrepute following its humiliating defeat by the smaller Austrian fleet off the Dalmatian island of Lissa in July 1866. In 1860–64, the Regia Marina had acquired 14 steam-powered ironclads – 11 being US, British or French-built. All had foreign armor, engines and cannon since the Italians could not produce such equipment. After Lissa, these purchases seemed wasted. The Italian Navy remained larger than the Austrian, however, providing security in the Adriatic. In contrast, the wider Mediterranean had become more threatening for Italy. French resentment over Italian failure to aid its former ally in the Franco-Prussian War required Saint Bon and Brin to plan for war with the French Navy, far superior in size and technology to the Regia Marina.[4]

The two sought solutions in innovation, stressing quality over quantity. Brin designed battleships with little armor or secondary armament but with high speed and heavy guns. The turret-mounted guns of Brin's battleships could outrange and overpower smaller, faster opponents; the Italian ships' speed would allow them to outrun any superior hostile squadrons or close rapidly on single ships. Italian commanders could use speed, or weight and range of fire, as circumstances suggested. Brin had anticipated by three decades Fisher's battlecruiser concept.[5]

Acquiring the infrastructure to transform Brin's designs into operational warships was problematic. Since 1861, the Italians had imported armor plate, mainly from the United States. The Regia Marina purchased low-quality US materials to afford the amount necessary. Even so, Italian warships cost more than foreign-built vessels. Hoping for better, Saint Bon applied his liberal economics, opening the armor contract for *Duilio* and *Dandolo* to international competition. The French firm, Schneider, won, becoming armor supplier to the Regia Marina in 1876. Brin succeeded Saint Bon as minister that March. He would hold the post five times until 1898, over 11 years in total. Brin would realize his mentor's concepts; but with generous budgets from 1883, he chose protectionism over liberalism.

Rivalry with Italy over Tunisia provoked French occupation in 1881. The invasion caused deep resentment in Rome and led directly to Italy's Triple Alliance with Germany and Austria-Hungary in 1882. The treaty offered no protection in the Mediterranean – such guarantees were included in the second treaty of 1887 – but it eased Italian fears of war with the Dual Monarchy. The Italians also obtained a declaration that the treaty was not directed against Britain. Royal Navy supremacy in the Mediterranean, British domination of the Strait of Gibraltar and the dependence of the Italian economy on maritime trade made the idea of war against the United Kingdom near-suicidal in Italian minds. British occupation of Egypt in the summer of 1882 and, with it, control of the Suez Canal, made the necessity for friendly relations with Britain even more essential to the Italians. But despite the Triple Alliance and good relations between Rome and London, the large French Army and Navy, as well as superior French technology, presented continued challenges to the Italians.[6]

Regia Marina could rely no longer on imported French armor. After Brin became minister for the second time in March 1884, he convinced parliament to establish a state-supported steelworks at Terni in the hills of Umbria. Terni adopted the Schneider system under license. Schneider was persuaded to sell the details of its armor making and the Terni complex made profitable by each receiving advances on government orders at guaranteed high prices. Terni commenced production in 1886. But its monopoly over Italian steel making allowed it to sell products of uneven quality, much to the distress of the naval shipyards. Furthermore, the Italians remained dependent on the French for nickel ore, essential for the Schneider armor-making process; at the time, French New Caledonia provided the only known source.

Italy possessed very little coal. But the island of Elba off the Tuscan coast contained some iron deposits. It made economic sense to ship ore from Elba to Livorno or Civitavecchia and from there by rail to Terni. But the vulnerability of such shipping routes to attack from French ships based at Ajaccio made such ore deliveries impractical. Instead, the Terni works imported the ingredients for steel making from Britain and Germany, while the products of Elba's mines were shipped abroad.

Italian warship construction prices were further increased by a lack of skilled workers. This led to cost inefficiencies and greatly slowed the pace of building. The need to purchase guns and engines from Britain raised other expenses, only partially alleviated after Brin built heavily subsidized but low-capacity arsenals and factories at La Spezia, Castellamare di Stabia, Naples, Taranto, and Venice. In 1884, Brin also persuaded Armstrong, the British naval gun manufacturer, to set up a production center at Pozzuoli, just west of Naples. Operations began in 1889. The government granted Armstrong, like Schneider, a long-term contract granting orders sufficient to repay the cost of investment, as well as providing very generous profit margins. Thus, the Italian Navy secured two modern production facilities within national borders. But the Italians paid heavily to sustain the system. Even so, the building of Italian warships still proceeded far more slowly than in richer, more technologically advanced countries. When Brin's vessels finally were combat ready, they remained fine warships, but they no longer represented the innovative marvels they had when first conceived.

Foreign navies took advantage of their intelligence about Brin's designs, and their superior resources and speed of construction allowed them to produce equivalent or better battleships by the time the Italian vessels entered service.[7]

Despite his stress on battleships, Brin had studied the growing potential of the torpedo boat. After deciding the light craft did present a danger to his capital ships, in 1883 Brin introduced protection against torpedoes and mines by an extensive system of water-tight compartments on *Re Umberto* class battleships. Finally convinced of their value, the navy minister ordered 93 torpedo craft during 1886–95, built under license from designs by the Schichau firm of Elbing. To obtain a source for their armaments, he persuaded the German torpedo manufacturer Schwarzkopf to open a factory at Venice in 1887. Brin also designed a torpedo boat destroyer to combat French *torpilleurs*. But the growing cost of Italian battleship construction, combined with persistent national poverty and Regia Marina concentration on acquiring capital ships, left it with ever fewer light craft as the decades passed.[8]

Brin dominated the Regia Marina for over 20 years and made engineering the great strength of his service, a tradition which endures. But he could not overcome single-handedly the technical and financial weaknesses plaguing the Italian Navy. The policies of Umberto I (1878–1900) and Prime Minister Francesco Crispi (1887–91, 1893–96) added to Brin's difficulties. Despite a depressed economy from the mid-1870s to mid-1890s, the king approved Crispi's lavish spending on the army and railways, while pursuing confrontation with France and aggressive colonialism in East Africa. Funding for the navy rose, too. But national poverty still placed a limit on the size of the fleet. Even when his budgets were at their highest in the 1880s, Brin considered a clash with the French Navy a near-hopeless proposition for the Regia Marina.

Within a decade, the imbalance between ends and means led the Italians to undertake an ill-advised invasion of Ethiopia and suffer humiliating defeat at Adowa in March 1896. The resulting social and political unrest culminated in Umberto I's assassination in June 1900. Italian naval spending dropped from its 1889 apogee to a level less than two-thirds as high by 1895. Only in 1899 did naval budgets rise again, owing to an economy that had begun unprecedented growth in 1896. But the Italian Navy had fallen from third place in the world in 1890 to seventh by 1900 and Brin's early battleships had become obsolete due to the advent of quick-firing naval guns.[9]

These developments and Brin's ideas made a lasting impression on Italian naval thinking. Italian warships would be designed for speed. Italians expected their navy would remain inferior in numbers to likely opponents, who from 1870 to 1915 generally were the French. Poverty and slow construction meant that losses could not be replaced quickly. Swift warships, however, would allow Italian commanders to seek or flee action as they saw fit, preserving precious assets for decisive actions. The navy would concentrate funds on battleship construction. Even if the navy possessed few capital ships, they could be concentrated. The vulnerability of Italy's coastline made its protection the paramount task of the Regia Marina. Thus, the navy adopted a defensive strategy even if it anticipated opportunities for offensive operations.

Italian geography forced the Regia Marina and the naval industries to build most bases, shipyards, arsenals, and ports on the west coast. If such facilities had been located in the Adriatic, they would have enjoyed safety from the French Navy. However, the Adriatic coast possessed few good harbors, especially compared with those on the west coast with their added advantage of easier access to Atlantic trade routes. The Ligurian and Tyrrhenian ports, their communications to the Po Valley and the Alpine rail lines, and the workforces they employed had been built up long before the deterioration in Italian–French relations. It would have been economically impossible to shift such facilities to the east coast, let alone expand ports there to contain them.[10]

These factors suggested that the French would divide their fleet to blockade Italy's widely separated ports and naval bases. Also, many Italian rail lines ran along narrow coastal plains, creating attractive naval gunfire targets. The scattered opportunities for French naval attack might encourage the formation of separate bombardment squadrons. Concentrated Italian forces could smash parts of a dispersed French Navy. In fact, the French did plan to attack the Ligurian coast, particularly where blocking tunnels and smashing bridges would stop troop movement to the French frontier. Other possible operations included shelling a large port by the combined French battle fleet to force the inferior Regia Marina to steam forth, in response, to its destruction, and an amphibious landing on Elba to provoke the same reaction or to seize the iron mines.[11]

While the Italians did not know the details of the French Navy's plans, strategic logic suggested French intentions. Emphasis on battleship construction seemed wise. By 1900, the acceptance of Mahan's ideas in Italy also encouraged capital ship enthusiasts. One was Umberto I's successor, Vittorio Emanuele III. Unlike his predecessors, the new king had studied naval matters and grown convinced of the primacy of battleships. Royal support and strong economic growth helped to double naval budgets from 1900 to 1910. Still, from the 1890s to 1914, French naval spending was twice that of the Italians. In 1901, the French parliament approved a program that included 28 battleships. But only in 1910 did the French completely abandon *Jeune École* concepts to construct a navy based on dreadnoughts.[12]

Meanwhile, Vittorio Emanuele Cuniberti, whose design and engineering genius rivaled Brin's, had entered naval service. In 1893, Cuniberti had gained attention by advancing arguments in favor of oil over coal as a preferable fuel for warships. As a result, the Italian Navy launched the armored cruisers *Vettor Pisani* and *Carlo Alberto* with oil- and coal-fired engines in 1895–96, placing itself in the vanguard of such developments. But lack of a secure source of petroleum for Italy restrained the naval leadership from approving the construction of battleships driven by naphtha.[13]

Cuniberti enjoyed more success with his 1899 battleship projects. Vittorio Emanuele III fervently approved of them, the first capital ships laid down in his reign. Cuniberti designed the *Vittorio Emanuele* class to engage French armored cruisers. The ships carried only 2 305 mm but 12 203 mm guns, a departure from Brin's emphasis on a monocaliber main armament. But the design included remarkably strong armor while retaining the Brin stress on speed: the *Vittorio Emanuele* class could make 21–22 knots. These warships could outrun any existing battleship and anticipated both the battlecruiser and the post-war German 'pocket battleship' in concept. Cuniberti designed even more innovative warships during 1899–1902. His first proposal was an armored cruiser of 8,000 tons mounting 12 203 mm guns, protected by a 6–8-inch armored belt and capable of 22 knots.[14] Cuniberti next presented a more extraordinary design: an 'invincible' all-big-gun battleship of unprecedented size, fire power, protection and speed: an extraordinary 24 knots.

The navy considered these ideas carefully. But they rejected them because of cost and their doubts about realizing such revolutionary designs. The speeds Cuniberti projected seemed impossible. Furthermore, Italian gun-laying and aiming devices did not allow accurate long-range fire, negating the main advantage of an all-big-gun design. Aware of those shortcomings, Cuniberti had argued that his projected warships would use their heavy main armament to devastate opponents at short range, while relying on thick armor to survive action at several thousand yards' distance. However, such tactics would make such Italian ships highly vulnerable to torpedo attacks launched from an opposing fleet at such close quarters.[15]

Cuniberti did gain permission to publish his ideas abroad. His article 'An Ideal Warship for the British Navy', appeared in Jane's *Fighting Ships* for 1903. The proposal helped solidify Fisher's ideas for *Dreadnought* and *Invincible*. Cuniberti's place in the Brin tradition became obvious with his 1907–08 design for Italy's first dreadnought, *Dante Alighieri*. The ship emphasized firepower with 12 305 mm guns, was powered by oil and coal combined, made 24 knots but had little armor.[16]

The contradictory pattern of innovative Italian design yet deficient construction continued into the new century. By 1900, Italian shipyards had increased work speed. But Terni produced high-quality steel only at high cost and in small quantities, delaying the mounting of turrets, armor, and guns. The Regia Marina had used foreign sources for some of these items, at added cost in time and money. Italian naval arsenals displayed similar weaknesses. In 1906, after a parliamentary inquiry, reforms were instituted. However, the results of protectionism, as well as shipbuilding industry corruption, continued to damage Italian warship quality. *Vittorio Emanuele* only entered service in August 1908, seven years after it had been laid down. By then, advances in ordnance had rendered its armament inadequate. *Dante*'s construction began in June 1909, over a year before the Austro-Hungarians laid the keel of their first dreadnought. But *Dante* was not ready until January 1913, three months after the Austro-Hungarian *Viribus Unitis*. Similar delays beset completion of Italy's next dreadnoughts, three of the *Giulio Cesare* class.[17]

The Regia Marina could expand due to the post-1896 industrial boom and the resulting rise in revenues. Increased demand for steel and continued unhappiness with the quality of Terni's products encouraged Armstrong to build a steel mill, dedicated to armaments, at Pozzuoli. It opened in April 1902 and used ore from Elba, indicating government confidence in sustained good relations with France and the navy's ability to protect coastal shipping. In 1906, a steel works commenced production at Piombino, directly across from Elba on the mainland. In 1910, Terni inaugurated a mill to produce naval equipment at Bagnoli near Pozzuoli. Meanwhile, several dozen steel mills had opened elsewhere, although largely for non-naval production. Soaring production figures reflected the proliferation of steel works.[18]

Acquiring heavy ordnance and high-quality armor for the dreadnoughts proved harder than producing steel to build them. From 1909 to 1916, the Italians completed six dreadnoughts of 147,000 tons total displacement. Designed armament required 77 12-inch (305 mm) guns. Producing such a number of heavy guns in such a short time lay beyond the capacity of Italian armaments firms. So did production of the latest types of armor plate. In late 1903, the Ansaldo shipbuilding company formed a consortium with Armstrong to construct cannon of superior quality to previous Italian manufacture. Two years later, encouraged by the naval ministry in order to increase naval gun production and to lessen dependence on the Pozzuoli works, Terni reached a similar agreement with another British arms manufacturer, Vickers. Their gun factory was erected at La Spezia. In early 1910, after the French government had dropped its previous objections, Ansaldo formed a second gun-building consortium with Schneider. Meanwhile, in early 1907, Ansaldo recalled the procurement practices of the 1860s by signing a contract with Bethlehem Steel for the provision of US-made armor plate for Italy's projected dreadnoughts. Continued reliance on British and French technology, as well as on the import of US armor which would have to pass through waters dominated by the Royal Navy and French Navy, had obvious foreign policy implications. None the less, the Italians had greatly reduced the direct import of naval armaments.[19]

In fact, major realignments of Italian foreign policy had taken place during the same ten years. For two decades after the formation of the Triple Alliance, the Regia Marina planning had focused on conflict with the French. But Italian weakness after the 1896 debacle prompted them to resolve their differences with France. French–British hostility after the Fashoda Crisis in the summer of 1898 encouraged Paris to restore good relations with Rome. The balance in a conflict pitting the French Navy against the Royal Navy and the Regia Marina hardly favored the former. French–Italian negotiations led to a 1902 understanding that each would remain neutral should the other be forced into war. Two years later, however, the growing German menace persuaded the French and British to form their *Entente Cordiale*. The possibility that France and Britain might join in a war against their German ally created great anxiety for Italy's government and navy. The Royal Navy set a standard the Regia Marina leadership could only dream of emulating. War between Italy and Britain was unthinkable for Italian admirals.[20]

But the possibility of war with the Dual Monarchy had returned to vex Italian naval planners. The assassination of Umberto I in 1900 and his succession by the far more liberal Vittorio Emanuele III signaled a shift of Italian sentiment away from the authoritarian Central European empires. The simultaneous surge in economic and military power strengthened Italian self-confidence and revived Italian nationalism. Commercial and political rivalry in the Balkans, followed by friction over the status of the Italian-speakers in the Habsburg Monarchy, reawoke Italian–Austrian hostility. Sponsored by Archduke Franz Ferdinand, the Hapsburg navy began a major expansion program in 1904. Four years later, Austria-Hungary annexed Bosnia but refused Italy compensation due under the Triple Alliance treaty. Germany backed Austria-Hungary. In May 1909, Vittorio Emanuele III told the British ambassador he believed the chances were growing for war between Britain and Germany, and between Italy and Austria-Hungary. The king insisted Austro-Hungarian naval leaders were preparing to fight Italy. His navy had to remain supreme in the Adriatic.[21]

Still, the king cringed at the high cost of his new dreadnoughts: triple that of *Duilio* and *Doria* 30 years before. But when in 1910 the Austro-Hungarians began their own dreadnoughts, the ironic result was to alarm the British and French, who saw threats in naval expansion by Germany's allies. Meanwhile, Rome's relations with Paris and London had worsened due to the Italian invasion of Libya in October 1911. The French had allowed arms across the Tunisian border to aid the Turks. In January 1912, Italian warships intercepted three French vessels to search for contraband. After the Regia Marina bombarded the Dardanelles forts in April, then landed an invasion force in the Dodecanese Islands, the British grew alarmed at Italian actions. These incidents promoted British–French discussions about naval cooperation.[22] The Regia Marina had taken a prominent part

10

in the war. It had conducted blockades, bombardments, minelaying, convoy escort, amphibious landings, raids, and reconnaissance from the Libyan coast, the lower Adriatic, the Aegean and the waters off Lebanon to the Red Sea; but no fleet actions took place. The Turkish battle squadron had fled from Beirut into the Dardanelles prior to the war's outbreak. Italian cruisers, destroyers and torpedo boats had proven more useful than battleships, calling into question navy policies. By early 1913, with war against either France or the Dual Monarchy possible, the navy's combat forces seemed clearly inadequate.

These deficiencies worried Admiral Paolo Thaon di Revel. He had commanded cruisers in the war, then became inspector general of torpedo boats in late 1912. In April 1913 he was appointed chief of staff, determined to redress the fleet's imbalances. The Habsburg Navy presented a lesser danger than the French and likely would operate only in the Adriatic in a conflict with Italy. None the less, the chief of staff believed the Austro-Hungarian fleet enjoyed distinct geographic advantages. The rugged Dalmatian coast with its outlying necklace of islands stretched southeast for some 270 miles from the main Austro-Hungarian naval base at Pola (Pula) at the tip of the Istrian peninsula to the port of Ragusa (Dubrovnik). Numerous passages through the islands could be secured by minefields. Heavy warship losses to mines by both sides in the Russo-Japanese War had shown the danger such weapons posed. Behind the Dalmatian Islands barrier, Austro-Hungarian battleships and cruisers could steam unobserved, then sally forth for surprise attacks. Especially at night or in poor visibility, destroyers – on which the Austro-Hungarians put special stress – could slip through the coastal islands to launch salvoes at Italian warships in the Adriatic.[23]

The naval battles of the Russo-Japanese War already had impressed the naval staff with Regia Marina weakness in light craft and scouting vessels. To offset the growing danger of greatly improved modern torpedoes, the navy had acquired the first true Italian destroyer in 1898. By placing five 57 mm guns and six torpedoes on a 340-ton displacement, the design represented an attempt to make up for lack of numbers with a particularly well-armed destroyer. But it only produced a top-heavy, unseaworthy ship that could actually steam at only 23 knots, three less than its designed speed. Humiliated by this failure, the Regia Marina once again had to look abroad for assistance. It purchased ten more German-built torpedo boats and destroyers, and built five British-designed destroyers under license in 1900–5. But the high costs involved reduced the number of such vessels the Italian Navy could afford. Meanwhile, the Regia Marina had placed so few orders for torpedoes that the Schwarzkopf torpedo factory in Venice had closed for lack of business in 1902.[24]

In 1910 the navy had two obsolete light cruisers, no large and only 13 small destroyers, just three of which were Italian-built. By then, Whitehead

11

torpedoes had achieved ranges beyond naval guns and continued to improve in reach, speed and warhead size. First the French, then the Austro-Hungarians, began acquiring new torpedo boats and submarines. Most Italian admirals recognized the need to limit battleship construction to buy more light craft. Even Cuniberti opposed building new battleships of 35,000 tons with 12 381mm guns, proposed in late 1912 for laying down in 1914. Cuniberti argued that the project would severely reduce purchases of the smaller warships the navy required. Thaon di Revel agreed. Despite the admiral's war experiences, he still wanted a fleet based on more dreadnoughts. But he advocated relatively small ones, to free funds for light cruisers, destroyers and submarines.[25]

One solution to the problem of confronting the French Navy with inadequate light forces lay in combining the naval assets of the Triple Alliance. Another swing in Italian foreign policy had taken place in late 1912. French and British annoyance with Italy's gains in Africa and the Aegean had pushed Rome closer to Vienna and Berlin. Simultaneously, the acquisition of Libya had concentrated Italian strategic concerns in the Mediterranean. But Libya could be cut off by French or British naval forces which the Regia Marina alone could not challenge effectively. Finally, the revival of Tsarist naval power after the Russo-Japanese War raised the threat of a Russian squadron eventually joining the French fleet in the Mediterranean. The Italians clearly needed the naval assistance of their allies. In fact, in late 1912, the Germans had initiated consultations to create a combined Triple Alliance naval operations plan in the Mediterranean. Meanwhile, between November 1912 and February 1913, the French and British had agreed that the Royal Navy would concentrate in the North Sea and that the French Atlantic fleet would be transferred to the Mediterranean. The understanding obviously implied naval cooperation against the Triple Alliance.[26]

A Triple Alliance naval agreement was reached in August 1913. If a crisis arose, the Italian and Austro-Hungarian battle fleets, and the German Mediterranean squadron, would meet off northeast Sicily. Austro-Hungarian Admiral Anton Haus would command the force. In a war with France alone, the admiral was to seek out and destroy the French battle fleet; turn back or destroy convoys carrying troops from North Africa; then cover the landing of an Italian army in Provence. In case of conflict with Britain and France, Haus would try to prevent the union of the two countries' Mediterranean naval forces, then seek to destroy each in turn. If this proved impossible, the combined fleet was to use La Maddalena and La Spezia to attack French troop convoys and the Riviera coastline. In either eventuality, older Italian and Austro-Hungarian warships would guard the entrance to the Adriatic.[27]

While the naval agreement alleviated the Regia Marina's need for light craft, it hardly addressed the problem of war against the Habsburg Monarchy.

Yet the Italian government decided to build four super-dreadnoughts. While smaller than originally planned, each of the new *Caracciolo* class would displace 29,000 tons, be driven by oil-powered turbines, achieve 28 knots and carry eight 15-inch (381 mm) guns. The 12-inch guns on Italy's dreadnoughts had been designed to their ballistics limits. Firing created great bore pressures and temperatures that rapidly wore out the barrels. The increased caliber of the new ships' main guns would provide far greater hitting and penetration power yet extend barrel life. Creusot, a Schneider subsidiary, successfully tested a proof gun in July 1914. But the outbreak of the First World War led the Regia Marina to shift the order to British-affiliated Armstrong-Pozzuoli. Work on the *Caracciolo* began in September. Its sisters were laid down in March–June 1915. The naval ministry had contracted Carnegie Steel to supply the latest vanadium steel armor for the class.[28]

Since 1873, the Regia Marina had been based on a few powerful battleships. Brin's quality before quantity concept still seemed valid, even with others planning or building super-dreadnoughts. The final *Caracciolo* design combined speed, armor and guns to provide superiority over any warships then conceived. To these ends, Italian designers had abandoned coal power and sacrificed radius of action. The latter presented no disadvantage, intended as the *Carraciolos* were for Mediterranean service. But their oil dependence ruled out all but a short war with Britain.[29]

The navy also laid down two light cruisers and seven destroyers in 1910–12, creating greater need for torpedoes. Negotiations between Ansaldo and Schwarzkopf to build a new torpedo factory at Taranto succeeded in April 1914. But the outbreak of the First World War prevented this. Instead, the Whitehead company – closely associated with Armstrong and Vickers – agreed to establish a torpedo plant in Naples.[30]

Meanwhile, the French had laid the keels of 12 dreadnoughts between 1910 and 1914. Four more were scheduled to be laid down in 1915. Another 12 were to be completed by 1922, giving the French Navy 28 modern battleships. If the Italians had laid down successors to *Caracciolos* in 1916–18, they still would have faced a French battleship force twice as large. Thaon di Revel faced a dilemma: expand the light forces the navy needed or continue to emphasize battleship construction? Even the vigorous new Italian economy could not fund both.[31]

Nevertheless, the admiral attempted the impossible. The navy received 429 million lire for 1913–14 and 550 million lire for 1914–15, the latter double the navy's 1911–12 budget. Thaon di Revel ordered the four *Caracciolos* at 100 million lire each, as well as four large and ten small destroyers, one torpedo boat and seven submarines. The Italians also laid down four large destroyers for Romania. The chief of staff could not know that the First World War would break out in July 1914, nor that Italy would intervene in May 1915, nor that the conflict would last until late 1918.

But with Italian naval industries already overwhelmed with orders, wartime demands drove up prices for materials and fuel. Furthermore, shipping rates soared due to war risks. Hampered by shortages and costs, Italian construction rates fell drastically. The navy went to war with far too few light craft. The *Caracciolo*s were suspended and never completed.[32]

By July 1914, Italian relations with Austria-Hungary had deteriorated. The governments had cooperated to prevent Albania's partition by Serbia and Greece in 1913. But Vienna and Rome then competed to dominate the country. Control of the Strait of Otranto would allow Italy to shut the Adriatic. Austro-Hungarian access to Valona would give access to the Mediterranean. By mid-1914, Italy and the Dual Monarchy were fighting a proxy war in Albania. That, combined with the Austro-Hungarian 23 July ultimatum to Serbia, refusal to compensate Italy and, above all, British entry into the war in August led to Italy's neutrality declaration on 2 August.[33]

Prime Minister Antonio Salandra instructed the navy to prepare contingency plans for war against Austria-Hungary on 5 August. The decision for war was not made for seven months but Thaon di Revel soon began worrying about the conflict after next. He feared victory over the Austro-Hungarians might cost the Regia Marina so many ships that it would lose the war with France for Mediterranean dominance that he considered inevitable. To reduce such losses and to guarantee post-war Italian control in the Adriatic, he helped persuade the government to secure the Strait of Otranto. Salandra directed the Regia Marina to seize Saseno (Sazanit) Island at the entrance to Valona harbor in October. He ordered occupation of the port itself on Christmas Day. Over the fall and winter of 1914–15, Thaon di Revel also obtained funds for emergency expansion of the ports at Brindisi and Taranto. He wanted adequate bases should the Austro-Hungarian fleet sortie from the Adriatic. Finally, he demanded that if Italy joined the *Entente*, the Regia Marina would receive considerable Allied warships to serve under his command and share the fighting in the Adriatic.[34]

After five months of naval operations had revealed how effective mines and torpedoes had become, Thaon di Revel approved war plans in January 1915 and issued final instructions in March. The aggressive but unimaginative Luigi di Savoia, the duke of the Abruzzi, received command of the battle fleet. The chief of staff had hoped to seize Curzola Island and the Sabbioncello Peninsula in southern Dalmatia to gain a base from which to deter Austro-Hungarian surprise attacks through the island chain. But the army command refused to release sufficient forces for the landing and the operation was abandoned. Thaon di Revel and the duke worked out a simpler plan. The battle fleet would remain at its bases while light craft operated in the Adriatic and Dalmatia. The latter would conduct aggressive operations to destroy enemy warships and submarines, gradually extending Italian control northward. Older pre-dreadnoughts escorted by light craft would operate out of Venice to provide the army with naval gunfire

14

support and protect it against bombardment from the sea. The two admirals expected that the army would advance on the main Austro-Hungarian fleet base at Pola by the end of the 1915 campaign season. Then, the Italian fleet would steam to Venice, cover the army's Adriatic flank and engage the Austro-Hungarian fleet when it fled Pola, an eventuality the duke eagerly anticipated.[35]

The Treaty of London, signed on 26 April, pledged Italian entry into the war against the Central Powers in a month. The treaty promised British and French naval aid to Italy but left the details for negotiation. The naval convention of 10 May gave Thaon di Revel far less than he had wanted: 12 French destroyers, six submarines, six minesweepers, and four British light cruisers. More Allied naval forces would be offered when circumstances permitted. But Thaon di Revel doubted that this promise would be kept. When Italy declared war on 23 May, he harbored many concerns.[36]

The Adriatic war proved altogether different than the Regia Marina leadership had expected. Rather than months, the conflict lasted three-and-a-half years. No fleet actions took place and only two significant surface engagements between cruisers and light craft occurred. Lack of victories brought about Thaon di Revel's dismissal in October 1915. No replacement was appointed and the duke of the Abruzzi became the effective head of the navy. His unswerving search for a Mediterranean Jutland led to nothing but warship losses. Thaon di Revel returned to command the navy with unprecedented authority in February 1917. He guided the Regia Marina to victory over the next 21 months with innovative use of light craft, airplanes and novel naval assault weapons. In doing so he proved the greatest Italian naval leader of modern times and the only one ever promoted to the exalted rank of grand admiral.[37]

Despite Thaon di Revel's accomplishments, Brin's tradition of battleship supremacy proved stronger than the lessons of the Adriatic war. Under Fascism, the navy neglected air power, radar, underwater assault and submarine technology and concentrated its limited funds on battleship construction. This anachronistic policy led directly to Taranto and Matapan. While the navy recovered to an astonishing degree in 1942, its continuing resource deficiencies and the ongoing weaknesses of Italian industry, led to collapse in 1943. The problems afflicting Italian shipbuilding, technology and seapower concepts accompanied the Regia Marina to its end.[38]

NOTES

1. Alberto Guglielmotti, *Marc'Antonio Colonna alla battaglia di Lepanto* (Florence, 1862); Guglielmotti, *La guerra dei pirati e la Marina pontificia dal 1500 al 1560*, 2 vols. (Florence, 1876); Guglielmotti, *La squadra ausiliaria della marina romana a Candida e alla Morea: Storia dal 1644 al 1699* (Rome, 1883); Guglielmotti, *Vocabolario marino e militare* (Rome, 1889); Augusto Vittorio Vecchj, 'Sulla

strategia navale dell'Italia', *Nuova Antologia* (April, 1876); Vecchj, *Storia generale della Marina militare*, 2 vols (Livorno, 1892); Domenico Bonamico, *La difesa marittima dell'Italia* (Rome, 1881); Bonamico, *La difesa dello Stato: Considerazioni sull'opera del tenente colonello Perrucchetti* (Rome, 1884); P. Innocenzo Taurisano, *Alberto Guglielmotti, La vita – Le opere – Le pagine più belle* (Rome, 1960); Ezio Ferrante, *Il pensiero strategico navale in Italia* (Rome: Ufficio Storico, 1988), pp. 10–31; Luigi Donolo, *Storia della dottrina navale italiana* (Rome: Ufficio Storico, 1996), pp. 34–7, 43–4, 190–5, 211–21; Alfred Thayer Mahan, *The Influence of Seapower upon History 1660–1783* (New York: Hill & Wang, 1985), pp. 26–8, 73–5, 475–82. Alberto Guglielmotti (1812–93), Augusto Vittorio Vecchj (1842–1932) and Domenico Bonamico (1846–25), whose most important works are listed above, created the theoretical basis for Italian naval doctrine in the period discussed in this article. Vecchj published frequently under the pseudonym 'Jack La Bolina'.
2. John Gooch, *Army, State and Society in Italy, 1870–1915* (London: Macmillan, 1989), pp. 23–48; Fortunato Minniti, *Esercito e politica da Porta pia alla Triplice alleanza* (Rome: Bonacci, 1984), pp. 41–7, 66–7, 92–108.
3. Ezio Ferrante, 'The Impact of the Jeune École on the Way of Thinking of the Italian Navy' in *Marine et technique au XIXe siècle. Actes du colloque international Paris. École militaire, les 10, 11, 12 juin 1987* (Paris: Service historique de la Marine, 1988), pp. 519–24; Raimondo Luraghi, 'Italy', in Bruce W. Watson and Susan M. Watson, eds, *The Soviet Naval Threat to Europe: Military and Political Dimensions* (Boulder, CO: Westview Press, 1989), pp. 268–70; Luigi Donolo and James J. Tritten, 'The History of Italian Naval Doctrine' (Norfolk, VA: Naval Doctrine Command, 1995), p. 15.
    Only when Admiral Ferdinando Acton served as navy minister, 1880–83, did the Italian version of *Jeune École* thinking guide Italian naval policy. See Mariano Gabriele, *Benedetto Brin* (Rome, 1998), pp. 43–58; Romeo Bernotti, 'Acton, Ferdinando', *Dizionario biografico degli italiani* (Rome: Enciclopedia Italiana, 1960) (hereafter *DBI*), vol. I.
4. Simone de Saint Bon, *Pensieri sulla Marina militare* (Naples: Classici, 1862); Gino Galuppini, *Guida alle navi d'Italia: la marina da guerra dal 1861 ad oggi* (Milan: Mondadori, 1982), pp. 8–18; Brian R. Sullivan, 'A Fleet in Being: The Rise and Fall of Italian Sea Power, 1861–1943', *International History Review* (February 1988), pp. 108–10; Jack Greene and Alessandro Massignani, *Ironclads at War: The Origin and Development of the Armored Warship, 1854–1891* (Conshohocken, PA: Combined Publishing, 1998), pp. 213–35; Philippe Masson, 'La marine française de 1871 à 1914' in Guy Pedrocini, ed., *Histoire militaire de la France*, 3 vols (Paris: Presses Universitaires de France, 1992), vol. III, *De 1871 à 1940*, pp. 119–24.
5. Gabriele, *Benedetto Brin*, pp. 17–20; Ezio Ferrante, *Benedetto Brin e la questione marittima italiano (1866–1898)* (Rome: Rivista Marittima, 1983), pp. 33–7; Ferrante, *Il potere marittimo: evoluzione ideologica in Italia, 1861–1939* (Rome: Rivista Marittima, 1982), pp. 37–41; Lucio Ceva, *Le forze armate* (Turin: UTET, 1981), pp. 100–1; Giuseppe Fioravanzo, *Storia del pensiero tattico navale* (Rome: USMM, 1973), p. 142; Giorgio Giorgerini, *Da Matapan al Golfo Persico: la Marina militare italiana dal fascismo alla Repubblica* (Milan: Mondadori, 1989), pp. 51–2; Lawrence Sondhaus, *The Naval Policy of Austria-Hungary, 1867–1918* (West Lafayette, IN: Purdue University Press, 1994), pp. 49–51; Siegfried Breyer, *Battleships and Battle Cruisers* (New York, Doubleday, 1973), p. 33; Theodor Ropp, *The Development of a Modern Navy: French Naval Policy 1871–1904*, ed. Stephen S. Roberts (Annapolis, MD: Naval Institute Press, 1987), pp. 82–6, 297–8, 304; Jon Tetsuro Sumida, *In Defence*

of Naval Supremacy: Finance, Technology and British Naval Policy, 1889–1914 (Boston: Unwin Hymen, 1989), pp. 38–45, 851–61; Nicholas A. Lambert, 'Admiral Sir John Fisher and the Concept of Flotilla Defence, 1904–1909', *Journal of Military History* (October 1995), pp. 641–4.

Brin's 1871–72 design of the battleships *Duilio* and *Dandolo* appears to have started young Jackie Fisher thinking as early as 1882 about concepts that he would realize as *Dreadnought* and *Invincible* a quarter century later.

6. Christopher Seton-Watson, *Italy from Liberalism to Fascism 1870–1925* (London and New York: Methuen, 1981), pp. 111–14, 121–5; E. T. S. Dugdale, ed., *German Diplomatic Documents 1871–1914*, 4 vols (New York and London: Harpers, 1928), vol. I, *Bismarck's Relations with England 1871–1890*, pp. 120–2; Alfred Franzis Pribram, *The Secret Treaties of Austria-Hungary 1879–1914*, 2 vols (Cambridge, MA: Harvard University Press, 1920), vol. I, *Texts of the Treaties and Agreements*, pp. 68–73, 104–15.

7. Gabriele, *Benedetto Brin*, p. 20; Ferrante, *Benedetto Brin*, pp. 41–8, 54–69, 76–88; Alfredo Capone, 'Brin, Benedetto', *DBI*, vol. XIV (Rome: Enciclopedia Italiana, 1972), pp. 312–16; Ugo Spadolini, 'L'Ansaldo e la politica navale italiana', in *Storia dell'Ansaldo*, 5 vols (Bari: Laterza, 1994–), vol. II, *La costruzione di una grande impresa 1883–1902*, Giorgio Mori, ed., pp. 68–71; Giorgio Mori, 'L'industria dell'acciaio in Italia', in ibid., vol. III, *Dai Bombrini ai Perrone 1903–1914*, pp. 34–5; National Archives, Record Group 38, Office of Naval Intelligence, Naval Attaché Reports 1886–1939 (hereafter NA, ONI), box 1082, K-9-b, report of 11 April 1899; Mariano Gabriele and Giuliano Friz, *La politica navale italiana dal 1885 al 1915* (Rome: Ufficio Storico, Marina Militaire, 1982), pp. 17–18, 29; Luciano Segreto, 'More Trouble than Profit: Vickers' Investments in Italy 1906–39', *Business History* (November 1985), p. 317; Segreto, *Marte e Mercurio: industria bellica e sviluppo economico in Italia 1861–1940* (Milan: Franco Angeli, 1997), pp. 21, 32 n.26; Ropp, *The Development of a Modern Navy*, pp. 79–80; René Greger, *Battleships of the World* (Annapolis, MD: Naval Institute Press, 1997), p. 138; Maurice Pearton, *Diplomacy, War and Technology since 1830* (Lawrence, KS: University Press of Kansas, 1984), pp. 114–16. Galuppini, *Guida alle navi*, pp. 46–61; Ceva, *Le forze armate*, p. 101; Giorgerini, *Da Matapan al Golfo Persico*, p. 45.

The Italians laid down *Duilio* and *Dandolo* in early 1873. They entered service only in January 1880 and April 1882 respectively. Construction of *Italia* and *Lepanto* began in mid-1876 but took nine years for the former, 11 years for the latter. The three *Sardegna* class battleships were begun in 1884–85 but required from nine to ten-and-a-half years for completion. Brin's finest designs, the two *Regina Margherita* class pre-dreadnoughts, were built more quickly but still took five-and-a-half and six-and-a-half years in the period 1898–1905.

8. Ferrante, *Benedetto Brin*, pp. 46–7, 73, 77, 81; Gabriele, *Benedetto Brin*, pp. 67, 70–2; Erminio Bagnasco and Achille Rastelli, 'L'attività e la produzione cantieristica', in Mori, *Storia dell'Ansaldo*, vol. III, pp. 90–1; Segreto, *Marte e Mercurio*, p. 21; Antonio Casali and Marina Cattaruzza, *Sotto I mari del mondo: La Whitehead 1875–1990* (Bari: Laterza, 1990), pp. 45–6.

9. Gabriele, *Benedetto Brin*, pp. 130–43; Seton-Watson, *Italy from Liberalism to Fascism*, pp. 98–195; Gianni Toniolo, *An Economic History of Liberal Italy 1850–1918* (London and New York: Routledge, 1990), pp. 60–102; Spadolini, 'L'Ansaldo e la politica navale italiana', pp. 72–6; Kenneth Bourne and D. Cameron Watt, eds, *British Documents on Foreign Affairs: Reports and Papers from the Foreign Office Confidential Print*, part I, *From the Mid-Nineteenth Century to the First World War*, Series F, *Europe, 1848–1914*, John F. V. Keiger, ed. (Frederick, MD: University Publications of America, 1983) (hereafter *BDFA*), vol. XXIV,

Italy, 1875–1903, p. 135; Sullivan, 'A Fleet in Being', pp. 111–12; Sullivan, 'The Strategy of the Decisive Weight', in Williamson Murray, MacGregor Knox, and Alvin Bernstein, eds, *The Making of Strategy: Rulers, States, and War* (New York: Cambri, 1994), pp. 313–17; Giorgerini, *Da Matapan al Golfo Persico*, p. 53; Gabriele, *Benedetto Brin*, pp. 64–6.

10. *Papers Relating to the Foreign Relations of the United States 1919: The Paris Peace Conference*, vol. I (Washington, 1942) (hereafter *FRUS*), pp. 480–1; Stefano Fenoaltea, 'Italy', in Patrick O'Brien, ed., *Railways and the Economic Development of Western Europe, 1830–1914* (New York: St Martin's Press, 1983), pp. 51–3, 94–6; Albert Schram, *Railways and the Formation of the Italian State in the Nineteenth Century* (Cambridge: Cambridge University Press, 1997), pp. 27–41, 99–110, 129–33, 147–52.

11. Ropp, *The Development of a Modern Navy*, pp. 200–1; Paul G. Halpern, *The Mediterranean Naval Situation 1908–1914* (Cambridge, MA: Harvard University Press, 1971), pp. 187–8; Schram, *Railways*, pp. 129–32; Gabriele and Friz, *La politica navale*, pp. 16–22.

12. *BDFA*, vol. XXIV, pp. 322–3; ibid., vol. XXV, *Italy, 1904–1914*, pp. 378–9, 382; Denis Mack Smith, *Italy and its Monarchy* (New Haven, CT: Yale University Press, 1989), pp. 147, 178, 180–1; Ceva, *Le forze armate*, p. 104; Raoul Gûeze, 'Bettolo, Giovanni', *DBI*, vol. IX (Rome, 1967), pp. 769–70; Ray Walser, *France's Search for a Battle Fleet: Naval Policy and Naval Power, 1898–1914* (New York: Garland Press, 1992), pp. 58–90, 151, 180–200, 220, 227.

13. Umberto D'Aquino, 'Cuniberti, Vittorio Emanuele', *DBI*, vol. XXXI (Rome, 1985), pp. 374–6; Galuppini, *Guida alle navi*, p. 70.

In the 1890s, the closest sources of oil to Italy were the Galician, Ploesti, and Baku fields, access to which could be easily blocked at the Straits. Inside the Mediterranean basin, even modest petroleum extraction began only in the mid-1930s with production from the small Albanian deposits. The major discoveries in Algeria and Libya took place in the second half of the 1950s. See Daniel Yergin, *The Prize: The Epic Quest for Oil, Money and Power* (New York: Simon & Schuster, 1992), pp. 25, 57–63, 281, 526–8.

14. In contrast, while the two Italian armored cruisers of the *Garibaldi* class under construction for the Italian Navy in the period 1898–1901 displaced 8,100 tons, their best speed was only a little over 19 knots and they carried a heterogeneous array of 254 mm, 203 mm, 152 mm, 76 mm, and 47 mm guns. Yet the *Garibaldi* design was considered so advanced that the Argentine, Spanish, and Japanese governments had ordered seven such cruisers for their own navies. See Erminio Bagnasco and Achille Rastelli, *Le costruzioni navali italiane per l'estero: centotrenta anni di prestigiosa presenza nel mondo*, supplement to *Rivista Marittima*, December 1911 (Rome, 1991), pp. 14–21; Galuppini, *Guida alle navi*, pp. 72–3.

15. Breyer, *Battleships and Battle Cruisers*, pp. 44, 372; Galuppini, *Guida alle navi*, p. 102; Giorgerini, *Da Matapan al Golfo Persico*, p. 60; Greger, *Battleships of the World*, pp. 136, 140.

16. Arthur J. Marder, *From the Dreadnought to Scapa Flow: The Royal Navy in the Fisher Era, 1904–1919*, 5 vols (London: Oxford University Press, 1961–70), vol. I, *The Road to War, 1904–1914*, p. 13 n.6; Sumida, *In Defence of Naval Supremacy*, pp. 45–6; Breyer, *Battleships and Battle Cruisers*, pp. 55, 373.

Cuniberti presented his armored cruiser concept in the German Navy's official journal in the spring of 1900. The article inspired the design of the *Scharnhorst* and *Blucher* classes of armored cruisers in 1903–5, marking a radical break with the slower, multicaliber *Prinz Adalbert* and *Roon* cruiser classes of 1899–1901. The *Prinz Adalbert* class displaced 9,100 tons, carried four 210 mm and ten 150 mm guns and had a maximum speed of 20.5 knots. The *Roon* class displaced

9,500 tons, had the same armament as the *Prinz Adalbert* class and was capable of slightly more than 21 knots. The *Scharnhorst* class displaced 11,600 tons, carried eight 210 mm and six 150 mm guns and could steam at 23.5 knots. *Blücher* displaced 15,800 tons, was armed with 12 210 mm and eight 150 mm guns and had a top speed of 25.4 knots. See V. E. Cuniberti, 'Der neue Typ des Schlachtschiffes', *Marine-Rundschau* (May and June 1900); Erich Gröner with Dieter Jung and Martin Maas, *German Warships 1815–1945*, vol. I, *Major Surface Vessels* (Annapolis, MD: Naval Institute Press, 1990), pp. 50–3.

17. Halpern, *The Mediterranean Naval Situation*, pp. 162–3, 184, 189–93, 200; Breyer, *Battleships and Battle Cruisers*, 372–4, 409–11; Gabriele and Friz, *La politica navale*, pp. 144–5; Ceva, *Le forze armate*, pp. 100–2; Giorgerini, *Da Matapan al Golfo Persico*, pp. 54–7, 60–1; Sondhaus, *The Naval Policy of Austria-Hungary*, pp. 203–4.

18. NA, ONI, box 854, E-11-a, reports of 5 April 1901, 28 April 1902, 25 June 1910; Mori, 'L'industria dell'acciaio in Italia', pp. 41, 64–6; Luciano Segreto, 'Partner e rivali nell'industria degli armamenti', in Hertner, *Storia dell'Ansaldo*, vol. III, p. 115.

Throughout the slump of the 1890s, Italian steel output had averaged 74,000 metric tons annually. It rose to 1.3 million tons in 1913. During the same decade, Italian coal imports – mostly from Britain – almost doubled from 5.5 to 10.8 million tons. See B. R. Mitchell, *International Historical Statistics: Europe 1750–1988* (New York: Stockton Press, 1992), pp. 456–7, 468.

19. Galuppini, *Guida alle navi*, pp. 56–61, 102–5; NA, ONI, box 854, E-11-a, report of 5 April 1901; Ludovica de Courten, 'L'Ansaldo e la politica navale durante l'età giolittiana', in Hertner, *Storia dell'Ansaldo*, vol. III, pp. 77, 79, 83; Segreto, 'Partner e rivali', pp. 116, 120–33; de Courten, 'More Trouble than Profit', pp. 317–20; de Courten, *Marte e Mercurio*, pp. 33–7; Erminio Bagnasco and Achille Rastelli, 'Le costruzioni navali dell'Ansaldo', in Hertner, ibid., pp. 187–90.

In 1884–1908, 11 Italian capital ships had advanced from keel laying to entry into service. These ships displaced a total of 153,000 tons standard and carried a total of 36 heavy guns.

20. Seton-Watson, *Italy from Liberalism to Fascism*, pp. 201–13, 325–33; Walser, *France's Search*, pp. 42–117; Masson, 'La marine française', pp. 134–42; Giorgerini, *Da Matapan al Golfo Persico*, pp. 57–8.

21. Seton-Watson, *Italy from Liberalism to Fascism*, pp. 333–8, 342–60; F. R. Bridge, *The Habsburg Monarchy among the Great Powers, 1815–1918* (New York: St Martin's Press, 1990), pp. 238–9; Milan N. Vego, *Austro-Hungarian Naval Policy 1904–14* (London and Portland, OR: Frank Cass, 1996), pp. 41–7, 188–9; Mack Smith, *Italy and its Monarchy*, p. 178.

22. BDFA, vol. XXIV, p. 323; ibid., vol. XXV, 239–41, 267, 306, 321–2; Sullivan, 'The Strategy of the Decisive Weight', pp. 318–22; Gabriele and Friz, *La politica navale*, pp. 132–42, 161–75; Halpern, *The Mediterranean Naval Situation*, pp. 67–110, 165; Sondhaus, *The Naval Policy of Austria-Hungary*, pp. 191–8; Vego, *Austro-Hungarian Naval Policy*, pp. 57–8, 100–4, 108–10; Mack Smith, *Italy and its Monarchy*, pp. 180–1; Giorgerini, *Da Matapan al Golfo Persico*, p. 61; Breyer, *Battleships and Battle Cruisers*, pp. 374–80; Marder, *The Road to War*, pp. 288–311; Bridge, *The Habsburg Monarchy*, p. 302; Walser, *France's Search*, pp. 207–8, 223; Seton-Watson, *Italy from Liberalism to Fascism*, pp. 374–7.

23. Mariano Gabriele, *La marina nella guerra italo-turca: Il potere marittimo strumento militare e politico (1911–1912)* (Rome, 1998), pp. 33–44, 195 n.3, 205–7; Luigi Fulvi *et al.*, *Le fanterie di marina italiane*, 2nd edn (Rome, 1998)

pp. 39–4; Ezio Ferrante, *Il Grande Ammiraglio Paolo Thaon di Revel* (Rome, 1989), 43–8; *FRUS*, pp. 479–80; Vego, *Austro-Hungarian Naval Policy*, pp. 22, 39.

24. Galuppini, *Guida alle navi*, pp. 82–6; Segreto, *Marte e Mercurio*, p. 36; Casali and Cattaruzza, *Sotto I mari*, p. 79.

25. Halpern, *The Mediterranean Naval Situation*, pp. 162, 182–6, 198–211; Ferrante, *Benedetto Brin*, pp. 46–7, 81; Ropp, *The Development of a Modern Navy*, pp. 82, 222; Capone, 'Brin, Benedetto', p. 316; Herwig, 'Luxury Fleet', p. 26; Galuppini, *Guida alle navi*, pp. 56–7, 64–5, 68–9, 80–8; Breyer, *Battleships and Battle Cruisers*, pp. 41–2, 381; NA, ONI, box 861, E-12-c, report of 23 December 1912; Lambert, 'Admiral Sir John Fisher', pp. 647–53; Marder, *The Road to War*, pp. 328–30; Sumida, *In Defence of Naval Supremacy*, p. 114.

26. Bridge, *The Habsburg Monarchy*, pp. 308, 314; Vego, *Austro-Hungarian Naval Policy*, pp. 114–16, 142–4; *British Documents on the Origins of the War 1898–1914*, G. P. Gooch and Harold Temperley, vols X, part II, *The Last Years of Peace* (London: Foreign Office, 1938), pp. 640–2.

27. Vego, *Austro-Hungarian Naval Policy*, pp. 117–32; Pribram, *The Secret Treaties of Austria-Hungary*, pp. 282–305; Halpern, *The Mediterranean Naval Situation*, pp. 224–73; Gabriele and Friz, *La politica navale*, pp. 226–30.

For 1914, the agreement stipulated that the combined fleet would consist of six dreadnoughts (three Italian and three Austro-Hungarian), the German battlecruiser *Goeben*, seven newer pre-dreadnoughts, ten older pre-dreadnoughts, nine armored cruisers, 11 light cruisers (three German), 44 destroyers and 66 torpedo boats. In fact, even by September 1914, the Italians and Austro-Hungarians had only two combat-ready dreadnoughts. Another new Austro-Hungarian was fit for war service by the very end of 1914 and three additional Italian dreadnoughts were by the late summer of 1915. Furthermore, at the outbreak of the First World War, the Germans had only one light cruiser in the Mediterranean. See Breyer, *Battleships and Battle Cruisers*, pp. 373–4, 378, 409.

28. Bagnasco and Rastelli, 'Le costruzioni navali', pp. 190–1; ONI, NA, box 861, E-12-c, reports of 24 March, 6 August, 4 September 1914; ibid, box 1253, O-11-b, reports of 11 June 1913, 17 Oct. 1914, 9 February 4 March, 29 March, 27 June 1915; Carlo Alfredo Clerici, Alfredo Flocchini and Charles B. Robbins, 'The 15″ (381 mm)/40 Guns of the "Francesco Caracciolo" Class Battleships,' *Warship International*, no. 2 (1999), pp. 151–3; Ian Hogg and John Batchelor, *Naval Gun* (Poole, UK: Blandford Press, 1978), pp. 117–18.

The Italians intended to acquire 40 15-inch guns for the four super-dreadnoughts: eight barrels and two spares for each ship. The proof piece and nine more guns were built by Ansaldo-Schneider. Twelve more were manufactured by Armstrong-Pozzuoli under British supervision and weighed about a third more than the Creusot-designed guns. Vickers-Terni appears to have built an additional three. The shift of priorities for arms manufacture during the First World War and the cancellation of the *Caracciolo* class afterwards halted further production. See Clerici *et al.*, 'The 15″ (381 mm)/40 Guns', p. 152.

29. Breyer, *Battleships and Battle Cruisers*, pp. 106, 141–2, 189, 230, 257, 280–2, 369, 381, 407, 411–13, 415, 426–30; Vego, *Austro-Hungarian Naval Policy*, pp. 173–4; NA, ONI, box 1253, O-11-b, reports of 11 June 1913, 8 July 1914.

The *Caracciolo* class would have had a speed advantage of 4–7 knots over other super-dreadnoughts, been more heavily armored than any except the German *Bayern* and American *New Mexico* classes, and fired a heavier broadside than any battleships save the projected French *Lyon* class. The range of its 15 inch guns would have been matched only by the British *Queen Elizabeth* class, which carried the same type and number of main guns. Of course, given the ongoing naval armaments race, the *Caracciolo* class would have been out-matched by the Japanese *Nagato* and American *Maryland* classes by 1921–22. See Breyer, *Battleships and Battle Cruisers*, for details.

Owing to the outbreak of the First World War and the consequent need for the French, Italians, and Austro-Hungarians to devote their scarce resources else-where, only the British and Germans completed any of the super-dreadnoughts being built or planned in 1914.

30. Galuppini, *Guida alle navi*, pp. 112, 115, 118; Casali and Cattaruzza, *Sotto I mari*, pp. 74–5; Segreto, 'Partner e rivali', pp. 134–5.
31. Breyer, *Battleships and Battle Cruisers*, pp. 419–31; Walser, *France's Search*, pp. 186–200, 222–32. For an assessment of the Mediterranean naval balance of power in 1914 see Paul G. Halpern, *The Naval War in the Mediterranean 1914–1918* (Annapolis, MD: Naval Institute Press, 1987), pp. 1–42.
32. Ferrante, *Il Grande Ammiraglio*, pp. 51–2; J. Scott Keltie, ed., *The Statesman's Year-Book 1916* (London, 1916), p. 1077; Giorgerini, *Da Matapan al Golfo Persico*, p. 72; Hugh B. Killough, *Raw Materials of Industrialism* (New York: Thomas Y. Crowall, 1929), pp. 227, 248, 287; Robert S. Manthy, *Natural Resource Commodities – A Century of Statistics* (Baltimore, MD and London: Johns Hopkins University Press, 1978), p. 115; Galuppini, *Guida alle navi*, pp. 113, 115, 124, 132, 135, 142–3; Camillo Manfroni, *Storia della marina italiana durante la guerra mondiale 1914–1918* (Bologna, 1925), pp. 2, 12; Breyer, *Battleships and Battle Cruisers*, p. 381.
33. Seton-Watson, *Italy from Liberalism to Fascism*, pp. 396–406, 409, 414; Bridge, *The Habsburg Monarchy*, pp. 319–32; Vego, *Austro-Hungarian Naval Policy*, pp. 158–60, 168–70; Gabriele and Friz, *La politica navale*, pp. 241–3; Geoffrey A. Haywood, *Failure of a Dream: Sidney Sonnino and the Rise and Fall of Liberal Italy 1847–1922* (Florence: L.S. Olschki, 1999), pp. 395–400; Ferrante, *Il Grande Ammiraglio*, pp. 53–4.
34. *I documenti diplomatici italiani*, series 5, vol. I (hereafter *DDI*, followed by series, volume and document number), no. 468, p. 257; ibid., vol. II, nos 508, 750; ibid., vol. III, nos 228, 577, 596; Seton-Watson, *Italy from Liberalism to Fascism*, p. 428; Gabriele and Friz, *La politica navale*, pp. 255–7; Manfroni, *Storia della marina italiana*, pp. 3–12.
35. *DDI*, 5, III, no. 334; Halpern, *The Naval War*, pp. 84–92; Giorgerini, *Da Matapan al Golfo Persico*, pp. 72–5; Gabriele and Friz, *La politica navale*, pp. 250–1, 257–9.
36. *DDI*, 5, III, nos 637, 644, 656; Halpern, *The Naval War*, pp. 93–101; Gabriele and Friz, *La politica navale*, pp. 259–64.
37. Halpern, *The Naval War*, pp. 125–64, 264–89, 333–49, 357–67, 374–411, 426–87, 498–541, 555–68; Sullivan, 'The Strategy of the Decisive Weight', pp. 337–8, 342; Ferrante, *Il Grande Ammiraglio*, pp. 56–114.
38. For a survey of the Italian Navy in the Fascist period, see Giorgerini, *Da Matapan al Golfo Persico*, pp. 146–549.

2

Japanese Naval Construction, 1878–1918

David C. Evans

At the outset of the 1880s, early in Japan's modern history, the Imperial Japanese Navy was an odd-lot collection of vessels acquired to provide for the nation's coastal defense. By the end of the First World War, barely four decades later, it had become the world's third most powerful fleet, an agent for the projection of Japanese power abroad.

Four essential elements influenced the course and pace of the rise of Japanese naval power during this period. To begin with, Japan entered the modern world as an essentially agricultural nation, with severely limited financial resources, largely without heavy industry, without a significant naval tradition, with negligible facilities for naval construction, and little understanding of modern naval technology. It was therefore greatly dependent on outside assistance in the acquisition of such technology.

Second, Japan's acquisition of a modern navy took place during a period of particular technological and tactical uncertainty. The second great wave of technological change (the first having been the displacement of sail by steam), largely that of weaponry, raised critical issues of force structure, warship design and tactical employment for all navies. Yet, though Japan had scant naval tradition or indigenous technological expertise to draw upon in meeting these issues, it was not, at least, burdened by a naval establishment resistant to change or a large fleet that rapid shifts in technology could make obsolescent and expensive to replace. Indeed, combined with the Japanese cultural propensity to accept and adopt technological advances, the flux of naval technology in these years offered the Japanese Navy particular opportunities for modern development. This was especially true given that the Japanese Navy had access to the latest technology and a leadership sufficiently perceptive and decisive to make wise choices as to the navy's force structure.

Access to the latest Western technology, tactical advances and capital markets for loans – which indirectly eased the burden of naval modernization – was the third critical element in the Japanese Navy's rise to power before the First World War. In these years of embryonic naval power, Japan was fortunate to have a mentor and later an ally in Britain which could offer assistance in training, technology, tactical guidance and loans on relatively easy terms.[1]

But such assistance would have meant little had Japan not had decisive and forward-looking leadership to take advantage of the opportunities available. Fortunately, the navy had such leadership, emerging from its middle echelon, but manifested most decisively in the person of Admiral Yamamoto Gombei. He swept away the moribund feudal remnants in the navy's command structure and, at the turn of the century, fought for the navy's interests in the halls of government and the court of public opinion, and made critical decisions as to the navy's mission and force structure. Others in the middle echelon were also quick to recognize the need to develop a strategy for industrial and technological development and, ultimately, independence.[2]

Lastly, lacking a tradition and thus without a doctrine, the Japanese Navy, through its conduct of two modern naval wars, nevertheless forged a set of doctrinal principles. These centered on a preference for offensive over defensive tactics and on qualitative rather than numerical strength, and based in part on Japan's ancient military traditions (in land warfare) and in part on its modern combat experience. These principles were to influence the development of Japanese naval technology from 1895 to the navy's annihilation by 1945.

1878–94

Emblematic of the primitive stage of Japanese naval professionalism and naval industry and technology at the time were the circumstances surrounding the purchase and delivery in 1878 of the first three warships to be built specifically for the Japanese Navy (two frigates and one corvette). Since Japan had no naval constructors of its own, these ships were designed by the distinguished British naval constructor Edward Reed. Because Japan had no yards suitable for their armored construction, they were launched and completed in British yards. And, as Japanese technological and navigational skills were inadequate to operate them halfway around the globe, British crews brought them to Japan, with Japanese aboard only as observers. But their construction gave Japanese naval architects the chance to go to Britain to learn the latest developments in protective armor and ordnance,[3] while naval officers like Lieutenant Tôgô Heihachirô (aboard one of the corvettes) gained vital experience in handling steam warships.

By this time, moreover, Japan had begun to take steps to create the professionalism, the basic industry and the technological base necessary to create a modern navy. The professionalism was introduced with the arrival in Japan of a series of advisors and instructors from the British

Navy, beginning in the late 1870s and continuing through until the early 1890s, supplemented by the training of selected junior officers in British naval schools. By these means the fledgling navy gradually became familiar with the latest developments in Western tactical and strategic thought and with a wide range of technical information.[4]

In striving to build an industrial base upon which Japanese naval construction could eventually become autonomous, the leaders of the Japanese government were perceptive enough to recognize (as China, for example, did not) the importance of making the civilian and military economies interdependent during these years. Specifically, the government sought to nurture private industry through the indigenization and diffusion of advanced foreign technology.[5] Throughout the last two decades of the nineteenth century, for example, the navy was instrumental in the development of an indigenous steel industry. It established blast furnaces and steel mills to accelerate the government's efforts to make Japan self-sufficient in steel and capable of providing this basic resource for naval construction.[6]

In the 1880s, the navy took the first steps to develop just such a naval arms industry when it established a number of shipyards for merchant vessels and constructed naval arsenals at Tsukiji in Tokyo Bay and at Yokosuka.[7] The Tsukiji arsenal had already begun to repair ships and guns and the Yokosuka Arsenal began to turn out a few warships of modest size, importing the necessary machinery and temporarily hiring several skilled workers from Britain. But Japanese naval arsenals did not simply build ships. They were also an important source of commercial technology for the nation as a whole and a critical source of technicians and trained management for the private sector, particularly after the sale of most of the government's shipyards to private entrepreneurs in the 1880s. Some of the largest and most successful of Japanese industrial giants in the twentieth century had their origins in this privatization of government arsenals and shipyards in the nineteenth century. By the 1920s, these private shipyards would produce the preponderance of construction for the Japanese Navy, a justification of the economic-industrial policies of Japan's early modernizing leadership.

But, in the 1880s, the navy was still hugely dependent on foreign industry and technology to build its fleet. In 1882, with a heightened sense of the nation's vulnerability to outside maritime pressure, the Diet passed the first naval expansion bill which called for a fleet of 48 warships (later reduced to 46). Owing to the influence of the French *Jeune École* in Japanese naval thinking during these years, 22 of these vessels were to be torpedo boats, assembled in foreign (mostly French) yards, broken down for trans-shipment and reassembly in Japan. For the time being, such a force structure signified the ongoing defensive posture of the Japanese Navy.

By the end of the decade, however, Japan's expanding concern with the Asian continent, particularly with the Korean peninsula, led to the promotion of public and governmental support for an expanded navy capable of projecting Japanese power into East Asian waters. In the emerging confrontation with China over Korea, the navy came to be seen as the sole means of protecting an army expeditionary force that might be sent to the peninsula to defend what Japan saw as its legitimate interests on the continent. Along with the formulation of the navy's first tactical doctrine and the establishment of standing fleets, therefore, the navy acquired its first naval units designed specifically to confront a particular opponent. In 1891–94, Japan looked once more to France and its eminent naval constructor Emile Bertin for the design of the three cruisers of the *Sankeikan* class to match the several large warships which the Chinese had recently acquired from Germany.

On the eve of Japan's war with China, 1894–95, the navy's newly established Combined Fleet was a foreign-built force centered on ten first-line warships, assembled at considerable economic cost to the nation.[8] While it was a makeshift force, its unified command and its superior speed, tactics and armament proved triumphant in the several engagements of the war, most notably in the battle off the Yalu, 17 September 1894. Those victories confirmed the navy in the lessons it had been taught by British naval instructors: the tactical importance of the column, strict station-keeping and the consequent concentration of gunfire; effectiveness of the torpedo and the quick-firing gun; and the necessity for an homogenous fleet able to maneuver together. In the navy's view the war also validated its insistence on primacy of place in Japan's armed services.[9]

1895–1904

In the period immediately following the war, Japan's humiliation by the Triple Intervention and the apparent Russian drive to achieve hegemony in East Asia underscored the nation's maritime weakness in relation to the West. These two reverses led to two initiatives to strengthen Japan's challenge to Russian ambitions. One of these was a diplomatic démarche to deal with the possible junction of hostile Western battle fleets in East Asian waters should Russia, the world's third greatest naval power, become allied with another maritime nation against Japan. The Anglo-Japanese Alliance of 1902 reduced this risk and gave Japan the freedom of action to plan hostilities against Russia without having to worry about the intervention of a second hostile power.

The second initiative was the acquisition of sufficient naval strength to defeat or blockade any enemy naval force – presumably Russian – in East Asian waters. This would necessitate securing the ongoing commitment of the nation to an unprecedented level of naval security and the consequent assembling of a battle force composed of state-of-the-art capital ships.

There were difficulties in each of these tasks. Despite the indemnity from China received at the end of the Sino-Japanese War, the economic costs of that conflict and the competition for funds by the navy's service rival would require a substantial campaign to garner support in the Diet and among the public for a massive new naval expansion plan. Beyond this, the navy's plans for a battle force emerged at a time of great technological and tactical uncertainty. The end of the nineteenth century saw the rapid development of naval technology, particularly ordnance, armor, torpedoes, propulsion and the concomitant development of various warship types. Without a decisive lead taken by any one technology, all navies, amid a fog of uncertainty, struggled to find the dominant weapon, the most efficient fleet organization and the most potent tactical system. For Japan, newly embarking on the path to naval power, the selection of the right mix among these categories in building a modern fleet was a stark challenge and required decisive and knowledgeable leadership.

Fortunately for Japan, the navy possessed such authority in the person of Admiral Yamamoto Gombei (1852–1933), whose influence and acumen exceeded his current position as chief of the Navy Ministry's Naval Affairs Department. It was Yamamoto who, exploiting and manipulating public opinion, floated his plans for massive naval expansion on the tide of popular enthusiasm for naval glory following the victory over China. Yamamoto's ten-year naval expansion program which he pushed successfully through the Diet in 1896, centered on the construction of Japan's first true battle fleet of six battleships and six armored cruisers. Yamamoto and his colleagues judged this the minimum level of naval security capable of dealing with either Russian or British naval power stationed in East Asian waters, aided in either case by the forces of any lesser naval power (France or Germany).[10]

In effect, therefore, Yamamoto's expansion plan committed the government to a theoretical standard of naval power not unlike Britain's 'Two-power Standard', one based on the capabilities rather than on the intentions of other nations. By doing so, it attempted to guarantee government support for a level of naval security unaffected by public support, political crises, or cabinet changes. The plan also represented a conscious effort to match the navy's qualitative strength against that of all other naval powers, for, in addition to two battleships already being built in British yards, it called for four new British-built battleships, more powerful than any others afloat. The specifications the navy thus called for in the *Mikasa* and her three sisters at the time of their construction, 1900–2, set the precedent for the Japanese Navy's overriding concern with superiority in every critical category – armament, armor, speed and range.[11] For the rest of the navy's existence qualitative superiority *vis-à-vis* the probable enemy was to be the navy's single greatest priority in the warships it acquired.

The six cruisers to augment the projected Japanese battle line were built abroad, between 1899 and 1901, under the 1897 revision of Yamamoto's ten-year plan: four in Britain at the famous Elswick works which had set a standard in cruiser construction for the past several decades, and one each in Germany and France. When they joined the Japanese fleet, Yamamoto's formidable 'Six-Six Fleet' was completed. Yet while construction of the battle line was the most dramatic feature of the 1896–97 expansion plan, Yamamoto had also urged the assembly of a balanced fleet. To this end the navy came to add protected cruisers to seek out and pursue the enemy's advance units, as well as a sufficient number of destroyers and torpedo boats capable of striking the enemy in its home ports.[12] Ninety per cent of the 234,000 tons of naval construction contracted for under the ten-year plan was foreign built and when completed would comprise 70 per cent of the Japanese fleet. Of this tonnage the overwhelming portion was built in British yards.

But Japan had already begun the process of acquiring the industrial facilities necessary for indigenous naval construction. Steel production was, of course, basic to such naval construction and Japan had begun to acquire integrated steel plants, furnaces and rolling equipment necessary for the construction of heavy armor plate and for the construction of the largest naval units. With British help, Japanese steel production had increased dramatically in the first years of the twentieth century and Japanese private capital had begun to move into the steel industry to supplement the efforts of the navy's own shipyards and arsenals. Hence, the capacity of Japanese industry and technology by this time made possible the construction in Japanese dockyards (though largely to foreign design), of five of the eight new protected cruisers called for in the Yamamoto expansion plan.

While purchasing warships from a range of foreign contractors in order to assure the highest standards of naval armament and then following this purchase with indigenous production of the same or an improved design, the navy had begun to pioneer the Japanese formula for technology transfer which it would pursue until the 1930s: copy, improve and innovate. This involved the purchase of specific foreign examples, the exhaustive analysis and testing of those models, their subsequent improvement where possible, and the allocation of production arrangements to either government or private facilities.[13] Using this formula, the navy was now able to produce a range of superior ordnance, machinery and lesser ship types.

In any case, the cost of naval construction, both foreign and domestic, placed a heavy strain on the Japanese economy which was still largely agricultural. To finance the burden of military preparations, including naval construction, the government increased domestic taxation (which fell largely on small merchants and on the agricultural class), imposed government monopolies on certain commodities, and used the ¥360,000,000 indemnity from China for armament expansion. To add to these revenues the government sought public loans within Japan and in 1898 began to scrutinize foreign capital markets. In 1899, Japan obtained a loan of £10,000,000 from British banks.[14]

With these industrial and fiscal resources, Japan, on the eve of its clash with Russia, was fourth among the world's maritime powers, with a well-balanced fleet of six modern battleships, eight armored cruisers, 16 protected cruisers, 20 destroyers and 58 torpedo boats. It had, moreover, a naval staff which kept abreast of the latest tactical thought and which provided the Combined Fleet (reconstituted on the eve of war) with detailed tactical planning for a major fleet encounter. It had kept up with developments in fire control and its principal units were well equipped with range tables and Barr and Stroud range finders. Its crews had been brought to peak efficiency with constant training at its main base at Sasebo and its leadership, particularly that of Combined Fleet commander Admiral Tôgô Heihachirô, had a keen appreciation of the strategic imperatives of the coming conflict.[15]

The navy was, of course, still the navy of a regional power. Its mission was to defend the seas around Japan, to blockade enemy (Russian) naval forces in their East Asian ports, and to protect the maritime communications of any Japanese land force placed on the northeast coast of Asia. In the war that followed, 1904–05, with few exceptions, the Japanese Navy demonstrated superior performance in carrying out these tasks. The culmination of this performance was the signal triumph scored by the Combined Fleet under Tôgô with the annihilation of the Russian Baltic Fleet in the straits of Tsushima, 27–28 May 1905. Following the battle, Russia dropped from third to sixth place among the world's maritime powers, while Japan leapt to third place. More importantly, based upon the apparent lessons of Tsushima, the victory fixated Japanese naval doctrine on the concept of the decisive battle at sea whose outcome would be determined by big ships and big guns. This dogma shaped the navy's force structure priorities for decades to come.[16]

1905–22

Despite the completeness of the victory at Tsushima, in the decade that followed the war the nation and the navy faced several formidable challenges. The first of these was the spreading naval arms race among the Western maritime powers which caused a decline in Japanese naval strength relative to that of the great powers: Japan sank from third to fifth among the maritime nations. The other challenge was the shift in Japan–US relations from cooperation to rivalry. This rift was provoked by Japan's resentment over the treatment of its nationals on the US west coast, by the emergence of competing ambitions in the western Pacific, and most of all by the fact that the two nations were now the foremost naval powers in the Pacific. Thus, each hypothetically posed the most dangerous naval threat to the other.

The Japanese response to these two challenges was articulated by the navy's foremost thinker of the period, Captain (later Admiral) Satô Tetsutarô. It was Satô who provided to the Japanese Navy the two concepts which were to have an indelible influence on Japanese naval policy and naval construction. The first, his designation of a hypothetical enemy based on that nation's capability to threaten Japanese security (rather than upon its intentions to do so), became a basic feature of Japanese naval policy from 1907 onward. By this criterion the US Navy was the Japanese Navy's obvious hypothetical enemy against which all Japanese naval plans, construction and force structure must be directed.

Second, based on this assumption and recognizing that lesser Japanese economic and industrial strength would make it impossible to match the United States ship-for-ship in naval power, Satô (probably in collaboration with Captain Akiyama Saneyuki at the Naval Staff College) worked out a formula which called for the maintenance of naval strength at least 70 per cent of that of the United States (in naval tonnage).[17] The 70 per cent ratio was founded on the widely held assumption of the day that it was necessary for an attacking fleet to hold a 50 per cent superiority in firepower over a fleet defending its territorial waters. For that reason Satô concluded, that in order to repel an attacking fleet a defending fleet had to possess 70 per cent of the strength of an attacking fleet; anything less than this percentage – say, 60 per cent of an attacking enemy's strength – would imperil the security of the defending nation.[18] Though its assumptions were badly flawed, the 70 per cent ratio was to become one of the principal pillars of Japanese naval policy for the next 30 years.

The difficulty in the navy's identification of the United States as its hypothetical enemy was that it ran directly counter to the grand strategic priorities of the Imperial Japanese Army which identified Russia as the nation's most likely hypothetical enemy. The 1907 Imperial Defense Policy represented an attempt to eliminate this dichotomy and to coordinate a national strategy for Japan's two armed services. In fact, it only served to highlight their fundamentally opposed approaches to grand strategy and thus merely resulted in the designation of two hypothetical enemies instead of one, Russia for the army and the United States for the navy.[19]

The institution of these fundamental policies – the United States as the navy's hypothetical enemy and the insistence on a 70 per cent ratio vis-à-vis US naval strength – was paralleled by the beginning of strategic and tactical planning for a naval conflict with the United States. These plans, which were to shape Japanese naval force structure and hence naval construction, centered on the assumption of a decisive big-gun duel at sea somewhere in the western Pacific. That grand encounter was to be preceded by attrition of the US battle line by Japanese light forces prior to the decisive battle, so as to reduce the US battle force to near equality with or even inferiority to its Japanese opponent.[20]

The navy, for its part, used the 1907 Imperial Defense Policy, or rather, one of its several codicils, to undertake a new round of naval construction which called for the building, over an eight-year period, of a battle force of eight battleships and eight armored cruisers. This, the 'Eight–Eight Fleet Plan' came to be the third pillar of Japanese naval policy for the next 15 years. [21] But in 1907, given the heavy strains on Japanese capital resources and a growing deficit in the nation's balance of payments that were legacies of the Russo-Japanese War, a fleet of this size was beyond the economic resources of the Japanese government which was already burdened with heavy debt stemming from foreign and domestic public loans floated during the war.[22] There was, moreover, little public enthusiasm for a massive augmentation of the navy, now that its most immediate enemy had been driven from East Asian waters. For these reasons, the Navy General Staff building plans for an Eight–Eight Fleet were whittled down successively by the Navy Ministry, the cabinet and the Diet. The staff was therefore obliged to proceed toward its goal by stages.

However, it was the advent of the revolution in naval technology represented by the completion of the British *Dreadnought* in 1906, and even more the completion of the three British battlecruisers of the *Invincible* class, that compromised the Japanese Navy's building plans. Inevitably, because of these British innovations, some of the capital ships under construction for the Japanese Navy during the Russo-Japanese War, and completed some years after it, were obsolete from the day they were launched. This was certainly true of the last two Japanese battleships (the *Kashima* and *Katori*) to be built abroad. It was less true of the first two battleships to be constructed on Japanese slipways – the *Aki* and *Satsuma* – since only Japan's tightened financial circumstances at the time of their launching (during the Russo-Japanese War) prevented them from being all-big-gun warships. In any event, it was not until 1909 that Japan was able to lay down its first two dreadnoughts.

That it was able to do so, says much about the progress of the Japanese industrial and technological base by this time. The First World War dramatically accelerated the growth of domestic steel production as private firms expanded capacity and new firms were established. The Japanese Navy, having helped to foster the steel industry, was quick to exploit these new capacities. While most of the navy's armor plate was imported from the West until the First World War, as early as 1900 the first 150 mm Krupp cemented (KC) armor was produced in Japan and by 1915 domestic industry had produced the first 200 mm Vickers cemented (VC) plates.[23] Along with steel, great advances were also made in these years in the

Japanese chemical and electrical industries, which were essential to the progress of Japanese naval technology.

The beginning of the twentieth century not only saw the broadening and deepening of the Japanese technological base, but a change in the process for acquiring naval technology. At the end of the nineteenth century Japanese naval research was concentrated on the identification and indigenization of foreign designs which would then be produced in Japan under license and using imported materials. In this way the technological gap between Japan and the West began to close with increasing speed after the 1894–95 war with China.[24] With the establishment of the Navy Technological Department (Kansei Honbu, Kanpon for short) in 1900, the navy acquired its first central facility for its own research, development, and diffusion of advanced technology. In this way, the navy began to develop its own technologies and to design materials across a range of machinery, weapons, explosives and instruments. It was in the domestic production of these items during these years that the government's policy of technological diffusion began to pay off. It was large private yards like those of Mitsubishi and Kawasaki that gradually but increasingly began to supply the navy with ships incorporating the same technologies that the navy had developed. [25]

With the growth of the steel industry and with the increasing sophistication of Japanese naval technology it became possible to increase the percentage of warship tonnage as well as the size of warships built in Japanese yards. Still, up until the First World War, the navy was dependent essentially on foreign (largely British) construction for its navy while domestic naval construction was produced largely in the navy's own yards. Between the latter half of 1904 and 1912, the nation's industrial and technological advances had enabled Japan to build the five protected cruisers already discussed (two of which were built in private yards), four battlecruisers and the battleships *Aki* and *Satsuma* mentioned above. In 1909, with the laying down of the *Kawachi* and *Settsu*, Japan became the fourth nation to build dreadnought-type battleships for its fleet. Designed and constructed in Japan (at the navy's Yokosuka and Kure yards respectively), the two ships incorporated some of the best features of British and German dreadnoughts already under construction, an indication of the Japanese Navy's obsessive drive for the latest in naval technology.[26]

In 1910, with the design and construction of the four battlecruisers of the *Kongô* class, a major chapter in the construction of the Japanese Navy came to an end. In order to give Japanese constructors an opportunity to observe the building techniques of the world's foremost naval power, the namesake ship of the class was built in the Vickers yard to specifications in certain respects more demanding than those of similar types being supplied to the Royal Navy.[27] But the *Kongô* was the last Japanese warship built abroad and the remaining ships of the class were built in Japanese

31

yards, one at the navy's Yokosuka yard and the other two in private yards. With their completion, Japan's naval construction industry and technology can be said to have come of age. Between 1912 and 1920, in pursuit of the 'Eight–Eight Fleet Plan', the navy added six dreadnoughts to its fleet, two each of the *Fusô*, *Ise* and *Nagato* classes, each, upon its completion, being among the most powerful of its type in any navy.

Yet, because of the lag-time between the authorization and the completion of a capital ship and because of the method by which the navy counted the effective life of such a warship, the goal of an 'Eight–Eight Fleet' remained outside of the navy's reach. Early during the First World War, emboldened by the prospect that a recovering Japanese economy could support a larger naval budget, the navy submitted an expansion plan that could realize an 'Eight–Four Fleet' as an interim stage to the final goal. But in the wake of a bribery scandal that provoked public distrust of the navy, it was rejected by the Japanese Diet. Then, in 1916, the sudden and apparent challenge of a massive US naval building program had a salutary effect where previously the navy's own arguments and publicity had failed to convince a skeptical Diet. In response to the Congressional navy bill that would have increased American tonnage superiority over Japan by 100 per cent (a project never completely realized), the Diet authorized an expansion plan which would have provided the navy with an 'Eight–Six Fleet'.[28]

In 1918, learning of an even more ambitious plan President Wilson had set before Congress to add ten more battleships to the ten already under construction under the 1916 bill, thus providing the United States with the world's greatest battle fleet, the Navy General Staff proposed the construction of 24 capital ships to be built over an eight-year period. But if the navy proposed, the Diet disposed. By this time, many in the cabinet and the Diet recognized what the navy chose to ignore: that while the Japanese economy had grown remarkably during the First World War, the navy's expenses had grown even faster, so fast indeed that the Finance Ministry warned that future naval budgets could spell the death of the Japanese economy.

In 1919, President Wilson, determined to achieve naval pre-eminence, not just parity, with Britain, set before Congress a plan for yet another 16 capital ships. This American *démarche* was sufficient to goad the Japanese Diet which, in 1920, approved an augmentation plan that would at last make possible an 'Eight–Eight' fleet: four battlecruisers of over 41,000 tons and armed with ten 16-inch guns and four battleships of over 47,000 tons armed with ten 18-inch guns – all units to be completed by 1927.

But the planning and construction of these super-battleships were overtaken by the Japanese decision in 1921 to participate in the Washington naval conference. That decision brought to an end the aspirations for an 'Eight–Eight Fleet' and, for the time being, forced upon Japan two critical restrictions; the acceptance of an inferior position among the three great fleets of the world and, seemingly, the hostage of its maritime security to the good intentions of the Anglo-US naval powers. It remained to be seen how Japan's naval leadership would deal with these new challenges during the rest of the decade.

NOTES

All Japanese-language publications cited are published in Tokyo.

1. For a good English-language summation of these matters, see John Curtis Perry, 'Great Britain and the Emergence of Japan as a Naval Power', *Monumenta Nipponica* , vol. 21 (1966), 305–21.
2. For a detailed study of these issues see David Evans, 'The Satsuma Faction and Professionalism in the Japanese Naval Officer Corps of the Meiji period, 1868–1912' (PhD dissertation, Stanford University, 1978).
3. Among those young constructors selected for this training was the future father of Japanese naval architecture, Sasô Sachû.
4. Shinohara Hiroshi, *Kaigun Sôsetsu-shi: Igirisu gunji komondan no kage* [History of the Founding of the Navy: Influence of British Naval Missions] (Tokyo: Riburopôto, 1986), 255–83.
5. For an expert explanation of this process see Richard Samuels, *Rich Nation, Strong Army: National Security and the Technological Transformation of Japan* (Ithaca, NY: Cornell University Press, 1994), 84–95.
6. In 1896, work on the Yawata iron and steel works was begun, the blast furnace was blown in 1901 with an annual capacity of 60,000 metric tons (more than doubling Japan's existing iron-making capacity), and modern steel-making and rolling equipment was installed. Yawata was to occupy a vital place in Japan's future naval construction.
7. For an English-language survey history of the Yokosuka naval base and shipyard see Tom Tompkins, *Yokosuka: Base of an Empire* (Novato, CA: Presidio Press, 1981).
8. Although Japan was obliged to be dependent on foreign naval construction during the decades in which it was developing its own industrial and technological base, it strove to maintain its economic autonomy. To this end, abjuring foreign loans, during 1874–96, it financed its industrialization and its national defense entirely from domestic savings. Its preparations and conduct of its war with China, 1894–95, was financed largely by domestic loans and from funds transferred from the Treasury. Toshio Suzuki, *Japanese Government Loan Issues on the London Capital Market, 1870–1913* (London: Athlone Press, 1994), 66.
9. David C. Evans and Mark R. Peattie, *Kaigun: Strategy, Tactics, and Technology in the Imperial Japanese Navy, 1887–1941* (Annapolis, MD: Naval Institute Press, 1997), 11–13.
10. Japan, Kaigunshô, ed., *Yamamoto Gombei to kaigun* [Yamamoto Gombei and the Navy] (Hara Shobô, 1966), 348–9.
11. Peter Brook, 'Armstrong Battleships Built for Japan', *Warship International*, vol. 22, no. 3 (1985), 269–70 and 278–82.
12. Kaigunshô, *Yamamoto Gombei*, 350.
13. This process is summarized in Christopher Howe, *The Origins of the Japanese Trade Supremacy* (London: Hurst, 1996), 283–4 and given greater detail in Samuels, *Rich Nation, Strong Army*, 42–56.
14. Suzuki, *Japanese Government Loan Issues*, 83–4.

15. Evans and Peattie, *Kaigun*, 74–84.
16. Ibid., 124–32.
17. Ibid., 141–44.
18. That is, a 1.5 to 1 superiority for the attacker would correspond to a 0.67 to 1 (67 per cent) inferiority for the defender. If the latter ratio is less than 0.67 then the probability favors a victory for the attacker; if it exceeds 0.67 the probability favors a victory for the defender. For Satô and Akiyama the 70 per cent figure may have been nothing more than a convenient rounding off of 67 per cent. Japan, Bôeichô Bôeikenkyûjô Senshishitsu, *Dai Hon'ei Kaigunbu: Rengô Kantai, ichi, kaisen made* [Japan Imperial General Headquarters, Navy Division, Combined Fleet, no. 1. To the opening of the Pacific War], Senshi Sôsho series (Asagumo Shimbunsha, 1975), 158–9.
19. In actual fact there was little reason to designate the US Navy as Japan's hypothetical enemy. There was, after all, no clash of fundamental interests between Japan and the United States nor any indication that either the Japanese or US governments desired a confrontation. The truth was that in the decade before the First World War, the US Navy provided to its Japanese counterpart a 'budgetary enemy' upon which the Japanese navy could claim an increasing share of the nation's defense expenditures. Far from providing a rationale for any particular force structure by way of a detailed explanation of a US naval threat, the 1907 Imperial Defense Policy arbitrarily selected the United States in order to justify the scale of naval strength it desired.
20. Ibid., *Dai Hon'ei Kaigunbu*, 187–91.
21. Ibid.
22. The Japanese government obtained huge loan issues in London, New York, Berlin and Paris, as well as public loans in Japan, by which the government had largely financed the war. This debt burden grew rapidly from 1906 and was nearing crisis proportions by the eve of the First World War. By 1913, Japan's total foreign indebtedness was about ¥2 billion. Fortunately for Japan, the nation's sudden spurt in trade caused by Western orders from Japanese industry during the war prevented the crisis and by the end of the war Japan had paid off its debts and, until the Kantô earthquake of 1923, the nation had no need to float more foreign loans. Suzuki, *Japanese Government Loan Issues*, 83–4; William Lockwood, *The Economic Development of Japan* (Princeton, NJ: Princeton University Press, 1954), 35–6.
23. Eric Lacroix and Linton Wells II, *Japanese Cruisers of the Pacific War* (Annapolis, MD: Naval Institute Press, 1997), 743.
24. One of the measures of the navy's procurement policy on technological progress in Japanese industry was gun manufacture. The navy assiduously monitored the development of naval ordnance in the West throughout the late nineteenth century and continuously provided this metallurgical information to Japanese industry for the manufacture of Japanese naval guns. By a combination of imports and import substitution (of parts and materials), it would appear that the navy had achieved parity with international standards in naval ordnance by 1907–10. Christopher Howe, *The Origins of the Japanese Trade Supremacy* (London: Hurst, 1996), 298–301. In other fields, such as steam propulsion, Japanese private industry was able to undertake forward engineering on imported technologies. Examples of this phenomenon were the Parsons and Curtis marine steam turbines lent to Mitsubishi's Nagasaki works and the Kawasaki shipyard respectively whose research and development of these mechanisms led eventually to the development of a wholly indigenous turbine which became the prototype for all Japanese engines to the end of the Pacific War. Miwao Matsumoto, 'Reconsidering Japanese Industrialization: Marine Turbine

Transfer at Mitsubishi', *Technology and Culture*, vol. 40 (January 1999), 74–97.

25. Examples of this indigenous naval technology were the Ijûin fuze, adopted in 1900 and used throughout the Russo-Japanese War; Shimose Smokeless Powder in 1913; the Ro-Go Kampon Boiler (1914), which remained the standard Japanese Navy boiler throughout the Pacific War; and the Kampon Turbine (1916–17) which became extensively used in Japanese naval propulsion by the end of the First World War. See Evans and Peattie, *Kaigun*, 63, 181–3.

26. Anthony J. Watts and Brian G. Gordon, *The Imperial Japanese Navy* (Garden City, NJ: Doubleday, 1971), 39–40.

27. The *Kongô* was sufficiently superior to the British *Lion* class battlecruisers to cause no more of that class to be laid down and to induce the battlecruiser *Tiger* to be redesigned before it was completed. Watts and Gordon, ibid., 40; Masataka Chihaya and Yasuo Abe, 'IJN Kongô, Battleship, 1912–1944', in *Warships in Profile*, vol. I, ed. John Wingate (Windsor, Berkshire: Profile Publications, 1971).

28. Evans and Peattie, *Kaigun*, 166–7.

3

The French Navy, 1880–1914

Paul Halpern

The French Navy in 1880 was still burdened by the aftermath of the Franco-Prussian War. It was decidedly the junior service as far as expenditure was concerned and its case was not helped by the fact that owing to the circumstances of the war in the public mind it had not been able to accomplish much at sea. Ironically, the navy did enjoy considerable popularity owing to its services on land in the defense of Paris. In 1880 it was operating under the framework of the program of 1872, a program whose goals the French legislature never came near to funding adequately. The French placed most emphasis on maintaining ships on distant stations and, in European waters, a 'squadron of evolutions' (*escadre d'évolutions*), plus ships considered essential for training. The number of battleships in commission was relatively small. The French planned for coast defence ships (*garde-côtes*) and gunboats (*canonnières*) to protect their coasts and cruisers and sloops (*avisos*) for foreign stations.[1] The primary potential enemy was still Germany and the first battleship laid down under the program and commissioned in 1878, the *Redoutable*, was designed with a shallow draught for operations in the Baltic and with a still sizeable amount of sail to minimize the need for coaling while executing a blockade of the German coast.[2]

The relative decline of the French Navy from its position during the Second Empire was all the more painful because in many ways the French had a good technological base. This was, after all, the navy that had introduced the ironclad *Gloire* and enjoyed the services of a naval constructor corps and naval artillery corps that attracted graduates from the elite École Polytechnique. The artillery-testing center at Gâvres was renowned for systematic experimentation involving artillery, explosives, projectiles and armor plate.[3] The situation was less happy with arsenals of the five French naval ports: Brest, Toulon, Cherbourg, Rochefort and Lorient. Rochefort and Lorient were really relics of an earlier age and their maintenance involved much duplication of effort, but political pressures kept them in existence and for a long time the French parliament was suspicious of and

36

reluctant to entrust work to private yards. The French Navy also had factories at Indret for the manufacture of steam engines and boilers, at Ruelle for the production of guns and at Guérigny for the production of anchors and chains. Unfortunately, the French administrative organization, often a hodgepodge left over from an earlier age, was notorious for its complexity and red tape. The navy also did not have control over the independent organization responsible for the manufacture of explosives, the *Service des poudres*, and there would be a nightmarish problem of unstable powder in the years before the First World War. The elite engineering background of the naval constructors also proved, perhaps, too much of a good thing. There were strong egos, competing schools of thought and a distinct lack of cooperation with engineers seeking an ideal engineering solution at the expense of practicality. These organizational difficulties would by the turn of the century inflict great harm on the navy, offsetting the potential advantages that might have been derived from the imaginative or technically daring constructors. The French, in summary, did not manage technology well and the French Navy would pay the price.[4]

The French Navy under the political and financial constraints of the Third Republic could have no thought of attempting to rival the Royal Navy. The standard of strength was to be the combined fleets of the Triple Alliance – Germany, Austria-Hungary and Italy. Fortunately, the German Navy was still small but by the 1880s Italian naval development was a cause for concern. To make the situation even worse, by the early 1880s Great Britain became a major colonial rival. This came at a time when the complex but masterful diplomacy of Bismarck was successful in ensuring that France was not likely to have an important continental ally. France was alone against a sea of potential enemies.

In the question of technological development it is often not clear whether technology drove the strategy or the strategic situation stimulated development of the technology. There is no question, however, that by the 1880s one technological development had had a major influence on French strategy and naval construction. This was the perfection of the self-propelled torpedo by the British engineer Alfred Whitehead. The French embraced the torpedo as a relatively cheap method for a poorer navy, in terms of finance or ships, to offset the advantages of its more powerful rivals.

The French had been interested in 'torpedoes' (*torpilles*) ever since the 1860s but initially these were the devices similar to present-day mines. In 1868 a school for *mineurs-marins* was established at Boyardville on the Ile d'Oléron, near Rochefort. The French were also intrigued by the spar-torpedo and until the performance of self-propelled torpedoes improved beyond their original relatively short range they were inclined to favor this device. The Russians used them in the Russo-Turkish War, 1877–78, and the French were successful with them against the Chinese fleet at Foochow and Sheï-Poo bay in 1884–85.[5]

37

In 1867 the French Navy had been informed by the French consul in Fiume of trials of the Whitehead torpedo and in 1868 sent a naval officer to investigate. The first talks with Whitehead did not succeed, the disruption of the Franco-Prussian War intervened and it was not until January 1873 that the French, perhaps stimulated by intelligence that other powers had acquired the device, proceeded with trials at Boyardville. Whitehead was present, jealously guarding his secret to the point of working behind a screen. The trials were successful and led to a contract being signed in April 1873 for licensed production in France.[6] The French then proceeded to experiment to find the best way to employ the device and which type of craft to use. The early torpedoes were disappointing in performance, hampered by difficulties in launching and relatively slow. Progressive development by 1880 made the torpedo a much more attractive weapon, with increased speed and explosive charge; they could then be launched by means of compressed air or steam from tubes mounted above the water. By 1881, and not counting rival designs or competition such as the German Schwarzkopf Company, Whitehead had sold 1,456 torpedoes to over a dozen navies. The French accounted for 218 but the British had purchased 254, the Germans 203 and the Russians 250.[7] The French Navy was therefore not different from other contemporary navies in seeking to exploit this new technology. However, in France a powerful and attractive line of naval, strategic and tactical thought emerged and struck a responsive cord with the French public outside of professional naval circles, and for a time had a dominant position with those who controlled the purse strings, the French parliament. The doctrine and its followers are generally grouped together under the name *Jeune École*.[8] The torpedo played an important role in its doctrine and its best-known exponent – but certainly not the only one – was Vice-Admiral Hyacinthe-Laurent-Théophile Aube (1826–90), minister of marine, January 1886–May 1887.[9] The torpedo, carried in a swarm of relatively cheap small torpedo boats was a weapon that naturally appealed to the French, forced by continuing military requirements to restrict spending on their navy and unable to compete directly with their colonial rivals, the British.

In his 1882 publication, *La guerre maritime et les ports français*, Aube anticipated that torpedo boats could defend the French coast by driving back blockading squadrons, thereby permitting French battleships to sortie and engage the weakened enemy ships of the line, now reduced in numbers. The torpedo boats would also facilitate the sortie of French cruisers to attack lines of communication and pursue the traditional *guerre de course*. Conventional squadron warfare with battleships would still have its place in the Mediterranean, assuring communications with North Africa. The torpedo boats would act primarily in the Channel and Atlantic along with cruisers conducting the *guerre de course*. Aube was confident that the electric telegraph and railways would permit rapid concentration of troops to repel an enemy landing, and that steam and the electric tele-graph would facilitate a concentration against the enemy blockading squadrons off the French ports.[10]

Aube's thought was popularized by the journalist Gabriel Charmes, a brilliant writer destined to die relatively young from tuberculosis. The two became fast friends in the last years of Charmes' life and Aube invited him for a cruise with the Mediterranean fleet. The ideas of Aube and Charmes became intertwined to the detriment in the long run of Aube's reputation, for the journalist went beyond what Aube had recommended and distorted the doctrine in favor of the torpedo boat.[11] The concept of 'division of labor' was introduced, that is the traditional battleship had combined in one ship the functions of the ram, the gun and the torpedo. Charmes argued that this ought to be divided among specialized ships, some with guns, some with torpedoes and some acting as rams. The *bateau-canon* or gunboat, approximately the same dimensions as the torpedo boat, would be armed with a single 5.5 inch (140 mm) cannon. There would be two types of torpedo boats, offensive (*torpilleurs d'attaque*) armed only with torpedoes and defensive (*torpilleurs de défense*), armed with revolver (quick-firing) canons and spar torpedoes to protect the offensive torpedo boats from attack by enemy light craft. The craft would form a '*groupe de combat*', composed of two gunboats and eight torpedo boats (four defensive and four offensive). The gunboats and defensive torpedo boats would in theory split the enemy line, firing rapidly and producing much smoke to enable the offensive torpedo boats to break through and attack the enemy battleships. To handle logistical needs there would also be 'mother ships' (*ravitailleurs*), each capable of supplying four gunboats and 16 torpedo boats.[12]

The popular imagery of torpedo boats as 'microbes' or 'fleas' or 'David's against 'Goliaths' is appealing but it also tends to obscure what was prob-ably the core of the *Jeune École* argument. This was the *guerre de course* where the real action would take place because the stronger fleet would be constrained to remain in its bases out of fear of the torpedo and the weaker fleet would naturally decline combat. Furthermore, the execution of a trade war would be merciless. The *bateau-canon* would, for example, attack Italian ports and not merely military installations but also open cities and undefended commercial harbors. At sea the 'autonomous torpedo boats' (*torpilleurs autonomes*), given their small size and complement, would be unable to take prizes in the traditional manner and would there-fore shadow much larger and perhaps better armed liners and under the cover of darkness send them to the bottom. This ruthless action obviously foreshadowed the unrestricted submarine warfare of the First World War. For Charmes it would be the means to bring England, much stronger at sea but absolutely dependent on overseas commerce, to its knees by inducing economic panic and social chaos.[13]

Aube was destined to be minster for only a relatively short time, but his influence, for better or worse, lived on. It lasted long enough for him to create the system of scattering torpedo boats about French ports under the designation of *défenses mobiles* and also order a competition for a submarine design that led to the experimental submarine *Gymnote* of 1888. Aube also began construction of what would be ultimately a large number of cruisers for commerce raiding, although his program would be drastically curtailed and the cruisers themselves would undergo many mutations with the final results, a generation later, far from satisfactory. Aube slowed construction of battleships and ordered large numbers of small torpedo boats. However, the experimental *bateau-canon*, appropriately named *Gabriel Charmes* after the latter's death, was a dismal failure. The small craft was simply too unstable a firing platform. Unfortunately for the French Navy the concept of 'autonomous torpedo boats' able to undertake serious operations in the Atlantic was hardly credible. The naval maneuvers of 1887 – France's first – demonstrated that one could not yet dispense with large ships, and construction of battleships was resumed. The 35 meter torpedo boats which were to play such an important role were plagued with a variety of problems including a lack of stability.[14]

The *Jeune École* was probably as much a political as it was a purely naval question. This accounted for the worst of its effects and its persistence almost until the end of the century. Advocates of big ships were regarded as reactionaries, anxious to find plush commands for superannuated officers of high rank. The relative scarcity of these commands in a navy facing economic constraints meant that a small oligarchy ruled the French Navy, monopolizing the best opportunities. Torpedo boats, in contrast, were the 'republican arm', inherently democratic in nature and by their very number offering junior officers ample opportunity for command. This also foreshadows 1914–18 when the U-boat war was regarded as a 'lieutenant's war'. In addition, torpedo boats were cheap – one could build many for the price of a single battleship – and politically correct. Politicians were attracted by the 'defensive' aspects of *Jeune École* policies. Torpedo boats could be grouped in the *défenses mobiles* and the coast could also be protected by the *garde-côtes* or coast defense ships, vessels of relatively modest dimensions able to operate in shallow waters and ostensibly cheaper than the larger and more conventional battleships. *Jeune École* doctrines divided the navy and in the ensuing decade we find ministers and officers of one school or the other alternating in office, while the lack of organization in the dockyards permitted endless experimentation with ships under construction. The effect was for one minister to undo the progress made by another.[15]

The lack of organization was most evident in the battleship program during the 1890s. The French constructed relatively small numbers of battleships (only five in the 1880s, 10–11 in the 1890s), very slowly and with little uniformity. Even when the ships were supposed to be of the same class the latitude given to each dockyard meant that they differed in many details. Constructors were free to indulge in that individualism and creativity upon which the French pride themselves. Cannon, ostensibly the same caliber, were not always the same model and gear and other apparatus differed from ship to ship. The mixture of guns led some ships to be described as floating artillery museums with the obvious disadvantages for the supply of ammunition. The constraints on tonnage and dimensions also resulted in solutions that were far from happy in terms of endurance, habitability and protection. The French also continued to divert resources to the politically correct *garde-côtes* or coast defense ships.[16] The small slow ships with limited armament would have been no match for a proper battleship and they found no real role at sea. Until the naval program of 1900 the French fleet was described as *la flotte d'échantillons* or 'fleet of samples'.[17]

The French built large numbers of torpedo boats; the orders that were passed or considered in 1887 aimed at doubling French torpedo boat strength in less than three years and by 1892 the French had 220 in service or under construction compared with 186 for Great Britain, 143 for Germany and 129 for Italy.[18] The *défenses mobiles* were politically popular, they were appropriately 'defensive' and could be scattered about the coast providing the maximum amount of constituents with the illusion that the government was doing something to protect them. Unfortunately, the real value of this large flotilla of small torpedo boats in time of war was questionable. The realities of the sea made a mockery of the most optimistic *Jeune École* expectations and the development of quick-firing cannon, nets and eventually the 'torpedo boat destroyer' meant that the torpedo boat would not be the magic and suitably cheap weapon that would transform naval warfare. The French were naturally obligated to emulate British destroyer developments and in August 1896 ordered the 300 ton *Durandal* from the private yard Chanters Normand of Le Havre. The ship was designated an *aviso torpilleur* and served as the prototype of 55 300-ton destroyers for the French navy in the following decade.[19]

The *guerre de course* naturally required cruisers but technology had imposed a heavy new burden on those who wanted to pursue trade warfare. In the age of sail, commerce raiders could keep to sea as long as their supplies of food and fresh water lasted, and these could be replenished in sparsely populated places employing a minimum amount of gear. In contrast, late nineteenth-century warships required great quantities of coal, a fuel that was difficult (but not impossible) to transfer at sea. Coal would be found only at relatively developed ports equipped with depots and loading equipment and probably in telegraphic communication with the rest of the world so that the presence of a cruiser would be rapidly reported. The French never really developed the infrastructure to support cruiser warfare. Admiral Aube lacked the financial resources to do so and the majority of plans for bases that followed him came to nothing. In 1890 the *Conseil supérieur de la marine* had envisaged ten coaling stations, literally a chain of French coaling stations, around the world. By 1900, this had been scaled down to five, with Diego Suarez (Madagascar) and Dakar (Senegal) the most important from the strategic point of view. The former was well located for commerce raiding in the Indian Ocean and the latter menaced strategic British routes in the Atlantic. The scarcity of coaling stations need not have mattered much against the Triple Alliance but it would be a crippling limitation in any war against Great Britain and the vast British empire.[20]

The French cruiser program produced interesting innovations but ultimately led the French down what would be an expensive dead end. In 1889, Aube's immediate successor Senator Edouard Barbey, ordered the *Dupuy de Lôme*, the world's first true armored cruiser, a 6,500-ton ship with hull completely encircled by a belt of side armor, armed with two 7.6-inch guns and six 6.4-inch quick-firing guns and capable of 20 knots. The ship was superior to Italian and British protected cruisers and was intended to either break through an enemy cruiser screen or force enemy cruisers to break contact with the French. Between 1880 and the Anglo-French entente of 1904, the French laid down 21 armored cruisers (plus four after the entente) and 33 protected cruisers. Only two were really designed for commerce warfare for which most of the protected cruisers would have been far from adequate because of their small size, modest speed and insufficient coal capacity.[21] Disputes between the Budget Committee of the Chamber, the minister of marine, the Conseil Supérieur and Conseil des Travaux continued in the second half of the 1890s, resulting in a bewildering variety of classes and capabilities. By the turn of the century the French were concentrating on large armored cruisers, notably five 9,800-ton *Gloire* class, three 12,350-ton *Léon Gambetta* class, the even larger *Jules Michelet* (13,105 tons), *Ernest Renan* (13,504 tons) and, finally, two 13,847-ton *Edgar Quinet* class. This gave the French no fewer than 18–25 (depending on what one counts and when one begins) armored cruisers, the majority with a primary armament of only two (four starting with the *Gambettas*) 7.6-inch guns and a maximum speed not exceeding 23 knots. The *Renan* was not completed until 1909 and the two *Quinets* in 1911, well after the first British battlecruisers were in service and just as the first of the German battlecruisers was completed. These French armored cruisers were large, expensive (especially the latter classes) but weakly armed and relatively slow, and the French had neglected or deferred the fast scout or light cruisers that would prove so useful during the war.[22]

Undersea warfare was the one area where the French ended the nineteenth century well ahead of the rest of the world in technology. The design submitted by Maxime Laubeuf, an engineer in the *Génie Maritime*, won the 1896 competition instituted by Edouard Lockroy, one of the more competent and imaginative ministers at the turn of the century, for a true submarine capable of military use.[23] Laubeuf's design was for a double-hulled craft, the water ballast between the outer hull and inner pressure hull, with good sailing qualities for acting on the surface, and generally considered the first true submersible capable of actual offensive employment. The craft entered service in 1899 as the *Narval*. Laubeuf later in life recalled that the desiderata for the submarine's performance in the competition had been relatively vague and that he had approached the problem from the point of view of what he wanted the submarine to be able to do, appending this suggested mission to his proposal. Laubeuf envisaged his craft leaving from Brest or Cherbourg at nightfall, arriving off British ports before daybreak, submerging and torpedoing ships entering or leaving Portsmouth, Plymouth or the Thames estuary.[24] Lockroy was impressed by the potential of submarines, for in November 1898 he had ordered trials in which the *Gustave Zédé*, launched in 1893, despite its manifest limitations and the fact it was forced to show its kiosk through lack of a periscope, was judged to have made a successful torpedo attack on the battleship *Magenta* in the bay of Salins. Lieutenant Mottez, the *Zédé*'s commander, declared in his report that if an enemy fleet appeared off Toulon or attempted a raid against the îles d'Hyères the *Gustave Zédé* would sortie with a good chance of success in torpedoing one or several enemy ships. Lockroy claimed that had he the funds he would have ordered a dozen *Narvals*.[25] The construction of the *Narval* was given added impetus by the Fashoda affair of 1898 that exposed mercilessly the weakness of the French fleet in comparison with the Royal Navy. The French embarked on a submarine building program that would on the outbreak of war in 1914 give them one of the largest submarine fleets in the world. They had 46 submarines or submersibles in service and another 28 under construction.[26] However, by this time they had squandered their initial advantage and the submarine fleet in 1914 resembled the battleship fleet in 1900, that is, it was in many respects a 'fleet of samples'. In 1905 there were already 16 different types among the 39 French submarines. Rival schools of engineers squabbled over the types of submarines in what a former French submarine commander described as 'Byzantine discussions between partisans of "submarines" and "submersibles"'. Laubeuf was the object of considerable scorn and jealousy and would resign from the navy in 1906.[27] French naval construction was notoriously slow and French submarine construction would also be delayed by the absence of French producers of diesel engines. For example, in the case of three of the *Brumaire* class submarines built at Toulon, the firm Sautter-Harlé had contracted to deliver the engines, based on the design of the German company MAN, between September and November 1909, but the actual deliveries took place between October 1910 and April 1912. The order to lay down the submarines had been signed in October 1906 but they did not enter service until May–October 1912.[28] In addition, reliance on German designs had obvious disadvantages. In the case of the ten *Clorinde* class (1909–12) the Germans may have deliberately slowed down deliveries and withheld critical technical information. French submarine construction suffered from an additional disadvantage. In this new arm, officers with submarine experience were too junior and lacking in seniority to influence constructors who had a tendency to seek engineering solutions and were ignorant of the practical necessities of actually employing submarines at sea.[29]

Exactly how were those submarines to be used in time of war? The French envisaged five major missions: (1) attacking enemy ships on the high seas; (2) the protection of friendly coasts; (3) barring narrow passages, notably the Dover Straits; (4) action against the enemy coast, primarily penetrating enemy ports; and (5) intervening in a battle between squadrons. The last mission was an illusive goal that would lead the Royal Navy to the dubious *K* class and the French at the outbreak of the war had nothing really capable of fulfilling the role.[30]

The Fashoda affair had demonstrated how far the French Navy was behind in terms of battleships and Jean de Lanessan, minister of marine June 1899–June 1902, in the Program of 1900 set the strength of the French fleet at 28 battleships, 24 armored cruisers, 52 destroyers, 263 torpedo boats and 38 submarines. He set no limits on battleship tonnage and the six *Patrie* class (14,860 ton) laid down in 1901–3 were supposed to be comparable to British contemporaries and would have given the French their first truly homogeneous battleship squadron.[31] Vice-Admiral Alfred Gervais, commander of the active squadron 1895–96, declared in July 1898 that 'the battleship was the soul of the fleet, the rest mere auxiliaries'.[32] After acting as commander-in-chief of the fleet during the grand maneuvers of 1900 he argued that they had discredited many of the *Jeune École* theories in that speed alone would never compensate adequately for lack of offensive power and that current French torpedo boat and submarine defenses could not deter the movements of the battle fleet, and had been unable to counter a simulated attack on the port of Cherbourg. With the turn of the century the French Navy returned to increasing emphasis on the gun, the battleship and squadron warfare.

The French Navy lost its most dangerous potential enemy when the *Entente Cordiale* of 1904 turned Great Britain to at worst a neutral and, as time went on, more likely an active ally. This was fortunate, for it proved very difficult for the French to restore their relative position. The three years (1902–5) when the radical Camille Pelletan was minister of marine saw a return to what many considered the worst excesses of the *Jeune École*, but it was only an interval. Nevertheless, it was damaging, for Pelletan slowed badly needed battleship construction at a time when the

German fleet was moving steadily ahead, and if this could be discounted because Britain was now friendly, the Italian and imminent Austrian challenge in the Mediterranean could not. The French had a long way to go to catch up.

The first two *Patries* were not completed until the end of 1906 and the remaining slightly modified quartet was completed only in 1908. During the protracted period that they were under construction the Russo-Japanese War had taken place, HMS *Dreadnought* had entered service and the long-delayed ships were now obsolete. Paradoxically, the Russo-Japanese War also gave partisans of submarines like Vice-Admiral François Fournier, who had commanded the combined maneuvers in 1905, the opportunity to recommend that they wait until its lessons had been absorbed before building large surface warships and for the intermediate term concentrate on submarine construction. Fournier was inclined toward some theories of the *Jeune École* but not its excesses; for example, he championed the armored cruiser for commerce warfare as well as truly seaworthy torpedo boats and submarines. He now claimed that with 40 submarines in the Mediterranean and 25 in the Channel, France would make itself master of its maritime destiny and be in a position to dominate European choke points such as the Straits of Dover, Gibraltar and Messina.[33] However, the admirals of both the *Conseil Supérieur* and naval staff favored de-emphasizing flotilla defense, suspending construction of new cruisers for the time being and actually increasing the standard of battleship strength from 28 to 34 or even 38. They voted to begin construction in the 1906 budget of the first group of three of a new class of battleships, the 18,300 ton *Dantons*. Unfortunately, they chose a design that called for a mixed armament of four 12-inch (305 mm) and 12 9.2-inch (240 mm) and maintained this decision even after the monocaliber and revolutionary characteristics of the *Dreadnought* were known. The French built six of what were charitably termed 'semi-dreadnought' *Dantons*. They at least had the potential to be a true class of powerful homogeneous warships but even this gain was squandered because their completion was long delayed. Why had the French persisted in such an obvious error? One likely answer is that they drastically underestimated the range at which future battles would be fought. They estimated it would be 2,000 to 4,000 meters and that the ability to fire at ranges over 5,000 meters was of only marginal value. Furthermore, their own 12-inch gun was not really effective at ranges beyond 3,500 meters and the rate of fire was comparatively slow. Therefore the French naval staff favored medium artillery, especially the 9.2-inch (240 mm) gun, as the best solution, theoretically able to maintain a curtain of fire. The naval staff even produced figures demonstrating that in the weight of broadside per minute the *Danton* would be superior (7,480 kilogram) to the *Dreadnought* (6,170 kilogram). This, of course, conveniently ignored the greater range at which the *Dreadnought* would be able to fight. The charge has been made that this backward thinking was due to a lack of experience and progress in naval artillery during the retrograde years of the Pelletan regime with its neglect of capital ships.[34]

France's naval unpreparedness was the occasion for more parliamentary criticism than usual in the years 1906–9 and concern over the state of the navy played at least some role in the fall of Georges Clemenceau's cabinet in July 1909.[35] The malaise was accentuated by the nightmarish problem with unstable powder that resulted in the loss of the battleship *Iéna* in March 1907 and later the *Liberté*, in September 1911. There were production delays due to the usual and bad French habit of excess changes in design after construction had begun, along with procrastination in ordering essential components such as boilers, artillery and turrets until after the ships were on the stocks. To these were added archaic bureaucratic and work rules in the dockyards and a shortage of workers, as well as antiquated equipment. The net result was that the *Dantons* did not enter service until 1911 by which time they were already obsolete compared with their British and German contemporaries.[36]

Despite all these difficulties, the French Navy was put squarely on the path to becoming a battleship navy that Mahan would have been proud of by the ministers of marine, Vice-Admiral Augustin Boué de Lapeyrère, July 1909–March 1911, and Théophile Delcassé, March 1911–January 1913. Although Lapeyrère had first gained fame in 1884 by attacking a Chinese gunboat at Foochow with a spar torpedo, he was now a convinced battleship man, and in 1909 even wanted to increase the program total to a staggering 45 until both financial and production constraints convinced him the 1900 program of 28 would be more realistic. In March 1912 the French legislature gave its final approval to the organic naval law calling for, by 1920, 28 battleships, 10 light cruisers or scouts, 52 destroyers, 94 submarines (a big increase from the 38 of the 1900 program and the 64 that were originally proposed for the new law) and 10 ships (cruisers) for foreign stations.[37]

The French were now committed to a battleship navy and a war between squadrons. The destroyers and cruisers in the program were for reconnaissance and working with the fleet and not for the *guerre de course*, and there was no provision for small torpedo boats. Furthermore, in the near term the French concentrated on battleships and submarines; the light cruisers and flotilla craft were postponed to a later date. The navy was authorized to lay down the first two dreadnoughts, the *Courbet* and *Jean Bart*, in August 1910, as an interim measure while waiting for approval of the organic law. Two more, *France* and *Paris*, were scheduled to follow in 1911, making use of private yards since the arsenals were unable to handle the additional work. In addition, the French scrapped six out of nine old coast defense ships in order to overcome a shortage of personnel and thereby keep a second squadron of older battleships permanently in commission: another indication of changed priorities.[38]

Having committed to true dreadnoughts, the French found themselves behind in some of the technologies associated with large warships. The *Courbets* were designed with twelve 12-inch (305 mm) guns at a time when British contemporaries had gone to 13.5 inch (343 mm). Unfortunately, there were only preliminary studies of the 340 mm gun and turret in France and to switch would have meant an 18-month delay in the construction of badly needed modern battleships. Consequently, the French built their first class of four with 12 inch guns and the *Conseil Supérieur* again under-estimated the range of naval combat, believing it would not exceed 12,000 meters. They therefore restricted the angle of elevation of the 305 mm to 12 degrees, thereby limiting the range compared with foreign contemporaries. This error was repeated with the 340 mm guns of the next class.[39]

The heavy construction demands of the 1912 program resulted in the different French engineering and construction services being overwhelmed with work and to add to the difficulties the naval artillery corps had only come under naval control in 1910. In a number of essential matters including artillery, turrets and propulsion the French found it hard to catch up in a limited period of time. One could only do what one could and leave the improvements for the next class. The three 23,230-ton *Bretagne* class, laid down in 1912, had ten 340 mm guns and the five 25,230-ton *Normandie* class, laid down in 1913–14 but never finished, were designed with 12 340 mm guns arranged in three novel quadruple-gunned turrets. The four even larger 29,000-ton *Lyon* class scheduled for 1915 would have had a formidable 16 340 mm guns in four quadruple gunned turrets, but this class was never laid down.[40] The French, with two dreadnought squadrons on the way, even toyed with plans for 28,000-ton battlecruisers which they thought of slipping into the budget in the autumn of 1914 as a slight 'technical adjustment' (*recificatif*) to the budget, substituting 'fast battleships' for the scouts (*éclaireurs d'escadre*) of the organic law.[41]

The French planned to use this slow in modernizing battle fleet in classic Mahanian fashion. Lapeyrère assumed command of the *1ère Armée Navale*, France's major battle fleet, in the Mediterranean, after leaving the ministry, and trained hard for war – a war of squadrons. His plans, such as they were, involved putting to sea after the declaration of war with all available forces to sweep through enemy waters in order to hinder the enemy's mobilization and *combattre à outrance* any enemy force that put to sea. Destroyers and minelayers would act against the Italian base at Maddalena.[42] The main French effort would then move south for a blockade of Taranto and the entrance to the Adriatic. Submarines and torpedo boats, aside from the obvious defense of the French coast, appear to have played little role, at least in the early operations.[43] There was little concern for logistical support – the short war illusion – and the question of the relative priority of the essential convoys from North Africa in this scheme was never really solved before the war.[44] Oddly enough, as long as Italy held true to the Triple Alliance, Lapeyrère was not as far off the mark as later events made him seem. The Triple Alliance naval powers had concluded a secret naval convention in 1913 calling for a union of the Austrian and Italian fleets (and whatever German ships might be around) in Sicilian waters to seek control of the sea under the command of the Austrian Admiral Anton Haus. Haus, when he studied the tables of strength and his own unprecedented chances of having dreadnoughts, realized he just might do it – at least he would not have been relegated to a hopelessly inferior and therefore defensive position in the Adriatic – and confessed to his diary that he became so excited he could not sleep.[45] It all turned out very differently, of course, and it is ironic that the French were steaming full ahead in this direction at the very moment there is evidence the British were rethinking their strategy in the North Sea and ready to slow battleship construction in favor of submarines and flotilla defense.[46] Italy's declaration of neutrality left the French battle fleet without a real role in the war and only seven dreadnoughts of the ambitious French program were ever completed.[47]

The French were on their way to creating a truly formidable force, especially toward the end of the program when the flotilla craft and light cruisers would finally join the squadrons. Their experience shows, however, that it is not enough to embrace new technology, however fervently. That new technology must be managed as well, with clearly laid out and consistently followed programs. The French also discovered that once one falls behind in technology it can be very difficult to catch up, particularly in a limited period of time and with budgetary restraints. And finally, one cannot count on events allowing one to finish a long-term program. This, of course, happened to every naval power and, in the French case, war came six years early and before an essential component of the program, the light cruisers, had been laid down.

NOTES

1. Theodore Ropp, *The Development of a Modern Navy: French Naval Policy, 1871–1904*, ed. Stephen S. Roberts (Annapolis, MD: Naval Institute Press, 1987), pp. 33–7. Ropp remains the best study of the French Navy in this period. For concise surveys see Henri Le Masson, 'La politique navale française de 1870 à 1914', in Masson, *Propos Maritimes* (Paris: Éditions Maritimes et d'Outre-Mer, 1970), pp. 183–7, and Philippe Masson, 'La marine française de 1871 à 1914', in Guy Pedroncini (ed.), *Histoire Militaire de la France*, vol. III: *De 1871 à 1940* (Paris: Presses Universitaires de France, 1992), pp. 120–1.
2. Ropp, *Development of a Modern Navy*, pp. 35–6. *Redoutable*, with her main battery in casement and with the ram bow typical of the period, was the first French warship to use mostly steel instead of iron construction. See William

Hovgaard, *Modern History of Warships* (London: Spon, 1920; reprint London: Conway Maritime Press, 1971), pp. 18–19. Exhaustive detail in the three-part article: Mark Saibene, 'The *Redoutable*', *Warship International*, vol. 31, nos 1–2 (1994), pp. 15–45, 117–39, and vol. 32, no. 1 (1995), pp. 10–37.

3. Ropp, *Development of a Modern Navy*, pp. 8–9, 14.
4. Ibid., pp. 55–8, 143–4; Ray Walser, *France's Search for a Battle Fleet: Naval Policy and Naval Power, 1898–1914* (New York and London: Garland Publishing, 1992), pp. 153–4, 156–61, 186, 217, 212–16; Masson, 'Marine française de 1871 à 1914', pp. 146–7. The fact that the naval artillery corps and *Genie Maritime* were autonomous was another disadvantage, especially since the artillery corps was until after the turn of the century responsible for colonial artillery and engineering works in the colonies. The navy was not authorized to form its own corps of artillery engineers until November 1909, Le Masson, 'La Politique navale française', pp. 197–8.
5. Etienne Taillemite, *L'Histoire ignorée de la marine française* (Paris: Librairie Académique Perrin, 1988), pp. 382–6.
6. Henri Le Masson, *Histoire du torpilleur en France* (Paris: Académie de Marine, 1966), pp. 5–9. On the Whitehead torpedo, but with virtually nothing on the French Navy, see Edwyn Gray, *The Devil's Device: Robert Whitehead and the History of the Torpedo*, rev. edn (Annapolis, MD: Naval Institute Press, 1991).
7. Gray, *The Devil's Device*, p. 122.
8. Good studies are Taillemite, *L'Histoire ignorée de la marine française*, ch. 19 and Volkmar Bueb, *Die 'Junge Schule' der französischen Marine Strategie und Politik 1875–1900* (Boppard am Rhein: Harald Boldt, 1971).
9. A succinct summary of his career is in Etienne Taillemite, *Dictionnaire des Marins Français* (Paris: Éditions Maritimes et d'Outre-Mer, 1982), p. 16. See also Ropp, *Development of a Modern Navy*, pp. 155–6 and Le Masson, *Histoire du torpilleur*, pp. 32–3. One of Aube's predecessors, Auguste Gougeard, a former naval captain who was minister of marine, November 1881–January 1882, advocated 1,800 ton sea-going protected-deck 'torpedo ships' (frequently called 'torpedo cruisers') as cheaper than battleships and a means to counter Italian large ships such as the *Italia* or operate against British lines of communication in the Mediterranean. See Ropp, *Development of a Modern Navy*, pp. 130–1.
10. Masson, 'La marine française de 1871 à 1914', pp. 128–9; Ropp, *Development of a Modern Navy*, pp. 157–67.
11. Rémi Monaque, 'Gabriel Charmes: Propagandiste, enthousiaste, mais parfois infidèle des idées de l'amiral Aube' in Hervé Coutau-Bégarie (ed.), *L'évolution de la pensée navale VI* (Paris: Economica, 1997), pp. 57–66. See also Masson, 'La marine française de 1871 à 1914', pp. 128–30.
12. Monaque, 'Gabriel Charmes', pp. 62–3; Ropp, *Development of a Modern Navy*, pp. 160–1; Le Masson, *Histoire du torpilleur*, pp. 33–4.
13. Ropp, *Development of a Modern Navy*, pp. 162–7; Masson, 'La politique navale française', pp. 129–30; Le Masson, *Propos Maritimes*, pp. 191–3.
14. Ropp, *Development of a Modern Navy*, pp. 171–8; Le Masson, *Histoire du torpilleur*, pp. 37–42. Aube moved the torpedo school from Boyardville to Toulon and also started a factory there for the manufacture of torpedoes.
15. Examined at length in Henri Le Masson, 'Douze ministres ou dix ans d'hesitations de la marine française', *La Revue Maritime*, no. 233 (June 1966), pp. 710–33, and largely included in his 'La politique navale française', pp. 181–239. See also Ropp, *Development of a Modern Navy*, pp. 178–80, 288–92.
16. In the 1880s they built two classes of four, the 1,100 ton *Fusée* class and 1,600 ton *Achéron* class armored gunboats armed with either a single 9.4-inch or 10.8-inch gun and capable of around 12.5 knots. These were followed in the

1890s by the two 6,476-ton *Jemmapes* class armed with two 13.4 inch guns and two 6,681-ton *Amiral Tréhouarts* armed with two 12-inch guns. Ships' data from *Conway's All the World's Fighting Ships, 1860–1905* (London: Conway Maritime Press, 1979), pp. 300–1. The French at the beginning of the 1880s also had a miscellaneous collection (approximately 22) of floating batteries, armored rams, breastwork monitors and barbette ships laid down in earlier years.

17. Le Masson, 'La politique navale française', pp. 208–10.
18. Le Masson, *Histoire du torpilleur*, pp. 37, 47.
19. Ibid., pp.123–8. The designer, Jacques-Augustin Normand, had proposed originally that they might carry two different armaments according to their employment. When used as a torpedo boat against large warships, they would have three torpedo tubes with six torpedoes and two 47 mm cannon. When acting as *torpilleurs divisionnaires* against other torpedo boats they would carry only one tube with three torpedoes but one 65 mm and seven 47 mm guns. In service they all had a uniform armament, one 65 mm and six 47 mm guns and two torpedo tubes.
20. Ropp, *Development of a Modern Navy*, pp. 171, 198, 352–3. The five defended coaling stations were: Dakar, Diego Suarez, Fort-de-France, Saigon and Nouméa. The French parliament later added Reunion. Those dropped from consideration were Obock, Tahiti and Libreville. Bizerte in the Mediterranean was also developed as a major base, but this was aimed more for naval action against the Italians than commerce raiding against the British.
21. The two commerce raiders laid down in 1895 and 1896 were the *Châteaurenault* and *Guichen*, large 23.5 or 24 knot ships with four funnels that made them appear at a distance like ocean liners, although they were not really likely to fool anyone and with only two 6.4-inch and six 5.5-inch guns they lacked the armament or armor protection to stand up to real warships.
22. Ropp, *Development of a Modern Navy*, pp. 286–90; details of ships from *Conway's All the World's Fighting Ships, 1860–1905*, pp. 303–13.
23. Lockroy makes his case in two works based on his ministries: Edouard Lockroy, *La Marine de Guerre: Six mois Rue Royale*, 2nd edn (Paris: Berger-Levrault, 1897) and *La défense navale* (Paris: Berger-Levrault, 1900). A short summary of his career is in Taillimite, *Dictionnaire des marins français*, p. 216.
24. Henri Le Masson, *Du Nautilus (1800) au Redoutable (Histoire critique du sous-marin dans la marine française)* (Paris: Presses de la Cité, 1969), pp. 137–43. The *Narval* is covered in great detail in Gérard Garier, *L'odyssée technique et humaine du sous-marin en France*, vol. I, *Du Plongeur (1863) aux Guêpe (1904)* (Bourg en Bresse: Marines édition, n.d.), pp. 110–21.
25. Lockroy, *La défense navale*, pp. 82, 250–3. See also Garier, *L'odyssée technique*, vol. I, pp. 55–9.
26. Le Masson, *Du Nautilus au Redoutable*, p. 222. There were around six other craft considered too old for operations.
27. Le Masson, 'Laubeuf, l'inventeur du submersible', *Propos Maritimes*, pp. 104–7. A critique written in July 1906 for *Le Figaro* is reproduced in Garier, *L'odyssée technique*, vol. I, pp. 232–3.
28. Gérard Garier, *L'odyssée technique et humaine du sans-marin en France*, vol. II, *Des Emeraude (1905–1906) au Charles Brun (1908–1933)* (Nantes: Marines Édition, 1998), pp. 110–12.
29. Le Masson, *Du Nautilus au Redoutable*, pp. 172–3, 183–4, 206–12, 403–4.
30. Ibid., pp. 212–15.
31. Walser, *France's Search for a Battle Fleet*, pp. 57–9. On de Lanessan, see Taillimite, *Dictionnaire des marins français*, pp. 193–4.

32. Quoted in Ray Walser, *France's Search for a Battle Fleet*, pp. 60, 92. Gervais also pointed out that the maneuvers demonstrated that fast light cruisers were needed for scouting but, in contrast to his recommendations for battleships, the light cruisers were reserved for the distant future.

33. Walser, *France's Search for a Battle Fleet*, p. 136. On Fournier see Taillimite, *Dictionnaire des marins français*, pp. 125–6.

34. On the introduction of the *Dantons*, see Walser, *France's Search for a Battle Fleet*, pp. 141–8; Masson, 'La marine française de 1871 à 1914', pp. 145–6; and *Conway's All the World's Fighting Ships, 1906–1921* (London: Conway Maritime Press, 1985), pp. 190, 196.

35. David Robin Watson, *Georges Clemenceau: A Political Biography* (New York: David McKay, 1976), pp. 195–6, 212; Jean-Baptiste Duroselle, *Clemenceau* (Paris: Fayard, 1988), pp. 542–4. Clemenceau was opposed to diverting resources from the army to the navy. He doubted that France would be alone in a war with Germany and proposed that the navy make extensive use of submarines to counter the German fleet, Walser, *France's Search for a Battle Fleet*, p. 512.

36. Walser, *France's Search for a Battle Fleet*, pp. 152, 173, 177–9.

37. Le Masson, 'La politique navale française', pp. 223–4; Walser, *France's Search for a Battle Fleet*, pp. 191–7, 209–12. The law also aimed at increasing the number of dry docks available to the French from a mere four in 1911 to 11 (five in the Mediterranean) by 1920. Docking restrictions kept the tonnage of the first dreadnoughts to 22,500 tons, smaller than their foreign contemporaries.

38. Walser, *France's Search for a Battle Fleet*, pp. 193, 196–8. See also Robert Dumas and Jean Guiglini, *Les cuirassés français de 23.500 tonnes* (Grenoble: Editions des 4 Seigneurs, 1980), pp. 17–19.

39. Masson, 'La marine française de 1871 à 1914', p. 158; Dumas and Guiglini, *Cuirassés de 23.500 tonnes*, pp. 80–1, 88.

40. *Conway's All the World's Fighting Ships, 1906–1921*, pp. 197–299; Le Masson, 'Les cuirassés à tourelles quadruples de la classe *Normandie*', in *Propos Maritimes*, pp. 243–62 (originally in *La Revue Maritime*, no. 203 (Oct. 1963)) and ibid., 'Des cuirassés qui auraient pu être...', ibid., pp. 265–71 (originally in *La Revue Maritime*, no. 204 (Nov. 1963)). One of the *Normandies*, the *Béarn*, was eventually completed after the war as an aircraft carrier.

41. Le Masson, 'La politique navale française', pp. 236–7. Given the expenditure likely to have been involved, one wonders if the navy really would have been able to get away with this.

42. Certain French destroyers were fitted to lay mines and in 1911–12 two old cruisers had been converted into minelayers with rather indifferent results. The 1912 program included four minelayers under 'miscellaneous ships' and in 1912–13 the French completed two 660-ton minelayers. On the whole, however, mine warfare was not emphasized. See Hubert de Blois, *La guerre des mines dans la Marine française* (Brest: Editions de la Cité, 1982), pp. 26–31.

43. For example, the forces in the north available to face the German fleet on mobilization in 1914 included 14 submarines at Cherbourg and seven at Dunkirk as well as two large and 20 small torpedo boats of the Dunkirk *Défense mobile* and the two new minelayers. See A. Thomazi, *La guerre navale dans la zone des armées du nord* (Paris: Payot, 1924), pp. 232–3.

44. On Lapeyrère and his plans, see Paul G. Halpern, *The Mediterranean Naval Situation, 1908–1914* (Cambridge, MA: Harvard University Press, 1971), pp. 130–5, 147–8. Etienne Taillemite comments on Lapeyrère's relative neglect of submarines and the lack of real French submarine doctrine in his introduc-

tion to Henri Darrieus and Bernard Estival, *Gabriel Darrieus et la guerre sur mer* (Vincennes: Service historique de la marine, 1995), pp. vi–vii.

45. Paul G. Halpern, *Anton Haus: Österreich-Ungarns Grossadmiral* (Graz: Verlag Styria, 1998), pp. 80–1.
46. Nicholas A. Lambert, 'British Naval Policy, 1913–1914: Financial Limitation and Strategic Revolution', *Journal of Modern History*, vol. 67 (September 1995), pp. 624–5.
47. On the French Navy during the war the most thorough studies remain the works of A. Thomazi, especially *La guerre navale dans l'Adriatique* (Paris: Payot, 1925) and *La guerre navale dans la Méditerranée* (Paris: Payot, 1929).

4

Technology, Shipbuilding and Future Combat in Germany, 1880–1914

Michael Epkenhans

In 1912, to the embarrassment of his fellow officers of the construction and weapons departments, Grand Admiral Tirpitz, the so-called 'father of the German High Seas Fleet', ruled that German battleships still were to have a ram, 'for in a mêlée the ram would give a feeling of security'.[1] With this rather astonishing statement Tirpitz created the impression that he still adhered to concepts of battle like that of Salamis between the Greek and Persian fleets in ancient times or that of Lissa, when Admiral Tegethoff, out of mere desperation and not through a well-planned tactical manoeuvre, sank the Italian flagship and secured victory over a superior fleet. Around the turn of the century, many admirals still clung to the idea of a battle at close range. At the end of the first decade of the twentieth century, as a result of the 'dreadnought' revolution, there could be no doubt that battles would be fought at increasingly greater ranges. Thus, fear of torpedoes and the firing range of big guns made Tirpitz's decision about rams seem rather strange, to say nothing of the cost and the weight of this useless military device.

It would, however, be wrong to conclude from this somewhat strange episode that, on the eve of the Great War, the German Navy still adhered to outdated principles of naval strategy, naval tactics and construction. Only 40 years after its founding, the Imperial Navy had indeed made vast strides.[2] The number of its vessels and the size of the naval corps had been increased many times; industry, a prerequisite of any attempt at becoming a real seapower, was now capable of building first-class warships in German yards. Last, but not least, unlike the 1860s and 1870s, when the navy even had great difficulty defending the German coast against enemy fleets, it now seemed capable of providing both the *matériel* as well as the tactical and strategic concepts[3] needed to realize the most important political aim of Wilhelmine Germany, to become a world power. As a result of these remarkable achievements, it was not astonishing that the Imperial Navy was soon proudly looked upon as a symbol of a new age and not 'merely the part of the army that happened to watch the sea-frontier'.[4]

THE IMPORTANCE OF SEAPOWER FOR GERMANY

In the 1870s, 1880s, and even in the early 1890s, naval power still did not seem very important in Germany.[5] In spite of its hegemonic status among the European great powers, Germany relied primarily on its strong army. Its long-lasting tradition as a land power, its geographical situation in the centre of Europe and its lack of important overseas interests were responsible for Germany's neglect of seapower. It is true that after unification in 1870–71, Imperial Germany began to build up a fleet. It is, of course, necessary to keep in mind that this fleet which, significantly enough, was commanded by army Generals Stosch and Caprivi until 1889, only aspired to second-class naval strength. The small size of the navy and the operations plans, which primarily aimed at defending the coast, protecting commerce and supporting the army in case of war, further underscore the fact that seapower was not yet an aim in itself.

In this respect, the accession of the young Emperor Wilhelm II to the throne in 1888 definitely marked the end both of a long era of land-power thinking and of a relative decline for the navy. In spite of many personal flaws, the emperor's extraordinarily persistent attempts to realize his naval plans finally paved the way for their approval by the government and the Reichstag. Furthermore, he helped to end a decade of incompetent naval planning, of uncertainties about both naval construction and naval strategy, and, finally, of a lack of precise aims.

The emperor's 'naval passion' and his direct or indirect pressure in support of a large navy, however, cannot sufficiently explain the shift in German politics and military thinking in the 1890s. It seems unlikely that the emperor would have been successful if the importance of seapower had not been realized by a steadily increasing number of people, and, above all, if he had not had a man like Tirpitz at his disposal. It was Tirpitz who dealt systematically with the political, military, strategic and economic aspects of becoming a seapower.

However, what were the reasons for this change and what did seapower mean to the advocates of this new course?[6] First, many contemporaries were proud of their political, economic and military achievements since unification and they felt that Imperial Germany was a vigorous young nation cracking at the seams in many ways. The ideas of imperialism, which had reached Germany in the 1880s, and the political and military events in East Asia as well as in other distant parts of the world in the mid-1890s, further enhanced the conviction that Germany had to embark on a 'world policy'. Such a policy would secure a 'place in the sun' in order to preserve German achievements and, above all, Germany's status in the concert of the great powers.

Second, apart from the vague but psychologically important notion that seapower was a symbol as well as a precondition of national greatness, the rising emphasis on world politics and seapower since the mid-1890s also had important power political implications. As Wilhelm II publicly declared at the launching of the pre-dreadnought *Wittelsbach* in July 1900, world politics and seapower meant that 'in distant areas [beyond the ocean], no important decision should be taken without Germany and the German Emperor'.[7] However, like other pithy speeches about the need to build a navy or statements like 'the trident belongs in our hands',[8] this claim only vaguely described the political and naval concept underlying Germany's 'new course'.

In spite of the vagueness of the German demand for equal entitlement (*Gleichberechtigung*) and the corresponding lack of a catalogue of precise aims, it would be wrong to assume that the Imperial government did not know what it wanted. Germany's main aim, apart from the acquisition of huge slices of dying empires like the Chinese Empire and Ottoman Empire, and islands in the Pacific Ocean, was to revolutionize European and world politics in a Napoleonic manner by replacing the Pax Britannica with a Pax Germanica either through a cold or, if necessary, a hot war against the supreme sea and world power.

Third, seapower or, as Tirpitz more often put it, naval presence (*Seegeltung*) was allegedly also a prerequisite for the protection of the German colonies as well as of economic wealth, industrial progress and commerce. Without a strong navy, Tirpitz kept on arguing, Germany would be unable to preserve its steadily rising 'sea-interests' and would inevitably decline to the status of a pre-industrial, 'poor farming country'. Many people believed him.

THE INDUSTRIAL BASE OF A FUTURE WAR AT SEA

Like all naval strategists and naval planners in the nineteenth century, General von Stosch and General Caprivi as well as Admiral von Tirpitz, were well aware of the fact that the strength of a navy, whether its main task was more of a defensive or an offensive nature, was much more dependent on industrial and technological developments than that of armies. Superiority in these areas translated directly into naval superiority.[9] As long as Germany had been divided into more than 20 sovereign states, this had not really mattered, for there were no important sea interests, as Tirpitz later used to put it, which had to be protected. After unification in 1871, these sea interests, however, quickly developed. Subsequently, a navy capable of defending them and, in return, a naval-industrial complex to build a fleet, were prerequisites of economic prosperity and social peace as well as the protection of German commerce and colonies. This was even more true with regard to Tirpitz's grand design, already outlined above.

In the 1860s, when Prussia transformed Germany into both a united modern nation-state and the most powerful country in the centre of Europe, a naval-industrial complex in any form whatsoever simply did not exist. Though industry had begun to expand in the late 1840s, the ship-building industry was still in a rather poor state. Of the yards on both the North Sea and the Baltic coasts, only two, the Vulcan yard at Stettin and the Schichau yard at Danzig, were capable of building iron hulls. The rest of them still built only wooden ships. Moreover, the iron and steel industries in the Ruhr area, in later years one of the leading and most modern industrial centres of the world, were neither experienced nor even interested in the manufacture of shipbuilding material, armour, armaments or machinery. As a result, the navy had to order its ironclads and armoured ships abroad, in Britain or even in France.

For political and strategic reasons any dependence upon foreign suppliers seemed inappropriate. In 1873, the chief of the Admiralty, General von Stosch, therefore ruled that all warships had to be built in German yards in the future. This rule, however, did not prevent the navy from ordering new types of warships like the torpedo boat, an almost revolutionary weapons system, in Britain in the 1880s, or a submarine in Italy even as late as 1914. Another important objective of Stosch's regulation was his intention to help German industry develop its own skills and facilities in warship building for economic reasons. Stosch and, later on, Tirpitz, were convinced that a flourishing shipbuilding industry would soon be as important for the German economy as the railway industry in the 1850s and 1860s. Accordingly, the Vulcan yard received orders for several armoured ships, while the Schichau, the Germania and the A. G. Weser yards at Danzig, Kiel and Bremen began building torpedo boats for the navy in the 1880s. As the skills of these yards improved, they were also given orders for cruisers, frigates and corvettes. In 1891, Blohm & Voss at Hamburg also entered the navy's suppliers list, when it contracted for the small cruiser *Condor*. In the mid-1880s these yards already performed so well that they even began competing with British yards in the international armament market by exporting all types of warships to Turkey, China, Japan and other countries.

In many ways, the 1890s were, however, a kind of watershed in naval–industrial relations. Tirpitz's grand design of challenging the world's most powerful navy required a fleet of 60 capital ships, a fleet which would renew itself every 20 years at an annual rate of three ships. When taking office in 1897, the new secretary of state for the navy immediately systematized and intensified relations with private industry. Since four of Germany's big yards met the navy's requirements, these were to form the industrial backbone of the Tirpitz plan. In return for modernizing and enlarging their facilities, they were promised regular naval orders, at least as long as prices seemed reasonable. To further competition and to lower contract prices, the number of yards on the suppliers' list increased from four to six in 1908. Although all yards possessed the technical know-how to build high-quality ships-of-the-line and armoured cruisers, some of them soon specialized in certain types of warships. While Blohm & Voss excelled in building cruisers of the *Invincible* type, for example, the Germania and Schichau yards had almost a monopoly in supplying the navy with modern and sophisticated torpedo boats. Until 1914, the Krupp-owned Germania yard was the only private supplier of submarines.

Though private suppliers were of great importance for the navy's effectiveness, the Admiralty and, later on, the Imperial Navy Office tried carefully to avoid becoming dependent on them. The best means of both securing its independence and of controlling prices were naval dockyards. Of these the navy possessed three, in Kiel, Danzig and Wilhelmshaven, and a workshop for the manufacture of torpedoes and torpedo tubes. Plans for building a fourth yard were given up because of a lack of funds. Although the repair, refitting and maintenance of the fleet were their main tasks, the Imperial yards also built the hulls and machinery of battleships, cruisers and submarines. Attempts to build torpedo boats had already been shelved in the 1880s when the navy realized that it could not compete with private yards like Schichau or Germania.

In 1898, after the passing of the first Navy Law, considerable efforts were made to raise the efficiency of the Imperial yards in order to enable them both to cope with the rapid expansion of the navy and to be competitive with private shipbuilders. Unfortunately, production costs were generally higher than in private yards. For this reason, and because Tirpitz regarded the shipbuilding industry as a kind of ally, the majority of warship contracts were soon given to private yards.

In contrast to the army, the navy depended completely upon Krupp for the manufacture of guns and armour plate. Although the Imperial Navy Office was conscious of this serious structural weakness, which was unique in comparison with other navies, all deliberations about establishing its own armour and ordnance works were thwarted by lack of experience, the technical difficulties of producing big naval guns and gun-mountings and the enormous costs of an efficient naval artillery and armour plate plant.[10] Repeated attempts to find a new private supplier also proved futile before 1914, for neither the Düsseldorf firm of Rheinmetall nor the Thyssen enterprise at Mülheim were able or willing to enter into the difficult and financially risky manufacture of armour or big guns. As a result the navy and Krupp formed a kind of alliance, in which the former was guaranteed the supply of high-quality armour at a high though not excessive price, if compared with foreign suppliers, while the latter received regular orders, which, in turn, secured relatively high gross profits.[11]

The machine-building and the electrical industries, ranking first in the world at the turn of the century, also participated greatly in Germany's naval build-up. In certain cases, for example, the development of the turbine or the diesel engine, naval orders even had a spin-off effect on further industrial development. Scientific research, either by universities, shipyards, or even the navy itself, which had established its own research centre near Berlin, further helped improve ship designs, ship propulsion, fire control, armament and armour. Moreover, this research provided the technology for new weapons, which, in turn offered new strategical and tactical options for future naval warfare.[12]

SHIP DESIGN AND OPERATIONAL PLANNING

Germany's most prominent as well as most notorious ship designer was, of course, the German emperor himself. Almost relentlessly, Wilhelm II harassed the Imperial Navy Office with proposals for new and better ships, complaints about the performance of those that were just being built, and designs of ships that looked marvellous but would never swim as the experts in the Navy Office repeatedly sighed. Well-known examples of his interferences in these technical matters are his orders – usually recalled after strong protests by Tirpitz – for fast battleships, or, as in 1912, his idea of building a heavily armoured, submarine-like battleship, whose main armament consisted of numerous torpedoes instead of big guns.[13]

The navy's ships, built in the Stosch and Caprivi eras, generally were copies of foreign designs.[14] More importantly from a political point of view was that their design and armament left no doubt that their main objective was the defence of the German coast. The protection of commerce was the task of a number of different types of cruisers and, later on, gunboats, stationed overseas since the 1870s. The fighting value of the big ships built under Stosch, the ships of the *Saxony* class laid down between 1877 and 1880, was rather low, for they lacked both range and seaworthiness.

Just as their design reflected the principle aims of German naval policy, so did the composition of the fleet itself. While General von Stosch had still built several armoured ships, his successor, General von Caprivi, emphasized the building of torpedo boats that, as he argued in 1884, were a weapon 'that is of particular value for a power that is weaker on the high seas'.[15] It would, however, be wrong to assume that the Imperial Navy had turned to the ideas of the *Jeune École* in the 1880s. In fact, the Admiralty, whose chief never felt at ease in his position and who was disliked widely by his subordinates, vacillated between different schools of naval strategy. In 1884, for example, the idea of cruiser warfare, an important element of the French school of naval thought, was rejected outright for lack of overseas stations. Only two years later, Caprivi concluded in a memorandum for the Reichstag that 'after the advances made in the technology of ship and machine construction, cruiser war, even if slow in its effects, can none the less become decisive'.[16] At the same time, although Caprivi doubted the value of naval battles, he nevertheless advocated the building of battleships to deliver offensive blows against blockading forces.

Despite these inconsistencies in fleet building and, subsequently, naval strategy, Caprivi played a pioneering role in the area of ship design. For example, new construction specifications for cruisers on foreign stations were drawn up immediately after their tasks had been defined. At the same time, he emphasized the need for practical experience in manoeuvres for the development of tactical theory as well as ship construction, as Tirpitz's extensive studies of the effectiveness of torpedo boats illustrate.

Apart from the torpedo boats, built in the 1880s, the big ships, launched in these years of frustration, as they were later, partly unjustly, called, were not very satisfactory. The *Oldenburg*, laid down in 1884, was nothing but an unfortunate experiment, derided as a 'flat-iron', while those of the *Siegfried* class, built between 1888 and 1892, had a main armament of three 24 cm guns, of which two were rather unusually and superfluously emplaced in two front-turrets. In comparison with the *Royal Sovereign* class, which displaced 14,000 tons and which had a main armament of four 34.3 cm guns, these ships with a displacement of only 3,600 tons had little fighting value. The battleships of the *Brandenburg* class, launched in 1891–92, only displaced 10,550 tons. Thus they were still inferior to all British battleships. With their main armament of six 28 cm guns in six twin turrets, they did, however, represent the first real German predreadnoughts and, to some extent, they were even the forerunner of the later 'all big gun one calibre battleships'.[17] More importantly, they were also the first ships designed by one of the navy's best designers, Alfred Dietrich.

In spite of this progress in battleship construction in the 1870s and 1880s and, partly, even the 1890s, the Imperial Navy was, in short, still hardly more than a 'museum of experiments', to use a phrase coined by Tirpitz himself.[18] This collection of ships revealed that the navy, first, had neither a clear idea of the nature of nor the principal objectives in a naval war, and, subsequently, of the type of vessels it should build. As a result of this lack of decision, precise aims and coherent strategic principles, it was not astonishing that the Reichstag repeatedly rejected demands for new ships.

It was only in 1897 that Tirpitz finally convinced the Reichstag, by putting forward a detailed plan, of the need for a powerful navy. Although one might expect that Tirpitz, who had been the leader of the so-called 'torpedo gang' in the 1870s and 1880s, would have favoured the ideas of the French *Jeune École*, he was in fact an advocate of a blue-water strategy.[19] Whether he had been inspired by the writings of Mahan or had come to the same conclusions by himself remains unclear. Since the 1870s, Tirpitz, in this respect, was a true disciple of Clausewitz and was deeply convinced that only a decisive battle could annihilate the enemy and thus help win a war. Accordingly, despite the tactical advantages of torpedo boats in battle, he did not regard them as a panacea for Germany's naval needs. Subsequently, a fleet consisting of battleships and heavy cruisers, as well as a considerable number of light cruisers and torpedo boats, was necessary to achieve the self-set goal.

These ships-of-the-line as well as the battleships of the dreadnought type were all designed by the construction department of the Imperial Navy Office. Whereas their main armament was generally inferior to that of foreign navies, it was nevertheless highly effective due to the development of armour-piercing shells. Moreover, intricate underwater compartmentation to localize flooding from shells greatly increased the steadfastness of German warships in battle. To fight torpedo boats, which became more effective at the turn of the century when faster and farther travelling torpedoes were introduced, the secondary armament of battleships was increased with the launching of the *Wittelsbach* class in 1899.

A solution to the cruiser question, which almost haunted the navy not the least because the emperor preferred this type of ship, which could show the German flag in the most distant parts of the world, to clumsy battleships of short cruising ranges, proved rather difficult. For lack of funds Germany simply could not afford to build two different types, a fast, unprotected cruiser for overseas duties and a heavily armoured one for service with the battle fleet. Eventually, a uniform class was developed which could fulfil both functions reasonably well. Generally speaking, owing to restrictions imposed upon cruiser construction by the limited size of docks and harbours, the heavy or armoured cruisers of the pre-*Invincible* era were never equal to their counterparts in Britain, France or even Russia. Moreover, they were badly constructed, wet and ill-protected, and their armament was both insufficient and, owing to the space required by the engines, not well arranged. As a result, the firing angle of the turrets of the heavy artillery was limited. Even the best ships of this type, the big cruisers of the *Scharnhorst* class were therefore still inferior to their British counterparts on the China station, the *Minotaur* and the *Defence*. In this respect, the quality of light cruisers and torpedo boats was much better. It is, however, important to notice that Tirpitz, unlike Admiral Fisher, regarded cruisers only as scouting vessels and not as a kind of fast battleship which was capable of hunting down, pursuing and destroying a crippled battle fleet.

The launching of HMS *Dreadnought* was in many ways a gauntlet which Tirpitz finally took up, although his masterplan came under pressure from many sides. First, the emperor again took this opportunity to harass Tirpitz with his project of a fast battleship, thus, in Tirpitz's opinion, menacing fundamental principles of German naval strategy. Second, the launching of battleships of the dreadnought type was to have a far-reaching impact on the empire's financial resources as well as on his own credibility, for the secretary of the navy had always maintained that the financial burden for the average taxpayer would be kept within certain limits. Third, unless he also began building dreadnoughts, his ships would no longer be a lever to force Britain to succumb to German wishes in the future. In short, in order to avoid political bankruptcy, Tirpitz had no choice but to follow Fisher's example.[20] From 1907 onwards, battleships and battlecruisers were laid down with the greatest secrecy ever attempted by German yards. With regard to protection, below as well as above water (the *Nassau*, for example, had 16, her successors even 19 watertight compartments), these ships were superior to all British types, whereas their armament was inferior both in calibre and metal weight of broadsides. The engines took up too much space at midlength, making it necessary to choose hexagonal mountings with two turrets at each side. Only in firing forward and aft were these ships able to bring a maximum number of guns to bear. The lack of space-saving turbines thus proved a great obstacle for increasing fire-power and laying down vessels equivalent to their future enemy. Only the third generation of German dreadnoughts, the *Kaiser* class, received Parsons turbines which, in turn, allowed them to arrange the heavy artillery according to the British one-centre line, one-wing system. Following British *matériel* developments, the Imperial Navy soon also turned to building battleships of the super-dreadnought type, increasing gun calibres, though rather reluctantly, from 30.5 to 38 cm. The introduction of triple turrets, already used by Italy, Austria and Russia, was rejected because of major technical difficulties.

Parallel to battleships of the dreadnought type, the Imperial Navy also began building highly sophisticated battlecruisers of the 'Invincible' type. These battlecruisers, most of which were built by Blohm & Voss, were fitted outright with turbines which gave them a best speed of 26 knots (SMS *Lützow*), and a main armament, which was increased from 28 cm to 35 cm.

In summary, by 1914, when German dreadnought building came to an abrupt end, the Imperial Navy, as it did in its infancy, had copied most British design innovations. Its aims, however, were fundamentally different. Battleships now possessed supplementary oil-burners, 38 cm guns, steam turbines, super-firing twin turrets, and centre-firing as well as end mountings. Only purely oil-burning ships alone were not adopted, partly because German planners insisted that side coal bunkers, in addition to the torpedo bulkheads, afforded greater underwater protection, and partly because Tirpitz could not ensure for Germany a steady supply of this fuel.[21] These achievements, however, formidable as they no doubt were, did not really improve the navy's chances of success in a future naval war. During the First World War, a young critic, Lieutenant-Commander Wolfgang Wegener, argued rightly that seapower not only required the possession of a powerful and effective fleet, but it needed an advantageous geographic position as well.[22] On the eve of the Great War, German operational planning, of which the navy's principles of ship design and construction were only a mere reflection, still adhered to the importance of a decisive battle, thus dooming itself to failure.

NEW TECHNOLOGIES AND INNOVATIONS

The second half of the nineteenth century was full of technical innovations, which revolutionized modern naval warfare in very short intervals. The development of the ironclad and the breach-loading big gun, of explosive shells and self-propulsion, of Krupp armour and torpedoes, of submarines, airplanes and airships had a far-reaching impact on tactical and strategic ideas of waging future wars at sea. All 'makers' of the German Navy were well aware of the fact that without adopting new technological achievements, they ran the risk of losing a war even before it had actually begun. The German Navy, especially the Tirpitz navy, had great difficulty in meeting these requirements for at least two reasons. First, naval technology progressed at a quickly accelerating pace with the effect that many ships were already outdated when launched. Second, any decision to follow the pace of technological progress increased the financial burden on the taxpayer, without guaranteeing more effective naval strength. Subsequently, those responsible for the navy always had to balance the need for the adoption of new technology with its repercussions on domestic politics. Under these circumstances, Tirpitz's assurance that warship construction and technological development had arrived at a stage which would make costly leaps forward improbable, was a precondition of the Reichstag's consent to his plan. For the implementation of his plan, this meant that Tirpitz suffered from severe financial constraints right from the beginning. Unless, as in the case of the dreadnought leap, he could argue convincingly that the navy had no choice but to follow international developments in order to achieve its aim, he could not afford to undermine the confidence placed in him by embarking on an expensive building policy. Apart from these political implications of introducing new technology, Tirpitz's almost paranoid apprehension that experiments with new weapons systems of questionable military value in a future naval war would inevitably divert funds from battleship construction (the core of his whole plan), into vague projects, further increased both his reluctance towards new technological developments and his opposition to strategic alternatives based on their adoption.

This notwithstanding, the Imperial Navy eventually introduced four important innovations, which were to have a deep impact on future naval warfare: the submarine, the seaplane, the airship and the diesel engine.

The best-known example of Tirpitz's attitude towards new technology is the submarine.[23] While the grand admiral was still in office, the unexpected success of a few submarines, which contrasted sharply with the failure of the costly ships of the High Seas Fleet to keep the sea lanes open, not to speak of gaining command of the sea, led to heavy criticism against Tirpitz's building policy and his neglect of this modern type of warship in favour of his beloved but useless battleships. To some extent this criticism was true, but it was also partly unfair. It is true, in comparison with other navies, the Imperial Navy was a latecomer in introducing submarines into the High Seas Fleet. Only after the Krupp-owned Germania yard had successfully built and tested a submarine, did the navy order its first one, commissioned in 1906. Tirpitz's hesitation in adopting this new technology was due partly to a number of technical problems which still had to be solved. For example, the available engines were neither reliable nor safe. However, there can be no doubt that Tirpitz did not regard the submarine as a useful weapon in a future war. His conviction that command of the sea, gained in a decisive battle of capital ships, was both the symbol of real seapower as well as a prerequisite of Germany's political and naval aspirations, simply did not allow him to invest money in a weapons system which would only protect sea lanes. Accordingly, he mercilessly pursued all critics within the navy who questioned the fundamental principle of his grand political and strategic design by suggesting alternatives to a naval policy, which, with its preference for capital ships and its operations plans, was obviously doomed to failure since the dreadnought leap.

Despite this opposition by Tirpitz, the navy continued its trials with submarines. Many improvements, especially the changeover from petrol to diesel engines, turned these double-hull boats, which had a range of 7,600 sm and an armament of two bow and one stern tube with six torpedoes stored, into decisive strategic units capable of decimating the enemy's battleship strength. The Imperial manoeuvres of 1912, in which they were allowed to take part because Tirpitz was absent from office and his deputy did not hesitate to include them, openly illustrated their military value. Tirpitz nevertheless remained extremely cool towards them, and it was only their surprising success in the first months of the Great War, which sharply contrasted with the poor role played by his beloved battleships, that finally changed his mind.

Naval aviation, either in the form of the airship or of the airplane, though then in its infancy, was another area which was to influence future fighting at sea to a so far unknown degree. Similar to the submarine, Tirpitz was reluctant to adopt naval aviation as an integral part of naval defence or even naval warfare. In 1908, he rejected the request of a naval officer who wanted to be attached temporarily to the airship department of the army, by telling him that 'at least for the time being we have to follow the sea'.[24] International developments, however, soon forced Tirpitz to change his mind. In a memorandum for the kaiser, the Imperial Navy Office argued that seaplanes, as well as messenger planes, might be useful for reconnaissance flights both along the coastline and on the high seas. The idea of building an aircraft-carrier like the French *La Foudre* was, though, not regarded as feasible. This principal decision for the intro-duction of the airplane notwithstanding, the funds provided for the further development of an effective seaplane in 1910 were too low to be an incentive for private enterprises to invest in its construction.[25] Due to this attitude, the development of seaplanes hardly made any progress. Only the naval yard at Danzig started a series of trials to convert airplanes, pur-chased from private industry, into seaplanes. The technical problems, which both the naval yard as well as private industry had to overcome, were considerable, for the navy wanted nothing less than a so-called 'amphibian'. This was a plane, which could be used either on land or at sea. Even two competitions with prizes failed to encourage progress. Even-tually, the navy had no choice but to buy a US seaplane, built by Curtiss, which had already performed successfully in a number of trials in 1911–12. The difficulties in the construction of a satisfactory seaplane however, should not obscure the fact that the navy lagged far behind, even in comparison with the notoriously conservative army. In December 1911, when the Anglo-German naval arms race was reaching its climax with the introduction of another naval law, the Admiralty staff urgently demanded airplanes, for, as its chief, Vice-Admiral von Heeringen, wrote to Tirpitz, 'as a result of the general political situation, it is advisable to exploit all achievements of modern technology which might be useful in a future naval war'.[26] In Heeringen's eyes, reconnaissance flights along the coast, the scouting of blockading forces, and the search for submarines and mines in the German Bight were tasks airplanes might fulfil successfully. More-over, airplanes were also regarded as a kind of substitute for scouting cruisers. Tirpitz, however, remained reluctant and ignored these justified demands, as even the official history later remarked critically.[27] Progress was therefore rather slow. In 1914, the navy possessed 36 seaplanes, of which only nine were operable. Compared with their British counterparts, their performance was poor, for they had neither bomb-sights, bomb bays or a camera for aerial photography, not to speak of a wireless set. As a result, their fighting value was almost zero.[28]

Strange as it may appear, in spite of the chronic shortage of funds, the Imperial Navy also permitted itself the luxury of developing two types of naval aviation at the same time: the airplane and the airship. Whereas the airplane quickly developed into a modern, sophisticated and effective weapon in spite of many disappointing setbacks in its infancy, the airship, which was so popular in Germany before the war, did not survive the Wilhelmine era. As usual, Tirpitz proved reluctant in introducing the airship into the navy, though the Admiralty staff had emphasized its military value for reconnaissance as early as 1901.[29] However, Captain von Müller, later chief of the Naval Cabinet, following a detailed evaluation of the whole question by two members of the Admiralty staff, also pointed out the serious disadvantages of airships. In his eyes, the airship was neither an offensive nor a very useful weapon due to its vulnerability, its low speed and the fact that it could operate only in good weather. While the navy hesitated to support the development of the airship despite the emperor's interest in this new weapon, naval journalists emphasized its potential value. They suggested that its offensive use might successfully cut Britain's sinews of power by bombing its cities, ports and dockyards, and destroying the Royal Navy's new dreadnought fleet. Moreover, they could be used to transport thousands of soldiers to conquer the British Isles.[30] In 1906, this was nothing but science fiction or propaganda for a flying device which had not yet proven its effectiveness. The Navy Office remained sceptical, in spite of some positive discussions in its own 'Marinerundschau' in 1908 and 1910.[31] This scepticism notwithstanding, Tirpitz changed his attitude towards the airship in late 1911. The Navy Law of 1912, then already under discussion, provided 8 million marks for airships. The reasons for this almost radical change in airship policy are difficult to explain. On the one hand, the relative success of airship development in 1911 obviously convinced the navy that the airship might be useful both for reconnaissance and offensive operations against Britain, which could damage the morale of English towns.[32] Its lower costs, compared with cruisers which the High Seas Fleet needed as a scouting force, but which it could not afford for lack of funds, increased the military value of the former. However, at least to some extent it also seems likely that the Imperial Navy Office ordered airships simply to disguise its own backwardness in the development of the airplane. As mentioned above, the navy thus took the lead in the development of an already outdated weapon. Unfortunately, moreover, the decision in favour of the airship soon proved fatal, for the first two airships crashed within weeks in 1913. On the eve of war only one airship was left. When war broke out, more airships were ordered, and, from 1915 onwards, they even raided the British and Russian coasts. Despite the damage caused by raids against Britain during the Great War, the airship, apart from the great number of losses, proved a total failure from a technical as well as a strategic point of view.

In shipbuilding, Tirpitz also had no choice but to follow international developments in order to build ships which could perform the task for which they were intended. Whereas the turbine only accelerated the speed of ships, the development of a new form of ship propulsion, the diesel engine, had almost revolutionary implications for German shipbuilding and naval strategy.[33] In the 1870s self-propulsion had given independence from the wind for both tactical and strategic mobility. The only disadvantage was that fuel dependence now made logistics an important part of naval warfare. In this respect the High Seas Fleet was at a great disadvantage compared with its future adversary, the Grand Fleet. As long as steam propulsion, however sophisticated the engines were, remained the basis of both speed and cruising range, the operational freedom of the Imperial Navy was hampered by Germany's geographical position and the lack of safe coaling stations all over the world. The diesel engine thus offered a solution to the dilemma of cruising the seas in search of the enemy and the limitations set by geography, for these engines greatly enlarged the range of ships. Again the navy was reluctant to adopt this technology. Only when the French Navy ordered diesel engines from Germany's most experienced supplier, the MAN works at Augsburg, did the Imperial Navy Office follow suit. However, both the technological potential and the strategic advantages of this new form of propulsion for battleships and, as a result, for strategic naval warfare, were realized only as late as 1909, when MAN offered to build an engine supplying 800 horsepower. Though such an engine seemed useless for the navy, the Imperial Navy Office now regarded this offer as an opportunity to enter into negotiations about a far more powerful engine suitable for battleships and big cruisers. The rapid increase of both the size and the cost of warships in the dreadnought era made it necessary to look for alternatives which could save cost as well as weight. Moreover, with the diesel engine the High Sea Fleet would be superior to its main enemy in the field of ship propulsion. In order to ensure that this superiority would not be imperilled by the sale or licence agreements with foreign enterprises like Vickers, which had already approached the Augsburg firm, the latter even had to agree not to sell its patent rights. These constraints notwithstanding, the firm of MAN started constructing a diesel engine with 6,000 horsepower more or less at its own risk, for the economic prospects of a technical break-through were tempting enough for the firm's management. Though the firm's hopes were not fulfilled because of technical difficulties before 1914, the navy had thus proven its willingness to take the lead in modern ship technology. Already in 1912, at the time of the Haldane mission, the Admiralty regarded the danger of German cruisers with diesel engines waging cruiser warfare in the Atlantic as a serious potential menace.[34] Though this was not true then, in 1914 Tirpitz did indeed toy with the idea of forming two 'flying squadrons' to menace Britain's sea lanes in the Atlantic.[35]

SUMMARY

Owing to the primacy of continental policy under Bismarck as well as lack of experience, the German Navy, was, at best, a second-rate navy until the 1890s. The political wind of change in the early 1890s, which coincided with the development of Tirpitz's remarkably sound masterplan promising to achieve great ends at relatively low costs, propelled the navy into the centre of German politics. An effective shipbuilding and armaments industry as well as a number of naval institutions and private enterprises, which provided the navy with the latest technology to improve its fighting value, were the solid basis of Germany's grasp for world power. Tirpitz's dogma of the importance of a decisive battle, however, lacked the flexibility necessary to avoid failure. Whereas his fiercest counterpart on the other side of the North Sea, Admiral Fisher, met Tirpitz's challenge by considering radical changes in his construction programme while his superiors in the government looked for political alternatives to answer the German threat, the German admiral clung stubbornly to his main idea until the outbreak of war. Alternative strategies were no option for him, although the technology, the industrial base and, moreover, the men, who like Admirals Galster or von Maltzahn were capable of further developing new strategic ideas and principles of naval warfare, were at hand. Thus he himself was largely responsible for his own failure when, as English rumour had it before the war, 'the day came, many German naval officers had longed for'.

NOTES

1. Protocol of a meeting, 16 January 1912, Bundesarchiv-Militärarchiv (BA-MA) RM 3/15.
2. Cf. V. R. Berghahn, *Der Tirpitz-Plan: Genesis und Verfall einer innenpolitischen Krisenstrategie unter Wilhelm II* (Düsseldorf: Droste Verlag, 1971); H. H. Herwig, *'Luxury' Fleet: The Imperial German Navy 1888–1918* (London: Ashfield Press, 1991 repr.); M. Epkenhans, *Die wilhelminische Flottenrüstung 1908–1914: Weltmachtstreben, industrieller Fortschritt, soziale Integration* (Munich: Oldenbourg Verlag, 1991).
3. Cf. now R. Hobson, 'Imperialism at Sea: Naval Strategic Thought, the Ideology of Sea Power and the Tirpitz Plan, 1875–1914' (Oslo: unpublished PhD thesis, 1999).
4. Cf. T. Ropp, *The Development of a Modern Navy: French Naval Policy 1871–1904* (Annapolis, MD: Naval Institute Press, 1987), p. 28.
5. Cf. I. N. Lambi, *The Navy and German Power Politics, 1862–1914* (Boston: Allen & Unwin, 1984), pp. 1–49.
6. For details see the works mentioned in n. 2 above.
7. See the speech of Wilhelm II in Wilhelmshaven, 3 July 1900, quoted in E. Johann, *Reden des Kaisers: Ansprachen, Predigten und Trinksprüche Wilhelms II*, 2nd edn (Munich: Deutscher Taschenbuch Verlag, 1977), p. 81.
8. See the speech of Wilhelm II in Cologne, 18 June 1897, in Johann, *Reden des Kaisers*, p. 71.

9. For naval–industrial relations cf. T. Schwarz and E. von Halle (eds), *Die Schiff-bauindustrie in Deutschland und im Ausland* (Düsseldorf: VDI Verlag, 1987, repr., L. U. Scholl); A. Hurd and H. Castle, *German Seapower: Its Rise, Progress, and Economic Basis* (London: John Murray, 1913), which is also still valuable, and Epkenhans, *Flottenrüstung*, pp. 143–312.

10. In 1913 the costs of an armour-plate plant were estimated at 35 million marks, those of an ordnance factory at 100 million marks. Cf. Epkenhans, *Flotten-rüstung*, pp. 171–2, 188.

11. For details see ibid., pp. 153–201.

12. Ibid., pp. 249–65.

13. Cf. Tirpitz, A. von *Erinnerungen* (Leipzig: Hase & Köhler, 1919), pp. 133–4.

14. For details of ship design and construction cf. E. Gröner, *Die deutschen Kriegss-chiffe 1815–1945*, vol. I (Munich: Bernhard & Graefe, 1982), pp. 7–143; S. Breyer, *Schlachtschiffe und Schlachtkreuzer 1905–1970: Die geschichtliche Entwicklung des Großkampfschiffs* (Munich: Lehmanns Verlag, 1970), pp. 276–304; A. Grießmer, *Große Kreuzer der Kaiserlichen Marine 1906–1918: Konstruktionen und Entwürfe im Zeichen des Tirpitz-Planes* (Bonn: Bernhard & Graefe, 1996), pp. 6–196; Herwig, '*Luxury' Fleet*, passim.

15. Quoted in Lambi, *The Navy and German Power Politics*, pp. 7–8.

16. Ibid., p. 9.

17. Herwig, '*Luxury' Fleet*, p. 26.

18. See ibid., p. 38.

19. See Hobson, 'Imperialism at Sea', pp. 227–401.

20. See H. H. Herwig, 'The German Reaction to the *Dreadnought* Revolution', *International History Review*, 13 (1991), pp. 273–83.

21. Herwig, '*Luxury' Fleet*, pp. 82–3.

22. See W. Wegener, *The Naval Strategy of the World War*, ed. H. H. Herwig (Annapolis, MD: Naval Institute Press, 1989).

23. See memo of the Inspection of Torpedo Boats on 'Der Stand des Untersee-bootwesens' (undated [1911]), BA-MA RM 3/10981, as well as the report on 'Militärische und technische Erfahrungen auf Unterseebooten während der Herbstmanöver in der Nordsee', 9 January 1913, ibid., RM 3/10992; Herwig, '*Luxury' Fleet*, pp. 86–8.

24. Undated note by Tirpitz, quoted in Militärgeschichtliches Forschungsamt (ed.), *Die Militärluftfahrt bis zum Beginn des Weltkrieges 1914*, vol. I (2nd edn, Frank-furt: E. S. Mittler & Sohn, 1965; 1st edn 1941), p. 200, n. 1.

25. Overall, by 1914 Germany had spent only 18.4 million marks on naval air development – compared with more than 50 million marks for only one modern battleship, cf. Herwig, '*Luxury' Fleet*, p. 86.

26. Heeringen to Tirpitz, 30 December 1911, quoted in Militärgeschichtliches Forschungsamt, *Militärluftfahrt*, vol. I, p. 230.

27. Ibid., p. 231.

28. Herwig, '*Luxury' Fleet*, p. 85–6.

29. For a detailed account of the Navy's attitude to the airship, see Cyrus Roÿeck, 'Die Entwicklung der Luftschiffahrt in Deutschland und deren Weg in die Kaiser-liche Marine', unpublished MS (Neubiberg, 1994).

30. Ibid., pp. 99–103.

31. For details cf. ibid., pp. 103–19.

32. Ibid., p. 149.

33. See Epkenhans, *Flottenrüstung*, pp. 256–65.

34. Ibid., p. 123.

35. Ibid., pp. 396–9.

5

Admiral Sir John Fisher and the Concept of Flotilla Defence, 1904–9

Nicholas A. Lambert

Admiral Sir John Fisher rarely explained his strategic views in writing, and papers of his that do exist on this subject date for the most part from the period before he became First Sea Lord.[1] The paucity of formal expositions of his strategic views and his known disengagement from the preparation of written war plans, have given some historians the impression that he had little interest in, or no capacity for, the conceptualization of strategy. Fisher, in their view, was too preoccupied with *'matériel* policy'.[2] Arthur Marder, for example,[3] believed it was Fisher's instinctive response to the challenge of a rapidly expanding German Navy that motivated him to improve the war readiness of the fighting fleet by concentrating naval resources in home waters, re-equipping the battle fleet with new model armoured warships, and other administrative reforms intended to enhance the war readiness of ships in reserve.[4] 'The efficiency and strength of the Navy, one ready for war at a moment's notice', Marder declared, was Fisher's 'megalomania'.[5]

Of the three initiatives just mentioned, Fisher's innovation in capital ship design has attracted by far the most attention. Historians generally accept that Fisher possessed a genius for anticipating inevitable changes in warship design resulting from advances in naval technology.[6] The testimony to this vision was the building of HMS *Dreadnought*, a warship of revolutionary design that seemed overnight to render all previous battleships obsolete.[7] Fisher's 'prescience', it is argued, enabled the Royal Navy to steal a march over its rivals in the impending race to re-equip navies with modern battleships.[8] The inference that Fisher's principal objective had been simply to equip the Royal Navy with a larger number of modern battleships in order to win a fleet action in the North Sea against the German High Sea Fleet, reinforces the idea that Fisher was a purely conventional and rather unimaginative strategist.[9] Again, where he did make some departures from traditional Admiralty policy, such as the decision in November 1904 to scrap a large number of gunboats and trade protection cruisers, this is usually construed by historians as further evidence of his determination to 'build up the Royal Navy's strength in home waters' and improve the fighting efficiency of the battle fleet, at any cost, even at the price of losing the Royal Navy the command of the ocean trade routes.[10]

Recently published work, however, has undermined the traditional interpretation of Fisher's naval policy as codified by Arthur Marder.[11] A number of historians have uncovered a mass of new evidence which proves that the impetus for the Edwardian naval reforms actually came from governmental pressure upon the Admiralty to find substantial savings in the naval estimates.[12] Indeed, Fisher was appointed first sea lord largely because he was one of the few senior officers in the service who accepted the need for economies.[13] The new scholarship also shows that the motives for the redistribution of the fleet in November 1904, were predominantly financial. It was not intended to affect a concentration of force against the German Empire.[14] Generally speaking, previous accounts of pre-1914 naval policy have greatly underestimated the complexity of the naval administrative decision-making process. This has resulted in the misreading of motives and intentions for some key policy decisions.[15]

Most notably, in 1989, Jon Sumida published his research on the relationship during the Edwardian era between British capital ship design and the Royal Navy's efforts to improve the control of naval gunfire. His book, *In Defence of Naval Supremacy*, proved conclusively that previous historians had completely misunderstood Fisher's capital ship policy. Far from encouraging development of the *Dreadnought*, Fisher was actually campaigning for a cessation in battleship construction. Instead, he wanted the Royal Navy to build a new type of armoured warship of his own conception, the battlecruiser.[16] But opposition from within the Admiralty obliged him to compromise his preferred construction policy and to continue building 'dreadnoughts'. The discovery of Fisher's preference for battlecruisers reveals much more than a serious difference of opinion within the Admiralty over capital ship design. The battlecruiser, it transpires, was not conceived simply as an alternative to the battleship.

Until now, historians have taken the superior fighting characteristics of 'dreadnoughts' over 'pre-dreadnoughts' and their proven success during the First World War to provide sufficient justification and explanation for the adoption of the all-big-gun battleship.[17] At the same time there has been considerable confusion over exactly what the function of the battlecruiser was.[18] New evidence uncovered by Sumida has shown that when Fisher began thinking about the new warships he would build for the navy on becoming first sea lord, he was far more concerned by the prospect of waging global cruiser warfare against the French and Russian navies than by the steady expansion of the German High Sea Fleet. The *Dreadnought*, moreover, was regarded as a prototype warship built to test a combination of revolutionary features in armoured warships including the mono-calibre armament designed to facilitate the control of gunfire at longer ranges, and an advanced new system of propulsion. 'It would be wrong to assume', noted the director of naval intelligence in October 1906, 'that we shall arrive at anything like a settled pattern of capital ship for some years to come.'[19] What is more, the completion of *Dreadnought* was accelerated purposely so as to allow the lessons learnt during her trials to be applied to the design of the other ships of the 1905 programme, the three heavily armed *Invincible* class armoured cruisers.

The all-big-gun cruisers, or 'battlecruisers' as they later became known, were conceived for imperial and trade defence missions. Fisher believed that they could also be deployed to form lines of battle.[20] In other words, he saw the battlecruiser as a 'multi-role' warship capable of performing the functions of both armoured cruisers and battleships. He further believed that, for a variety of reasons, a force of qualitatively superior battlecruisers could be constructed and maintained at significantly less cost than the traditional combination of battle fleet and cruiser squadrons. Reviewers should note that, at this stage, the battlecruiser concept had not yet been associated with the highly sophisticated system of fire control being developed by the civilian inventor Arthur Pollen. Fisher's confidence in the ability of *Invincibles* to engage battleships was based upon the recent introduction of capped armour-piercing shells which meant that projectiles fired from the battlecruiser's 12-inch guns could penetrate the main armour of any existing battleship at then anticipated battle ranges; the thinner armour protecting the battlecruiser would not be a tactical liability because it was sufficient to keep out high explosive shells.[21] Even after Fisher learnt of the Pollen system in September 1906, he continued to argue that the appropriate response to thicker armour and longer battle ranges was to introduce more powerful guns firing heavier shells.[22]

While *Dreadnought* was still under construction, Fisher campaigned secretly for the navy to discontinue the building of more battleships in preference to battlecruisers.[23] In December 1905, he ordered the formation of what amounted to a second Committee on Designs to consider formally the merging of the battleship and the armoured cruiser into a single 'armoured vessel'. Unfortunately, Fisher's so-called 'fusion design' (alias battlecruiser) projected for the 1906 construction programme was not endorsed by his handpicked committee of experts.[24] They felt the cementing of the *Entente Cordiale* with France during the (1905) Moroccan Crisis, and the annihilation of the Russian fleet at the Battle of Tsushima the previous May, had diminished the likelihood of the Royal Navy having to fight the global cruiser war for which fast battlecruisers had been originally required. To fight Germany, regarded now as Britain's most likely foe, the Royal Navy required battleships, the German threat to British trade being seen as negligible. And battleships – even 'dreadnoughts'

– were cheaper to build than 'fusion' battlecruisers.[25] Fisher was not discouraged by this setback and continued to agitate for a switch to battlecruisers.[26] He was much less concerned about the magnitude of the German threat than most of his Admiralty colleagues.[27] Fisher also possessed a more 'imperialist perspective'.[28] 'For the moment', he reasoned, 'it would be safe to build against Germany alone. But we cannot build for the moment: the Board of Admiralty are the trustees of future generations.'[29]

In fact, John Fisher's dream of a battlecruiser revolution came much closer to realization than even Sumida realized. In September 1908, the first sea lord informed his friend Lord Esher that he had set the director of naval construction to work on the design of a new 'Nonpareil' battlecruiser 'that will make your mouth water when you see it', armed with eight new model 13.5-inch guns.[30] At the end of March 1909, Fisher used new intelligence on the German building programme to justify his suggestion that the Board of Admiralty lay down all eight capital ships of the 1909/10 programme as battlecruisers.[31] 'We have to work hard in the next two years', he urged the first lord of the Admiralty, Reginald McKenna, 'and build 8 "Nonpareils" to meet [battle] cruisers "E", "F", "G", and "H".'[32] That same day Fisher also informed Lord Esher of the projected German 'battlecruisers', and explained the paramount necessity for the Admiralty to respond 'at once' by ordering '8 big cruisers – 84,000 H.P. at least' – capable of steaming at 28 knots.[33] The first lord was persuaded. On 18 April, he was reported as having told the prime minister about 'Germany's plans to build fast cruisers to destroy commerce etc. and obviously we must not now commit ourselves to [building] dreadnoughts'.[34]

Once again, however, Fisher appears to have been hampered by the reluctance of a majority of the other sea lords 'to plunge'. Vice-Admiral Sir Francis Bridgeman, who had recently replaced Vice-Admiral Sir William May as second sea lord, was adamant that all eight ships of the 1909 programme should be constructed as battleships.[35] Although one of Fisher's protégés, Bridgeman had never liked the battlecruiser concept.[36] On 28 May, a wistful John Fisher reported to McKenna that 'our colleagues tried to scalp me after the Board meeting over the 10 guns! I think Mac[namara] is the chief savage! I think we had better give them the 10 guns in the July ships!'[37] This decision, however, was not final. Throughout the summer the question of capital ship design was discussed repeatedly by the sea lords.[38] On 17 June, Fisher was again overruled by the rest of the Board, this time over the design of the ten-gun battleships. On this occasion the first sea lord formally 'recorded his protest' at the decision to build 21-knot battleships instead of the faster armoured vessels he favoured.[39] In October a new compromise was reached: initially only four ships would be laid down, two as battleships (*Colossus* and *Hercules*), and two as battlecruisers (*Lion* and *Princess Royal*). The design of the other four ships would be settled later. Significantly, Fisher managed to have the battlecruisers armed with new model 13.5-inch guns, while the battleships were equipped with 12-inch guns of an older experimental pattern.[40] There is every reason to believe that Fisher still hoped to build the second tranche of four ships as battlecruisers.[41]

A number of commentators have found Sumida's explanation of Fisher's capital ship policy hard to accept. A fleet comprised only of battlecruisers, they assert, would have been quite incompatible with the clearly stated objectives of British naval policy during this period. Navies, the critics assume, had to have a battle fleet with which to defeat rival battle fleets. The battlecruiser could never have been considered as a replacement for all battleships because the type had such weak armour protection. But if such a policy had been adopted, they argue, the disastrous performance of the battlecruisers at the Battle of Jutland demonstrates that it would have been a major, maybe even fatal, blunder by the British Navy. Much of this appraisal, however, appears to be counterfactual reasoning. The practicability of Fisher's ideas may be open to criticism, but that is a question quite separate and apart from whether or not Fisher was trying to engineer a battlecruiser revolution. Yet it must be admitted that Sumida's interpretation of British capital ship policy clearly does not fit into the broader picture of naval policy during this period painted in the generally accepted core histories. However, Fisher's preference for battlecruisers does not become fully comprehensible until one understands how exactly the concept of the battlecruiser fitted in to Fisher's strategic vision of modern war at sea.

The object of this chapter is to show that when Sir John Fisher became first sea lord he was very far from being an orthodox naval strategist, and was a man whose naval policy has been totally misunderstood. The single most important reason for the distortion of Fisher's views on naval strategy is that many historians have tended to view the available evidence from the wrong perspective. For instance, Marder's investigation of pre-1914 naval policy was framed upon a theoretical model of naval warfare developed at the end of the nineteenth century by a group of naval analysts led by Captain Alfred Mahan. The naval theorists of the 'historical school', as they were known, sought to clarify many prevailing uncertainties over the application of naval force in a major conflict by studying the use of navies in the age of sail. Marder accepted unquestioningly that the assumptions and conclusions of the historical school were valid, and that their model was applicable for studying the British Edwardian Navy. More importantly, he also assumed that before 1914 Mahan's ideas were accepted by most 'educated' British naval officers.[42] A closer examination of these assumptions, however, suggests that the Mahanian model is inappropriate for analysing British naval policy in the early twentieth century.

A key assumption made by the historical school was that strategic principles of naval warfare transcend scientific and technical advances in warship design. Belief in the existence of unchanging strategic principles led theorists to the conclusion that the focus of naval policy should always be the creation of a fleet organized to win a decisive engagement against a rival fleet of battleships.[43] Naval planning and operational performance are regarded generally by historians to form the heart of naval history – judging by the emphasis placed on these subjects in most core naval studies. As a result largely of oversimplified analysis, important issues during the late nineteenth and early twentieth centuries, such as the impact of the rapid advances in naval technology upon the formulation of naval strategy and the influence upon naval policy of financial, economic and industrial considerations, too often have been dismissed as being of only marginal importance. Improvements in science and technology did not simply translate into improved warship or weapon system performance. The rapid pace of technological innovation during this period meant that new warships quickly became obsolescent, which in turn had a significant impact upon naval finances. Navies were compelled continually to modernize their fleets if they wished to remain competitive. Equally expensive was the need to improve the infrastructure necessary for the development of naval weapon systems. Advances in technology and continually rising costs of warship development also encouraged navies to devise brand new weapons as a cheaper alternative to constructing fleets of battleships.

Arguably, the most significant naval invention of this period was the Whitehead locomotive torpedo. It was a cheap weapon which could sink a battleship. Early torpedoes possessed an effective range of only about 400 yards which meant that torpedo-carrying boats had to pass within the effective range of quick-fire artillery carried by battleships before launching their weapons. After 1896, however, the relative difference between the effective ranges of naval artillery and the torpedo narrowed considerably.[44] And the gap continued to narrow. When Fisher accepted the post of first sea lord in May 1904, he was informed by the first lord that recently 'Messrs Whitehead have produced a torpedo which ran straight for 3,000 yards, and I understand that, in the opinion of the *Vernon* [R.N. Torpedo school], before long we shall have torpedoes that will run accurately for 5,000 yards at the rate of 25 knots'.[45] Experiments with early 'heater' torpedoes later in 1904, suggested that the range of this engine might soon exceed 7,000 yards, a range which many considered to be the maximum effective range of naval gunfire.[46] As early as December 1908, the director of naval ordnance was predicting that 'we now have it in our power to construct a torpedo which should effect considerable damage on a line of ships outside practical gunnery range'. Armed with these weapons, destroyers 'would be able safely to fire torpedoes at ranges which render effective reply by gunfire even in daytime extremely doubtful'.[47] It was not then, as Marder believed, such an easy matter for Fisher to anticipate advances in naval technology. Exploiting new technology was a complex and subtle problem: the effectiveness of different weapon systems improved at different rates. With only limited resources, the Admiralty had to decide not only how much the navy should invest in each system, but also to calculate which weapon system showed the most promise of fulfilling the navy's requirements in the long run, given the set of circumstances facing the Royal Navy at that time. Furthermore, the fact that technology was evolving in new ways and at an uncertain pace meant that the context in which decisions were made was itself evolving continuously and unpredictably.[48]

Marder's interpretation of what Fisher was trying to achieve was fundamentally flawed largely because he interpreted the admiral's policies in the light of Mahanian theories of naval warfare. Many papers which allude to Fisher's radical strategic theory were dismissed by the historian as mere speculative writing, probably because the ideas they postulated on the conduct of war at sea did not conform with classic Mahanian theory. That Fisher himself claimed not to believe in historical principles of naval war was also ignored. When, however, the documentary evidence is viewed from a different perspective, it shows that Fisher was aiming to reconstitute British naval strategy: no less. He was convinced that the introduction of technologically advanced 'new types of fighting ships',[49] such as battlecruisers and submarines, permitted the navy to adopt different and more effective methods of conducting naval warfare. Consequently, a Navy centred around a stronger fleet of battleships was no longer the best force structure to protect British maritime interests. Instead, Fisher envisaged the creation of two distinct and independent fleets: a main fighting fleet equipped with battlecruisers to protect imperial interests around the globe;[50] the other, a force comprised mainly of submarines and torpedo craft whose capacity to inflict serious losses on troop transports and their escorts would deter or prevent invasion across the narrow seas around the British Isles. The viability of the battlecruiser concept thus hinged upon Fisher's concept of 'flotilla defence', a strategy which will be explained in greater detail below.

THE ORIGINS OF FLOTILLA DEFENCE

Traditionally, the foundation of British naval strategy was to maintain an effective blockade of all enemy naval bases by stationing observation squadrons off the enemy coast. The security of the inshore squadrons, of course, rested upon (close) support being provided by elements of the battle fleet. Effectively, the purpose of close blockade was to allow the Royal Navy to know the whereabouts of most enemy ships most of the time, and to provide early warning of aggressive movements. An effective blockade enabled the Admiralty to keep its battle squadrons more or less concentrated in a position to inflict a decisive defeat on the enemy's main fleet if the opportunity arose. At the same time, early warning allowed the Royal Navy to match hostile movements by small squadrons with economy of force. Also, if an invasion convoy left port, advanced warning from the observation force allowed the British battle fleet to intercept it long before it reached the English coast. The inshore squadron was also in a position to intercept commerce raiders attempting to escape to the oceans, and merchant ships trying to enter enemy ports.[51]

During a long war, the Royal Navy could rely upon the very existence of its stronger fleet of battleships to intimidate the enemy from using his significant naval units aggressively. The high degree of probability that ships leaving port would be observed and the reasonable certainty they would be quickly brought to action by a superior force tended to encourage the weaker naval power to await developments and keep its fleet in being. By establishing this 'moral superiority' near home, the Royal Navy was able to deploy relatively few cruisers in distant waters to protect British interests where they were most vulnerable. Using the battle fleet as a weapon of strategic deterrence, however, was dependent upon the Royal Navy keeping in home waters a significantly greater number of battleships than the enemy. This may have restricted the application of naval force in other theatres of operations, but the dividend was greater safety for commerce on the trade routes.

By the time Fisher became first sea lord he had been convinced that the Royal Navy would not be able to deploy large armoured warships in the 'narrow sea' around Britain. By far the most serious challenge came from the development of the locomotive torpedo. Progressive developments of this cheap weapon and improvements in the seaworthiness of the torpedo boat were gradually weakening the effectiveness of the blockade, by forcing the observation squadron to take station further and further away from the coast during the hours of darkness.[52] As already explained, the application of the gyroscope to the torpedo guidance mechanism in 1896, increased greatly the chances of French torpedo boats successfully engaging British armoured vessels in daylight. This invention at a stroke more than doubled the effective range of the torpedo. By contrast, Percy Scott's efforts to extend the effective range of naval artillery during the same period proceeded only slowly. Consequently, the relative gap between the effective range of the torpedo and naval artillery narrowed considerably.

As the effective range of the torpedo continued to be steadily increased, Fisher and other senior naval officers including Harry Rawson, Arthur Wilson, and Charles Beresford were persuaded that this engine had become a significant consideration in fleet tactics.[53] Possibly as early as 1900, but certainly by 1903, all three had been convinced that future naval engagements against a French squadron accompanied by torpedo boats, would have to be fought outside the effective range of the torpedo.[54] The wisdom of this precaution was emphasized by the discovery that existing British armoured vessels were unexpectedly vulnerable to underwater damage. The Admiralty tried desperately to improve the underwater protection of British warships, but experiments proved repeatedly that a single torpedo hit was likely to sink or cripple a battleship. In September 1903, the Admiralty conceded defeat after the old battleship *Belleisle*, which the experts thought had been made torpedo proof, sank to the bottom of Portsmouth harbour in eight minutes. 'I regret very much', concluded the controller, Rear Admiral William May, 'but I fear we must accept the position that with our present knowledge it is not possible to make a ship invulnerable against attack of the 18″ Whitehead [torpedo], without going to a prohibitive size.'[55]

The Royal Navy had a powerful incentive to contemplate the destructiveness of torpedoes. Across the English Channel the French Navy had been for many years investing heavily in the development of the torpedo craft. Gradually, the French managed to improve the sea-keeping qualities of their torpedo boats, thereby extending their effective radius of action beyond inshore waters. Towards the end of the 1890s, the French Navy adopted a coherent strategy for retaliating against a blockade of the French coasts which involved the extensive use of torpedo boats.[56] The plan involved the building of large numbers of flotilla craft, to produce eventually a mosquito fleet capable of threatening any hostile warships which tried to operate in their territorial waters. French naval doctrine called for torpedo craft day and night 'to harry' British warships, and especially the armoured vessels patrolling the English Channel in support of the blockade squadron. British intelligence correctly guessed the French 'expect more from this organization which they have taken such vast pains to perfect, than a mere increase of their defensive powers'.[57]

The main function of the *Défenses Mobiles* was to weaken the British blockade sufficiently to allow commerce raiders to escape to the high seas. For the *guerre industrielle* the French Navy had specially developed a totally new type of armoured warship. By exploiting major improvements in the process of manufacturing armour plate during the early 1890s, the French were able to build a cruiser protected with new lightweight side armour capable of stopping the projectiles of medium-calibre, quick-firing guns mounted on British cruisers, yet still able to steam at high speed. They also carried huge quantities of coal which enabled them to outpace and outdistance any British warship then afloat. The side-armoured cruisers, which were ordered in large numbers from 1897, rendered obsolete all existing British trade-protection cruisers.[58] The British response was conventional – to build large armoured cruisers of its own. Armoured cruisers, however, were almost as costly as battleships and even more expensive to maintain. Between 1897 and 1904, the Royal Navy laid down a total of 63 large armoured vessels – more than half of which were armoured cruisers: this phenomenal pace of construction could not be sustained. From 1899, the Admiralty struggled increasingly to persuade the government to appropriate adequate funds to sustain the Royal Navy's commitment to maintaining a two-power standard in battleships, in addition to building adequate numbers of armoured cruisers for trade protection duties.[59]

The advent of the submarine as a practical weapon of war had a profound impact upon Fisher's vision of the future. As commander-in-chief in the Mediterranean (1899–1902) he had been the first senior British officer forced to contemplate the threat of attacks on his fleet by submarines. Toulon was the main testing ground for French submarines. Later, while serving as commander-in-chief at Portsmouth (1903–4), he had been in a unique position to watch the development of the Royal Navy's own embryonic submarine service. Subsequently, he came to believe that technology could revolutionize the method of conducting war at sea.[60] 'Only those who have seen a flotilla of submarine boats as at Portsmouth practising out in the open sea', he wrote to the prime minister in November 1903, 'can form the right conception of the revolution they have caused'.[61] 'The pith and marrow' of his faith in the submarine was its ability to attack unseen, without warning, and to remain invulnerable to counterattack. These unique fighting characteristics, in his view, gave the submarine a moral advantage over surface warships, which was far more valuable than the vessel's actual fighting capabilities. In 1904, Fisher could barely contain his glee when he reported to a friend that 'six submarines we have here of the original type succeeded in the recent manoeuvres in sinking millions of £'s of battleships and cruisers and established such a funk as to keep the Home Fleet miles away from Portsmouth'.[62]

Lord Selborne, the first lord of the Admiralty, was absolutely convinced that Fisher really did believe that a revolution in naval warfare had occurred.

> I always said that the battleship held the field, that the battleship counted for more than anything else, and that no number of cruisers could be substitutes for them. Fisher did not believe this when I left the Admiralty [in March 1905], though he believed it before all other opinions when he was Commander-in-Chief in the Mediterranean. Fisher believed that the torpedo as used by torpedo boats and the submarine was going to make the narrow seas (they widely interpreted) impossible for battleships, that the torpedo was going to be the lord and master of the narrow seas under all conditions.[63]

In reaching this conclusion, Fisher also knew the results of the Royal Navy's highly secret and hitherto unknown programme of anti-submarine experiments.[64] These trials, conducted between 1900 and 1904, confirmed that to all intents and purposes submarines were undetectable and consequently unattackable; and that for the foreseeable future there was little prospect of developing effective countermeasures against them. The depth charge had been tried and rejected. Also, Fisher had seen reports by Captain Reginald Bacon, the officer in charge of the Royal Navy's own submarine flotilla, which indicated that the range and performance of the submarine was certain to develop very rapidly.[65] By the end of 1903, the Royal Navy already had under construction a new type of submarine designed to operate anywhere in the Channel for up to a week.[66]

Fisher may not have been the first officer to realize the implications of a submergible warship being able to sink a surface ship without warning, but he was the first senior British officer to accept that it would be impossible to maintain an effective close blockade of enemy ports defended by submarines, and to recognize the implications.[67] Submarines would not be used to attack the inshore blockade squadron, but the heavy units further out to sea. Deprived of close support, the inshore squadron would be vulnerable to forays by the enemy's own armoured warships. The impossibility of maintaining an effective blockade not only assisted commerce raiders to escape to the oceans, it also appeared initially to render Britain more vulnerable to surprise invasion or 'a bolt from the blue', by allowing the convoy to sail without detection.

When, during 1903, the Committee of Imperial Defence examined the practicability of a French invasion, British naval and military experts agreed that a successful invasion of the British Isles would depend upon the capture of a port on the mainland. This was recognized as essential, even by army officers, in order to facilitate the rapid disembarkation of troops necessary to secure the bridgehead and more importantly to permit the landing of military stores and heavy equipment. Before Fisher took office in 1904, the Admiralty argued that an invasion convoy would never attempt to cross the Channel unless it could be guaranteed protection from interference *en route*. This, the admirals insisted, would be impossible so long as the Royal Navy battle fleet remained intact.[68] Fisher disagreed. Realizing that the French would probably use only their torpedo boats and submarines to contest control of the Channel, he feared that if the Admiralty deployed the Royal Navy along traditional lines then its armoured warships would be sunk by 'unattackable' submarines by day and 'invisible' small craft at night. He was convinced, 'that in the course of a few years no Fleet will be able to remain in the Mediterranean or in the English Channel' for any period of time.[69] Without support from armoured warships close blockade was impractical; without a blockade, the difficulties in protecting the trade routes and preventing invasion would be increased enormously; which in turn would prevent the British fleet from remaining concentrated, thus significantly weakening its value as a weapon of strategic deterrence.

Fisher's solution was to reconstitute naval strategic policy. He approached the question of how to protect British Imperial interests by looking at 'the defence of the 'Narrow Seas' ... the English Channel and the western basin of the Mediterranean, as a question quite apart and separate from the working of the main fighting fleets'.[70] Accordingly, he proposed that the twin objectives of naval policy, the protection of ocean trade and the defence of the country from invasion, would in future be accomplished by two quite separate fleets. After his appointment as first sea lord in October 1904, Fisher initiated a programme of radical innovation in warship design, proposing innovative operational concepts, and redeployed existing warships with a view to conducting war along very different lines. He believed that his new force structure would protect British maritime interests more efficiently and at far less cost than a traditionally balanced fleet.

Instead of relying upon squadrons of armoured warships to deter invasion, Fisher proposed that the narrow seas around Britain should be guarded ('infested' was his term) by a large force of torpedo boats and submarines patrolling far out to sea. Any invasion convoy which attempted to approach a British port, he believed, would be sighted and attacked by a swarm of torpedo craft. In marked contrast to previous doctrines which identified the enemy main fleet as the principal objective, Fisher ordered that the flotilla craft should ignore escorting battleships and make straight for the troop transports.[71] 'Imagine', he wrote,

> the effect of one such transport going to the bottom in a few seconds with its living freight. Even the bare thought makes invasion impossible! Fancy 100,000 helpless, huddled up troops afloat in frightened transports with these invisible demons known to be near ... nothing conceivable more demoralising.[72]

It followed that an invasion convoy would be deterred from approaching the English coast until the defence flotilla had somehow been neutralized.[73] Fisher was confident that the 'moral threat' of the submarine would prevent an invasion convoy from ever sailing. In effect, submarines would become the new force of strategic deterrence.[74]

This idea was not completely new. Twenty years earlier, the *Jeune École* in France had advanced similar arguments to justify a halt in the construction of battleships. At that time, however, the French had not yet mastered the art of submarine navigation, and their torpedo boats were so unseaworthy as to make them little more than local defence craft tied to a single port. The development of quick-fire guns, moreover, provided battleships with an effective weapon to fend off torpedo craft during the hours of daylight. Furthermore, while the French torpedo boats had to remain dispersed, an enemy could concentrate his forces to attack a single point and overwhelm the local defence force. Obviously, the cost

of building a comprehensive network of local defence flotillas was prohibitive.

In 1904, however, Fisher was confident that recent improvements in ship
design allowed the Royal Navy to build torpedo craft with much better
sea-keeping abilities capable of operating as a truly mobile force anywhere
in the English Channel.[75] The concept of flotilla defence called for the
narrow coastal waters around Britain to be saturated with torpedo craft,
deployed offensively, forward into the middle waters of the Channel. In
one of the very few papers in which he clearly explained his ideas on flotilla
defence, Fisher argued that 'offensive strategy must be held to include the
circumspection of the free movements of the enemy. Any action that
limits their free movement of action is an action of offence.'[76] This was a
completely new way of thinking. Equally radical was his assertion that the
objective of flotilla defence was not to win or contest command of the sea
but to achieve (mutual) sea denial:

> The position in the Channel is the same to us and France when opposed
> to one another. The submarine is the only answer to the submarine(!)
> since they should be able to elude all craft and no one particular
> vessel can be built which can be relied upon to destroy them. This being
> so, by the use of these craft it may be made impossible to keep large
> units in the Channel, or other confined waters. If we cannot do so but
> the enemy can, then invasion is a certainty; hence the necessity for the
> provision of these craft on our sea frontiers. But having them for this
> purpose they become instantly available for further extended use ...
> our ships are liable to attack both by day and also by night. Before
> many years navigation in the western basin of the Mediterranean in
> wartime (equally with the English Channel) will be a very dangerous
> undertaking owing to the offensive action of this class of boat.[77]

In March 1905, Fisher's revolutionary ideas on the use of submarines
in war were disclosed to the Cabinet in surprising detail. 'Their main
attribute is their invisibility,' explained Earl Cawdor, the new first lord of
the Admiralty.

> This invests them with a subtle power of producing great uncertainty
> and apprehension in the minds of officers and crews of vessels work-
> ing in certain waters. We have only to recognise the disturbing effect
> produced by the presence of fixed blockade mines during the present
> [Russo-Japanese] war to foreshadow the increased mental strain that
> would be produced by mobile submarines.[78]

Cawdor went on to give his Cabinet colleagues a summary of his first sea
lord's ideas on how exactly submarines would be employed, and to dispel
the impression created by press reports that submarines were just
defensive craft. The Admiralty, he revealed, fully expected submarines

to blockade enemy ports. But undoubtedly the most interesting admission was:

> We must also not neglect the possibility of certain waters being denied to large ships from the danger of being attacked in daylight by submarine-boats, and at night by torpedo craft. The only way, at present, of meeting such an investment is by following suit and denying the waters in turn to the enemy, thereby neutralising these areas for offensive operations. Such a case may be far, at present, from actual realisation: but affairs move quickly these days, and we must be ready to forestall any dangerous contingencies.[79]

Fisher's strategy of 'flotilla defence' was dependent upon quantitative rather than qualitative superiority (although both were sought).[80] To this end, he immediately sought to procure for the navy, as quickly as possible, a large number of modern flotilla craft. In November 1904, he cancelled a contract for 13 *River* class destroyers.[81] In their place, he ordered vessels he termed 'coastal destroyers'. These were highly seaworthy torpedo boats with only a short radius of action, but which could be built for half the price of a full size destroyer.[82] Hitherto, no historian has ever managed to explain why 36 of these craft were built, while over the same period only four ocean-going 'fleet' destroyers were ordered. Fisher also endorsed the continued construction of large numbers of small, but again comparatively cheap, submarines when he knew that larger more efficient vessels could have been built.[83] 'This', explained the inspecting captain of submarines, Sydney Hall, 'was merely a question of money policy – Admiralty said they preferred to have twelve single screw rather than eight or nine twin screw' submarines.[84] Quality was not so important. Before he was appointed first sea lord, Fisher had repeatedly condemned the Admiralty for not ordering more submarines. 'We strain at the gnat of perfection, and swallow the camel of unreadiness!' We forget that 'half a loaf is better than no bread!' he moaned, 'some people think [that in wartime] you can go round the corner and buy a submarine like a pound of sugar!'[85]

During Fisher's administration, spending on the purchase of new flotilla craft rocketed from £1 million to over £2 million. This increase is all the more significant because over the same period, the total naval construction budget had dropped by £2 million, almost 20 per cent.[86] Put another way, when Fisher arrived at Whitehall in 1904 less than 10 per cent of the constructions budget was allocated to flotilla craft. In 1909 the proportion had grown to over 20 per cent.[87] In fact, if Fisher had been allowed, this shift would have been even more pronounced. Sketch naval estimates for the next four years compiled in July 1905 show that expenditure on flotilla craft was forecast to comprise a full one-third of the construction budget.[88]

In addition to building new torpedo craft, Fisher also took steps to make better use of existing resources. In November 1904, the Admiralty announced a redistribution of the fleet after the decommissioning of a large number of old trade-protection cruisers and gunboats. The principal motive for the famous decision to scrap 154 ships was to alleviate an acute shortage of trained personnel.[89] Subsequently, in February 1905, the Admiralty ordered that 'every effective torpedo vessel' be 'henceforward commissioned with a crew of two fifths full strength'.[90] Hitherto, the torpedo craft in reserve, a force comprised of 18 torpedo gunboats and 80 destroyers, had been left in the hands of dockyard care and mainte-nance parties and would have been manned only at the outbreak of war.[91] In addition, all destroyers in commission were grouped together under the command of a single rear admiral (D), Alfred Winsloe, a trusted member of the 'fishpond'. In April 1907, the flotilla was further strength-ened; first, all torpedo craft in home waters, both in commission or in reserve, were placed under the command of a rear admiral (D); and second, all torpedo craft in reserve were manned to 80 per cent of their war complement. Out of an effective fleet manpower of approximately 80,000 between October 1904 and April 1907, the number of personnel allocated to man the flotilla rose from 8,064 to 12,486.[92]

The biggest obstacle Fisher faced with respect to implementing flotilla defence was persuading senior fleet commanders to accept his strategic views. Admiral Lord Charles Beresford, commander-in-chief of the Channel Fleet (1907–9) and designated to command the combined fleets in the event of war, was consistently dismissive of the capabilities of submarines, and refused point blank to accept any War Orders from the Admiralty which did not include a close blockade of the German coast.[93] The bitter dispute between these 'two old men' was not simply a person-ality clash, as it is generally portrayed by historians. When Fisher realized Beresford had no intention of carrying out his orders, he tried desperately to have him dismissed for insubordination, but he was prevented from doing so by the Liberal Cabinet led by H. H. Asquith.[94] It must be said, however, at the same time even some of Fisher's closest supporters ques-tioned the extent to which the flotilla should be relied upon to defend Britain from invasion. Most believed that armoured warships would still be needed to support the flotilla. If so, they argued, then climactic 'Mahanian' battles between rival fleets would probably still occur. For instance in April 1909, during a discussion on the role of submarines in the event of war with Germany, Rear Admiral John Jellicoe insisted that eventually 'the time must come when our own battle fleet will be forced into the North Sea to endeavour to bring the German fleet to action'. Fisher did not agree.[95]

Whether or not the concept of flotilla defence was accepted by the fleet does not alter the fact that the strategy had been adopted by the Board of Admiralty. Relying upon the flotilla to deter invasion was the key to the

Admiralty's willingness to accept a much smaller margin of superiority in armoured warships than previously. Flotilla defence meant that the navy no longer had to maintain an overwhelmingly stronger battle fleet in home waters. 'It has really been on the superiority of our fleet of torpedo craft', stated Lord Selborne in November 1904, 'that the Committee of Imperial Defence has felt able to advise that the strength of the home army may be calculated apart from any serious fear of invasion.'[96] Quite simply, battleships were no longer required to the same effect.

The switch to flotilla defence also produced overall savings in the naval estimates which, during the Edwardian era, was the Admiralty's single most important goal. Submarines and torpedo boats were much cheaper to build and maintain than armoured warships.[97] In addition to savings in the construction budget, the adoption of the flotilla strategy also allowed further savings to be made by large reductions in the reserve fleet. The scrapping of old ships saved not only maintenance costs but also released crews and berthing space, thereby eliminating projected increases in spending on personnel and works. Marder argued these savings were made possible by improvements in the efficiency of the battle squadrons of the British fleet (both active and nucleus crew), thus diminishing the requirement for a large reserve.[98] In fact, much of the reserve fleet was supplanted, at lesser cost, by the expansion of the flotilla.

Strategically, the ability to rely upon the flotilla to protect the United Kingdom from invasion – independent of the main fleet, although probably supported by units of the reserve fleet – was supposed to give the Admiralty unprecedented flexibility in wartime to deploy squadrons of armoured warships to reinforce the outer marches of the Empire.[99] It was the strategy of flotilla defence, therefore, that enabled Fisher to build battlecruisers. These fast, powerfully armed, long-range warships were far better suited than battleships to protect British Imperial interests around the globe. Of course there was never any real chance of Fisher being able to equip every squadron in the navy with battlecruisers, even if he had been allowed. The operational life of pre-dreadnoughts was calculated at 20–25 years. After 1905, they may have been obsolescent but they were not obsolete. Fisher, therefore, must have envisaged deploying battlecruisers in conjunction with old battleships and cruisers.

The key to understanding Fisher's naval policy cannot be found just by looking at the warships in the fleet, or by analysing the Royal Navy's building programmes during this period. Comprehension depends upon recognition that Fisher's views on the conduct of naval warfare, and his ideas for the deployment of warships, were radically different to conventional or 'historical' operational doctrines. His innovative perceptions of the character of naval war represented a fundamental shift in British naval policy. Under Sir John Fisher, no longer was it the aim of the Royal Navy to seek out and destroy the enemy fleet in the blue water; because he believed that the navy could accomplish its 'ends' without necessarily employing the 'means' of defeating the enemy fleet in a decisive battle. This represented a switch towards an essentially reactive form of naval warfare as opposed to the active defence implicit in the concept of the offensive use of the battle fleet to attain command of the sea. Fisher's submarine and flotilla strategy in conjunction with the concept of the battlecruiser marked a complete turn around in the ethos of the Royal Navy.[100]

NOTES

In preparing this chapter, I have deliberately used only contemporary documents to support my argument, that is, papers written by Fisher before his retirement in 1910. This paper was originally presented to the 1993 Annapolis Naval History Symposium. It is based on a chapter from a much larger monograph, nearing completion, comparing the impact of the submarine upon naval strategies in Britain, France and the United States, provisionally titled *A Revolution in Naval Strategy: The Influence of the Submarine upon Maritime Thought, 1898–1914* (forthcoming). I thank Professors Charles Fairbanks, Paul Kennedy, Mark Shulman, Ronald Spector and Jon Sumida for helpful comments on earlier drafts of this chapter. I am also grateful to the Olin Foundation for their financial support.

1. 'Naval Necessities, Volume l', FISR 8/2, FP 4703a, Fisher Papers, Churchill College, Cambridge; reprinted in *The Papers of Admiral Sir John Fisher*, ed. Peter Kemp, 2 vols (London: Naval Records Society, 1960–64); 'The Mediterranean Fleet, 1899–1902', extracts from lectures by John Fisher, FISR 8/10, FP4702.

2. Ruddock Mackay, *Fisher of Kilverstone* (Oxford: Clarendon Press, 1973), 314–16, 367–74; Paul Haggie, 'The Royal Navy and War Planning in the Fisher Era', in P. Kennedy (ed.), *The War Plans of the Great Powers* (London: Unwin Hyman, 1979), 118–32; P. M. Kennedy, *Strategy and Diplomacy* (London, 1983), 114, 121–2; Aaron Friedburg, *The Weary Titan* (Princeton, NJ: Princeton University Press, 1988), 193.

3. The principal works of Arthur J. Marder include *The Anatomy of British Sea Power: A History of British Naval Policy in the Pre-Dreadnought Era, 1880–1905* (reprinted Hamden, CT: Archon, 1964), hereafter referred to as *Anatomy*; *Fear God and Dread Nought: The Correspondence of Admiral of the Fleet Lord Fisher of Kilverstone*, 3 vols (London, 1952–59), hereafter referred to as *FGDN*; and *From the Dreadnought to Scapa Flow: The Royal Navy in the Fisher Era*, 5 vols (London, 1961–70), hereafter referred to as *FDSF*.

4. 'Fisher: reforms and the German fleet', *Anatomy*, chapter 26, especially 489–91; *FDSF*, I, 36–45; *FGDN*, II, 15–45.

5. *FDSF*, I, 87. Also see I, 25, 40.

6. *FDSF*, I, 57. Also most recently, Rhodri Williams, *Defending the Empire* (New Haven, CT: Yale University Press, 1992), 75.

7. Kemp, *Papers of Admiral Sir John Fisher*, I, 198–297, 'Report of the Committee on Designs' (1905).

8. *FDSF*, I, 69.

 9. *FDSF*, I, 57; *FGDN*, II, 18–20, 24.
10. Typically, Paul Kennedy, *The Rise and Fall of British Naval Mastery*, 3rd edn (London: Fontana, 1991), 257–8; Friedburg, *Weary Titan*, 135–9, 204–8; P A. Towle, 'The Effect of the Russo-Japanese War on British Naval Policy', *Mariner's Mirror*, 60 (1974), 383–94.
11. Jon Sumida, *In Defence of Naval Supremacy: Finance, Technology and British Naval Policy, 1889–1914* (Boston, MA: Unwin Hyman, 1989), 18–28, 37–61. (compare with Marder's interpretation in *FDSF*, I, 232–6; *Anatomy*, 487); Williams, *Defending the Empire*, 62–9; Friedburg, *Weary Titan*; Keith Neilson, *Britain and the Last Tzar: British Policy and Russia, 1894–1917* (Oxford: Oxford University Press, 1995).
12. Charles Fairbanks, 'The Origins of the Dreadnought Revolution: A Historiographical Essay', *International History Review*, 13 (May 1991), 262; Sumida, *In Defence*, 18–28.
13. Ibid.; for an example of Fisher's views on the need for economy, see 'A Brief Precis on the Principal Considerations That Must Influence Our Future Naval and Military Policy', by John Fisher (n.d.), Additional Manuscripts (hereafter Add. MSS) 49710, 3–7, British Library, London. Admiralty stationery indicates this was written before September 1903. For Marder's view, see *Anatomy*, 486–9.
14. Ruddock Mackay, 'The Admiralty, the German Navy, and the Redistribution of the British Fleet, 1904–1905', *Mariner's Mirror*, 56 (August 1970), 341–6; see also Keith Neilson, 'The British Empire Floats on the British Navy: British Naval Policy, Belligerent Rights, and Disarmament, 1902–1909', in B. J. C. McKercher (ed.), *Arms Limitation and Disarmament*, (Westport, CT: Praeger, 1992), 23–4; Nicholas Lambert, *A Revolution* (forthcoming).
15. Jon Sumida, 'Sir John Fisher and the Dreadnought: The Sources of Naval Mythology', *Journal of Military History*, 59 (October 1995); Sumida, *In Defence*.
16. Sumida, *In Defence*, 37–61.
17. *FDSF*, I, 56–66, and especially 69–70.
18. Mackay, *Kilverstone*, 321–5.
19. 'Admiralty Policy', memorandum by Charles Ottley (DNI) dated 15 October 1906, 15, paragraph c, MSS 2/22, Crease Papers, Naval Library, Ministry of Defence.
20. Sumida, *In Defence*, 51–61; also, Jellicoe to Captain Reginald Tupper, 24 January 1906, Tupper MSS, Royal Navy Museum, Portsmouth.
21. Sumida, *In Defence*, 55–6.
22. Ibid., 60, 161–2.
23. Ibid., 58–61; 'Meeting held at Admiralty Saturday, 2nd December 1905', Part 3, 'Fusion design of battleships and armoured cruisers', and 'Naval Estimates Committee, 1906/07', 10 January 1906, 18–31, Crease MSS, Prints.
24. Characteristics of *Dreadnought*: displacement 17,900 tons, speed 21 knots, armament 10 × 12 inch; *Invincible*: 17,250 tons, 25 knots, 8 × 12 inch guns; 'fusion design', 22,500 tons, 25 knots, 10 × 12 inch guns.
25. 'Naval Estimates Committee 1906–07', 10 January 1906, Report of committee, 18–31, Crease MSS, Prints.
26. Fisher to McKenna, 14 August 1908, MCKN 3/4, f.19, McKenna Papers, Churchill College, Cambridge; Fisher to Arnold White, 15 August 1908, Fisher to Watts, 17 September 1908, and Fisher to McKenna, 5 March 1909, *FGDN*, 2, 189, 195, 229.
27. Mackay, *Kilverstone*, 387–91.
28. Nicholas Lambert, 'Economy or Empire: The Fleet Unit Concept and Quest for Collective Security in the Pacific, 1909–1914', in Keith Neilson and Greg

Kennedy, eds, *Far Flung Lines: Studies in Imperial Defence* (London: Frank Cass, 1995).

29. 'Admiralty Policy', October 1906, Crease MSS, 2122.
30. Fisher to Esher, 8 September 1908, *FGDN*, II, 195; see also Fisher to Watts, 17 September 1908, ibid.
31. McKenna to Asquith, 29 March 1909, MCKN 3/19, f. 13.
32. Fisher to McKenna, 30 March 1909, *FGDN*, II, 239.
33. Journal entry, 30 March 1909, ESHR 12/1, Esher Papers, Churchill College, Cambridge.
34. I am indebted to Professor Charles Fairbanks for this quotation from Cameron Hazelhurst, *A Liberal Chronicle: The Journal of J. A. Pease* (London: Historian Press, 1994), 8.
35. 'Notes on Interview with F.B.', 12 May 1909, Sanders MSS 758, f. 216, Sanders Papers, Bodleian Library, Oxford. Bridgeman became second sea lord in May 1909.
36. Ibid.; Nicholas Lambert 'Admiral Sir Francis Bridgeman-Bridgeman', in Malcolm Murfett (ed.), *The First Sea Lords: From Fisher to Mountbatten*, (Westport, CT: Praeger, 1995), 60.
37. Fisher to McKenna, 28 May 1909, FISR 1/8, FP390. Dreadnoughts were armed with ten guns, *Invincible* with eight.
38. Bridgeman to Sanders, 30 July and 2 August 1909, Sanders MSS 759, f. 49.
39. Minute by Sir Phillip Watts (DNC), 17 June 1909, on CN0440/09, Ships Covers 248 (*Orion* class battleships), f. 5, National Maritime Museum, Greenwich.
40. Ibid. See also 'Memorandum' by John Jellicoe (Third Sea Lord), 3 May 1909, Add. MSS 48990, f. 71; also Fisher to McKenna, 5 March 1909, *FGDN*, II: 229.
41. Fisher to Esher, 13 September 1909, and Fisher to Arnold White, 13 November 1909, *FGDN*, 2, 266, 277.
42. *FDSF*, I: 344, 364–8.
43. John Hattendorf, 'Alfred Thayer Mahan and his Strategic Thought', in *Maritime Strategy and the Balance of Power*, John Hattendorf and Robert Jordan, eds (New York: St Martin's Press, 1989), 83–92.
44. Annual Report of the Torpedo School, 1900, 'Report on trials of Gyroscopes Carried out in Channel Squadron', January 1900, 36–48, ART1, Priddy's Hard Collection, Hampshire Record Office, Winchester.
45. Memorandum by Selborne, 14 May 1904; Kemp, *Papers of Admiral Sir John Fisher*, I, xxi.
46. Ibid.; also 'Third Report of the Torpedo Design Committee', Priddy's Hard, ART 1, 1904, Appendix D; also Submarine Museum HMS *Dolphin*, BR 1696, 'Torpedo Manual, 1929', 'Historical Sketch of the Torpedo', 15.
47. 'As to allowance of 21-inch torpedoes in ships' (G18176/8), minutes by Reginald Bacon (DNO) and Bernard Currey (assistant director of torpedoes), both dated 17 December 1908, Ships Covers 224 (Australia and New Zealand) f. 34.
48. This point was made to me by Commander James Goldrick, Royal Australian Navy.
49. Fisher to Esher, 21 August 1904, *FGDN*, I, 325.
50. Sumida, *In Defence*, 54–61.
51. The best classical interpretation of the theory of seapower is Julian Corbett's *Some Principles of Maritime Strategy* (London and Annapolis, MD: Brassey's and Naval Institute Press, 1988).
52. *FDSF*, I, 369; also 'Great Britain Torpedo Craft Manoeuvres 1904', 70–8, ADM 231/43, N.I.D., report 794.

53. Fisher to Selborne, 29 July 1901, and Fisher to Selborne, 19 July 1902, *FGDN*, I, 202, 251.
54. Priddy's Hard, ART 1, 1900, 36–7; ibid., 1903, 49; Fisher to Selborne, 19 July 1902, *FGDN*, I, 251; Beresford to Selborne, n.d. [*c.* September 1903], Selborne MSS 18, f. 16, Selborne Papers, Bodleian Library, Oxford.
55. Minute by Controller, 2 December 1903, G13107/03, ADM 1/7687 HMS *Belleisle* (DNO 1:8:03), Admiralty Archives, Public Record Office, Kew.
56. Edouard Lockroy, *La Défense Navale* (Paris, 1900), 400–50; Theodore Ropp, *The Development of a Modern Navy* (Annapolis, MD: Naval Institute Press, 1987), 327–36.
57. 'Navy Estimates, 1901–1902: Memorandum on Shipbuilding', Selborne, 17 January 1901, 6–11, CAB37/53/8, Cabinet Archives, Public Record Office, Kew; 'The Navy Estimates and the Chancellor of the Exchequer's Memorandum on the Growth of Expenditure', Selborne, 16 November 1901, 9–15, CAB37/59/118.
58. Sumida, *In Defence*, 20–5; see especially 'Navy Estimates, 1899–1900', Goschen, 31 January 1899, 5–7, CAB37/49/7.
59. D. G. Boyce, *The Crisis of British Sea Power: The Imperial and Naval Papers of the Second Earl Selborne, 1898–1910* (London, 1990), 106–56.
60. Fisher to May, 20 April 1904, and Fisher to Esher, 23 April 1904, *FGDN*, I, 308, 310.
61. Fisher to Balfour, November 1903, enclosing comments on Balfour's paper 'Serious Invasion', Add. MSS 49710, f. 56; see also ibid., f. 57, Fisher to Sanders, 5 December 1903.
62. 'Submarines: Second Post-script', April 1904, Add. MSS 49710, f. 139.
63. Selborne to Balfour, 23 August 1905, Add. MSS 49707, f. 88.
64. 'Principal Questions Dealt with by Director of Naval Ordnance', May 1900, 109–13, Priddy's Hard; ibid., ART 1, 1901, Appendix C, 171–3; Memorandum by Admiral William May, 5 January 1904, ADM1/7717; Report on Submarines submitted by Captain Reginald Bacon, 31 May 1905, ADM1/7795; HMS *Thames*, 'Report on the Manoeuvres Recently Carried Out Between Submarine-boats and One Division of the Portsmouth Destroyer Flotilla', May 1904, ADM1/7719; Submarine Museum HMS *Dolphin*, 'Captain Bacon's Notebook', 57–9; 'Trial in Starfish of Swinging Outrigger to T.B.s and T.B.D.s to Destroy Submarine Boats', 1900–3, Ships Covers 185A, f. 26.
65. 'Reports on the Running of Submarine Boats', by Reginald Bacon, 31 May 1903, ADM 1/7795. Sadly the docket containing the original report has been lost, although some of the minutes written by Admiralty officials on the original docket are quoted by Marder in *Anatomy*, 365; Bacon, 'Report on Running of Submarine Boats, 30 June–31 December 1903', 16 January 1904, enclosed in Portsmouth submission No. 258/45, of 25 January 1904, ADM 1/7725.
66. Bacon to DNC, 7 November 1903, and 'Type of submarine boat for 1904', N.B. minute from May to Kerr, 14 December 1903, Ships Covers 185A, S30250/03.
67. Kemp, *Papers of Admiral Sir John Fisher*, I, 43, 68–72.
68. 'Our Position as Regards Invasion on the Supposition that our Battle Fleet in Home Waters has Sustained a Reverse and is Unable to Leave Port in Face of a Hostile Fleet in Superior Strength', Admiralty, 31 March 1903, CAB 38/2/19, 3/1/11A; 'Remarks on M.I.D. Paper 13A', Admiralty, 14 July 1903, CAB 38/3/60, 3/1/16A; 'Draft Report on the Possibility of Serious Invasion: Home Defence', Balfour, November 1903, CAB 3813171, 3/1/18A.
69. Fisher to Balfour, 5 January 1904, Add. MSS 49710, f. 79; Fisher to Arnold White, 12 March 1904, *FGDN*, I, 305. Contrast Fisher's views with those of

other senior Admiralty officers in Minutes by Kerr, 1 July 1904, and May, 30 June 1904, ADM 1/7719, HMS *Thames*.

70. Kemp, *Papers of Admiral Sir John Fisher*, II: 6.
71. Comments by Fisher on Balfour's paper 'Serious Invasion', November 1903, Add. MSS 49710, f. 55.
72. 'Invasion and Submarines: The effects of submarine boats', November 1903, Fisher, ADM 116/942.
73. Compare Fisher's paper with Balfour's 'Draft Report on the Possibility of Serious Invasion: Home Defence', November 1903, 7–9, 14–15, CAB 38/3/71, 3/1/18A.
74. Selborne to Balfour, 23 August 1905, Add. MSS 49707, f. 88.
75. 'The Defence of Naval Ports', Fisher, November 1904, Add. MSS 49710, ff. 156–60.
76. Enclosure with Fisher to Balfour, 24 January 1905, 'Submarines Used Offensively', Add. MSS 49710, f. 170.
77. Ibid.
78. 'Submarine Boats', Admiralty, March 1905, CAB37/75/57.
79. Ibid., 4–5.
80. Memorandum 1904, Selborne MSS 158, f. 158.
81. Edgar March, *British Destroyers* (London, 1966), 82.
82. Memorandum by Dunston and Watts, 22 December 1904, Ships Covers 214 (Torpedo boats 1–12), CN25464/4. A typical short-range torpedo boat cost £41,000. A *River* class destroyer cost about £75,000.
83. Chief of N branch to first sea lord, 23 June 1905, Minute by Jackson (Controller) 19 July 1905, and Minute by Fisher, 10 August 1905, Ships Covers 212 (General Cover for Submarines), f. 10; see also 'Meeting of Submarine boat design Committee', 23 June 1905, remarks by Bacon and Jackson on the significance of the cost of submarines, Ships Cover 290, CN10951/05.
84. Hall to Keyes, 7 October 1911, Keyes MSS 4/22, Keyes Papers, British Library, London.
85. Fisher to Esher, 23 April 1904, *FGDN*, I, 310.
86. Parliamentary Papers, Annual Naval Estimates, 1903–5. Total spending on new construction, 1904, £11,593,646; 1909, £9,796,233.
87. Figures taken from Sumida, *In Defence*, Tables 8 and 10.
88. 'Memorandum on the First Meeting of the Committee on Naval Estimates, 1906/07', Appendix 2, Add. MSS 49711, f. 37–43; see also 'Naval Estimates Committee 1906/07', 10 January 1906, Crease MSS, Prints.
89. Lambert, *A Revolution*.
90. 'Organisation of Torpedo Craft in Home Waters', Admiralty, 21 February 1905, ADM1/7725, D342/04, Print.
91. 'Navy and Dockyards – a statement of Admiralty Policy', 14 November 1905, 1–15, Cawdor MSS, Prints, Naval Library, Ministry of Defence, London.
92. 'The Home Fleet – Part 2 for office use only', February 1907, 9, Crease MSS, 2/27(2). Personnel figures compiled by Nicholas Lambert.
93. CAB16/9A, 62, Q.664; 51-52, Q.582; 314, Q.2598; 187-89, Q.1814-22; see also 'Plan of Campaign–Channel Fleet', Charles Beresford, 9 May 1907, 3–16, ADM116/1043B/2.
94. Knollys to Fisher, 19 September 1909, *FGDN*, II, 267.
95. Jellicoe to Fisher, 18 April 1909, FISR 1/8, FP382. Also enclosure with Fisher to McKenna, 24 September 1909, FISR 1/8, FP413, marginal comments by Fisher.
96. 'Memorandum', November 1904, Selborne MSS 158 f. 158.

97. For detailed figures on the cost of maintaining various classes of warships, see 'Australian Naval Defence Force', 15 June 1908, appendix, reel 3, Slade Papers (microfilm copies), National Maritime Museum, Greenwich. Lambert, 'Economy or Empire'.
98. *FGDN*, II, 23.
99. 'Home Defence: Raids and Small Invasions', 1906, Add. MSS 49698, f. 208; 'War Arrangements', Admiralty, 25 June 1907, Crease MSS 3/16.
100. See especially Nicholas Lambert, 'British Naval Policy 1913/14: Financial Limitation and Strategic Revolution', *Journal of Modern History* (September 1995).

PART II

PREPARING FOR THE
SECOND WORLD WAR

6

Japanese Naval Construction, 1919–41

Mark R. Peattie

In Chapter 2 of this volume, David Evans limned for us the formative four decades of the Japanese navy, the years of its apprenticeship as a naval power. As he has explained it, Japan not only mastered the complexities of modern naval technology with foreign guidance and assistance during this period, but through its own astute policies and intelligent leadership developed the skills and facilities to design and build warships in Japanese yards that, by the end of this period, were equal and even superior to those being built by Western naval powers.[1]

By the First World War, therefore, the Japanese Navy had largely ended its dependence on foreign technology. This new technological independence was exemplified first by the construction between 1912 and 1915 of three of the world's most powerful battlecruisers and, subsequently, by the design and construction of six battleships between 1912 and 1921, of even greater protection and firepower.[2] All of these vessels were to contribute to the navy's goal of a fleet of eight battleships and eight battlecruisers. Collectively, these warships provided dramatic evidence of the broadening of the industrial base on which Japan's naval construction rested and of the progress of Japanese naval technology.

The First World War had served as a dramatic impetus to Japanese industry in general and to the shipbuilding industry in particular. The general economic surge enjoyed by the nation as a whole due to the orders placed by both belligerents and neutrals was felt particularly in the shipbuilding industry. Between 1913 and 1919, annual launchings of merchant ships increased from 55,000 gross tons to 636,000 gross tons, the number of commercial yards grew from six to 57, the number of slipways rose from 17 to 157, and the number of workers from 26,000 to 95,000. Moreover, by the end of the war, so rapid had been the growth of Japanese industrial technology and facilities that the shipbuilding industry could at last obtain machinery – turbines, boilers, reciprocal engines and other propulsive equipment – from indigenous suppliers.[3]

The degree to which Japanese government facilities, in combination

93

with the capabilities of commercial shipbuilding firms, had achieved near technological sufficiency for the navy was the most salient aspect of Japanese naval technology at the end of the First World War. This development was in striking contrast to the navy's situation on the eve of the Russo-Japanese War. Whereas in 1904, Tôgô had taken a British-built fleet to sea, nearly all the warship types and weapons systems could now be constructed in Japan solely with Japanese materials and labor and according to Japanese design.[4]

The process of warship design and construction was normally initiated by the Navy General Staff. Once funds were appropriated by the Diet, the staff handed down the specifications for warships it believed the navy required. These specifications were passed on to the Navy Ministry, which in turn relayed them to the Navy Technical Department. The department, Kansei Hombu (literally 'Ship Administration Headquarters', sometimes shortened to Kampon), was the central agency under the navy minister responsible for the design and construction of warships, equivalent to the Bureau of Ships in the US Navy. Between the world wars, the department's functions came to include the planning, research, design, testing and maintenance of ships, weapons and machinery. Two of the department's most important branches were the Basic Design Section, which was at the heart of the navy's work on warship design, and the Navy Technical Research Center which conducted various experiments on materials, hull designs, electrical systems and other warship components.[5]

The actual task of ship design was the responsibility of constructors working in Basic Design. Over the course of four decades, Japanese constructors had undergone a period of apprenticeship, both at home under the guidance of foreign naval architects, such as Emile Bertin, who had been invited to Japan to lead the design and construction of major fleet units, and abroad, as Japanese were sent to observe and study the construction of warships in foreign, particularly British, yards. In this way, naval constructors like Fukuda Umanosuke, Hiraga Yuzuru and Fujimoto Kikuo came to amass the technical skills necessary for mastery of the enormous complexities of contemporary warship design. Indeed, the six battleships laid down between 1912 and 1921 were the result of their expertise.

By the end of the First World War, Japan had yards sufficiently large and well equipped in which to lay down the largest warships of the day. The navy had led the way in the construction of such facilities with its three principal yards at Yokosuka, Kure, Sasebo,[6] each equipped not only with multiple slipways but a complex of arsenals, foundries, research laboratories and testing facilities. Five of the capital ships mentioned above were laid down on the navy's slipways (three at Yokosuka and two at Kure). Construction at navy yards was supplemented by work undertaken at certain private shipyards, of which those of the Kawasaki Shipyard

Company at Kobe and the Mitsubishi Shipbuilding Company at Nagasaki were capable of building capital ships and cruisers. Lesser vessels were laid down at the Fujinagata Dockyard at Osaka, the Uraga Dockyard near Tokyo, Ishikawajima Heavy Industries at Tokyo and the Harima Dockyard at Hyôgo.

By the 1920s, therefore, the skills available at both naval and commercial dockyards made Japan capable of turning out a range of warships that in design and construction were equal or superior to those of any navy in the world. Only in certain specialized fields such as submarine technology, aircraft design, optics and fire control were Japanese technicians still dependent on foreign ideas and models. At the outset, the dominant influence was British, though during the 1920s, after the termination of the Anglo-Japanese Alliance and the cessation of special favors that had been extended to the Japanese over a range of fields, the navy turned largely to defeated Germany for expertise in optics and submarine design.[7]

Yet, if Japanese naval technology was now generally autonomous in concept and design and partly so in material, it was nevertheless subject to powerful constraints. First, of course, were the limitations in design and construction imposed by the Washington Treaty by which the navy was forced to abandon its plans for an 'Eight–Eight' fleet and by which the Japanese battle line was fixed in permanent numerical inferiority to that of the United States.[8] There were, as well, domestic restrictions on the development of naval technology within Japan. One such constraint was the generally negative and frugal attitude of the Diet, filled in the early 1920s with business-minded politicians averse to vast expenditures for military and naval purposes. Just as important was a post-war economic slump that put the government in a difficult financial situation. The great Tokyo earthquake and fire of 1923 which required extraordinary reconstruction costs strained government budgets even further. Together, these circumstances served as a serious check on Japanese naval construction in the 1920s.[9] Again and again, during the decade, naval construction programs drafted by the Navy General Staff were subjected to successive diminution and sometimes outright rejection by the Navy Ministry, the Finance Ministry, the Cabinet and the Diet. Yet, despite these impediments, the navy did a remarkable job, within the confines of the treaty, in designing and building the warships for the kind of combat it believed it would have to conduct.

THE INFLUENCE OF DOCTRINE AND STRATEGY

The Japanese Navy's force structure and, in consequence, its shipbuilding program in the period between the world wars, were shaped by two determinants: the doctrinal concepts in place since the Russo-Japanese War and its evolving strategy against the US Navy which it had come to conceive of as its most likely hypothetical enemy. Together, these determinants rested on six basic assumptions about the nature of a naval conflict with the United States.

The first of these, drawn from the annihilation of the Russian Baltic Fleet at Tsushima in 1905 and seemingly confirmed by the character of the Battle of Jutland 1916, was that victory in naval warfare would be most likely determined in a single great encounter between battle fleets and victory in that engagement would be decided by superiority in big ships with big guns.

The second assumption was that, in the event of a protracted naval war with the United States, Japan, with its far smaller industrial capacity, would eventually be overwhelmed by the ships and weapons produced by US arsenals and factories. A short conflict was thus a critical imperative for Japan.

Third, in order to be successful in any naval war with America, the Japanese Navy must maintain a minimum force level of 70 per cent of the strength of the US Navy.[10]

Fourth, the most likely scenario for a Japan–US naval war would begin with Japanese offensive operations against the Philippines followed by the despatch of the American battle fleet, with an accompanying fleet train and transports, westward across the Pacific. The US fleet might possibly be directed toward Japan, but more probably would head toward the Philippines to support or rescue US garrisons and naval units there. Somewhere in the western Pacific the Japanese fleet would be obliged to meet its American enemy in a great-gun duel that would decide the course and duration of the war.[11]

Fifth, at the outset of its movement westward across the Pacific, the American battle fleet would be numerically superior to its Japanese counterpart. Thus, it was imperative that the Japanese Navy devise the tactics and the weapons to undertake a strategy of attrition against the US battle line to reduce it to numerical inferiority or at least to parity before the decisive battle.[12]

Sixth and last, for most of the 1920s, the Japanese Navy was also convinced that the US numerical superiority in capital ships would be complemented by certain steaming formations and tactical arrangements which would make the US fleet more difficult to attack as it moved westward across the Pacific.[13]

For the entire treaty era of naval limitations, the navy's strategic and tactical planning, as well as its warship construction and weapons development, were directed to dealing with the stark issues posed by these assumptions. As in the past, the navy's solution was to attempt to achieve qualitative superiority to overcome quantitative inferiority. In other words, it sought to create better weapons and better tactics that would enable the navy to pit its fewer numbers against the greater US enemy and emerge victorious. All the measures of the Japanese Navy that aimed to counter the quantitative superiority of the US fleet were subsumed under the principle of 'using a few to conquer many' (*ka o motte shû o seisu*) which had been invoked as early as the Sino-Japanese War of 1894–95. Sometimes, this took the form of simply exceeding the capabilities of tactics and technologies known and possessed by other naval powers and sometimes it meant the development of new tactics and weapons systems, most of which were held as a closely guarded secret.[14]

NAVAL DESIGN AND CONSTRUCTION IN THE TREATY ERA, 1922–36

During the 1920s, with the freeze on capital ship construction enforced by Japan's adherence to the Washington Treaty, the navy's force structure priorities and thus its orders for naval design and construction were principally channeled toward three ship types: cruisers, destroyers and submarines, all of which were subjected to intensive efforts to achieve technological superiority.[15]

The evolution of the Japanese heavy cruiser during the 1920s was largely the story of the Navy General Staff's quest for an all-purpose warship. Conceived as retaining its traditional reconnaissance function, the heavy cruiser was also seen both as a substitute for the battleship in the decisive fleet encounter and as a central element in Japanese torpedo operations. Its fire power – both of its main batteries and of its torpedo tubes – was to enable it to blast its way through enemy defenses and its speed to enable it to lead the destroyer squadrons which were to deliver the main torpedo attacks. In the outstanding capabilities of the cruisers of the *Yubari*, *Furutaka* and *Myôkô* classes of the 1920s, the Japanese led the way in cruiser design and, in so doing, initiated what was probably an inevitable world-wide competition in this type. They were followed at the end of the decade by the *Takao* class whose speed and firepower made them the most powerful heavy cruisers of the time.[16]

If the cruiser was designed to be a jack-of-all-trades in Japanese fleet operations, the Japanese destroyer emerged as a highly specialized type of attack vessel. A critical feature of the decisive mid-Pacific surface encounter envisioned by the navy was the reduction of the US battle line by torpedo attacks delivered the night before the daylight surface engagement. By the end of the First World War, the main warship type for torpedo operations was the destroyer and thus, during the 1920s, the Japanese Navy gave intensive study to the design of destroyers of outstanding speed and firepower. The result was the construction of the 24 destroyers of the *Fubuki* class built between 1926 and 1931. Huge in size and remarkable in firepower (particularly in deck guns, but even more in the weight of their torpedo broadsides), the ships of the *Fubuki* class were the most advanced and powerful destroyers of their day, presenting a foremost example of the Japanese drive for a qualitative lead among the world's navies.

The Japanese development of the submarine as an offensive element of the fleet was, again, a consequence of Japan's determination to make up for the inferiority in capital ships. Discarding the passive role of the submarine as a coastal defense vessel, by the 1920s the Navy General Staff came to view the submarine as a potent weapon in carrying out the staff's attrition strategy against the westward-moving US fleet proceeding across the mid-Pacific. For this long-range interceptive strategy the navy needed a submarine of great range and endurance. Without expertise in designing such craft, the navy turned to Germany, whose U-boats had almost brought Britain to its knees in the recent war. Through the study of those U-boats allotted to Japan as part of German reparations after the war, through the despatch of selected officers to Germany for observation and consultation, and through the hiring under contract of German constructors, technicians and former U-boat commanders, Japan was eventually able design and construct a force of submarines of great size and range (often referred to as 'I-boats' due to the prefix given to their individual identification numbers).

Unlike the first 40 years of the navy's warship design and construction, all these warship categories were built in Japan's own shipyards. It was critical for the Japanese shipbuilding industry that this was so, since the Washington naval arms limitations agreements had canceled the large orders for construction of capital ships, with sharp repercussions for Japanese industry and labor. Moreover, the Japanese shipbuilding industry was already in dire straights in the first years immediately after the First World War. While Japan had been the third-ranking shipbuilding nation in the world at the end of that conflict, the world depression in the shipbuilding market had caused Japanese merchant ship production to plummet. The measures by which the Japanese government dealt with this crisis are indicative of the importance that it continued to place in the shipbuilding industry and the industry's relationship with Japan's naval construction. The first was a series of efforts in the 1920s to support commercial shipyards, including subsidies for Japanese producers of shipbuilding steel, tariffs on imported merchant vessels and low-interest loans for Japanese shipping firms that purchased Japanese vessels.[17] But most importantly, while the navy still built a good number of its warships in its own yards, its construction contracts were placed increasingly with the Japanese private shipyards mentioned above, so that by the end of the decade the larger portion of the navy's construction was completed by the commercial sector.

In 1928, anticipating the convening of the London Naval Conference slated to take up the issue of limitations on categories lesser than capital ships, a special committee established to review the navy's needs in light of Japan's strategic situation, the capabilities of its most likely opponents, and the past and anticipated limitations in naval armaments. As a result, it recommended the addition of 12 heavy and 12 light cruisers to the fleet. The next year, on the eve of the conference, the Navy General Staff issued a statement on the importance of maintaining a ratio of 70 per cent in heavy cruisers.

In the event, the London Treaty obliged the Japanese Navy to accept a lesser percentage and, ultimately, a reduction in strength across the board (as opposed to the terms of the Washington Treaty that merely froze the strengths of the three major naval powers as they existed). In so doing, the treaty increased the temper and influence of the anti-treaty faction within the navy.[18] Yet, for the mounting frustration of the entire Japanese Navy with the naval limitations system, in 1930, there were six years to go before Japan could leave that system. Until then, the navy was obliged to deal with the new realities created by the London Treaty. Its response, undertaken with considerable skill and ingenuity, was to strengthen those naval weapons and services not covered by the treaty and to build to its allotted tonnage limits in each of the restricted warship categories.

The first of these efforts constituted a series of modernizations and innovations, the latter kept in great secrecy, to improve the navy's qualitative edge over its putative US enemy; the modernization of existing warships, particularly the refitting and reconstruction of its four battlecruisers as fast battleships; the retrofitting of most of its capital ships to give their guns greater elevation, consistent with the navy's doctrine of outranging the enemy; the adoption of a special AP shell in the navy's experiments with 'underwater shots'; initial research on what would become the navy's formidable oxygen torpedo; and the first steps in the development of midget submarines to be carried by larger submarines for use in the projected main-force battle.

In 1930, immediately following the London Treaty, the navy also planned new construction under the first of what were to be called the 'circle plans'.[19] They were the culmination of a long process of negotiation between the navy and the Finance Ministry that had begun in 1928 and had been interrupted by the London Conference and Treaty. They were also the result of pressure from the navy brass to provide additional funds to minimize the limitations on Japanese naval strength in return for acceptance of the arrangements of the London Treaty. 'Circle One' covered the years 1931–36 and was the only one of the plans subject to the limitations of the treaty era.

NAVAL DESIGN AND CONSTRUCTION IN THE
POST-TREATY ERA, 1937–41

The remaining three 'circle plans' drawn up in 1934, 1937 and 1939, were carried out in the post-treaty era (projects under the 1934 plan did not get under way until after Japan had abrogated the treaties) and were thus restrained only by the financial, material and industrial limits of Japan. Between 1939 and 1941 there were as well a number of supplementary plans which attempted to accelerate certain projects within the 1937 plan.[20]

The naval shipbuilding programs carried out under these plans between 1931 and 1941 took place during a decade of forced-draft expansion of heavy industry that matched Japan's territorial expansion on the Asian continent in the face of what it perceived as its growing isolation in a hostile world. The growth in military expenditures during the decade particularly stimulated those sectors in heavy industry related to naval construction: the production of ingot steel, for example, rose from 1.8 million tons in 1931 to 6.8 million tons in 1941 and merchant ship production rose from 92,093 gross tons in 1931 to a peak of 405,195 gross tons in 1937.[21]

While space does not permit a detailed discussion of the construction between the end of the treaty era and the start of the Pacific, it may be said that the two dominant projects of the period – seemingly contradictory in the strategic concepts which lay behind them – were the building of the two super battleships, *Yamato* and *Musashi*, which were at the heart of the 'Circle Three' plan, and the great expansion of the navy's air arm, particularly its land-based air units, which constituted the main focus of the 'Circle Four' program.

In their size, armor and firepower the super-battleships were the apotheosis of the navy's fixation on quality as a battle winner and the culmination of the navy's fixation on big ships and big guns. They are also an extreme example of the validity of a technological concept being overtaken by the reality of other technologies before it is brought to fruition.[22] With its goal of doubling Japan's naval air strength in just five years, the 'Circle Four' plan was ferociously ambitious and aimed at achieving air superiority in East Asia and the western Pacific within a few years. Despite the tremendous increase in naval aircraft under the plan, giving Japan a total of 3,000 by 1941, it was not sufficient to overtake the US aircraft industry that enabled the US Navy to have 5,000 aircraft by the same year.[23]

At all events, Japan, having abrogated the naval arms limitations agreements and freed itself from the Anglo-US imposition of a 60 per cent ratio, believed that it had at last recovered the essential element of its naval security – the ability to build at least 70 per cent of the US Navy's naval tonnage. But a world without naval arms limitations proved more threatening to Japan than its naval leadership had foreseen. The United States, freed from treaty restrictions as well, could now not only build up to the old treaty limits, but put its industrial might into naval rearmament that surged far beyond those limits. The successive US naval expansion plans eventually extinguished Japanese hopes of attaining a 70 per cent ratio and Japanese naval leaders began to fear that their naval strength might even sink below 60 per cent *vis-à-vis* the United States. Given that ominous possibility, the Japanese Navy's only recourse, as its leaders saw it, was the development of exceptional weapons, improvement of its skills and 'making up for quantity by means of quality'.

While new construction was continuing during the five years before the Pacific War, the navy was also energetically pushing through refitting projects for warships in need of modernization.[24] All these modernization and new construction projects were undertaken in the navy's own four yards and in eight commercial yards, though the latter undertook the bulk of this work.[25] To facilitate further experience in naval construction, the Navy Technical Department allotted construction of particular categories of warships to specific yards, both navy and commercial.[26]

By December 1941, the Imperial Japanese Navy constituted a formidable force: 10 battleships,[27] 10 aircraft carriers, 38 cruisers, heavy and light, 112 destroyers, 65 submarines, numerous auxiliary warships of lesser size, and more units planned and under construction. The capabilities of many of these ships put them in the front rank of naval design. Nevertheless, for the war upon which Japan was about to embark, its shipbuilding facilities, its technology and its force structure were to prove disastrously inadequate.

JAPANESE INTERWAR NAVAL CONSTRUCTION IN RETROSPECT

The United States' industrial might and, in consequence its eventual wartime ability to overwhelm Japan with a seemingly endless line of ships of every kind is too commonplace an assertion to need detailed explanation or proof.[28] It may be sufficient to repeat H. P. Willmott's assertion that 'such was the scale of American industrial power that if, during the Pearl Harbor attack the Imperial Navy had been able to sink every major unit of the entire US Navy and then complete its own construction programs without losing a single unit, by mid-1944 it still would not have been able to put to sea a fleet equal to the one the Americans could have assembled in the intervening thirty months'.[29]

But explanations of a superior US ability to build ships in quantity go beyond matters of greater wealth and industrial resources. There were some indirect and long-range causes of the more limited naval construction of Japan compared with that of the United States. To begin with, in the Pacific War, Japan could utilize significantly fewer shipyards, both naval and private (27 as compared with the US 325), and thus had smaller space devoted to slipways and graving docks. Moreover, building capacity in most Japanese yards was simply inadequate even for the building programs that the navy actually undertook, and construction schedules for one type of ship were frequently delayed by those of another. The expansion of shipbuilding facilities from 1937 to 1941 was quite modest in light of the national emergency. In large part this was because the mountainous terrain of much of the Japanese islands and the rugged coasts along them meant that there was very little level land alongside deep water. The older shipyards where such land did exist were located in port cities, usually on the waterfront where it was difficult and expensive to clear space for shipbuilding. These older yards were congested, poorly organized and too often devoted to clumsy and antiquated construction methods. These difficulties, all of which made mass-production techniques impractical, were exacerbated during the Pacific War when combat losses had to be made up, repair work was constantly necessary, and new ship types had to be developed to respond to the changing tactical situation. These requirements threw regular building schedules into disarray.[30]

Turning to the broader perspective of Japanese naval technology in general, one can see that the navy's technological acquisitions process which had served it so well in the pre-First World War period,[31] and which it continued in the development of its air arm in the first decade after the First World War, was subject to some severe impediments during the inter-war decades. Some of these stemmed from the unavoidable consequence of Japan's historical circumstances and some were the result of an incomplete understanding of the requirements for the development of complex technological systems.

There was, to begin with, the inadequacy of Japan's resource base, particularly in certain high performance metals, such as high-strength alloy steel. This retarded the development, for example, of Japanese aircraft engines (with consequent limitations on engine power) and Japanese steam engineering (with consequent limitations on steam pressures). The limited nature of the Japanese transport system, particularly auto-transport, restricted the flow of vital materials to shipyards and arsenals and impeded the distribution of industrial products to military units.[32]

While the Japanese Navy had in the past gained proficiency in assimilating new naval technologies from abroad, once access to such technology was severely curtailed in the deepening enmity between Japan and the Anglo-US maritime nations after the First World War, it was forced to operate from a smaller and temporally shorter base of technological expertise.[33] This lesser technical experience as compared with Western navies resulted in technologies that may have been superior in one or more aspects but were less innovative – warships that were simply larger, faster and more heavily armed, for example. The Japanese base of technological expertise thus provided an initial superiority in certain 'first stage' technologies – torpedoes, optics, ordnance, for example – but could not sustain that lead against US technology as the war progressed and was inadequate to develop the critical 'second stage' technologies, such as radar, the VT (proximity) fuse and forward-thrown ASW weapons that were so much part of the Allied victory in the Second World War.

Raising the level of generalities about Japanese naval technology still higher, one can see that in the Japanese Navy perhaps more than any other, it was doctrine – particularly the concept that quality could always overcome quantity – that drove technology.[34] But 'quality' is a complex proposition when it comes to naval technology. One way to assess it is to judge it in terms of how effectively a system confronts all the problems it might meet. The design concept behind most Japanese warships emphasized some functions at the expense of others. An example, as noted earlier, was the Japanese concept of the destroyer solely as an all-out attack vessel which made it less than effective in convoy escort or ASW functions which were needed desperately by Japan as the Pacific War went on.[35]

Moreover, the navy's pre-war confidence that it could overcome a numerically superior enemy with its own qualitative superiority was a dubious proposition from the beginning. In modern history no major conflict has ever been won by technologically superior weapons alone. Indeed, it was the US capacity to produce crushing numbers of ships, aircraft, weapons and equipment, even if they were sometimes inferior in quality to those of the Japanese Navy, which made the difference in the US victory. In this sense, the US triumph in the Pacific seems to confirm the dictum attributed to Lenin: 'Quantity has a quality all its own.'

Last of all, I turn to the force structure produced by the Japanese shipbuilding programs in the interwar years. While it is probably true that no fleet that Japan could have assembled could have been ultimately victorious over the US enemy, it is clear that the Japanese building plans of 1919–41 had produced a force structure that was particularly ill-suited to the kind of extended naval conflict that Japan was obliged to wage.[36]

Most important, the navy's planning for a short war and its long fixation on the decisive surface encounter contributed to its neglect of vital logistical elements in what would be a war of great distances. The Japanese Navy never did develop a fleet train of the kind organized by the US Navy, a deficiency that meant that it could not remain on station far from its bases for any great length of time. Its inadequate sea transport capacity, particularly its shortage of fleet tankers, was to become critical when the fleet operated at the far perimeters of Japan's conquests in the Second World War.

Even more serious was the failure of the navy to lay down sufficient numbers of smaller vessels that could act as convoy escorts or could serve in an ASW capacity. Indeed, the most relevant criticism of the navy's super-battleship strategy does not concern the building of the two super-battleships themselves. Its pernicious effect was rather the consequent diversion of the navy's attention and the nation's resources from the most essential problem that the navy and the nation would face: Japan's utter dependence on its overseas sea routes and the need to build the vessels and develop the doctrine, organization and training that would be most effective in protecting those routes and in beating back the US undersea offensive that threatened them.[37]

In the end, the shipbuilding program of the Japanese navy from 1919 to 1941 failed because it was centered on the mistaken assumption that the outcome of a Japan–US naval conflict would be decided by a single battle at sea. That assumption created a fighting force that was both one-dimensional and brittle. Superbly armed and trained by 1941 to launch a thunderbolt strike and ready to risk all in furious combat, the Japanese Navy was ill-prepared to sustain the effort or injuries of extended war.

NOTES

1. These matters are discussed in greater detail in Chapter 2 of this volume by David Evans.
2. The namesake of the *Kongô*-class battlecruisers was designed and constructed in the Vickers yard at Barrow in Furness, the last Japanese warship constructed abroad. The remaining three ships of the class, the *Haruna*, *Hiei* and *Kirishima* were built in Japanese yards with gun mountings supplied by Vickers. The six battleships were: two of the *Fusô* class, two of the *Hyûga* class and two of the *Nagato* class. The origins of the 'Eight–Eight Fleet' concept are discussed in David C. Evans and Mark R. Peattie, *Kaigun: Strategy, Tactics, and Technology in the Imperial Japanese Navy, 1887–1941* (Annapolis, MD: Naval Institute Press, 1997), 150–1.
3. Seymour Broadbridge, 'Shipbuilding and the State in Japan since the 1850s', *Modern Asian Studies*, 2, 4 (1977), 607–8.
4. With the tightening control of information concerning warship design by the British during the First World War, the Japanese would have been forced back on their own designs in any event.
5. Nihon Zôsen Gakkai, eds, *Shôwa zôsen shi* [History of Ship Construction in the Shôwa Era], vol. I (Tokyo: Hara Shobô, 1977), 735–6.
6. A fourth yard at Maizuru was equipped to handle only the construction of destroyers, submarines and other lesser ship types.
7. Arthur Marder, *Old Friends, New Enemies: The Royal Navy and the Imperial Japanese Navy*, vol. I: *Strategic Illusions, 1936–1941* (New York: Oxford University Press, 1981), 296, and Carl Boyd, 'Japanese Military Effectiveness: The Interwar Period', in Allan Millett and Williamson Murray, eds, *Military Effectiveness*. vol. II, *The Interwar Period* (Winchester, MA: Unwin and Hyman, 1988), 136–7; and Sadao Asada, 'The Japanese Navy and the United States', in Dorothy Borg and Shumpei Okamoto, eds, *Pearl Harbor as History: Japanese–American Relations, 1931–1941*, (New York: Columbia University Press, 1973), 229.

8. While the terms of the treaty are too well known to occupy space here, it is worth noting the scale of the additions to the Japanese battle line which were planned, launched or under construction at the time that Japan signed the treaty in 1922: six battleships (one of which was converted to a carrier) and eight battlecruisers (one of which was also converted to a carrier).

9. In this period of reduced naval budgets, the navy nevertheless was able to garner greater financial support than its service rival. Indeed, except for the years 1932 and 1933 naval expenditures outpaced army expenditures from 1919 until the outbreak of Japan's war in China.

10. The 70 per cent ratio, a dogma in the Japanese Navy for over three decades, is thought to have originated in the research undertaken at the Naval Staff College by Captain (later Admiral) Satô Tetsutarô, on the force levels necessary for the Japanese Navy to have a chance against an attacking American or German fleet. Satô started with the widely held assumption of the day that it was necessary for an attacking fleet to hold a 50 per cent superiority in fire-power over a fleet defending its territorial waters. For that reason, Satô concluded, in order to repel an attacking fleet, a defending fleet had to possess 70 per cent of the strength of an attacking fleet; anything less than this percentage – say, 60 per cent of an attacking enemy's strength – would imperil the security of the defending nation. Bôeichô Bôeikenshûjo Senshishitsu, *Kaigun gunsembi, ichi, Shôwa jûrokunen jûichigatsu made* [Naval armaments and war preparations, no. 1, up to November 1941], hereafter *KG, Senshi sôsho* series (Tokyo: Asagumo Shimbunsha, 1969), 158–9.

11. Over the course of three decades the navy's plans moved the venue for this decisive battle continually eastwards, since the increasing navy emphasis on distant operations was meant to keep the enemy from quickly bringing the war to the home islands. Thus, in 1910, the projected location for the battle was near the Ryûkyû Islands whereas in 1940 it was placed as far east as the Marshalls.

12. In the 1910s, the strategy was conceived to be largely the task of light cruisers and destroyers. After the First World War, it became the responsibility chiefly of submarines and aircraft based (in wartime) in Japan's mandated islands in the Pacific.

13. These centered on the US Navy's 'circle formation' in which screening forces were deployed around the main force, fleet train and convoy in four concentric circles. During the 1920s, much of the Japanese Navy's planning was devoted to the tactics and the warship types needed to break into this formation. Evans and Peattie, *Kaigun*, 203–7.

14. Outstanding examples of the tactics and technology developed by the navy and held in tight secrecy were the tactics of underwater shooting and long-distance torpedo firing, the Type 93 oxygen ('Long Lance') torpedo, the midget submarine and the two super-battleships *Yamato* and *Musashi*. Evans and Peattie, *Kaigun*, 263–73.

15. While the navy constructed two fleet carriers during this period (both as conversions from capital ship hulls), neither represented a solid advance in design, perhaps because the capabilities, function and requirements of carrier aircraft were still in a state of flux and possibly because the ambiguous role of carrier aviation gave it no established place in Japanese plans for the decisive surface battle.

16. The ultimate authority on Japanese cruisers is the recent monumental work by Eric Lacroix and Linton Wells II, *Japanese Cruisers of the Pacific War* (Annapolis, MD: Naval Institute Press, 1997).

17. Tuvia Blumenthal, 'The Japanese Shipbuilding Industry', in Hugh Patrick, ed.,

Japanese Industrialization and its Social Consequences (Berkeley, CA: University of California Press, 1976), 138–9

18. *KG*, 158–60. The best English-language overview of the London Treaty from the Japanese perspective is Tatsuo Kobayashi, 'The London Naval Treaty, 1930', in James William Morley (ed.), *Japan Erupts: The London Naval Conference and the Manchurian Incident, 1928–1932*, (New York: Columbia University Press, 1984), 3–117.

19. The circle plans are summarized in Saburô Toyama, 'The Outline of the Armament Expansion of the Imperial Japanese Navy During the Years 1930–1941', in *Revue Internationale d'Histoire Militaire*, no. 73 (1991).

20. *KG*, 219–20, 396–400; and Asada, 'The Japanese Navy', 238–9.

21. Jerome B. Cohen, *Japan's Economy in War and Reconstruction* (Minneapolis, MN: University of Minnesota Press, 1949), 3.

22. Hindsight has not been kind to Japan's super-battleship strategy of the 1930s and even Japanese Navy men have referred to their construction as foolish. In the main, criticism has focused on the obsolescence of the very concept of super-battleships in the age of air power and has pointed to their consecutive destruction by aerial attacks in 1944 and 1945. But when they were planned in the mid-1930s the still primitive capabilities of aircraft (particularly carrier aircraft) and the inconsequential payloads they could carry did not invalidate the concept behind these ships. Less often remarked upon was the nature of the actual means of their destruction, the aerial torpedo, a threat neglected by their designers. During their construction, tests showed that their hulls could withstand the explosive force that any American torpedo, whether air- or sea-launched, could provide. By 1944–45, US development of a new and a powerful explosive, Torpex, was able to exploit, fatally, certain structural flaws in the protective belts of both ships. Evans and Peattie, *Kaigun*, 379–82.

23. Ohmae Toshikazu, 'Nihon kaigun no heijutsu shisô no hensen to gumbi oyobi sakusen' [Changes in tactical thought in the Japanese Navy in relation to armaments and operations], part 2, *Kaigun Bunko geppô*, no. 7 (July 1981), 40, and Clarke Van Fleet, *US Naval Aviation, 1910–1980* (Washington, DC: USGPO, 1981), 382.

24. So thorough were the navy's modernization efforts, 1936–40, that only a single vessel – a destroyer – was in need of a major overhaul at the beginning of the Pacific War.

25. Navy leaders enhanced their arguments for increased naval expenditures by asserting that large naval expenditures would not only advance naval technology, but would help revive the national economy and stimulate related industries, even if the government were forced into deficit financing to build a fleet of the size that the navy wanted. Yoshiaki Katada, 'The Political Economy of the Japanese Navy: The Navy and the Economy in the Early Twentieth Century', unpublished PhD dissertation, University of California at Los Angeles, 1998, p. 132.

26. This allocation system for naval orders was instituted with the expectation that specialization in warship construction would improve the knowledge and skill of individual shipyards and that, with the increasingly sophisticated understanding of the construction of limited types of warship, they could reduce construction costs and save on less than a complete inventory of shipbuilding materials. Katada, 'Political Economy', 153–4. This effort was only a partial success, since, during the Pacific War, with ongoing repairs and constantly changing force structure priorities, shipyards became congested and construction schedules became chaotic.

27. The two super-battleships would soon join the fleet: the *Yamato* eight days after Pearl Harbor and the *Musashi* the following May.

28. For a detailed elaboration of all the factors involved in this industrial supremacy see William McNeill, *The Pursuit of Power: Technology, Armed Force, and Society Since A.D. 1000* (Chicago, IL: University of Chicago Press, 1982) and Paul Kennedy, *The Rise and Fall of the Great Powers: Economic Change and Military Conflict from 1500 to 2000* (New York: Random House, 1987). One can note in passing that of the $68 billion of the national income of the United States in 1937 only 1.5 per cent was being spent on national defense, whereas in the same year, Japan was already devoting over 28 per cent of its relatively puny $4 billion national income to the same purpose. The industrial resources available to each power were correspondingly disproportionate. Steel, the central component of naval construction, demonstrates this clearly. Production of ingot steel in the United States in 1940, for example, was 61 million metric tons; in Japan, 7.5 million metric tons. Paul Tiffany, *The Decline of American Steel: How Management, Labor, and Government Went Wrong* (New York: Oxford University Press, 1988), 27, and *US Strategic Bombing Survey* (hereafter *USSBS*), Military Analysis Division, *The Effects of Strategic Bombing*, 112.

29. H. P. Willmott, *The Barrier and the Javelin: Japanese and Allied Pacific Strategies, February to June 1942* (Annapolis, MD: Naval Institute Press, 1983), 522.

30. Cohen, *Japan's Economy*, 257, and *USSBS*, *Japanese Naval Shipbuilding* (Washington, DC: USGPO, 1946), 2. For a detailed comparison of Japanese and US shipbuilding techniques in one type of ship, destroyers, see Evans and Peattie, *Kaigun*, 363–70.

31. See the Evans chapter earlier in this volume.

32. The way in which the disparate character of the Japanese economic infrastructure affected the process by which industrial products were developed, tested and transported is exemplified by the fact that, after the prototype Mitsubishi Zero fighter was completed at the Mitsubishi plant in Nagoya, it was transported for its flight tests at Kagamigahara airfield in Gifu Prefecture by oxcart. Jirô Horikoshi, *Eagles of Mitsubishi: The Story of the Zero Fighter*, translated Shojirô Shindo and Harold N. Wantiez (Seattle, WA: University of Washington Press, 1981), 64–5.

33. For example, in the critical field of electronics, most, though certainly not all of the research in Japan was done in the navy's own facilities, since there were few commercial laboratories in prewar Japan. In the United States before the Second World War, in addition to the Naval Research Laboratory, the research laboratories of at least four large commercial firms – General Electric, AT & T, Westinghouse and RCA – were involved in relevant research in this field.

34. One sees this in the extreme demands made by the Navy General Staff for the design specifications for certain ships and aircraft in the pursuit of a particular tactical objective – superior firepower, range or maneuverability. Their demands for one or more extraordinary capabilities often failed to give adequate attention to balanced design and resulted in ships that had unprecedented armament and armor, but were dangerously top-heavy and unstable and aircraft that lacked all but the most minimal pilot protection and damage tolerance for the sake of lightness and attendant maneuverability and range.

35. In justice to the navy's force planners, it should be pointed out, of course, that much of the ASW and convoy escort tasks of the US Navy in the Second World War were undertaken by destroyer escorts not destroyers, though American destroyers, as all-purpose warships, had excellent ASW capabilities. The Japanese Navy, however, had few vessels for either ASW or convoy escort functions.

36. From a national, rather than merely a naval, point of view, of course, the major defect was that increasing naval demands on Japanese slipways, 1937–41,

caused a substantial decline in merchant ship construction. While this did not seriously affect the Japanese war effort in the first several years of the Pacific conflict, the shrinking of the Japanese merchant fleet by the US submarine offensive, which grew in scale and ferocity in the second half of the war, meant that the home islands were gradually cut off from the strategic resources of Japan's conquered territories in Southeast Asia. A shortage of oil tankers became a particularly critical problem. Mark Parillo's *The Japanese Merchant Marine in World War II* (Annapolis, MD: Naval Institute Press, 1993) is the most authoritative English-language source on this critical issue for Japan.

37. In this, the Japanese misreading of the naval lessons of the First World War was catastrophic, in large part because their participation in the conflict had been so marginal. Fixated (as admittedly were other navies) on the tactical and technological aspects of Jutland, they almost entirely ignored the fact that Britain, an island nation like themselves, was almost brought to its knees by a determined submarine campaign against its maritime commerce and communications.

7

German Naval Strategy and Armament, 1919–39

Werner Rahn

THE SETTING OF 1919–22

In the course of drafting the Paris Peace Treaty, Britain was successful in gaining acceptance for its security interests: removal of the German colonies as potential naval bases, elimination of Heligoland as a naval base and the drastic limitation of naval armament, reducing Germany to the status of a third-rate naval power.

Under Article 181 of the Peace Treaty of Versailles,[1] the active forces in the German Navy could not exceed the following size: six elderly battleships, six light cruisers, 12 destroyers and 12 torpedo boats. Since the Treaty had not stipulated how many warships Germany was to be allowed to keep on reserve, the Conference of Allied Ambassadors determined in March 1920 the exact number of reserve units: two battleships, two light cruisers, four destroyers and four torpedo boats. To a certain extent, this decision contradicted Article 192, which permitted reserves of arms, munitions and naval war material only for units in commission. The reserve units now approved were allowed to keep their guns on board, although they were not allowed to have crews, munitions or other stocks.[2]

Thus, the navy, in contrast to the reduction of the army, was reinforced by one-third in terms of armament. Since the Peace Treaty did not mention minesweepers, training vessels or auxiliaries, the Conference of Allied Ambassadors also laid down specific figures for these units. Submarines and military aircraft were forbidden altogether. As a result, the navy lacked those weapons that modern naval warfare required. However, the British and US attempt to abolish the submarine was thwarted by France's opposition; Paris became the champion of minor naval powers by emphasizing the importance of the submarine as a naval weapon of weaker nations.[3]

Germany was allowed to replace naval forces after they had reached the age of 15–20 years, however, new ships were not to exceed certain displacements – for example, armoured ships no more than 10,000 tons after 20 years, and light cruisers no more than 6,000 tons after 20 years. The armament of ships intended for replacement was not specified, nor was there a precise definition of displacement. These omissions subsequently offered advantages following the 1922 Washington Naval Agreement with its definitions for the displacement of warships. Naval personnel was limited to 15,000, with officer and warrant officer strength not to exceed 1,500. This figure, however, was arrived at without examining in detail whether it made any sense in relation to the permitted naval forces and coastal fortifications.[4]

The German government initially rejected Allied demands to limit the army to 100,000 men, but a mitigation of the terms relating to the navy was never seriously discussed. The burdens imposed on Germany by the Peace Treaty were so great, and the navy was in such a weak position, that the government even considered renouncing the six old battleships in order to obtain concessions in other areas.[5] However, the Allied and Associated Powers rejected this proposal, pointing out that Germany had to retain naval forces 'for her protection and for naval police services'.[6] Thus, Germany's former enemies helped to ensure that the German Navy remained in existence, albeit on a modest scale.

In Germany, strategic deliberations regarding national defence after 1919[7] had to take into consideration the country's glaring inferiority in terms of personnel and *matériel* compared with the armed forces of the major neighbouring states. When it became apparent after 1920 that the arms limitations of the other powers announced at Versailles were not going to materialize, Germany consistently aspired to parity and national sovereignty in the military sphere, in order to be able to develop its armed forces into an effective instrument for 'the preservation of national security'. However, it was not clear what the government and the *Reichswehr* Command actually meant by 'security', and under what conditions 'security could be guaranteed at all'.[8] In its national defence planning the military took as its starting point the war potential of those countries immediately adjacent to Germany.

Given the restriction of ground forces to 100,000 men, the army constantly viewed naval personnel as possible reinforcements for land warfare. Rebutting this view, the Naval Command argued that naval forces were necessary because of the territorial changes in Eastern Europe after 1918, referring primarily to Poland and the isolation of East Prussia. In 1918–19 Germany had lost territories to the newly proclaimed Polish state, and by 1920–21, a Polish–Russian border dispute had led to war. Future conflicts could not be ruled out. If Germany did not have any naval forces at all, it would be impossible to defend East Prussia. Without naval protection, Poland could cut the sea route across the Baltic, the only reliable line of supply for East Prussia.

The navy's deliberations soon moved on to consider other possible conflicts. As early as 1922, the Naval Command took into account Poland's ties with France and naval strategy once again focused on the North Sea. Given the dependence of Germany's economy on sea-borne supplies, the prerequisites for the conduct of defensive operations could be achieved only if German shipping in the North Sea and the Baltic continued unimpaired.

NAVAL ARMAMENT AND THE PEACE TREATY OF VERSAILLES

All military planning and command takes as its starting point both friendly and enemy war potential. In the sphere of naval warfare, the *matériel* aspect has always played a decisive role, but the most effective means of naval warfare cannot be replaced by improvisation. Both personnel and equipment need lengthy periods of preparation and training. The construction of warships necessitates several months for motor torpedo boats and small submarines and years for cruisers and capital ships. Once construction has been completed, however, a warship is still not ready for action. It has to go through a lengthy trial and training phase. For these reasons, the *matériel* limitations which the Peace Treaty imposed on the German armed forces impaired the operational capabilities of the navy to a far greater extent than the army.

While the German Navy never regarded the Polish Navy as a serious threat, the French Navy was a potential enemy. The small and largely obsolete German fleet would have stood no chance whatsoever in a confrontation with the French fleet. Germany's chances to conduct successful naval warfare depended to a considerable extent on how quickly it could overcome the restrictive armament limitations in the event of a conflict. From 1923 onwards, the navy secretly prepared to be able to reinforce naval forces within a period of a few months. First and foremost, this concerned small units, especially submarines and aircraft. The Naval Command developed its secret activities mostly through cover firms.[9] Given the need to conceal and disguise, supervision by the government was limited from the outset. Even the *Reichswehr* Command did not intervene in the activities of its subordinate organizations, but rather acted along the lines of 'do what you want as long as I don't know anything about it'.[10]

Fierce attacks by the press in summer 1927 revealed some of the secret activities. The minister of defence [*Reichswehrminister*], Dr Otto Gessler, assumed political responsibility and resigned in January 1928, thereby drawing to a close an affair that had cost Germany approximately 13.3 million Reichsmarks without any useful military effect.[11] His successor, former Lieutenant-General Wilhelm Groener, liquidated all activities which were not entirely devoted to national defence. However, he was aware of the importance of developing modern naval weapons such as submarines, therefore the navy was allowed to continue preparations for constructing and later testing three submarine prototypes in Spain and Finland.[12]

Given the unfavourable situation in modern armament, the navy was anxious to make an immediate start on modernizing the forces it had been allowed to retain. Initially, the Naval Command concentrated on replacing its light naval forces with new vessels. There were two reasons for choosing this course: first, financial considerations and, second, the realization that this was the best way to construct efficient units within the displacement limits for cruisers and destroyers. In order to be able to start constructing a cruiser as soon as possible in 1920, the navy did not design a new type, but used the improved draft plans of the last vessels built during the war.[13] This meant that it would be possible to use at least some parts from scrapped cruisers, such as boilers, turbines and conning towers, in order to cut construction costs. But appropriate requests by the Naval Peace Commission were rejected by the Naval Interallied Commission of Control (NIACC). Complications also arose because of armament. The modern light cruisers of the Imperial Navy all had 15 cm guns at the end of the war, whereas the old cruisers that the navy was allowed to retain had only 10.5 cm guns. Naturally, the Naval Command was anxious to arm its first new vessel as heavily as possible and decided on eight 15 cm guns. The NIACC appealed to the Conference of Allied Ambassadors, which, while approving this armament, stipulated that in future this calibre should not be exceeded on cruisers. Thus, the Naval Command's hands were tied as far as further planning was concerned. When it subsequently constructed its new vessels, it had to forgo the introduction of the 19 cm calibre for a 6,000-ton cruiser.

In 1923, the Naval Command presented plans for the construction of an 800-ton destroyer. In its endeavours to make the vessel as large as possible, the Design Division had proposed that the standard displacement of the Washington Naval Agreement be adopted, as this provision allowed

> the trial displacement to be increased by more than 100 tons. Thus, a destroyer with a designed displacement of 800 tons in conformity with the Washington Agreement would have a trial displacement of over 900 tons calculated according to our previous formula.[14]

Using this method, there was thus a difference of approximately 43 per cent between the designed displacement (not including fuel and feed water) of approximately 800 tons and the maximum displacement of approximately 1,150 tons. The chief of the Naval Command, Admiral Paul Behncke, approved this calculation in the summer of 1923, and it was also tacitly accepted by the Allied Powers. From 1925 a series of 12 large torpedo boats was built. The designation 'torpedo boat' was chosen because their low level of ordnance (three 10.5 cm guns) meant that they were not comparable with the destroyers of other navies.

112

However, the Naval Command was anxious to upgrade the combat effectiveness of these boats. Since it was not possible to increase the number of guns without reducing the torpedo armament, the new chief of the Naval Command, Admiral Hans Zenker, decided in October 1924 to increase the calibre to 12.7 cm. Solely from the point of view of military necessity, it was a mistake for the navy to take this decision alone, without consulting the Foreign Ministry. The reaction of the Conference of Allied Ambassadors to the armament of the first cruiser should have been a warning. In December 1927 the British naval attaché inquired about the armament of the new torpedo boats; the information he was given by the German Naval Command was accurate. A short time later, the French naval attaché took the line that a calibre larger than 10.5 cm was not admissible for the torpedo boats since the Conference of Ambassadors had consented to an increase of calibre only for cruisers. The Naval Command was not convinced by this reasoning, but realized that a candid discussion of the problems involved in interpreting the Peace Treaty was better than adhering rigidly to its own legal viewpoint.[15] Admiral Zenker decided that the guns should not be mounted until the matter had been settled. He informed the British, Italian and Japanese naval attachés accordingly and requested them to communicate this to their governments. The British ambassador in Berlin, Sir Roland Lindsay, advised the Foreign Ministry that his government understood the situation and did not want to cause difficulties. However, on this question there could be no bilateral discussion, as it was an issue for the Conference of Ambassadors to decide. However, he encouraged his interlocutor not to give up hope that the Peace Treaty could be revised in the long run. 'He knew', he said, 'that the Treaty of Versailles contained many unpleasant provisions that Germany was pressing to remove. This would be possible in due course, but only if we attempted to do it at the right moment.' However, the time was not yet ripe.[16]

After a later *démarche* by the British ambassador, the only way out for the German government was either to persist in its own legal viewpoint or to forgo the heavier guns with which it wanted to arm the vessels. As a result of further British warnings, Minister of Defence Groener decided to modify the guns. His decision was probably determined by the realization that the armament of the torpedo boats played only a minor role within the larger context of naval armament as a whole. This incident illustrated clearly to the Naval Command that all planning, especially in a period of arms limitation, could not be the sole concern of the military, but rather required the government's participation.

The systematic renewal of light naval forces made steady progress from 1925 onwards. The first new light cruiser, *Emden*,[17] started her trials in summer 1925. The same year saw the laying down of a series of three new light cruisers, mounting three 15 cm triple-turrets. To increase endurance, the ships were given cruising diesel engines in addition to their main turbines. The first cruiser of the series, *Königsberg*, was completed in April 1929.

However, developing a 10,000-ton armoured vessel, as permitted by the Peace Treaty, with sufficient combat power to survive an engagement with French capital ships was a tough nut to crack. Given the displacement limitation, it was not possible to meet the requirements for heavy armament and armour plating. When the Naval Command's hoped-for change of the armament limitations failed to materialize, the navy was forced to concentrate on planning a ship which was in fact more like a cruiser than a battleship.

The decisive elements that influenced this change in planning lay on two different levels: the tactical-operational and the political-military. In the tactical-operational sphere, fleet exercises showed that heavy naval forces needed more speed. In the political-military sphere, the Naval Command thought it imperative that Germany construct a ship which 'was always superior in one respect' to the warship categories of the 1922 Washington Naval Agreement. It sought 'speed in the case of battleships' and 'heavy guns in the case of cruisers'. To replace the old battleship under the terms of the Peace Treaty, the Naval Command now planned a ship carrying six 28 cm guns and reaching a top speed of 28 knots.[18]

To understand better the German line of reasoning, we need to take a brief look at the status of international naval armaments at the end of the 1920s. The countries which had signed the Washington Naval Agreement (the United States, Great Britain, Japan, France and Italy) had fleets that were dominated by capital ships with 8–12 heavy guns (calibres between 30.5 and 40.6 cm) and a speed of 20 to 23 knots. Only Great Britain and Japan had battlecruisers with six to eight heavy guns. Some of them were more lightly armoured than other capital ships, but they had a top speed between 27 and 31 knots. The Washington Naval Treaty of limited the total tonnage and construction of battleships and aircraft carriers until 1930. For cruisers, on the other hand, the treaty established ceilings only for displacement and armament of the individual vessel, not total fleet size.

Thus, cruisers with a standard displacement of 10,000 tons and light armour were built. Their main armament comprised six to ten 20.3 cm guns and they had a top speed of 33 knots. Although they could evade the slower capital ships, they had to avoid contact with battlecruisers, which were far superior to them in terms of armament and were capable of almost the same speed.

Since the core of the French fleet consisted of nine slow capital ships and five fast heavy cruisers, the German Naval Command deliberately endowed its 10,000-ton vessel with the characteristics of a 'small battle-cruiser'; thus it was at least superior to cruisers in gunnery and to capital

114

ships in speed.[19] With six 28 cm guns in two triple-turrets and a speed of 26 to 28 knots, the armoured ship (also known as the 'pocket battleship') came very close to the concept of the battlecruiser. Moreover, diesel engines would give the ship a maximum range of up to 20,000 miles, vastly exceeding that of any cruiser or capital ship. Owing to its combat effectiveness and endurance, the 'pocket battleship' was suitable for both large-area warfare in the North Sea and offensive operations in the Atlantic. The construction of the ship attracted the immediate attention of foreign naval experts. In April 1929 the British ambassador in Berlin, Sir Horace Rumbold, reported to his government:[20]

> From a naval technical point of view, the building of this vessel is to be welcomed, as its design promises to include a number of new features in warship construction. The principal of these are reported to be a comparatively heavy armament of six 11-inch guns, eight 5.8-inch and twenty anti-aircraft guns, six torpedo tubes, adequate armour protection, special Diesel engines giving a cruising speed of 26 knots, the extensive employment of light metals and electric welding in place of riveting and the highest degree of unsinkability.

However, the Naval Command regarded the construction of 'pocket battleships' not just as a military necessity, but also as a political-military lever with which to upset the system of international naval armament established without German participation at Washington in 1922. The Naval Command hoped that this step would give Germany the chance to be readmitted to the group of major naval powers. Of course, if Germany had been included in the Washington Naval Agreement, this would have been tantamount to a wholesale abrogation of the naval arms limitations laid down by the Treaty of Versailles. The Washington agreement would have given Germany a tonnage of between 100,000 and 175,000 for capital ships and total freedom in designing individual vessels. Moreover, submarines and aircraft, which had hitherto been forbidden, would have been permitted.

SHIFT IN STRATEGY AND OPERATIONAL PLANNING

Being aware of Germany's limited resources and its high degree of dependence on sea imports, the Naval Command had always tried to bring this overall strategic approach home to the army when the latter was drawing up its own operational plans. However, from 1928 onwards, the new Minister of Defence, Wilhelm Groener, set new standards for all operational planning by the army and navy. He stressed that for the *Reichswehr*, the idea of a large-scale war had to be ruled out from the start and military operations against foreign powers limited to two possible types of conflict:

(1) repelling raids by neighbouring states onto German territory, and (2) armed neutrality during a conflict between foreign powers.[21]

Groener demanded that the *Reichswehr* should be immediately combat ready to oppose a sudden Polish invasion. For the navy, this new concept meant that it had to be able, on 72 hours' notice, to begin to destroy the Polish Navy and neutralize the port of Gdynia as a naval base. Such a demonstrative strike was clearly intended to be part of a strategy of deterrence. With this 'form of calculated escalation', the German government could react quickly to a possible invasion and, at the same time, refer the conflict to the League of Nations without delay. Thus, the government assigned to the navy, for the first time, the role of an effective instrument of crisis management.

In spring 1929 Groener asked the Naval Command to review whether Germany needed for its maritime defence any surface units that would go beyond the ceiling of the Versailles Treaty. In doing so, Groener undoubtedly got to the heart of the self-perception of the navy's leadership – which saw its service not merely as an instrument of national defence but also, in the long run, as an indispensable prerequisite for a future German maritime position of power. Under no circumstances would a return to the status of a brown-water navy be acceptable; rather it was intended to build ocean-going units, thus proceeding in accordance with the traditional concept of naval prestige and expressing the hope for a better future.[22] Naturally, it was not possible, nor was it intended, to explain this to a minister who – although he had pushed the 'pocket battleship' through the *Reichstag* – had otherwise often expressed his critical attitude towards the build-up of the High Seas Fleet before 1914.

In his reply to Groener's question, 'Does Germany need large warships?', the chief of the Naval Command, Admiral Erich Raeder,[23] therefore put forward his arguments in accordance with the former concept, which focused on a potential conflict with France and Poland.[24] The attitude of the navy 'must not be determined by wishful thinking to re-establish an outstanding naval power'. Its most important task in war was to prevent at all costs enemy blockading forces from restricting German sea lanes. The world war had proved the connection between German endurance on the ground and naval blockade: 'Cutting off our sea lanes is the simplest and safest way, without any bloodshed, of defeating us. Our enemies know this as well.' England had the most powerful fleet world-wide and 'its geographical position is disastrous for Germany'. Therefore, 'any armed conflict has to be avoided that would turn England into one of our enemies. We would be doomed to failure right from the start.' Raeder's memorandum concluded that the navy – even without the limits set by the Treaty of Versailles – could only fight a fleet of a second-class naval power, such as France.

WAR LESSONS AND STRATEGY DISCUSSION

The year 1925 witnessed the beginning of a discussion on the fundamental problems of naval strategy.[25] Rear-Admiral Wolfgang Wegener[26] criticized the navy for seeking to solve its problems in purely tactical ways. His calculus defined the terms 'seapower' and 'strategy':[27]

> Two things are required for seapower and naval warfare:
> 1. The tactical fleet,
> 2. The strategic-geographical position from which this fleet can operate, that is, control the sea lanes and thereby exercise sea control. Strategy, therefore, is the doctrine of strategic-geographical positions, their changes, and their deterioration. Offensive strategy is the acquisition, defensive strategy is its deterioration of a geographical position.

In 1926 Wegener presented a memorandum entitled 'The Naval Strategy of the World War'. Therein, he detailed an alternative concept with which Germany would have had a better chance in the naval war against Great Britain. This centred on the strategic-geographical position as the indispensable element of any seapower whose strategy would concentrate on the struggle for naval supremacy. In order to control the Atlantic sea lanes, Germany would have had to improve the geographic basis. According to Wegener, if Germany had been unable to secure the French Atlantic coast, Denmark, Norway, the Faeroes and Iceland would have been the crucial positions on the way to the Atlantic Ocean. He did not reject the battle fleet as an instrument of naval warfare, but he wanted to give it a clearly defined strategic aim. This aim, however, had been lacking because 'our politics knew no world-political, geographical goal' and thus had not deployed the fleet in a strategic offensive.[28] However, Wegener 'overlooked the pressing matter of *how* the weaker fleet was supposed to gain victory after it had challenged the Royal Navy to battle'.[29]

Having analysed the war's lessons, Wegener formulated the political demand that the Germans 'once more have to take the road to world and seapower, but this time with a matured instinct for sea power'.[30] Without seapower, 'Germany would be left at the mercy of Great Britain. But once our people and state are in good shape again, we will feel this drive to go out to sea and establish our position at sea where we will encounter the Anglo-Saxons as enemies.'[31] When Wegener published his memorandum in 1929, he moderated these aggressive formulations.

However, his far-reaching deliberations evidently assumed that Germany would regain its former posture in power politics. Therefore, his theories, as Rolf Hobson observed recently, 'represented one of the most important bridges within the ideology of sea-power between the imperialism of the Tirpitz generation of naval officers and the fascism of the one that followed'.[32]

This variant of thinking about sea and naval power had its repercussions during the French–German naval antagonism following the building of the first 'pocket battleship', the *Deutschland*, which was launched in May 1931. France was aware of the German concept of the 'pocket battleship' even before the first vessel had been completed, and moved quickly to construct battlecruisers which, with eight 33 cm guns and approximately 30 knots best speed, were superior to the German 'pocket battleships' in every respect. The subsequent *Dunkerque* was already casting her shadows before her. The German reaction showed diverging views. Some officers wanted to improve the 'pocket battleship' type in such a way that it would stand a chance in a duel with the *Dunkerque*, while others advocated the renunciation of the ship-versus-ship comparison of combat power. As early as March 1931, the latter discussed a new tactical concept of organizing the existing naval forces into battle groups. Using a sizeable number of small but highly combat-effective ships with 28 cm guns, these officers thought it would be possible in a future conflict to place a French battlecruisers in a difficult situation.[33]

However, as soon as it became apparent that it would be possible to overcome the limitations imposed by the Treaty of Versailles, the traditional principle of *similia similibus* came to the fore again. Naval officers wanted to build ships 'which are at least the equal of those of our potential enemy'.[34] The demand for equal rights overshadowed the obvious strategic and operational problem of what functions capital ships should and could assume in performing the navy's most important wartime tasks protecting supplies in large areas of the North Sea and of attacking enemy sea lines of communication. The military and political-military reasoning favouring the 'pocket battleship' type also supported the navy's power-policy calculation. The navy did not want to be reduced to the status of a 'coastal navy', but rather to pursue a course that would take Germany to a position of power which, in the eyes of the Naval Command, was commensurate with the country's economic potential.[35] However, this did not become feasible until after 1933, when the political leadership came to use the German armed forces primarily to achieve power-policy goals.

NAVAL ARMAMENT UNDER HITLER, 1933–37

A few weeks after seizing power in 1933, Adolf Hitler made it clear to military and naval commanders that he intended to develop the armed forces into an instrument of his power politics.[36] As far as the translation of this objective into armament was concerned, however, Hitler was initially cautious. The Navy therefore had to make do with compromises regarding the displacement and armament of its future capital ships and, in view of the long-term build-up of the fleet, these compromises seemed to be acceptable. The last of three 'pocket battleships', the famous *Admiral Graf Spee* was launched in June 1934 and completed 18 months later. The next two units were upgraded to battlecruisers (31,000 tons, 31 knots, nine 28 cm guns) in answer to the French *Dunkerque* and *Strasbourg*. The *Scharnhorst* and *Gneisenau* were launched in October and December 1936 and commissioned in January 1939 and May 1938, respectively.[37]

Following the conclusion of the Anglo-German Naval Agreement on 18 June 1935, which allowed Germany to have a surface fleet with a tonnage up to 35 per cent of that of the British Empire, German naval leaders now believed that they had attained their goal of equal rights. The 35 per cent ceiling applied not only to the total tonnage but also to the individual categories of warships. Only in the case of U-boats was Germany allowed to achieve, first, 45 per cent and, later, even 100 per cent of British submarine strength[38]. The navy's planning was thus based wholly on the structure of the other naval powers. Its motto was: What the other navies, with their rich traditions, consider proper, and what Germany is now permitted within the 35 per cent ceiling, is what Germany will now build. The navy started to build a so-called 'normal fleet': capital ships, heavy and light cruisers, aircraft carriers, destroyers and, for the first time after 17 years, submarines. One week after the Anglo-German Naval Agreement was announced, the navy commissioned the first small 250-ton U-boat, uncovering the long-term secret activity in this matter. Although the basic design of the U-boat had not been improved since 1918, substantial developments had been made in a number of areas, as Rear-Admiral Eberhard Godt wrote in an essay for the British Admiralty after the Second World War:[39]

> better torpedoes with bubble-less ejection, trackless and with non-contact pistols; the ability to lay mines from all U-boats, to transmit and receive signals both surfaced and submerged, greater diving depths, and increased power of resistance through welded pressure hulls.

Nevertheless, widespread opinion prevailed in all navies, including the German, that the U-boat had lost the role it had achieved in the First World War as one of the most effective naval weapons. Contrary to this opinion, the small German U-boat staff, centred around Captain Karl Dönitz,[40] was convinced that ASW weapons were greatly overrated and had not made decisive progress since 1918. However, the U-boat staff was unable to persuade the Navy High Command to get the best type of medium-sized boat in sufficient numbers. German U-boat construction policy seemed to remain 'unclear and without definite direction' and was sometimes 'determined neither by military nor by political calculations, but by economic possibilities'.[41]

119

The German shipbuilding industry faced great difficulties accelerating the naval rearmament constantly demanded by Hitler. After years of inactivity in warship construction the shipyards needed time to acquire the necessary experience. Even before the Anglo-German Naval Agreement had been signed, the Navy Command came to the conclusion that

> an acceleration of the construction of 'pocket battleships', cruisers, destroyers, support ships, patrol boats, minesweepers, and aircraft-carriers is not possible, as construction periods cannot be shortened any more, the shipyards are operating at full capacity, and all available skilled workers are fully employed.[42]

From 1928 onwards, the navy's thinking was determined by an officer who was to command it until early 1943, Admiral Erich Raeder.[43] In his study of the cruiser campaign in the First World War, Raeder had come to the conclusion that there had been a strategic correlation between the operations of the cruiser squadron in the Pacific and South Atlantic and in the North Sea campaign in autumn 1914.[44] Raeder based his concept of naval strategy on the realization that all naval theatres of war formed a homogeneous whole and that consequently any operation must be viewed in its correlation with other sea areas. Accordingly, cruiser warfare overseas and operations by the battle fleet in home waters were integral components of a single naval strategy which, by exploiting the diversionary effect, sought to weaken the enemy's forces and to disrupt supplies.[45]

Raeder formulated his strategic thinking most clearly in a briefing he gave Hitler on 3 February 1937.[46] Analysing the war's experiences, he pointed out the correlation between strategy and a country's military-geographical situation. Raeder was aware of the totality of a future war, which would be a struggle not just between forces, but of 'nation versus nation'. He emphasized the negative consequences for Germany 'if she is unable continually to procure the raw materials she lacks'.[47] Thus, Raeder had pointed out the glaring weaknesses in Germany's war potential, but without being able to influence Hitler's policy of confrontation.

BUILD-UP OF THE NAVY AGAINST BRITAIN, 1938–39

A fundamental change in the Navy's strategic planning commenced in the spring of 1938 when it became apparent that the Western powers opposed German expansion. Hitler issued the directive that all German war preparations should consider not only France and the Soviet Union, but also Great Britain, as potential enemies. A second confrontation with Britain now influenced all further planning for the next naval war. Raeder followed Hitler's hazardous course of confrontation willingly and without protest, neglecting his strong statement on this matter to Groener in 1929 and assuming erroneously that the navy would still have several years of peace to continue its build-up.[48]

In the summer of 1938 the Naval Staff's strategic study concluded that, given a geographical starting position similar to that of 1914, only oceanic cruiser warfare with improved 'pocket battleships' and U-boats could hold any prospect of success.[49] Despite this realization, a planning committee of senior officers busied itself with the question of what task battleships could perform in a cruiser war in the Atlantic. The result was paradoxical and revealing: 'the chief of staff of the naval staff concluded at the end of the discussion that all participants agreed that battleships were necessary, but that no consensus regarding their use could be achieved for the time being'.[50]

To the traditionalists, who considered capital ships to be the most important arm of a naval power, this meant that the concept of sea denial was pushed into the background by the concept of sea control. Unlike Tirpitz, the Naval Staff had repeatedly proposed a sea denial strategy in the 1930s. However, the new suggestion to develop a German strategy of sea control constituted a second approach to sea and world power in the twentieth century, as the then commander-in-chief of the fleet, Admiral Rolf Carls, noted in September 1938:

> If, in accordance with the will of the Führer, Germany is to achieve a firm world-power position, it will need, in addition to sufficient colonies, secure sea routes and access to the high seas … A war against Britain means a war against the Empire, against France, probably also against Russia and a number of countries overseas, in other words against one-half or two-thirds of the whole world.[51]

Nevertheless, Raeder was more inclined towards a sea denial strategy in an oceanic cruiser campaign with 'pocket battleships', and he intended to give this strategy priority in the future armament programme. In November 1938, however, he was unable to gain Hitler's support for his plans. The dictator did not accept the cruiser warfare strategy, and insisted instead that the navy step up the pace of its battleship construction so that he would have at his disposal an instrument of power which could be employed globally as soon as possible.

The navy accepted this decisive change and formulated a new armament concept, the so-called Z-Plan, which centred on the construction of six capital ships by 1944. In addition, battlecruisers, 'pocket battleships', aircraft-carriers, fast light cruisers and 247 U-boats were to form the backbone of German naval forces for the future Battle of the Atlantic. On 27 January 1939, when Hitler ordered that the 'build-up of the Navy' was to take precedence over 'all other tasks, including the rearmament of the other two Wehrmacht services',[52] he heralded a gigantic increase in naval forces. Within a few months the planning of a series of six newly designed diesel-driven battleships was completed; the construction of two units began in summer 1939.

Disillusionment came in September 1939. The navy was by no means in a position to fight the next naval war, either in terms of material or personnel. Raeder resigned himself to the fact that neither the few U-boats nor the surface forces on hand would have any decisive effect on the outcome of the war. All they could do, he noted, was to 'show that they know how to die gallantly and thus are willing to create the foundations for later reconstruction'.[53] The German Navy faced a hopeless situation.

CONCLUSION

After 1919, the navy regarded itself as an essential element of national defence. As long as the interdiction of major German maritime communications in a conceivable conflict was looming, countermeasures that could not be taken with the fleet allowed under the terms of the Treaty of Versailles would undoubtedly be necessary. However, the navy's steadfast demand for parity between Germany and France served not only German naval defence, but also aimed at long-term objectives. To prevent itself from falling back to brown-water status, it was important to the navy – as Vice-Admiral Zenker had already reflected in September 1924 – 'mentally to become and remain a seapower and to keep their eyes fixed on the ocean looking beyond coastal waters'.[54] The building of the 'pocket battleship' was a symbol for this new approach to seapower.

Moreover, the navy eventually became subject to Hitler's long-term ambitions for dominating the world, and the seas in particular. At first, the Anglo-German Naval Agreement of 1935 influenced naval development strongly. However, even with the right to build capital ships, the navy did not find a convincing solution to the obvious strategic and operational problem of what the function of capital ships was in performing the most important wartime tasks of the navy – protecting German supplies over large areas and attacking enemy sea lines of communication. Nevertheless, in their endeavours to achieve a stronger position of power for Germany, Hitler and his naval commanders operated with different assumptions as far as their strategic thinking was concerned. For Hitler, strategy and ideology were linked to each other and geared to the forthcoming struggle for hegemony in Europe, whereas the navy believed that Hitler would take into consideration the necessary industrial constraints and time required to build a new fleet.

In 1938, neglecting his strong statement of 1929 that in a new conflict with Britain Germany 'would be doomed to failure right from the start',[55] Admiral Raeder followed Hitler's hazardous course of confrontation. He accepted that Hitler had overturned the sea denial concept for the navy, but did not resign. Misjudging the weak resources of his country and the industrial constraints, Hitler ordered the build-up of a massive fleet that concentrated one-sidedly on battleships. However, the Second World War broke out before his naval plans could take effect. As a result, the navy was totally unprepared to fight the next war at sea.

NOTES

This chapter is based mainly on my publication *Reichsmarine und Landesverteidigung 1919–1928: Konzeption und Führung der Marine in der Weimarer Republik* (Munich: Bernard & Graefe, 1976). Cf. also Michael Geyer, *Aufrüstung oder Sicherheit: Die Reichswehr in der Krise der Machtpolitik 1924–1926* (Wiesbaden: Steiner, 1980), Jost Dülffer, *Weimar, Hitler und die Marine: Reichspolitik und Flottenbau 1920–1939* (Düsseldorf: Droste, 1973), and Wilhelm Deist, 'The Rearmament of the Wehrmacht', in *Germany and the Second World War,* vol. I: *The Build-up of German Aggression* (Oxford: Oxford University Press, 1990), pp. 372–540.

1. Articles of the Peace Treaty of Versailles quoted from *Major Peace Treaties of Modern History 1648–1967,* ed. Fred L. Israel, vol. II, (New York and Toronto 1967), pp. 1265–385.
2. NIACC (Naval Interallied Commission of Control) to Mafri (Marinefriedenskommission, i.e. German Naval Peace Commission), 26 March 1920: 'the Principal Allied Powers have decided that, although Article 192 of the Treaty with Germany does not admit of Ships in Reserve retaining their guns, the German Government may retain the following number of surface warships in reserve (with guns on board, but no crews, munitions or stores)', cited by Rahn, *Reichsmarine,* pp. 22–3.
3. Cf. Arthur Marder, *From Dreadnought to Scapa Flow,* vol. V, *From Victory to Aftermath* (London: Oxford University Press, 1970), p. 258, and Stephen. W. Roskill, *Naval Policy Between the Wars,* vol. II, *The Period of Anglo-American Antagonism 1919–1929* (London: Oxford University Press, 1968), p. 92.
4. Cf. R. A. Chaput, *Disarmament in British Foreign Policy* (London, 1935), p. 58, and Michael Salewski, *Entwaffnung und Militärkontrolle in Deutschland 1919–1927* (Munich, 1966), p. 201, note 6.
5. Cf. minutes of cabinet meeting, 30 May 1919, nos 6 and 7, *Das Kabinett Scheidemann,* ed. H. Schulze (Boppard: Boldt, 1971), document no. 91; minutes of the German Peace delegation, 11 May 1919, ibid., document no. 87, note 2; and *Die Gegenvorschläge der Deutschen Regierung zu den Friedensbedingungen* (Berlin, 1919), pp. 23, 93.
6. Auswärtiges Amt (German Foreign Office), *Antwort der Alliierten aund Assoziierten Mächte auf die Bemerkungen der Deutschen Delegation zu den Friedenbedingungen nebst Mantelnot* (Berlin, 1919), p. 51.
7. This part is based on Rahn, *Reichsmarine, passim.* Cf. also Gerhard Schreiber, 'Die Rolle Frankreichs im strategischen und operativen Denken der deutschen Marine', in K. Hildebrand and K. F. Werner, eds, *Deutschland und Frankreich 1936–1939,* (Munich and Zurich, 1981), pp. 167–213 (Supplement to *Francia,* vol. X).
8. This problem is discussed by Geyer, *Aufrüstung oder Sicherheit, passim,* and Michael Salewski, 'Zur deutschen Sicherheitspolitik in der Spätzeit der

Weimarer Republik', *Vierteljahreshefte für Zeitgeschichte*, vol. XXII (1974), pp. 121–47.

9. The problem of secret armaments is discussed in detail by Rahn, *Reichsmarine*, pp. 208–32, and by Bernd Remmele, 'Die maritime Geheimrüstung unter Kapitän z. S. Lohmann', *Militärgeschichtliche Mitteilungen*, vol. LVI (1997), no. 2, pp. 313–76.

10. Remarks of Reichwehr Minister Groener, 10 April 1930, cited by Rahn, *Reichsmarine*, p. 231.

11. In comparison, the costs for building a light cruiser were 36 million Reichsmarks. The balance account of the whole operations was 35.17 million marks. The debit for the government was 25.9 million marks, but this sum included 12.7 millions mark of investment in real defence matters. See Rahn, *Reichsmarine*, p. 227.

12. Allison W. Saville, 'The Development of the German U-Boat Arm, 1919–1935' (DPhil. dissertation Washington, 1963), and 'Entwurf einer Denkschrift über den Flottenaufbau 1926–1939', written by Wilhelm Treue in 1942–43, published in Wilhelm Treue, Eberhard Möller and Werner Rahn, *Deutsche Marinerüstung 1919–1942. Die Gefahren der Tirpitz-Tradition* (Herford, Bonn: Mittler, 1992), pp. 41–142, in this context pp. 139–49.

13. Light cruiser *Cöln II*, 5,620 ton, 29 knots, eight 15 cm guns, commissioned in January 1918, scuttled in Scapa Flow at 21 June 1919.

14. Marineleitung (Naval Command)/BK (Construction Dept.), I d 1799, 23 June 1923, cited by Rahn, *Reichsmarine*, p. 200.

15. Minutes of Völkerbundgruppe Marine about a conversation with the French naval *attaché*, 19 January 1928, quoted by Rahn, *Reichsmarine*, p. 201. In this context it should be mentioned again that the Peace Treaty did not specify the armament of warships.

16. Minutes of a conversation with the British ambassador, 24 March 1928, quoted by Rahn, *Reichsmarine*, pp. 201–2.

17. *Emden*, 5,600 tons stdd, 29 knots, eight 15 cm guns, four torpedo tubes, commissioned in October 1925.

18. Naval Command/Operations Division to Construction Dept., 20 June 1926, quoted by Gerhard Sandhofer, 'Das Panzerschiff A und die Vorentwürfe von 1920 bis 1928', *Militärgeschichtliche Mitteilungen*, vol. 3, no. 1 (1968), p. 50.

19. The designation 'small battlecruiser' was used by the Naval Command in its study 'Der militärische Wert der Panzerschiffneubauten' (2 October 1928). See in this context Rahn, *Reichsmarine*, pp. 240–1.

20. Annual Report on Germany for the Year 1928, 25 March 1929, PRO FO 311/1364, p. 33.

21. Speech of Reichswehr Minister Groener in Reichstag, 15 November 1928, *Stenographische Berichte des Reichstages*, vol. 423, p. 342. Cf. Geyer, *Aufrüstung oder Sicherheit*, pp. 202–3, and Keith W. Bird, *Weimar, the German Naval Officer Corps and the Rise of National Socialism* (Amsterdam, 1977), pp. 235–7, 265–71.

22. See address of the Head of Operations Division (*Flottenabteilung*) within the Naval Command, Captain Assmann, delivered at the Berlin Skagerrak Gesellschaft on 2 November 1928, cited by Rahn, *Reichsmarine*, p. 243. For the continuity of the long-term notion of power politics of the navy, see in particular Schreiber, *Die Rolle Frankreichs*.

23. Raeder was born in 1876, joined the navy in 1894; during the First World War was chief-of-staff to Vice-Admiral Hipper; 1918 commanding officer of a light cruiser for nine months; 1919–20 head of central department within the Admiralty; 1920–22 naval historian within the Naval Archive, writing on cruiser warfare;

in 1922 promoted to rear-admiral, inspector of naval education; 1924 flag officer Light Naval Forces North Sea Area; 1925–28 flag officer Baltic Naval Station; October 1928 chief of naval command within Ministry of Defence; 1935 commander-in-chief of the navy; in April 1939 promoted to grand-admiral; resigned in January 1943; in October 1946 sentenced by the International Military Tribunal at Nuremberg to imprisonment for life; in October 1955 released from prison for health reasons; died 6 November 1960.

24. Memorandum of the Naval Command of 28 May 1929: 'Braucht Deutschland grosse Kriegsschiffe?' (Does Germany Need Big Warships?), published in Rahn, *Reichsmarine*, pp. 281–6.

25. For the following discussions see Rahn, *Reichsmarine*, pp. 126–32. Cf. Holger H. Herwig's 'Introduction' in Wolfgang Wegener, *The Naval Strategy of the World War* (Annapolis, MD: Naval Institute Press, 1989), pp. xv–lv, and Rolf Hobson, 'The German School of Naval Thought and the Origins of the Tirpitz Plan 1875–1900', *Forsvarsstuddier*, no. 2/1996, ed. Institutt for Forsvarsstudier, (Oslo), pp. 5–93.

26. Wegener was born in 1875 and joined the Imperial Navy in 1894 together with Erich Raeder; during the First World War Wegener was a senior officer on the staff of a battleship squadron; from 1917 commanding officer of a light cruiser; in March 1923 promoted to rear admiral and was inspector of Naval Artillery; retired in September 1926, and died on 29 October 1956. For more details, see Herwig, 'Introduction', pp. xv–lv.

27. 'Reflections Concerning the Concepts of Our War Games and War Studies', submitted to the Chief of Naval Command, Vice-Admiral Hans Zenker, 25 September 1925, cited by Rahn, *Reichsmarine*, p. 129; for a translation see Wegener, *Naval Strategy*, p. 200.

28. Wolfgang Wegener, *Die Seestrategie des Weltkrieges* (Berlin, 1929), p. 83, 2nd edn (Berlin: E.S. Mittler & Sohn, 1941), p. 79; for a translation see Wegener, *Naval Strategy*, p. 126.

29. Hobson, 'The German School', p. 61.

30. Wegener, *Seestrategie*, p. 84 (2nd edn, p. 80; for a translation see Wegener, *Naval Strategy*, p. 127.

31. Wegener, 'Seestrategie' (2nd extended edn, Berlin, 1941), p. 81. This edition is nearly identical with the original 1926 version, see C. A. Gemzell, *Raeder, Hitler und Skandinavien* (Lund: CWK Gleerup, 1965), pp. 15–27. The latent anti-British attitude of the Navy's leadership is particularly stressed in Schreiber, *Die Rolle Frankreichs*. As a semi-official 'response' by the Naval Command to Wegener's theses, the following can be considered: Otto Groos, *Seekriegslehren im Lichte des Weltkrieges* (Berlin: E. S. Mittler & Sohn, 1929). Between 1920 and 1925, Groos (rear admiral from 1 December 1930) was the author of the first volumes of North Sea theatre official naval history and, from 1931 to 1934, he was chief of the *Marinekommandoamt* (Naval Command Office).

32. Hobson, 'German School', p. 62.

33. Memo of commander Schuster, Staff Officer Operations Division (*Flottenabteilung*) within Naval Command, 20 March 1931, quoted by Rahn, *Reichsmarine*, pp. 245–6.

34. Memo of captain Boehm, head of Operations Division, 30 July 1932, quoted in ibid., p. 246.

35. See lecture of Captain Kurt Assmann (head of Fleet Dept.), 2 November 1928, quoted by Rahn, *Reichsmarine*, p. 243. The following part is based on my chapter, 'German Naval Power in the First and Second World Wars', in N. A. M. Rodger, ed., *Naval Power in the Twentieth Century* (London: Macmillan, 1996), pp. 88–100.

36. Dülffer, *Weimar,* pp. 237–9. See also Bird, *German Naval Officer Corps,* pp. 291–3.
37. For the planning of these two battlecruisers see Jost Dülffer, 'Die Reichs- und Kriegsmarine 1918–1939', *Handbuch zur deutschen Militärgeschichte 1648–1939,* ed. Militärgeschichtliches Forschungsamt, part VIII (Munich: Bernard & Graefe, 1977), pp. 463–6; and Deist, 'The Rearmament', pp. 458–62.
38. See Deist, 'The Rearmament', pp. 462–72.
39. Essay by Rear Admiral Godt on the 'War at Sea', November 1945 (N.I.D. 1/GP/17), Naval Historical Center, Operational Archives Branch (Washington, DC); see also Clay Blair, *Hitler's U-Boat War: The Hunters 1939–1942* (New York: Random House, 1996), pp. 30–9.
40. Dönitz was born on 16 September 1891 and joined the navy in 1910; in the First World War was CO of *UB-68,* sunk in 1918; prisoner-of-war, 1934–35; CO of cruiser *Emden,* chief of U-boat Command from 1935 until January 1943; promoted to captain in 1935; rear admiral in October 1939; grand admiral February 1943; 1943–45 commander-in-chief of the navy; in October 1946 sentenced by the IMT at Nuremberg to imprisonment for ten years; in October 1956 released from prison; died 24 December 1980, see Blair, *Hitler's U-Boat War: The Hunters,* pp. 35–49, and Peter Padfield, *Dönitz, The Last Führer: Portrait of a Nazi War Leader* (New York: Harper & Row, 1984).
41. Deist, 'The Rearmament', p. 467; see also Treue, 'Entwurf einer Denkschrift über den Flottenaufbau 1926–1939', in Wilhelm Treue, *et al., Deutsche Marinerüstung 1919–1942,* pp. 139–49.
42. Memo of Naval Command/General Navy Office, 9 April 1935, quoted by Dülffer, *Weimar,* p. 315; for a translation see Deist, 'The Rearmament ', p. 465.
43. See above, note 24.
44. Erich Raeder, *Der Kreuzerkrieg in ausländischen Gewässern,* vol. I: *Das Kreuzergeschwader,* 2nd edn (Berlin: E. S. Mittler & Sohn, 1927), pp. 253, 265, 339, 341. Compare Klaus Schröder, 'Zur Entstehung der strategischen Konzeption Großadmiral Raeders', *MOV-Nachrichten,* vol. XLVI (1971), pp. 14–18, 45–8.
45. Schröder, 'Entstehung', p. 48, and Michael Salewski, *Die deutsche Seekriegsleitung 1935–1945,* vol. I (Frankfurt: Bernard & Graefe, 1970), pp. 32–3.
46. Lecture of the commander-in-chief navy, 3 February 1937: 'Grundsätzliche Gedanken der Seekriegführung', BA-MA RM 6/53. Compare in this context Salewski, *Seekriegsleitung,* vol. I, pp. 32–3; Dülffer, *Weimar,* pp. 435–6; and C. A. Gemzell, *Raeder, Hitler und Skandinavien* (Lund: CWR Gleerup, 1965), pp. 49–51.
47. Ibid., pp. 64–5.
48. See Deist, 'The Rearmament', pp. 472–80.
49. Memorandum of Commander Hellmuth Heye: 'Seekriegführung gegen England und die sich daraus ergebenden Forderungen für die strategische Zielsetzung und den Aufbau der Kriegsmarine' (Conducting a naval war against Britain and the resulting requirements for strategic objectives and the build-up of the navy). See also Salewski, *Seekriegsleitung,* vol. I, pp. 43–6; Dülffer, *Weimar,* pp. 471–3; and Deist, 'The Rearmament', pp. 473–5. The final version of the memorandum is published by Salewski, *Seekriegsleitung,* vol. III (Frankfurt, 1973), pp. 28–60.
50. Deist, 'The Rearmament', p. 474. Cf. Salewski, *Seekriegsleitung,* vol. I, pp. 51–4; and Dülffer, *Weimar,* pp. 481–5.
51. Comment of the commander-in-chief of the fleet, Admiral Carls, on Heye's memorandum of September 1938, cited by Deist 'The Rearmament', p. 475; see also Dülffer, *Weimar,* pp. 486–7.
52. Quoted in ibid., p. 502.

GERMAN NAVAL STRATEGY AND ARMAMENT, 1919–39

53. 'Gedanken des Oberbefehlshabers der Kriegsmarine zum Kriegsausbruch am 3 September 1939', in Gerhard Wagner, ed., *Lagevorträge des Oberbefehlshabers der Kriegsmarine vor Hitler 1939–1945*, (Munich: J. F. Lehmann Verlag, 1972), pp. 19–20. For the translation see *Fuehrer Conferences on Naval Affairs, 1939–1945* (Annapolis, MD: Naval Institute Press, 1990), pp. 37–8.
54. Concluding reflections of Vice-Admiral Zenker on the 1924 autumn exercises, 12 September 1924, cited in Rahn, *Reichsmarine*, pp. 113–14.
55. See above, note 25.

127

8

British Naval Procurement and Technological Change, 1919–39

Jon T. Sumida

During the Second World War, carrier-borne aviation displaced battleship heavy artillery as the final arbiter of sea control, surface ships needed a combination of effective anti-aircraft guns and fire control in order to maximize the chances of survival against hostile sea- or shore-based air strikes, and well-armed, relatively speedy and long-range light warships in large numbers were required to defend convoys on the high seas against attacks by groups of submarines. The Royal Navy, however, was ill-prepared in all three areas. At the outbreak of hostilities, the aircraft on British carriers were substantially inferior in terms of both numbers and quality to those of the US Navy and Japanese Navy, British warships were armed with significantly less potent fire control gear than was standard in US ships, and high-performance anti-submarine escorts were too few in number to protect adequately Britain's trans-Atlantic trade routes. These defects in *matériel* limited the offensive power of the fleet and created vulnerabilities that caused heavy naval and mercantile casualties.

Weaknesses in British air, anti-air and anti-submarine *matériel* have reflected badly on British naval procurement between the world wars. Many have attributed Admiralty mistakes in technical policy to its supposed inability to assess accurately the capabilities of important weapons innovations.[1] This chapter takes a different approach. Its primary concern is not the explanation of defective decision-making as such, but the analytical description of the problems posed by technological change in relation to larger policy questions, and the response of Britain's naval leadership to these interconnected issues. The present brief study, in other words, will examine complicated processes as a whole rather than focus narrowly on the particular causes of simple outcomes.[2] The main general arguments are that British naval technical shortcomings had multiple causes, and that decisions regarding the ultimate worth of untried weapons had to be made within the context of difficult, complex and contingent circumstances, which made 'correct in light of the future as it happened' choices unlikely if not practically impossible.

From the conclusion of the war in late 1918 until rearmament began in 1936, the direction of British naval affairs was heavily influenced, if not practically determined, by chronic severe financial limitation. This was caused by the First World War. The direct fiscal burden imposed by support of the fighting effort was enormous. During hostilities, Britain spent more on war-related activity every two weeks than it had on the navy in any single year before 1914. Most expenditure was borrowed, more than tripling the proportion of state revenue devoted to the annual servicing of the national debt. The indirect fiscal effects of the war had no less punishing implications for the navy. Popular demand for improved social services after years of war-induced privation and sacrifice resulted in government spending on domestic amelioration in 1921–22 that was five times greater than in 1913–14. Moreover, the formation of an independent Royal Air Force created an additional competitor (besides the army) for the reduced resources available for defence purposes (see Table 8.1).[3]

Table 8.1
British Defence Expenditure, 1920–39 (thousands of £)

Fiscal Year	Army	Navy	Air Force	Total	Navy % of Total
1920–21	181,500	88,428	22,300	292,228	30
1921–22	95,110	80,770	13,560	189,440	43
1922–23	45,400	56,200	9,400	111,000	51
1923–24	43,600	52,600	9,600	105,800	50
1924–25	44,765	55,625	14,310	114,700	49
1925–26	44,250	59,657	15,470	119,377	50
1926–27	43,600	57,600	15,530	116,730	49
1927–28	44,150	58,140	15,150	117,440	50
1928–29	40,500	56,920	16.050	113,470	50
1929–30	40,500	55,750	16,750	113,000	49
1930–31	40,243	52,274	17,632	110,149	48
1931–32	38,624	51,042	17,869	107,535	48
1932–33	36,137	50,165	17.057	103,359	49
1933–34	37,540	53,444	16,701	107,685	50
1934–35	39,692	56,616	17,608	113,916	50
1935–36	44,654	64,887	27.515	137,056	47
1936–37	55,015	80,976	49,996	185,987	44
1937–38	72,676	101,892	81,799	256,367	40
1938–39	121,543	132,437	143,500	397,480	33
1939–40	242,438	181,771	294,834	719,043	25

Sources: Sir Bernard Mallet and C. Oswald George, *British Budgets: Third Series, 1921–22 to 1932–33* (London: Macmillan, 1933), pp. 425–53; and Robert Paul Shay, Jr, *British Rearmament in the Thirties: Politics and Profits* (Princeton, NJ: Princeton University Press, 1977), p. 297.

The war also weakened the Admiralty's claim on government income by both eliminating all European threats to Britain's naval position and precipitating a warship construction boom that by 1919 had created a fleet that was in numbers and quality overwhelmingly superior to any other. The Versailles Treaty not only stripped Germany of its large battle fleet, but barred its replacement. War had seriously delayed or even halted major naval construction in Russia, France and Italy, and political upheaval and financial prostration ensured that lost ground would not be recovered quickly, if at all. The United States and Japan possessed substantial navies and the former was fiscally powerful, but both were more or less friendly, and in any case distant. British finance had been severely strained by the war, but against this could be set an enormous gain in naval capital. Between August 1914 and November 1918, 842 warships amounting to over 1.6 million tons displacement were added to the fleet, to which must be added 571 naval auxiliaries that came to nearly 800,000 tons, for a grand total of almost 2.5 million tons of construction, or more than that carried out during the quarter century that preceded the war.[4]

Most of the major warships built before the war were obsolescent or weakened by strenuous deployment, while many of the vessels constructed during the war for anti-submarine and other flotilla work were light craft whose effective service life was relatively short. But some 45 per cent of the fighting tonnage laid down in 1917 and 1918 consisted of fleet units, that is, one battlecruiser, three big cruisers, 25 light cruisers, three aircraft carriers, 18 fleet submarines, and no fewer than 90 large destroyers. The heavy commitment of resources to such vessels had interfered with the construction of escorts and merchant vessels needed to counter the German submarine campaign. Although the Admiralty had justified the policy as a necessary precaution against German building, its real motive was probably to obtain as many high-value warships as possible before the onset of the fiscal famine that was bound to accompany the end of hostilities. In any case, the late war programmes produced a large cohort of new units capable of operating for many years.[5]

The combination of financial austerity, absence of danger and large stock of fresh warships worked against Admiralty demands for substantial new construction. These factors largely explain the amenability of the British government to US proposals in 1921 for a comprehensive naval arms limitation agreement. The resulting Washington Naval Conference Treaty of 1922 imposed a moratorium on new capital ships and restricted the building of aircraft carriers and cruisers. Such provisions encouraged naval economy by preventing or restraining the construction of many more expensive warships, stabilized the friendly relations of the three great naval powers which might otherwise have been soured by an open-ended warship building competition, and extended the effective life of existing warships by preventing the introduction of radically improved models in significant numbers.[6]

The Admiralty believed the treaty settings of building maximums represented imperial security minimums that should be reached as quickly as possible. While treaty tonnage quotas for surface capital ships and aircraft carriers were filled or nearly so by existing units, that for large cruisers was not. Historically, Britain had matched or even overmatched the cruiser construction of potential enemies with superior numbers of at least equal and often qualitatively better units in order to defend the extended lines of maritime communications that were vital to its economic existence. British cruisers were also supposed to be capable of interdicting the trade routes of opponents and of reinforcing the battle fleet.[7] The fact that large cruisers were the only venue for major new warship construction only reinforced powerful and long-standing predilections. Britain's naval leadership thus focused their hopes upon the construction of cruisers of the largest type and in the greatest numbers allowed by the Washington accords.[8]

The Admiralty's aspirations were not shared by either the Labour or Conservative parties. The short-lived first Labour government of 1924 had cut naval spending to well below that approved by its Conservative predecessor. The Conservative government that followed from late 1924 to mid-1929 could do little more than restore naval spending to the level of 1923, because tax reductions and increases in social spending were needed to garner votes in the next general election.[9] As a consequence, a quarter of the navy's cruiser programme was cancelled between 1927 and 1929. This sacrifice, which was made in the hope that continued Conservative rule would temper naval economies over the long run, was in vain – a Labour victory in the spring of 1929 was followed by the suspension and then cancellation of additional cruisers. The onset of the Great Depression in 1929 drastically increased pressure on the navy to reduce expenditure, which was reinforced by the negotiation of a second Naval Arms Limitation Treaty in London in 1930.[10]

From 1930 to 1933, British naval spending authorizations were well below the previous record interwar low set in 1924, the replacement of the Labour government by a Conservative–Labour coalition in 1931 notwithstanding.[11] At the nadir, in 1932, the navy's budget came to only 6 per cent of the government's total expenditure, as compared with the 25 per cent share it had enjoyed before the First World War. While the absolute amount was more or less the same as in 1914, costs since that time had risen dramatically. And while orders for cruisers were actually much higher than in the late 1920s, the funds used for new shipbuilding were obtained by economies in other critical areas.[12]

In 1933, the Admiralty was alarmed by reports that the United States had spent five times as much, and Japan three times as much, as Britain on battleship modernization. While all 15 US capital ships were equipped or about to be equipped with first-class fire-control gear, aircraft equipment and gun mountings, only two out of Britain's 15 heavy units could

131

be considered up-to-date in these areas.[13] The situation with regard to naval aircraft procurement was even worse. By 1926, the US Navy had surpassed the Royal Navy in terms of naval aircraft numbers. During the late 1920s, British plans for new carrier construction were cancelled and carrier aircraft acquisition reduced, in part to preserve the cruiser building programme in spite of the economies in overall naval spending demanded by the government. By 1930, the Royal Navy's fleet air arm of 150 planes was numerically half the size of that of the US Navy. Between 1929 and 1934, the strength of Britain's carrier air force increased by a mere 18 planes, while that of the United States rose by some 80 machines.[14]

On the other hand, the numerical contraction of the battle fleet induced by financial circumstances and arms control brought certain strategic and tactical benefits. During the First World War, the expansion and maintenance of the enormous force of capital ships created by a decade of Anglo-German rivalry had imposed a heavy economical and logistical burden. Navy consumption of steel, dockyards and skilled workers curtailed sharply merchant ship construction and repair, which made Britain much more vulnerable to the German submarine campaign of 1917.[15] Although the distances by land or sea between coalfields in Wales and the main fleet in Scotland were not great, fuel transport consumed large quantities of scarce shipping and rail resources. A battle fleet anywhere near the size of that deployed during the war was for all intents and purposes unsustainable outside of home waters.[16]

In the absence of any serious naval rival in Europe, and with the presumption that war with the United States was unthinkable, British naval strategic planning after the First World War was directed toward the threat posed by Japan to imperial holdings in the Far East. The 15-unit battle fleet mandated by the Washington treaty was only one-third the size of Britain's wartime force at its peak, but this meant that it would require commensurately less logistical support.[17] With the prospective enemy fleet comparably reduced in size, the danger of being critically outnumbered was eliminated. The treaty limitations, in other words, made the projection of significant naval power far from home waters practical when it otherwise might not have been the case.

A numerically smaller battle fleet was also desirable for tactical reasons. At the battle of Jutland in 1916, the actions of the 39 British capital ships in three separate groups were difficult to coordinate, while the centralized direction by flag signal of the main body of 24 battleships reduced manoeuvrability, compromising both offensive flexibility and increasing vulnerability to torpedo attack. Britain's treaty battle fleet of 15, of which no more than ten to 12 were likely to be operated collectively, was subdivided into divisions of three to five. Groups of this size could be manoeuvred without flag signals, and thus were far more capable of exploiting offensive opportunities; avoiding either surface, sub-surface, or air-launched torpedoes; and operating at night. Exercises and experiments in the 1930s revealed the advantages of divisional tactics, which were adopted as standard by the end of the decade.[18]

The effectiveness of divisional tactics was greatly enhanced by improvements in naval technology and method. The value of long-range naval gunnery was enhanced by the advent of fire control equipment that was far more sophisticated than the gear available during the First World War, and by the development of air artillery spotting. The coordination of independently acting divisions was facilitated by mechanized course plotters that kept track of the relative positions of friendly warships, and by the creation of bureaucratized operations management in the form of the Action Information Centre (Combat Information Centre). Surface ship vulnerability to air attack was further reduced by the improvement and proliferation of anti-aircraft guns. The considerable increases in surface ship offensive and defensive capabilities evident by the early to mid-1930s, coupled to the fact that Britain planned to deploy its fleet within range of friendly land-based aircraft during the initial stages of a Far Eastern war with Japan, were significant compensations for Royal Navy weaknesses in carrier aviation.[19]

Besides strategic, logistical and tactical considerations, Admiralty hope, if not confidence, in the sufficiency of even a reduced, ageing and in many ways defective fleet rested upon the assumption that many new vessels would be available before or not long after the outbreak of hostilities. Between 1923 and 1927, the Principal Supply Officers Committee (PSOC), a body made up of the senior procurement executives of the three services and the president of the board of trade, was developed to resolve in advance potentially debilitating conflicts between the army, navy and air force and civilian economy over access to raw materials, skilled labour and manufacturing plant. The most important functions of the new body were to improve the armaments producing potential of industrial firms that in peace produced for the civilian market, and to create a coordinated scheme for a swift and efficient transition from peace to war production.[20]

As a result of the deliberations of the PSOC and the work of the Defence Requirements Committee from 1933 to 1935,[21] the Admiralty retained priority access to skilled labour and manufacturing resources over the army and air force during peacetime (see Table 8.1). In practice, this meant the navy's share of defence spending was more or less equal to the combined expenditure of the other two services prior to rearmament, and remained disproportionately high (that is, well above a third) during the first two years of preparatory industrial mobilization. This gave a reasonable assurance that substantial numbers of new battleships, carriers and cruisers – that is, heavy units that required several years to build – would be available to reinforce the existing fleet in time. In return, the navy was expected to concentrate its wartime productive effort on the construction of light craft and to allow the building of the large numbers of merchant ships, both of which could be accomplished with unskilled labour and relatively low-grade industrial materials. This would leave free high-value manufacturing assets needed to facilitate the rapid equipment of the army and air force.[22]

The careful planning and serious interservice political negotiation devoted to the national armaments production problem was partly a reflection of an awareness of the degree to which unrestrained competition between the army and navy for the output of a large but ill-prepared manufacturing base had disrupted Britain's industrial effort during the First World War. But more importantly, careful planning and coordination was necessary because by the 1930s British capacity to build weapons in quantity was only a fraction of what it had been in 1914. Between 1922 and 1935, new construction for the Royal Navy was less than a third that of the 14-year period from 1897 to 1910 (see Table 8.2). Beginning in 1929, the Bank of England in cooperation with shipbuilding firms began a conscious policy of reducing the number of yards through closure or consolidation in order to ensure the profitability of the industry. By 1933, of the 12 naval shipbuilding and armaments firms that had been prosperously engaged in work in 1914, only one, Vickers, remained capable of fulfilling large orders for major warships.[23]

The steep decline in government purchases exacerbated the negative effects of a slump in merchant shipbuilding. After a brief construction boom to replace ships that were lost or worn out during the war, a combination of foreign competition and chronic world-trade recession, followed by depression, ruined the market for new vessels. During the decade before the First World War, Britain produced some 60 per cent of the world's shipping. During the 1920s, its market share dropped to 45 per cent, and during the 1930s to little more than 20 per cent. During the latter period, Britain's merchant tonnage declined by nearly 10 per cent while the volume of sea-borne international trade increased by almost a third. Protracted bad times resulted in the closing of shipyards and the evaporation of skilled worker pools, which reduced the ability of the commercial shipbuilding industry to serve as a manufacturing reserve for both the navy and merchant marine in the event of war.[24] By the mid-1930s, British skilled shipbuilding labour was half what it had been in the previous decade, and many of the reduced number of shipyards were out of date or poorly maintained.[25]

The careful planning and effective management of rearmament to a great degree rectified the navy's deficiencies in up-to-date units. In response to the re-emergence of Germany as a major threat and Japanese aggression in China in the mid-1930s, Britain began rearming in 1936. The naval programmes of 1936, 1937, 1938 and 1939 provided for the construction of nine battleships, seven carriers, 33 cruisers and supporting flotilla craft.

Table 8.2

Pre-World War/Inter-World Wars Comparison of New Construction
Large Warships

Year	New Battleship and 1st Class Cruiser Tonnage	Year	New Battleship, Carrier and Cruiser Tonnage
1897	128,650	1922	67,850
1898	192,380	1923	–
1899	46,140	1924	68,250
1900	67,500	1925	39,360
1901	111,855	1926	28,150
1902	58,270	1927	8,390
1903	124,555	1928	7,270
1904	75,980	1929	7,175
1905	69,650	1930	20,845
1906	55,800	1931	19,215
1907	57,750	1932	19,215
1908	38,400	1933	18,200
1909	219,540	1934	33,170
1910	118,270	1935	50,200
Subtotal	1,303,990	Subtotal	387,290
1911	128,430	1936	163,250
1912	137,500	1937	201,900
1913	140,000	1938	168,750
Subtotal	405,930	Subtotal	533,900
Total	1,709,920	Total	921,190

Sources: Jon Tetsuro Sumida, *In Defence of Naval Supremacy: Finance, Technology and British Naval Policy, 1889–1914* (Boston, MA: Unwin Hyman, 1989), Appendix, Tables 16 and 17, and H. T. Lenton and J. J. Colledge, *Warships of World War II* (London: Ian Allan, 1964).

These orders promised an increase in the surface fleet by more than half, and doubled the number of aircraft carriers. In addition, three of the oldest battleships and one battlecruiser were practically rebuilt, and the anti-aircraft armament of the remaining old capital ships and most of the cruisers heavily augmented. The need to rebuild shipbuilding capacity with large investments in capital plant and the retraining of labour before actual construction of war vessels could begin,[26] the competing demands of a strong upswing in commercial shipbuilding,[27] and the outbreak of war in the fall of 1939, disrupted and delayed completion of the units ordered in 1936 and 1937, and the four battleships authorized for 1938 and 1939 were eventually cancelled, but ultimately most of the projected increase in naval strength was brought into service (see Table 8.3).[28]

Table 8.3
Major Warship Construction: Britain, United States, Japan, 1920–39

Programme Year	Britain	United States	Japan
1920–21	–	–	–
1921–22	1 CM	–	–
1922–23	2 BB	–	8 CA
			1 CL
1923–24	–	–	–
1924–25	7 CA	–	–
1925–26	4 CA	2 CA	–
1926–27	3 CA	–	–
1927–28	1 CA	6 CA	1 CVL
			4 CA
1928–29	1 CL	–	–
1929–30	1 CL	5 CA	–
1930–31	3 CL	1 CV	–
		1 CA	
1931–32	3 CL	1 CA	2 CV
			4 CL
1932–33	3 CL	–	2 CL
1933–34	2 CL	3 CV	1 [CVL]
		2 CA	
		4 CL	
1934–35	1 CV	1 CA	2 [CVL]
	4 CL	3 CL	
1935–36	3 CL	1 CV	–
		2 CL	
1936–37	2 BB	–	–
	2 CV		
	7 CL		
1937–38	3 BB	2 BB	2 CV
	2 CV		5 BB
	7 CL		4 CL(T)
1938–39	[2 BB]	4 BB	–
	1 CV	4 CL	
	1 CVL		
	10 CL		
1939–40	[2 BB]	2 BB	1 CV
	1 CV	1 CV	
	5 CVE		
	9 CL		

Sources: H. T. Lenton and J. J. Colledge, *Warships of World War II* (London: Ian Allan, 1964), pp. 11–12; Paul H. Silverstone, *US Warships of World War II* (Garden City, NY: Doubleday, 1965), p. 13.

The combination of much greater spending on armaments in general (see Table 8.1) and efficient industrial policy, however, did not rectify shortcomings in the three critical areas of naval aviation, fleet anti-aircraft defence, and anti-submarine escorts. In 1939, the Royal Navy deployed 230 aircraft at sea, compared with the 600 aboard the ships of the US and Japanese fleets; numerical inferiority, moreover, was compounded by the antiquated design of many of Britain's ship-based airplanes. British provisions for naval anti-aircraft fire control lagged far behind those of the US Navy. And long-range anti-submarine escorts were few, and production of what was to become the mainstay of convoy defence during the early war years had not even started.

The deplorable state of the Royal Navy's air force on the outbreak of war was at bottom the product of service organizational circumstances peculiar to Britain. In the United States and Japan, the army and navy retained control over the development of aircraft and personnel, but in Britain an independent air force was mainly responsible for aircraft supply to the two senior services, and exercised significant authority over navy air personnel, as well as taking care of its own requirements. In the United States and Japan, the natural rivalry of the army and navy stimulated the development of the aviation components of each. In Britain, an insecure air service looked after its own needs and discouraged initiatives from the other two. The navy, for its part, had good reason to downplay the importance of air operations, on the grounds that arguments in this direction only reinforced the claims of the air force for wider responsibilities and more funding, and distrusted the service loyalty of its own air officers, which undermined their ability to influence policy.

By the time the Royal Navy was able to re-establish complete control over its own aircraft procurement and air personnel in 1938, great damage had been done. During the 1920s and much of the 1930s, the combination of severe financial austerity and air force obstruction on the one hand, and the lack of well-informed and determined air-mindedness in the navy on the other, had resulted in a Fleet Air Arm that was equipped with unsatisfactory aircraft in insufficient numbers. These defects retarded the development of the operational doctrine, techniques and supporting equipment required to exploit the capabilities of large numbers of high-performance carrier aircraft. In the absence of both the appropriate *matériel* and experience, the Admiralty did not appreciate the full potential of sea-based aviation and acted accordingly. Although the carrier building programme was large, the aircraft-carrying capacity of the new vessels was substantially less than that of comparable US and Japanese units. Aircraft procurement, moreover, was limited by inadequate fiscal support.[29]

But the production of large numbers of suitable aircraft might well have been impossible regardless of the Admiralty's attitude toward the

137

importance of carrier aviation. Air Ministry connections to Britain's air-craft building firms were well established, and the rearmament expansion of the Royal Air Force was well under way by the time the navy had regained control over its own aircraft procurement. The leading design teams of the air industry were thus preoccupied with work for their primary customer, and existing and planned production facilities already heavily committed to the fulfilment of its orders. Even the assignment of first priority to the production of naval aircraft by the Admiralty and the allocation of funds to carry it through would not have changed the fact that the necessary design staffs and manufacturing plants were engaged in other work and thus, for practical purposes, unavailable.[30]

The shortcomings of British naval aviation were matched by no less critical deficiencies in anti-aircraft equipment. On the outbreak of war in 1939, British warships were equipped with fire control outfits that were incapable of dealing with rapidly moving aircraft, while the low-angle main armament of most destroyers – whose intended targets were other ships – was virtually useless against high-flying and dive bombers. British provisions in the areas just mentioned were strikingly less efficient than those in the US Navy. All major US warships, including most destroyers, were fitted or about to be fitted with advanced fire-control computers whose outputs automatically controlled the movement (remote power control) of dual-purpose (that is, anti-ship and anti-air) medium-calibre guns, which greatly improved the effectiveness of anti-aircraft fire. In 1942, the chief technical adviser to the director of naval ordnance attributed no less than half of the heavy British warship casualties caused by airplanes in the Mediterranean and the Far East to the lack of remote power control alone.[31]

The Admiralty was solely responsible for the condition of fleet ordnance systems, and thus the division of authority between competing services cannot be blamed as the fundamental cause of flawed anti-aircraft defence as in the case of naval aviation. Financial limitation was undoubtedly a major factor. During the 1920s, the United States spent nearly 50 per cent more on its navy than did Britain, and during the 1930s before the begin-ning of rearmament (1930–35), US naval expenditure was more than a third higher.[32] While the United States had to contend with steeper ship-building costs, and spent a great deal more on naval aviation and battle-ship modernization, it obviously devoted significantly larger sums to the development of naval fire control in general, and naval anti-aircraft fire control in particular, than Britain.[33]

The atmosphere of financial stringency promoted the attitude that more had to be done with less – that is, new systems under design were expected to be capable of much higher performance than their predecessors in order to eliminate supposed inefficiencies that would be generated by the design and production of a larger number of instrument types that improved in smaller increments. The result was that British anti-aircraft fire control projects were overambitious, and thus either were delayed, or compromised by excessive complications that caused unreliability. In the United States, the general practice was to go forward steadily in short stages, while allowing manufacturers to spend whatever was necessary to achieve comparatively modest performance goals. In effect, the US practice was to pay greater amounts to achieve less but more frequently, an expensive approach that none the less produced equipment in quantity that was much better than that of the British.[34]

The United States' advantages over Britain with respect to the much greater size of its engineering higher education and corporate manufacturing establishments do not seem to have favoured more productive design activity.[35] Shortcomings in the management of weapons procurement, on the other hand, were probably a serious problem. The development of fire-control systems usually required contributions from separate departments – for example, ordnance and electrical – but in the absence of supra-departmental direction of technical programmes, important projects – of which remote power control was one – were compromised by poor coordination. Although the formation of the Admiralty Research Laboratory and the expansion of older technical departments improved enormously the Royal Navy's fire control design capability over pre-First World War levels, communications between naval officers and civilian engineers – that is, between users and producers – remained poor. This meant that requirements for new equipment were frequently formulated with insufficient technical input, and then unmodified by continuous technically expert review.[36]

The case of naval radar – a success story – is perhaps an indicator of how much the factors just described mattered. Much of the basic research was undertaken by the air force, whose pioneering efforts formed a strong point of departure for the Royal Navy's relatively late recognition of the significance of electronic weapons. The critical period for the development of naval radar coincided with rearmament, which meant that fiscal restraints may have been less severe than in naval anti-aircraft gunnery. But, in addition, radar development was the responsibility of the Signals School rather than the Ordnance Department, where academic scientific participation was strong, cooperation between officers and scientists was close, organization – especially after 1937 – unusually good, and executive direction clear and robust.[37]

For the reasons just given, the performance of British anti-aircraft fire control equipment was unsatisfactory.[38] Thus, although rearmament production enabled the Royal Navy to double the medium-calibre anti-aircraft gun armament of post-war cruisers and all unmodernized battleships, and provide powerful new dual-purpose batteries to all the new battleships, carriers, anti-aircraft cruisers and many new destroyers,[39] the anti-aircraft capability of British warships was far less effective than it might otherwise have been.

The protection of maritime lines of supply were vital to Britain's survival, yet in spite of the warning provided by the near war-winning achievements of German submarines in 1917, the Royal Navy was ill-prepared in 1939 to deal with underwater attacks on Atlantic convoys. The corvette, Britain's main anti-submarine warship during the early years of the Second World War, lacked speed and endurance, was poorly armed and difficult to inhabit for extended periods. The combination of inadequate fighting performance and crews exhausted by debilitating living conditions significantly increased the vulnerability of merchant shipping to submarine attack. Much more capable escorts became available in large numbers beginning in 1943, but not before German submarines had inflicted heavy losses on inadequately protected convoys.

The design shortcomings of the corvette were attributable to pre-war staff requirements, which had called for a vessel suitable for the defence of coastal shipping. At the time, Admiralty planners not unreasonably assumed that German access to the Atlantic would be restricted by geography as had been the case during the First World War. Under these circumstances, the combination of minefields and vigorous patrol of the English Channel and North Sea passages by aircraft and relatively few surface anti-submarine warships would have been sufficient to prevent Germany from mounting a large-scale submarine campaign against British Atlantic shipping. The Admiralty, therefore, believed that a modest programme of sloops would meet the anticipated moderate requirements of escorting long-distance mercantile traffic, while the mass-produced corvettes, with the support of aircraft, would be capable of providing adequate protection to short-haul convoys and of undertaking short-range patrol work.[40]

The fall of France in 1940 invalidated the fundamental assumptions upon which Admiralty anti-submarine preparations, and indeed all naval plans, had been based. German submarines, deployed from bases on France's Atlantic coast, outflanked Britain's intended containment zone, and exposed its shipping routes in the Western hemisphere to serious attack. The neutralization of the French Navy also deprived Britain of the support of substantial anti-submarine forces. Manufacturing resources that might have been devoted to the production of many more sloops had to be allocated to repairing the heavy equipment losses of the British Army in France and meeting the needs of outnumbered British military forces in North Africa, while building up the air force to counter air bombing attacks launched from France. In the face of such disastrous circumstances, the Royal Navy had no choice but to deploy corvettes as ocean escorts, whatever their shortcomings. But if the continental military debacle compromised British naval plans in the short run, it also precipitated activity in the Western hemisphere that promised a remedy for the Royal Navy's lack of a satisfactory convoy protector, and defects in aircraft and anti-aircraft fire control as well.

The collapse of France forced the British government to abandon all fiscal restraint and place massive orders for US manufactured armaments. It also prompted the United States to begin industrial mobilization in earnest and to increase economic support. When British credit was exhausted in the spring of 1941, the United States began financing British government purchases through Lend-Lease, which magnified enormously the British ability to acquire US production.[41] While the contribution of US arms to the total produced by British factories in 1940 and 1941 was relatively small, and the Royal Navy's share miniscule in comparison to that of the air force,[42] the early stages of US naval equipment supply were significant because they addressed British weaknesses in aircraft, anti-aircraft equipment and anti-submarine escorts.

By late 1941, Britain had received some 220 American Wildcat carrier fighters (known as Martlets in British service), which was little more than 10 per cent of total British production of naval aircraft in 1940 and 1941,[43] but nearly as many machines as had equipped the entire Fleet Air Arm at the start of the war.[44] During the spring, summer and autumn of 1941, the British light cruiser *Delhi* was rearmed with US dual-purpose guns and the latest anti-aircraft fire control equipment, the success of which prompted a large order for the director component (Mark 37 director), which was far superior to comparable British gear.[45] And over the course of 1941, Britain ordered from US shipbuilders over 300 anti-submarine escorts of two designs much superior to that of the corvette, which was double the number of the older type then built or being built in domestic shipyards.[46]

The flow of US naval *matériel* was disrupted by the entry of the United States into the war as an active belligerent. US Navy requirements for all available anti-aircraft fire control production ruled out the possibility of the re-equipment of the British fleet with the Mark 37 director (a few new British vessels, such as the battleship *Vanguard*, received them after the war).[47] Most of the British anti-submarine escorts were taken over by the US Navy, although 78 were eventually delivered to the Royal Navy.[48] British orders for naval aircraft also suffered at first, but such was the bounty generated by US factories that even limited largess had far-reaching effects. By the spring of 1943, the United States had provided nearly a quarter of the Fleet Air Arm's bombers and over half of its fighters. At the end of the war in 1945, the Royal Navy deployed more than five times as many combat aircraft as it had in 1939, of which over half were US built. No less than two-thirds of Britain's naval single-seat fighter squadrons – the premier type of naval air combatant formation – were equipped with US machines.[49]

In other important categories of naval equipment, such as radio and radar, light anti-aircraft cannon and anti-submarine aircraft carriers, US production for the Royal Navy was significant.[50] Even where US *matériel* was not forthcoming, it was not because it was unproduced, but because output was assigned to equip a powerful friendly fleet. In 1945, the United States had 41,000 naval aircraft (including training and utility machines) in comparison with Britain's 11,300,[51] its major warships – which heavily outnumbered those of the Royal Navy – were all equipped with anti-aircraft fire control that was superior to that mounted in most British vessels, and it had virtually equalled the combined anti-submarine escort production of Britain and Canada. In the Second World War, US aid and then alliance had come in spite of Anglo-American antagonism in the 1920s, and the effects of neutrality legislation in the 1930s.[52] Admiralty planners before 1939 could not count upon large-scale US redress of British naval industrial weakness.[53] None the less, a combination of US supply and active belligerence was ultimately required to win the war at sea.

From 1919 to 1939, the Admiralty was not faced with simple choices between supporting or not supporting the development of aircraft or countermeasures against aircraft and submarines because the policy problem was not predicting a singular future, but having to prepare under difficult conditions for a multitude of possible and in some cases more probable futures. Naval policy then, as now, was driven by the need to maximize strengths and minimize weaknesses while confronted by financial restraint, technical complexity and uncertainty, and, above all, strategic contingency. Challenged by severe fiscal limitations and arms control, and handicapped by a weakened armaments industry and certain inefficiencies in its own technical departments, the Admiralty responded with a succession of teleologically conditioned trade-offs that were based upon reasonable as opposed to worst-case strategic assumptions. These may be summarized as follows.

The cruisers deemed essential to trade defence, attacks on enemy trade and augmentation of the treaty restricted battle fleet, were obtained at the cost of battleship modernization and weaker naval aviation. Improved surface warfare technique and the probability that a war against Japan would initially be fought within range of friendly land-based airpower were accepted as compensations in the short run for inferior strength in naval aviation, at least during the early stages of a war. Efficient industrial mobilization on several years' warning with respect to a major conflict was intended to provide the battleship modernization and new construction essential to exploit the full potential of improved surface warfare technique and to increase anti-aircraft capability, and over a longer term to redress the deficiencies in naval aviation. The diversion of energy to the mass production of high-performance anti-submarine escorts was unnecessary and therefore an extravagance that could not be afforded, because Britain, it was reasonably assumed, would be allied to France, a major naval power, which meant that geography would disfavour an effective German submarine campaign against British shipping and substantial French naval forces would be available to assist the Royal Navy.

Given a functioning Anglo-French partnership, British preparations to deal with the changes in fighting at sea brought about by improvements in aircraft and submarines would have been – if not wholly satisfactory – at least minimally adequate. Pre-war underestimation of the power of air and underwater weapons meant certain weaknesses in equipment countermeasures and dangerously optimistic tactical mindsets.[54] That being said, in the absence of German control of French Atlantic ports, the engagement of the bulk of the German Army on the French frontiers, and French naval containment of the Italians, the Royal Navy should have been more than equal to the task of maintaining sea control in Europe while putting up a credible deterrent to Japanese aggression in the Far East, the actions of German and Italian air and submarine forces notwithstanding. Before 1940, the sudden French military collapse would have been considered practically impossible, and thus could not have been the basis for serious naval planning,[55] particularly because the fiscal circumstances of the interwar period made the task of preparing for the next major conflict extremely difficult even when based on more favourable assumptions.

The dilemmas of prediction between the world wars with respect to new forms of weaponry may be stated as general propositions. Even the most promising devices require years – if not decades – of improvement before their full potential can be assessed accurately and appropriate forms of application definitively established. During this period, other technical developments, either independently, or in combination with older *matériel*, might offer an effective operational alternative to immature new technology. In addition, fiscal austerity might privilege the adoption of less capable alternative equipment because of short-run but none the less significant cost savings, or wreck promising projects through insufficient funding. The advantages of large commitment to the adoption of adolescent new technology – economies of scale in production and illuminating experience with substantial forces – must be set against the disadvantages of investing heavily in the production of hardware that was bound to become obsolete rapidly and the diversion of funds from projects of equal and even greater importance. And, finally, while perceptions of probable strategic circumstances unavoidably exert a strong influence upon decisions related to armaments, the history of war indicates that what are regarded as improbable strategic circumstances before the event often come to pass.

NOTES

1. See, for example, Stephen Roskill, *Naval Policy Between the Wars*, 2 vols (London: Collins, 1968–76), vol. II, 334; and Bryan Ranft, *Technical Change and British Naval Policy 1860–1939* (New York: Holmes & Meier, 1977), p. xi.
2. In addition to Stephen Roskill's *Naval Policy Between the Wars*, still the standard comprehensive account, and Arthur J. Marder's *Old Friends, New Enemies: The Royal Navy and the Imperial Japanese Navy; Strategic Illusions 1936–1941* (Oxford: Clarendon Press, 1981), this chapter's general view of the period was informed by the following recent articles and essays: Malcolm H. Murfett, '"Are We Ready?" The Development of American and British Naval Strategy, 1922–39', in John B. Hattendorf and Robert S. Jordan, eds, *Maritime Strategy and the Balance of Power: Britain and America in the Twentieth Century* (New York: St Martin's Press, 1989), pp. 214–42; Andrew Gordon, 'The Admiralty and Imperial Overstretch, 1902–1941', in Geoffrey Till, ed., *Seapower: Theory and Practice* (London: Frank Cass, 1994), pp. 63–85; Daniel A. Baugh, 'Confusions and Constraints: The Navy and British Defence Planning 1919–39', in N. A. M. Rodger, ed., *Naval Power in the Twentieth Century* (Annapolis, MD: Naval Institute Press, 1996), pp. 101–19; John Ferris, 'The Last Decade of British Maritime Supremacy, 1919–1929', Orest Babij, 'The Royal Navy and the Defence of the British Empire, 1928–1934', and Greg Kennedy, '1935: A Snapshot of British Imperial Defence in the Far East', in Greg Kennedy and Keith Neilson, eds, *Far-Flung Lines: Essays on Imperial Defence in Honour of Donald Mackenzie Schurman* (London: Frank Cass, 1996), pp. 124–70, 171–89, 190–215; Phillips Payson O'Brien, *British and American Naval Power: Politics and Policy, 1900–1936* (Westport, CT: Praeger, 1998); and Joseph A. Maiolo, *The Royal Navy and Nazi Germany, 1933–39: A Study in Appeasement and the Origins of the Second World War* (London: Macmillan, 1998).
3. B. R. Mitchell, *Abstract of British Historical Statistics* (Cambridge: Cambridge University Press, 1971); Paul M. Kennedy, *Rise and Fall of British Naval Mastery* (New York: Charles Scribner's Sons, 1976), pp. 271–2.
4. D. K. Brown, *A Century of Naval Construction: The History of the Royal Corps of Naval Constructors, 1883–1983* (London: Conway Maritime Press, 1983), pp. 121–3.
5. Jon Tetsuro Sumida, 'Forging the Trident: British Naval Industrial Logistics, 1914–1918', in John A. Lynn, ed., *Feeding Mars: Logistics in Western Warfare from the Middle Ages to the Present* (Boulder, CO: Westview Press, 1993), pp. 229, 249.
6. Roger Dingman, *Power in the Pacific: The Origins of Naval Arms Limitation, 1914–1922* (Chicago, IL: University of Chicago Press, 1976).
7. Jon Tetsuro Sumida, *In Defence of Naval Supremacy: Finance, Technology, and British Naval Policy, 1889–1914* (Boston, MA: Unwin Hyman, 1989; London: Routledge, 1993), pp. 19–20, 42–4.
8. John Robert Ferris, *The Evolution of British Strategic Policy, 1919–26* (London: Macmillan, 1989), pp. 132–3, and 'Last Decade of British Maritime Supremacy', pp. 137–8.
9. For navy spending authorizations of the Conservative and Labour governments in question, which differed substantially from the actual spending amounts tabulated in Table 8.1, see Sir Bernard Mallet and C. Oswald George, *British Budgets: Third Series, 1921–22 to 1932–33* (London: Macmillan, 1933), pp. 430–1.

10. Ibid. See also Jon Sumida, 'Churchill and British Sea Power, 1908–29', in R. A. C. Parker, ed., *Winston Churchill: Studies in Statesmanship* (London: Brassey's, 1995), pp. 5–21.
11. Mallet and George, *British Budgets*, pp. 446–53. See also Table 8.1.
12. Kennedy, *Rise and Fall of British Naval Mastery*, p. 272.
13. Alan Raven and John Roberts, *British Battleships of World War Two: The Development and Technical History of the Royal Navy's Battleships and Battlecruisers from 1911 to 1946* (London: Arms & Armour Press, 1976), p. 165.
14. Geoffrey Till, *Air Power and the Royal Navy, 1914–1945: A Historical Survey* (London: Jane's Publishing Company, 1979).
15. Sumida, 'Forging the Trident'.
16. Jon Tetsuro Sumida, 'British Naval Operational Logistics, 1914–1918', *Journal of Military History*, 57 (July 1993), pp. 447–80.
17. Although a smaller battle fleet still posed enormous difficulties – projected oil consumption of a Far Eastern battle fleet for one year was nearly equal to the quantity of oil issued to the fleet during the entire First World War (7.2 million tons compared with 9.1 million tons), a large load even though coal transport was eliminated. For estimated fuel consumption, see Great Britain, Admiralty, Oil Fuel Board, *First Annual Report* (December 1926), Cab. 4/16, Public Record Office, Kew. For British naval oil consumption during the First World War, see Sumida, 'British Naval Operational Logistics', p. 471.
18. Jon Tetsuro Sumida, '"The Best Laid Plans": The Development of British Battle-Fleet Tactics, 1919–1942', *International History Review*, 14 (November 1992), pp. 661–880, and Andrew Gordon, *The Rules of the Game: Jutland and British Naval Command* (Annapolis, MD: Naval Institute Press, 1996).
19. Ibid.
20. G. A. H. Gordon, *British Seapower and Procurement Between the Wars: A Reappraisal of Rearmament* (Annapolis, MD: Naval Institute Press, 1988), chs 4, 6, 20, 23.
21. Ibid., pp. 112, 124, 140, 143, 172.
22. Ibid.
23. Ibid., p. 79, and Ferris, 'Last Decade of British Maritime Supremacy', pp. 142–5, 160. See also Hugh B. Peebles, *Warshipbuilding on the Clyde: Naval Orders and the Prosperity of the Clyde Shipbuilding Industry, 1889–1939* (Edinburgh: John Donald Publishers, 1987), chs 8 and 9.
24. R. H. Thornton, *British Shipping* (Cambridge: Cambridge University Press, 1945), pp. 100–2, and Edward H. Lorenz, 'An Evolutionary Explanation for Competitive Decline: The British Shipbuilding Industry, 1890–1970', *Journal of Economic History*, 51 (December 1991), pp. 911–35.
25. M. M. Postan, *British War Production* (London: HMSO, 1952), p. 4. See also Ferris, 'Last Decade of British Maritime Supremacy', p. 144.
26. Gordon, *British Seapower and Procurement*, chs 19 and 21.
27. Peebles, *Warshipbuilding on the Clyde*, pp. 140–1.
28. For a recent general account of British naval rearmament, see David K. Brown, 'Naval Rearmament, 1930–1941: The Royal Navy', in Jürgen Rohwer, ed., *The Naval Arms Race 1930–1941* (Stuttgart: Revue Internationale D'Histoire Militaire, 1991), pp. 11–30.
29. Till, *Air Power and the Royal Navy*, and Norman Friedman, *British Carrier Aviation: The Evolution of the Ships and their Aircraft* (Annapolis, MD: Naval Institute Press, 1988).
30. Till, *Air Power and the Royal Navy*, p. 104, and tables of planned and actual aircraft deliveries to the Royal Air Force and Navy, the figures for the latter

always coming to less than 10 per cent of the total, in Postan, *British War Production*, pp. 472–85.

31. H. Clausen, 'A Report on Questions Concerning the Gunnery Efficiency of His Majesty's Navy' (1942), p. 1024, Naval Library, Ministry of Defence, London; and Lt J. V. P. Goldrick, 'For Want of a Nail ...: Royal Naval Anti-Aircraft Gunnery 1919–1939', *Journal of the Royal United Services Institute of Australia*, 6 (April 1983), pp. 62–8.

32. Roskill, *Naval Policy Between the Wars*, vol. II, pp. 489–1.

33. 'Report of Dr. C. Dannatt on American Fire Control Practice and Developments (Visit of USA and Canada – July, 1943)', p. 12, HMS *Excellent*, B15 20 (courtesy of Dr Nicholas Lambert).

34. 'Report of a Visit to USA by Commander M. J. Ross, RN of Naval Ordnance Department, June–July 1945', p. 31, HMS *Excellent*, B 15 52 (courtesy of Dr Nicholas Lambert).

35. 'Report of Dr. C. Dannatt', p. 12.

36. Ibid.

37. F. A. Kingsley, ed., *The Development of Radar Equipments for the Royal Navy, 1935–45* (London: Macmillan, 1995), pp. 16–21, 69–70.

38. John Campbell, *Naval Weapons of World War Two* (Annapolis, MD: Naval Institute Press, 1985), pp. 15–21.

39. Ibid., pp. 52–7, and Gordon, *British Seapower and Procurement*, pp. 175, 209–12.

40. Peter Elliott, *Allied Escort Ships of World War II: A Complete Survey* (Annapolis, MD: Naval Institute Press, 1977), pp. 14–16, 136–7; A. W. Watson, 'Corvettes and Frigates' (27 March 1947) in *Selected Papers on British Warship Design in World War II* (London: Conway Maritime Press, 1983), p. 85.

41. W. K. Hancock and M. M. Gowing, *British War Economy* (London: HMSO, 1949), pp. 382–8; H. Duncan Hall, *North American Supply* (London: HMSO, 1955), chs 3–5; and David Reynolds, *The Creation of the Anglo-American Alliance 1937–1941: A Study in Competitive Co-Operation* (Chapel Hill, NC: University of North Carolina Press, 1981), chs 3–7.

42. Postan, *British War Production*, pp. 231–2; and Hall, *North American Supply*, pp. 39, 116.

43. Postan, *British War Production*, pp. 484–5.

44. Owen Thetford, *British Naval Aircraft since 1912* (London: Putnam, 1958).

45. Alan Raven and John Roberts, *British Cruisers of World War Two* (Annapolis, MD: Naval Institute Press, 1980), pp. 230–2; Campbell, *Naval Weapons*, p. 19.

46. Elliott, *Allied Escort Ships*, pp. 20, 32. In 1939, the Admiralty had proposed the purchase from American shipbuilders of 16 destroyers, 70 corvettes and 136 smaller warships at a cost of $132 million; low shipping losses to submarines prior to the fall of France were the main reason the proposal failed, but the financial aspect was important. See Hall, *North American Supply*, p. 116.

47. Raven and Roberts, *British Cruisers*; Campbell, *Naval Weapons*.

48. Elliott, *Allied Escort Ships*, p. 32.

49. Thetford, *British Naval Aircraft*; Till, *Air Power and the Royal Navy*, pp. 109–10.

50. Postan, *British War Production*, pp. 358–65; Hall, *North American Supply*, pp. 413–14; Buford Rowland and William B. Boyd, *US Navy Bureau of Ordnance in World War II* (Washington, DC: GPO, 1953), ch. 11; Campbell, *Naval Weapons*, p. 75; and H. T. Lenton, *British Battleships and Aircraft Carriers* (Garden City, NY: Doubleday, 1972), pp. 131–44.

51. Thetford, *British Naval Aircraft*, p. 25; Till, *Air Power and the Royal Navy*, p. 110.

52. Roskill, *Naval Policy Between the Wars*, vol. I, and Reynolds, *Anglo-American Alliance*, pp. 54–8.
53. For the small ambitions of the Admiralty with respect to American supply of manufactured articles (as opposed to critical raw materials) as late as the autumn of 1940, see Hall, *North American Supply*, pp. 50, 110–12, 177–8.
54. See, for an especially egregious example, the testimony of Admiral A. E. M. Chatfield to the Committee of Imperial Defence on 30 July 1936, in Great Britain, Committee of Imperial Defence, *Sub-Committee on the Vulnerability of Capital Ships to Air Attack, Report, Proceedings & Memoranda: 1936*, Cab 16/147, PRO, Kew. Chatfield's testimony about aircraft and submarines, however, was conditioned by political expediency – namely, fending off the Air Force – and may not have been an accurate representation of the professional judgement of the naval staff.
55. Gordon, *British Seapower and Procurement*, p. 274.

9

Politics, Arms Control and US Naval Development in the Interwar Period

Phillips Payson O'Brien

Before the Second World War, getting new ships built was never a straight-forward task for the US Navy. More than any other great power's fleet, the US Navy's fate was subject to the unpredictable whims and fashions of a notoriously fickle political process. This was mainly because there was one extraordinary difference between the United States' naval needs for self-defence and those of any other power. The United States did not need a large navy.

To naval supporters this might seem like heresy. From the time of Alfred Thayer Mahan and Theodore Roosevelt there was a vocal segment of American society that was convinced that the country would be in the greatest danger without one of the largest fleets in the world. Before the First World War most Americans, on the other hand, were far from persuaded of this danger and in many ways they were right. It would be hard to say who represented a naval threat to the United States. The rest of the world's great powers could point, with some sincerity, to another nation that could threaten its sovereignty through sea control. Supporters of a large US fleet, meanwhile, often resorted to entities such as the Philippines or the Monroe Doctrine to support their arguments for a big navy. While these arguments carried some force, they were not ones that revolved around the national survival of the United States.

The fact was that naval issues generated little or no interest among many Americans, especially those living in the midwestern or southern parts of the country. For instance, in 1910 and 1912 when the Republican Party clearly portrayed itself as the party most in favour of increased naval construction, the Republican vote slumped.[1] It was not that the American population actively opposed naval construction, it was just that it did not care. This being the case, American congressmen often felt little political need to support a consistent naval policy. The US Navy was thus left in the perennially uncomfortable position of having little idea of what it would be allowed to build year after year. Congressional interference was not limited just to the numbers of ships built, for at times it even extended to the technological specifications of US warships. In 1903 Senator Eugene Hale of Maine, the chairman of the Senate's Naval Appropriations Committee who had a phobia of large battleships, forced the navy to build two 13,000-ton capital ships instead of the 16,000-ton vessels the fleet wanted.[2] These ships, known as the *Idaho* class, had never been conceived of by the naval professionals, so a mad scramble ensued to design a heretofore unplanned-for vessel. The results were disastrous.

By the time of the First World War some of these defects had been made good. Though the fleet still had little influence over Congress's annual building programmes, for the most part the US Navy had gained control over the technical specifications of its vessels. When this occurred the US Navy generally strove to build the most heavily armed and protected vessels possible. *Jane's Fighting Ships* referred to this American tendency for battleships as an 'everything or nothing' philosophy.[3] Certainly, when the fighting began in Europe the United States was building the largest battleships in the world.

By the US Navy's own estimations the United States' 32,000-ton *New Mexico*-class battleships, approved in 1914, were 25 per cent stronger than Germany's 28,000-ton *Bayern* class and a remarkable 38 per cent stronger than Britain's 25,750-ton *Royal Sovereign* class, both of which were approved at about the same time.[4] While these figures might have been inflated by American overoptimism, the United States' preference for vessels that were larger and stronger than anyone else's continued into the First World War. The most potent indicator of this tendency was the famous 1916 programme.

The First World War was a great boon to supporters of increased US naval strength. Before the war US naval power had been built up under Theodore Roosevelt's presidency, but had then unceremoniously stalled under the presidencies of William Howard Taft and Woodrow Wilson. The First World War, however, created a powerful domestic coalition in favour of a US Navy 'Second to None'. Two years after the commencement of hostilities, Congress passed and President Wilson signed the 1916 programme, which called for the construction of 10 battleships, six battle-cruisers, ten scout cruisers, 50 destroyers, 67 submarines and 13 other vessels. In technological terms these vessels were the crowning achievement of the American notion of overwhelming force. Each class of vessel proposed was the largest and most powerful type heretofore built anywhere in the world. Had all of these ships been built the US Navy would have become the most powerful maritime force on the globe.

The First World War was not, however, an unmixed blessing for the US Navy. Indeed, the war posed far more naval questions than it answered. It provided glimpses of a future where new technologies had the possibility of changing almost every aspect of sea fighting, but these glimpses were incomplete and somewhat ambiguous. For the US Navy, the challenges posed by the First World War would lead it to question a number of its fundamental rationales.

To begin with, however, the US Navy left the First World War much as it had entered it, by designing some of the largest and most powerful vessels around. By 1919 the United States was building *Omaha* class cruisers which weighed about 7,050 tons and sported ten 6-inch guns, vessels which were 30 per cent heavier and had a main battery 40 per cent larger than Britain's *Diomede* class cruisers. The US Navy's support for gargantuan ships can perhaps best be seen in its plan for a new class of battlecruisers, first approved in the summer of 1919. These ships, which were never built, were expected to weigh 43,500 tons and carry 12 16-inch guns.[5] Most interestingly, the lessons of the First World War were employed to create a new and very powerful kind of battlecruiser.

As first designed by the famous British Admiral John (Jacky) Fisher, battlecruisers were supposed to carry a heavy battery of guns, but be lightly armoured. This lack of armour was to be compensated for by increased speed, which in Fisher's eyes meant that a battlecruiser could fight whom it wanted when it wanted. Before the First World War began, this concept reached the point where the British were designing vessels carrying 18-inch guns, with only minimum protection.

In 1919 the Americans were turning this concept on its head, keeping the heavy battery and relatively high speed, but protecting the battlecruiser so heavily that it was, for all intents and purposes, a very fast battleship. The US Navy had been alarmed by the performance of battlecruisers during the First World War when, for instance, at the Battle of Jutland, the only major warships sunk were battlecruisers. The thin armour of HMS *Queen Mary*, HMS *Indefatigable* and HMS *Invincible* left them unable to stand up to heavy bombardment while none of the better pro-tected British battleships suffered significant damage. In 1919 the US Navy was trying to correct this battlecruiser defect by designing vessels with far greater protection, particularly from vertical damage.

One of the other lessons learned from the First World War was that combat between major vessels usually occurred at close to maximum range, so that few vessels were hit in the side, but that killing blows could be delivered vertically, onto the top of a vessel. These 1919 battlecruiser designs, therefore, saw turret protection raised by between 50 and 90 per cent, with other vertical protection, including conning towers, having their armour increased by over 100 per cent.[6] To put these changes into perspective, these 1919 US battlecruisers were to have vertical protection equivalent to, and sometimes stronger than, British battleships designed and laid down in 1913.[7]

There remains, however, an air of unreality draped around many US designs in this period. Many in the fleet seemed to believe that the First

World War and the 1916 naval programme had initiated an entirely new era in US naval history. In this new era, Congress and the presidency would annually support very substantial naval appropriations containing provision for a large number of new vessels. Nothing could be farther from the truth. Many of the navy's basic political weaknesses remained in the interwar period, and they would soon re-emerge.

In truth, the 1916 programme was an anomaly in US naval history. Only the threat of the ongoing world war was able to stir the president and Congress into such a dramatic action on the fleet's behalf. Once peace returned, it was an open question just how long this commitment would remain. To begin with, the omens seemed good. In January 1919 the House of Representatives agreed to double the 1916 programme. At the same time in Europe, during the stormy negotiations at the Paris Peace Conference, President Wilson was using the threat of more US naval building to convince the British to support a League of Nations.[8] It seemed that the US Navy could look forward to a period of increased political security.

This period, however, never materialized. Between the signing of the Versailles Treaty and the Republican Party's capture of the presidency and both houses of Congress in 1920, support for a continuing US naval build-up evaporated. In its place there appeared, within the American population in general and the political class in particular, a strong desire for a negotiated settlement to the growing international tensions over naval strength. The complexities of these international tensions cannot be fully discussed here, but one of the outcomes of American concerns about them was the famous naval arms control process which dominated much planning in the interwar period.

This process, which began at the Washington Conference of 1921–22, stretched through the Geneva Conference of 1927 and the first London Conference of 1930 and ended with the Second London Conference of 1935–36, had a profound influence on US naval building and technology. Yet, the US Navy was in many ways marginalized in the process of negotiating these agreements. Before the Washington conference, the American secretary of state, Charles Evans Hughes, politely noted the US Navy's positions, and then proceeded to disregard most of them.[9] Before the First London Conference, President Herbert Hoover was desperate to reach a deal with the British that would pre-empt an expensive cruiser construction race. Like Hughes nine years earlier, he simply disregarded the navy's advice when he thought it inconvenient and instead cut a deal with the British to limit further construction.[10]

Existing in such a world was extremely frustrating for the US Navy. Yet, it is impossible to understand the construction of the US fleet in these years without delving into the impact of the arms control process on US naval power and the navy's concurrent political weakness. There have already been a number of very substantial works, especially by Norman Friedman, which detail the host of technical changes debated within the navy during these years.[11] Instead of re-ploughing these furrows, this chapter will mostly discuss the relationship between the political situation of the US fleet in the interwar years, the naval arms control process and the eventual fleet with which the United States entered the Second World War.

Needless to say, the US Navy had an internal process for designing its naval vessels. There were, in essence, three different groupings that had some say over the matter, and they often disagreed. To start there were the various 'bureaus', committees that had existed since the nineteenth century, which still exercised real power in the US Navy. The Bureau of Construction and Repair, in particular, wielded considerable influence over the process of designing US ships. This bureau not only was responsible for producing the final plans for all vessels, it also served as a conduit of debate, through which other bureaus or even individual officers argued for different technological changes. This bureau was not, however, the only body with influence over the design process. The Bureau of Ordnance often made recommendations on such things as turret design and armour placement, while the Bureau of Aeronautics quickly became a key player in the development of naval air power.

Beyond the individual bureaus, however, the venerable General Board still retained in many ways the greatest authority over the design of new ships. Founded by executive order in 1900, the General Board had never been officially approved by Congress. However, it quickly became something close to a professional naval staff, and from its inception until 1916 was the primary forum for debating most strategic questions. In the interwar period the General Board was the body that made the final recommendations on the characteristics of new vessels and the incorporation of new technologies.

The reason the General Board began to lose some of its influence after 1916, however, was because of the creation of the post of chief of naval operations (CNO). Starting with William S. Benson, the first CNO, all individuals named to the post accumulated great authority over the existing fighting units of the navy. While the area of shipbuilding was one where a CNO's influence was actually somewhat limited, the person holding this office could exercise power when he thought it necessary.

The potential for disagreement between these different power centres became apparent not too long after the First World War ended. In 1921, when the next generation of US battleships was being planned, the different centres began to squabble. The General Board began to press for far stronger anti-aircraft protection, the Bureau of Ordnance called for side belt protection, and the Bureau of Construction and Repair put stress on the dangers posed by 'mines and depth charges' as well as the threat posed by poison gas.[12] There are two ways to look at the disparate nature of this design process. On the one hand, there was a certain amount of bitter bureaucratic infighting, which saw different elements of the navy pitted against each other. On the other hand, the system also seemed to foster a certain 'creative tension' within the US Navy. The number of different designs and technological possibilities that were discussed was quite large, due in part to a system that created power centres with quite different agendas.

The problem for the navy, however, was that at the beginning of the interwar period, it lost control over certain crucial areas of planning in the US government's rush for naval arms control. As the war receded in the early 1920s the new Harding administration, prodded along by arms control supporters in Congress, like the well-known Senator William Borah of Idaho, developed a great reluctance to finish building the behemoths of the 1916 programme. It made little economic sense to spend the millions needed to complete these vessels when US security seemed barely threatened. While the navy tried to create a sense that real threats existed from the Japanese and, to a certain degree, from the British, they were never really able to create the climate of fear needed to fund their extremely large building programmes. By 1921 Charles Evans Hughes felt confident enough in US security to offer to scrap all of the United States' 1916 programme vessels, and this offer formed the basis of the Washington Treaty signed in 1922.

The most famous agreement reached at Washington was the ratio system. Henceforth, US, British and Japanese capital ship and aircraft carrier strength was to be maintained at a level of 5–5–3. This could be seen as a public relations victory for the US Navy for it was officially recognized as the equal of the Royal Navy. Technically, however, the limits imposed by the Washington treaties upset many of the US fleet's assumptions. Future battleships, whose construction was to be delayed by a ten-year 'holiday', were henceforth to be limited to 35,000 tons and could carry nothing greater than 16-inch guns. Cruisers, which were not subject to numerical limitations, now had a treaty displacement limit of 10,000 tons and could carry nothing greater than 8-inch guns. Aircraft carriers, meanwhile, were originally going to be limited to 27,000 tons but because the United States wanted to rebuild two of the 1916 programme's battle-cruisers as aircraft carriers, this figure was raised to 33,000 tons.

These agreements were just the beginning. Since there had been no over-all cruiser limitation agreed to at Washington, the United States was eager to reach such an agreement at the next naval arms control conference, held in Geneva in 1927. Between Washington and Geneva, however, the political weakness of the US fleet returned with a vengeance. The general American view, shared by most politicians and the public, was that the Washington agreements meant that hardly any new US ships needed to be built. The British and Japanese governments, meanwhile, both recognizing

153

that there were no limits on the numbers of cruisers that they could build and both believing that they had special needs for trade protection cruisers that the United States did not, pressed ahead with new construction.[13]

The US Navy would have liked very much to join in this cruiser race, but was treated rather dismissively by Congress. Between the end of the Washington Conference and 1926, Congress did authorize the construction of eight 10,000-ton cruisers, but only provided enough money for one to be built. This one cruiser, along with a single submarine and six river gunboats, made up the sum total of US naval construction between 1922 and 1926.

The US Navy's political weakness had let it fall further and further behind the British and Japanese in cruiser strength, a deficit that the Coolidge administration hoped to paper over at the Geneva Conference by extending the 5–5–3 ratio to all auxiliary vessels including cruisers. However, at this point the British government, led by its chancellor of the exchequer, Winston Churchill, came unwittingly to the US Navy's rescue. The United States' soporific cruiser policy lulled the British into thinking that they could reject US claims to parity and they refused to let the negotiators reach a deal at Geneva.[14] Their behaviour was considered so insulting that President Coolidge, who up to this point had been a rabid supporter of reductions in naval spending, unexpectedly sprang into life. Believing that the British had insulted the United States grievously, Coolidge called for the construction of 25 new 10,000-ton cruisers, a programme that would have left the United States with the most modern and powerful cruiser force in the world.

Congress, while also feeling shabbily treated by the British, could not stomach such a massive appropriation and instead supported a plan calling for 15 new cruisers. For a while it seemed like the US Navy had broken free from its political isolation, and that naval issues once again were a topic of national debate. Yet, this period of optimism was to prove even more short-lived than the period between the passing of the 1916 programme and the Washington Conference. Soon, Coolidge's anti-British animosity was replaced in the White House by Herbert Hoover's Quaker sensibilities. By nature Hoover had no desire to engage in a naval building race, an instinct that was further reinforced by the economic downturn that began in late 1929. This Great Depression led the new president to call for new economies in military and naval spending, and negotiations with the British government were soon reinvigorated. Prime Minister Ramsay MacDonald visited the United States and the two leaders hammered out the framework for a yardstick agreement, whereby Britain would be allowed a larger overall tonnage allowance in smaller cruisers to offset the fact that the United States could build a larger number of 10,000-ton vessels.

This compromise formed the basis of the agreements reached at the First London conference of 1930, which has been seen as the highpoint of the naval arms control process. By this point, many supporters of a larger US Navy seemed gripped by despair. In the aftermath of the London conference Hoover pressed for even more economies in the fleet. Soon a number of retired American admirals and the US Navy League launched bitter attacks on the Hoover administration's policies.[15] It seemed that in ten years the navy had been routed on almost every front by the naval arms control process and the general indifference of American politicians.

Had the relatively prosperous conditions and relatively stable international outlook of the late 1920s continued on into the 1930s, there is no telling how long the US Navy's stay in purgatory would have lasted. However, soon after the first London Conference, the international consensus upon which the naval arms control process rested, began to unravel. The Great Depression caused the Japanese to chafe against the naval limitations even more than they had previously, and helped support the rise of Adolf Hitler to power in Germany. Also, the poor economic situation in the United States helped erode public support for Herbert Hoover (no bad thing as far as the US Navy was concerned) and in 1932 he lost his bid for re-election to Franklin D. Roosevelt. Roosevelt was the most consistently pro-navy president to hold the office since his distant cousin Theodore had been chief executive, between 1901 and 1909.

Franklin Roosevelt viewed the relationship between the depression and naval spending very differently. He saw increased spending on naval construction as a way to relieve unemployment in crucial industrial cities and to help reflate the national economy. Soon Congress, with the passage of the Vinson–Trammel Act, had appropriated enough money to build the US Navy up to its full treaty complement. Thus, when the great naval powers reassembled in London in 1935, the fortunes of the US Navy seemed to be on the upswing. They were further aided by the results of the conference itself, which witnessed the beginning of the end for the arms control process. The Japanese delegation came to London with an uncompromising demand for a 'common upper limit', or complete naval parity with the United States and Great Britain. It was a concession that neither of the dominant naval powers was willing to make, and the Japanese duly withdrew from the process.

The end of the naval arms control process was something that many in the navy had wanted for years. From Washington onwards critics had arisen to savage this or that injustice that the process had supposedly imposed on US naval power.[16] Now, with it lifted, so it seemed, the US Navy could finally fight for and gain the kinds of building programmes that it had always wanted and needed. Yet, one should not accept the navy's relief at being freed from the naval arms control process as a proper verdict on the process itself. Far from holding the navy back, it is quite possible that the naval arms control process played an important role in preparing the US Navy to fight the next war at sea.

There are a number of reasons why this is possible. In the first place had there been a great deal of naval building immediately after the First World War there was no guarantee that the US Navy would have built the 'proper' vessels for the next great sea war. The 'lessons' of the First World War needed time to be digested. Indeed, the First World War opened up the prospect of a far 'broader' future for naval technology than had heretofore existed. Going into the war most powers seemed content to rely on battleship strength as the primary indicator of overall naval strength. The war itself, however, opened up the possibility, without confirming the likelihood, that submarines and naval airpower could displace battleships as the most important elements of national naval strength. The effectiveness of Germany's submarine offensive against British trade and the increasing use of aircraft in a military capacity, convinced some, but certainly not all, in the US Navy that the fleet should entrust its future to whole new classes of warships.

With hindsight it is easy to view some of the advocates of submarine warfare or naval air power almost as visionaries. Yet, at the time, trying to guess which new technologies would have the greatest impact on any future naval war was very much a 'hit or miss' proposition. The US Navy, like many large bureaucratic institutions, had a strong conservative streak. To begin with, the navy returned to its pre-war battle doctrine of relying on large battleships to dominate an enemy.[17] The extra construction of such vessels in the early 1920s would have done relatively little to add to US naval strength in the Second World War, and quite possibly would have soaked up many dollars that were spent usefully in other areas. There are a number of other instances where supposedly obvious lessons learned from the First World War turned out to be flawed. One of the most interesting, for the Americans, was the torpedo frenzy of the early 1920s.

The origins of this movement were simple. The effectiveness of the torpedo in the First World War led many in the US Navy to push for extra torpedo tubes on almost every class of warship, except for aircraft carriers. By the summer of 1921, the General Board was even arguing that battleships should be fitted with a far stronger complement of underwater torpedo tubes.[18] On the other hand, fear of torpedo attacks was leading many in the fleet to call for drastic protective measures. Large blisters were fitted to many vessels and some were even fitted with anti-torpedo netting, long strips of wire netting that were suspended a few metres from the ships' side.

Eventually, this movement petered out almost as quickly as it started. While many ships did retain anti-torpedo blisters, most of the other changes were relatively quickly scaled back. By 1928 all torpedo tubes either had been removed or were in the process of being removed from every US capital ship.[19] By 1937 the General Board was recommending the removal of all torpedo tubes from light cruisers.[20] Of all the innovations, only anti-torpedo blisters seemed to have a future.

The US Navy's experiences with torpedo and anti-torpedo technology remains a salutary warning to those who see almost all technological change as something to be incorporated immediately into naval building. It also shows the difficult questions that naval planners in the interwar period were trying to answer. By looking briefly at some discussions over submarine and aircraft carrier development, two of the most contentious areas of interwar period naval debate, the peculiar pitfalls lurking for naval shipbuilders in these years becomes more apparent. Perhaps the best way to see how this worked is in the different debates that surrounded US submarine construction in the 1920s. The possibilities which submarine technology seemed to offer the US Navy led to discussion of a wide range of issues. Different groups arose to argue for the development of buoyant mines, underwater guns, sonar torpedoes or 'listening devices' (sonar detection).[21] There was also one group of officers, centred around Lieutenant Commander F. S. Craven, who began to argue that submarine development spelt the end of the traditional surface vessel. They began pressing for the construction of submarine 'capital ships', vessels more than 20 or even 25 times as large as the typical German submarine afloat at the end of the First World War. In April 1920, Craven came up with plans for a 20,000-ton 'submersible cruiser', which sported four 12-inch guns, 14 torpedo tubes and four anti-aircraft guns.[22] This underwater behemoth was also capable or travelling at a very respectable 25 knots per hour and had a cruising radius of approximately 20,000 miles. After the Plans Division of the Bureau of Construction and Repair criticized the practicality of such a design, new ideas were hatched for submersible cruisers of more than 13,000 tons which sported four 8-inch guns and, interestingly enough, carried a number of aeroplanes.[23]

The backers of such a plan, and there were a significant number, argued that submarines had made surface ships redundant. A submarine, they argued, could inflict almost as much damage as a battleship, but remain practically immune to attack from other vessels and even aeroplanes.[24] It could also, because of its enormous range and offensive punch, stretch an opponent's fleet to breaking point.

The problems with building such vessels, however, were clear. Constructing an underwater platform with the stability needed to fire large naval guns seemed almost impossible to the vessel's critics. Ultimately, and probably wisely, the General Board lacked the stomach for such a grand project. Yet, to write off the submersible cruiser as merely a flight of fancy is a disservice. While gargantuan submarines as such were never built, the idea of a submarine with a huge cruising radius, which could exhaust an enemy's resources, was enormously appealing. Such a vessel fitted perfectly into the US Navy's greatest and most developed war plan of the interwar period, War Plan Orange. These plans, for an offensive war in the western Pacific by the US fleet against the Japanese, were based on the assumption that a powerful US force could be shepherded safely across vast distances. If the US Navy could develop a submarine with the range necessary to help protect such a force and at the same time threaten Japanese naval assets, it would have benefited enormously.

With this in mind the navy began to develop the idea of a smaller cruiser. Such a vessel would not mount a battery of huge guns but would be capable of travelling great distances and inflicting real damage on enemy commercial and military vessels. In 1923, plans for a 2,600-ton submarine with two 6-inch guns were developed.[25] As time went by even more of the exotic touches first thought of in 1920 were dropped, but the basic plan remained. In 1925 the General Board came out against cruiser submarines capable of carrying planes and in 1928 the submarine's battery was reduced to one 4-inch gun.[26] Yet, the concept of the long-distance cruiser submarine persisted throughout the 1930s. At that point, however, its method of attack was more traditional, relying overwhelmingly on torpedoes. However, the idea of a long-range attack sub formed the basis of many US submarine designs of the 1930s, including the famous *Gato* class, first approved as part of the 1939 building programme. When the Second World War began in the Pacific, the ability of the Americans to project submarine power into the western Pacific was a crucial element in the defeat of Japan.

If the cruiser submarine debate began in the 1920s and quietened in the 1930s, the debate over US naval air power moved to the forefront in this latter decade. The discussion over the United States' aircraft carriers is relatively well known. At the end of the First World War there were plans for both large and small carriers.[27] In 1920, plans were assembled for a 34,500-ton carrier with an 840-foot flight deck, a vessel far larger than anything heretofore constructed.[28] Yet, the carriers with which the fleet eventually ended up came directly out of the Washington conference. When the US delegation agreed to scrap all its large capital ships under construction, the navy was given the unfinished hulls of the battlecruisers *Lexington* and *Saratoga* to develop as aircraft carriers. When these vessels were converted, a process that was completed in 1927 and 1928, they weighed approximately 33,000 tons, and could each carry a complement of almost 100 planes. They were by far the fastest and most powerful aircraft carriers in the world, and it seemed for a time that the US Navy was, with hindsight, making all the right technological choices. The General Board, for one, was constantly pushing naval aviation. One of the reasons it was reluctant to support the construction of a large cruiser submarine in the early 1920s was that it afforded a higher priority to building up US naval aviation.[29] It seemed as if the Americans were moving towards the idea of a powerful fleet of strike carriers.

It was at this point, interestingly enough, that the whole notion of large, US strike carriers was called into question. The notion that the main role of carriers was to serve as scouts for a fleet of battleships had persisted since the First World War.[30] From this perspective, the United States, for a number of reasons, needed a large number of smaller carriers. The *Lexington* and *Saratoga* were attacked as an unnecessary drain on US aircraft carrier tonnage, which was limited to 135,000 tons by the Washington agreements. By the late 1920s and early 1930s a powerful movement began in the navy for the United States to build a new class of very small carriers. In 1928 the General Board approved the construction of a 13,800-ton vessel, one barely more than 40 per cent as large as the *Lexington* and *Saratoga*.[31] In 1931 the USS *Ranger*, a carrier of little more than 14,000 tons was actually laid down, to be successfully completed in 1934. The *Ranger* was slow, extremely lightly armed, but could carry a relatively high number of planes. Many in the fleet believed that the *Ranger* design, even with its slow speed, was to be preferred to large carriers.[32]

A few years of working with such a vessel, however, were enough to make the US Navy revert to more traditional notions. The *Ranger*'s drawbacks, which did not show up well on paper, proved a real handicap when operating with the fleet. Its unreliability and lack of speed made it difficult for the *Ranger* to keep up with the main battle fleet and impossible for it to function as a strike carrier. When the next round of carrier construction began with the building of the *Yorktown* and *Enterprise*, the US Navy compromised. It opted for vessels of 20,000 tons that could steam as quickly as the *Lexington* and *Saratoga* and carry a complement of over 80 aeroplanes. Only at this point, according to Friedman, did the United States actually begin to construct 'modern' carriers.[33]

These examples are but some of the debates about naval technology that swirled around the US fleet in the interwar period. Undoubtedly some decisions were rightly taken and some were less successful, though in many ways deciding which choices were right or wrong is of little interest here. What is important is how, because of the different decisions possible, the naval arms control process actually served the US Navy's interest. The final reason that this was true has to do with the fleet's political weakness. Had there been a naval race it was quite possible that the United States might have been left behind. What is apparent from interwar period history, at least until the mid-1930s, is that the US Navy remained extremely vulnerable. George Baer has correctly described the fleet's role as 'passive', and even this might be too kind.[34] Once the excitement of the First World War began to subside, the US Navy seemed helpless in its fight to secure new ships from Congress. With the exception of the cruiser programme approved after the collapse of the Geneva Conference, the navy received almost nothing until the advent of Franklin Roosevelt. Without the arms control process restraining naval building in the other powers, particularly Britain and Japan, there was no guarantee that the US Navy would have retained the status it won at the Washington Conference.

Also, as the navy of world's largest and most productive economy, the US fleet wanted other powers to be kept relatively as weak as possible. Naval ships were the most complex and technologically advanced machines of warfare in the pre-atomic, industrial age. US economic strength meant that it could produce naval vessels at a far greater rate, and in far larger quantity, than any other power. Therefore, in preparing for the next war it made great sense to keep every other power's peace-time building to a minimum. This lesson was borne out in the Second World War. The Japanese Navy, which ran riot in the Pacific for the first few months of the war, was actually dependent upon a relatively small number of major surface ships to maintain its momentum. Between 1930 and 1935, when they were still restrained by the limits of the naval arms control process, the Japanese began the construction of only one aircraft carrier, the *Soryu*, and no battleships.[35] Between the end of the naval arms control process and 1939, the Japanese built at a far higher pace, beginning three front-line aircraft carriers, *Hiryu, Shokaku* and *Zuikaku*, and the two largest battleships ever constructed, the massive *Yamato and Musashi*.[36] The fact that the Japanese were reliant upon so few major naval units meant that when they suffered one major defeat, which they did at the Battle of Midway in June 1942, they could never fully recover. From that point on, the United States' economic strength allowed them to construct far more vessels with which the Japanese could not contend. While the naval arms control process did not allow the US fleet to develop in the ways that many would have wished, it helped make the next war at sea 'winnable' for the US Navy.

NOTES

1. In 1910 the Republican Party lost control of the House of Representatives and in 1912 it lost the presidency and control of the Senate.
2. Phillips O'Brien, *British and American Naval Power: Politics and Policies 1900–1936* (Westport, CT: Praeger Press, 1998), p. 21.
3. *Jane's Fighting Ships of World War I* (1990), p. 134.
4. General Board Subject File (GBSF), National Archives, Washington DC, 420, Memorandum, 4 December 1914.
5. Design Data for US Vessels, Bureau of Construction and Repair (BCR), Memorandum, 17 June 1919.
6. Ibid.
7. *Jane's Fighting Ships*, p. 35.
8. Harold Sprout and Margaret Sprout, *Toward a New Order of Seapower* (Princeton, NJ: 1943; New York: Greenwood Press, 1969), pp. 62–72; Arthur Marder,

From the Dreadnought to Scapa Flow, vol. V (London: Oxford University Press, 1970), pp. 234–7; O'Brien, *British and American Naval Power*, pp. 142–5.

9. O'Brien, *British and American Naval Power*, p. 161.
10. Ibid, pp. 211–13.
11. See Norman Friedman, *US Aircraft Carriers: An Illustrated Design History* (London: Arms and Armour Press, 1983); *US Battleships: An Illustrated Design History* (London: Arms and Armour Press, 1986); *US Cruisers: An Illustrated Design History* (London: Arms and Armour Press, 1985); *US Destroyers: An Illustrated Design History* (Annapolis, MD: Naval Institute Press, 1982).
12. BCR, Design Data, Memorandum, 8 June 1921.
13. By 1925 the British had 49 cruisers either built or being built, while the United States had ten. The Japanese, meanwhile, had laid down 19 cruisers between 1919 and 1924.
14. O'Brien, *British and American Naval Power*, pp. 186–94.
15. In President Hoover's papers there is list of the attacks made against his policies. See Hoover MSS, Herbert Hoover Presidential Library, West Branch IA, C/P, Statements by Naval Officers, 25 August 1930.
16. O'Brien, *British and American Naval Power*, pp. 169–70.
17. George Baer, *One Hundred Years of Seapower: The US Navy 1890–1990* (Stanford, CA: Stanford University Press, 1994), p. 83.
18. GBSF 420-11, GB to secretary of the navy, 29 August 1921.
19. GBSF 420-11, GB to secretary of the navy, 14 February 1928.
20. GBSF 420-8, CNO to Ordnance Bureau, 30 June 1937.
21. GBSF 420-15, Memorandum, 25 January 1918. See also GB to secretary of the navy, 11 February 1921.
22. BCR, Design Data, Joint Letter, 18 May 1920.
23. Ibid., Plans Division Memorandum, 5 December 1920. See also 'Cruiser Submarine' plans, BCR, 23 October 1920.
24. GBSF 420-15, Hopkins Report, 24 April 1940.
25. GBSF 420-15, GB to secretary of the navy, 10 April 1923.
26. GBSF 420-15, GB to secretary of the navy, 13 May 1925; GB to secretary of the navy, 14 May 1928.
27. BCR, Design Data, AC memorandum, 17 March 1919.
28. Ibid., 24 November 1920.
29. GBSF 420-15, GB to secretary of the navy, 25 May 1921.
30. BCR, Design Data, Goodall to BCR, 22 August 1918.
31. GBSF 420-7, GB to secretary of the navy, 16 March 1928.
32. GBSF 420-7, much discussion of Ranger design.
33. Friedman, *US Aircraft* Carriers, p. 79.
34. George Baer, *One Hundred Years of Seapower: The US Navy 1890–1990* (Stanford, CA: Stanford University Press, 1994), p. 117.
35. O'Brien, *British and American Naval Power*, Appendix II.
36. Ibid.

PART III

PREPARING FOR THE COLD WAR

10

The Russian Navy in the Gorshkov Era

Evan Mawdsley

The build-up of the Russian Navy in the post-war years is now an historical event with a beginning and an end. The cruiser *Sverdlov* and the aircraft carrier designed under the code-name 'Eagle' (*Orel*) entered service at an interval of nearly 40 years and are symbols of post-war Russia's naval programme and ambitions. The handsome 17,970-ton *Sverdlov*, completed in May 1952, took part in the 1953 British coronation review at Spithead. She seemed to mark, with her 13 completed sister ships of the Project 68 *bis* class, the naval coming of age of the Russian superpower. The first carrier of the 67,500-ton 'Eagle' design, also known as Pr. 1143.5, was laid down in 1982 as *Riga* (now *Kuznetsov*). Meanwhile, in the building yard at Nikolaev, 'leaked' US satellite photographs and artists' reconstructions made her a centrepiece of the Reagan administration's campaign against the expansion of Soviet military power. As with the navies of other countries, the Russian experience is often identified with one particular individual. The Tirpitz or Fisher of post-war Russia was Admiral S. G. Gorshkov, who was commander-in-chief for a remarkable period of nearly 30 years, from 1955 to 1985. The basic questions asked here are why the Russians embarked on an ambitious naval programme in the 'Gorshkov era', and what factors shaped that programme. Although much has been written about the Soviet Navy's development, the present chapter has the advantage both of hindsight, and of new information, mainly about ships and weapons systems,[1] but also about aspects of naval policy.[2]

The first phase in the post-war history of the navy, falling before the 'Gorshkov era' proper, was covered by a 1946–55 Ten-Year Plan. This was a conventional, even old-fashioned, naval build-up, projecting 4 battle-cruisers, 30 light cruisers, 188 destroyers, 177 frigates and 367 submarines.[3] Technically, many of the units that were actually completed in the early Cold War, including the *Sverdlov* class, were 'corrected' versions of pre-war designs.[4] The shipyards also produced large numbers of destroyers to pre-war (Pr. 30-*bis*/SKORY) and post-war (Pr. 56/KOTLIN) designs, and 215 medium submarines of the Pr. 613/WHISKEY class, a massive programme for peacetime.[5] Naval policy in this period was dominated by Stalin and by Admiral N. G. Kuznetsov, who was commander-in-chief of the navy from 1939 to January 1947, and from July 1951 to January 1956.

The years 1955 and 1956 were a break in the history of the post-war navy, the beginning of a second phase. Admiral Kuznetsov was sacked in December 1955, essentially because he protested against delays in confirming the 1956–65 Ten-Year Plan, an ambitious programme which included aircraft carriers and amphibious ships.[6] His replacement was the 45-year-old former commander-in-chief of the Black Sea Fleet, Admiral Gorshkov. The years when Nikita Khrushchev dominated the Kremlin as CPSU first secretary – essentially 1955–64 – were volatile and contradictory in politics, economics and foreign and security policy. The new party leadership, which consolidated its power in 1955–57, was interested in economic reform, and this demanded cuts in the huge military establishment inherited from Stalin. The armed forces high command, dominated by the army and from February 1955 by the person of Marshal Zhukov as head of a unified Ministry of Defence, was concerned with other military priorities, including modernization and the rapid deployment of strategic nuclear forces. Neither was prepared to continue paying for the upkeep and development of a conventional fleet, which was taking up a very large share of defence expenditure.[7]

One senior naval officer, Admiral Nikolai Amel'ko, called this the 'dark period',[8] and modern Russian writers on the navy are unanimous in their condemnation of Khrushchev. The most bitterly remembered victims of the cuts were the final 13 *Sverdlovs*; the building programme was suspended in 1955 and in 1959 seven hulls in an advanced stage of construction were scrapped. Other naval building was cut back, including a huge diesel submarine programme.[9] The navy lost control over its large (land-based) fighter and attack-plane force and the naval infantry was disbanded. Khrushchev argued that in an age of missiles and nuclear weapons surface warships were obsolete; the Soviet Union could be defended by missile-carrying land-based bombers and by nuclear submarines. Naval construction was greatly reduced. Several years were spent within the navy determining how to proceed, and the 1959–65 naval Seven-Year Plan, its start and end matching the national economic plan, was modest. A few destroyers (Pr. 57/KRUPNY) were converted to carry surface-to-surface missiles, but the only new major surface ships were four destroyer-sized vessels of Pr. 58/KYNDA; four 7,600-ton ASW ships were also approved under Khrushchev, the Pr. 1134/KRESTA I.

The navy's complaint was that Khrushchev was a 'voluntarist'; in Western terms he was looking for a 'quick fix' to the USSR's security problems. On the other hand, key existing lines of development **were** vigorously pursued in these years. The first Soviet nuclear submarine, *K-3*, entered service in March 1959, the lead boat of 13 Pr. 627/NOVEMBER class. Cruise and ballistic missiles were introduced into the fleet, and even the first nuclear weapons. The navy began a strategic role with the commissioning from 1959 of 23 Pr. 629/GOLF class diesel submarines, and a year later the first of eight nuclear Pr. 658/HOTEL class; each was armed with three ballistic missiles.[10] These were followed in 1960 by the first of five purpose-built diesel cruise-missile submarines of Pr. 659/ECHO I. Naval sources (including Gorshkov in his memoirs) now make relatively little of another aspect of maritime power, the development of a whole new branch of naval service, the so-called 'Naval Missile-Carrier Command' (*Morskaia raketonosnaia aviatsiia* or MRA). The MRA with its anti-shipping missiles was responsible for *oceanic* attack while the fighters, strike aircraft and bombers of the Soviet Air Force proper (the *VVS*) were now responsible for attacks in coastal areas and enclosed seas. The MRA inherited many of the Air Force's medium-range jet bombers, which had in turn been replaced after a short operational life by ballistic missiles; the most important 'missile-carrier' (*raketonosets*) was the Tu-16/BADGER, of which some 500 were to operate in the maritime role from 1954.[11]

The navy became increasingly active towards the end of the Khrushchev years, with a number of port visits. The first large-scale 'oceanic' manoeuvres were held in the Norwegian Sea in 1961, code-named 'Poliarnyi krug' (Polar Circle). Submariners competed for national attention with cosmonauts as *K-3* visited the North Pole in July 1962, although three months later the only warships that could be deployed to support the Cuban missile adventure were Pr. 641/FOXTROT class diesel submarines.

The third stage, roughly from 1965 to 1980, involved a more steady build-up, with a smaller number of types and longer production runs. Khrushchev had been ousted in October 1964, and Leonid Brezhnev replaced him as first secretary. The navy found him more sympathetic to its case, and easier to deal with.[12] The naval build-up was covered by rolling Ten-year Plans for 1966–75 and 1971–80. Most notable was the development of the nuclear submarine force. The Soviet Union built 70 Pr. 667/YANKEE-DELTA class ballistic missile submarines between 1967 and 1981, four to five boats a year. At the same time there was a very long production run of a hunter-killer nuclear submarine, 47 Pr. 671/VICTOR, between 1967 and 1987, two a year. Surface ships were also built in this way, to more advanced designs. Compared with two earlier small batches of missile ships, Soviet yards produced long runs of 'Large ASW Ships' (*BPK*), some 17 more Pr. 1134 (actually two different classes, known in the West as KRESTA II and KARA) in 1967–79, and 20 smaller gas-turbine powered Pr. 61/KASHIN class during 1964–73. Soviet interest in ship-board aviation developed, and *Moskva* and *Leningrad*, two 14,655-ton Pr. 1123 class helicopter carriers, entered service in 1967 and 1969. There was further development of the MRA. The first version of the Tu-22M (BACKFIRE) missile-carrier entered service in 1972, but significant numbers became available in the late 1970s and 1980s, up to a total of 200 aircraft.[13] This period was also, strikingly, one of much greater activity at sea – especially the *Okean* exercise in 1970 and the 1973 Arab–Israeli war.

The late Brezhnev and late Gorshkov years, roughly 1975–85, were a fourth period. Although this coincided with what has been called the 'Second Cold War', the units which entered service were built to specifications dating back to the late 1960s. New classes of large surface ship entered service from 1980, including the Pr. 1155/*Udaloi* ASW ship (the first unit was commissioned 1980), Pr. 956/*Sovremennnyi* class destroyer (1981), and the 11,300-ton Pr. 1164/*Slava* class missile cruiser (1983). A fourth class was the 28,000-ton missile cruiser (ARKR) Pr. 1144/*Kirov*, the USSR's first nuclear-powered surface warship, which entered service in 1980. These were related to the 'submarine heavy cruisers' of the Pr. 949/OSCAR class of 17,000 tons (1986) in that both were platforms for the big P-700 ('*Granit*') surface-to-surface missile. Size was also a feature of the 33,800-ton Pr. 941/TYPHOON class submarine, the first of which entered service in December 1981, built around a large solid-fuel multiple-warhead ballistic missile. An even more remarkable feature of this fourth period was the deployment of Soviet aircraft carriers: Pr. 1143/*Kiev*, equipped with a vertical take-off and landing (VTOL) jet strike aircraft, entered service in 1975, and the *Eagle* conventional carrier design was taking shape.

The post-script was the collapse of the Soviet Navy in the late 1980s. This came from the economic and political dislocation of the country, and a reorientation of foreign policy. Gorshkov was removed as commander-in-chief in December 1985; he died in May 1988 and was spared seeing the worst. The USSR disintegrated in 1991, major surface-ship building yards in Ukraine were lost, and the Russian Federation and Ukraine had a bitter dispute about the Sevastopol naval base. The 1981–90 Ten-Year Plan was uncompleted. The second conventional carrier, *Variag*, the sister of *Riga/Kuznetsov*, would be written off, incomplete, in 1993. The fourth nuclear-powered missile cruiser of the *Kirov* class, *Petr Velikii* ('Peter the Great', formerly *Iurii Andropov*), was commissioned only in May 1998, having been laid down in 1986 – and to a design dating back to 1972. Many of the ships constructed at great cost in the era of Brezhnev and Gorshkov had short service lives. *Novorossiisk*, the third *Kiev*-class VTOL carrier, commissioned in August 1982, was struck off in June 1993, and scrapped in South Korea. With no replacement for their aircraft, *Kiev* and *Minsk* also left service in the 1990, along with the older helicopter carriers *Moskva* and *Leningrad*.[14] Ironically, even a carrier named after Gorshkov himself suffered a difficult fate; the VTOL carrier *Admiral Flota Sovetskogo Soiuza Gorshkov* (formerly *Baku*, the fourth *Kiev*) took nine years to build, and at the time of writing is most likely to be sold abroad.

Going beyond this waste has been a terrifying environmental problem. Some 249 nuclear submarines were built and, by the late 1990s, 149 had been decommissioned. A number of these had been irresponsibly scuttled and the great majority lay rusting in port awaiting de-fuelling. Many of the ballistic missile submarines were dismantled under the US 'Cooperative Threat Reduction' programme, and even the Pr.941/TYPHOON class may be part of this.

Such was the course of the rise and fall of the Soviet Navy. What were the driving forces? The objectives of Soviet foreign policy and the operational objectives of the combined-arms forces deployed on land in Central Europe can be debated, but the strategic posture of the Soviet Navy, at least relative to the US Navy, was defensive throughout most of this period. Many of the technical developments were reactions to developments initiated by the *veroiatnyi protivnik* (likely opponent).[15] The Americans (and British) had huge fleets built in the Second World War; Stalin's pre-war building programme had been fatally interrupted in 1941, and much of what had been built was lost. The danger was not only Western task forces of the kind seen in the Second World War and Korea but also, for a period in the 1950s, nuclear strikes from US carriers. The Americans laid down five more giant carriers in the 1950s alone. Although we still know little about Soviet naval war plans, the stress in the early Soviet planning was on medium-range and short-range forces to defend coastal waters. The large numbers of naval units resulted in part from the need to face potential threats in four different areas, the Baltic, the Black Sea, the Arctic Ocean and the Pacific, which could not readily reinforce one another. The nature of Russian policy was reflected in an asymmetric approach; the Russians did not attempt to match the West ship for ship, at least not for much of the era. From the mid-1950s the Soviets developed a range of forces – surface, submarine and air – particularly designed to deal with the US carrier task forces; a special feature was the development of anti-ship missiles. The Soviet Navy also had to respond to a new type of threat with the US deployment of submarine-launched ballistic missiles (SLBMs) from 1960.[16] Much of the Soviet build-up in the 1960s can be seen as an attempt to counter Polaris, notably in the helicopter carriers, 'large ASW ships', hunter-killer nuclear submarines and long-range ASW aircraft. This effort was, however, constantly outpaced by the growing range of the new American SLBMs.

The defensive mission of the Soviet Navy resembled what had been developed with the submarines and shore-based bombers of the early 1930s – albeit with weapons of much greater power and longer range. A completely new mission for the navy, and another determinant of its development, was the strategic nuclear one.[17] In the 1940s and 1950s, the USSR was within range of US bombers based on the Eurasian periphery but had only the most limited means of attacking North America. The Pr.

169

627/NOVEMBER class nuclear submarine was originally conceived to carry the massive 1550mm T-15 strategic nuclear torpedo,[18] but in the end, as we have seen, reliance was placed on missiles. The rationale for initially building up the early SLBM force is clear enough, given the slow deployment through the mid-1960s of Soviet land-based ICBMs. What is less obvious is the continuation of this programme at a time when the USSR had other kinds of strategic nuclear missiles, especially a huge force of land-based ICBMs. This strategic role mixed subtly with the reactive nature of Soviet policy. The USSR turned from finding (asymmetrical) counters to the US bomber force in the 1950s, to copying the Polaris SLBM force in the 1960s. The second generation of Soviet strategic missile submarines was an analogue of the 16-missile *George Washington* class Polaris boats of 1960. The Pr. 671/YANKEE class were unofficially known in Soviet service as *Ivan Vashington* and *Dzhorzhik* (Little George).[19] The Soviet leadership evidently found it important symbolically to compete with Americans in all types of strategic forces. Meanwhile SLBMs were a bargaining chip in the Strategic Arms Limitations Talks which began in 1969, and, during the negotiations, the Americans encouraged the Soviets in the direction of less vulnerable sea-based systems, which many theorists regarded as inherently less likely to trigger off a nuclear exchange. The last word in the Gorshkov era were the Pr. 941/TYPHOON 'submarine heavy cruisers', intended to match the contemporary *Ohio* class with their 24 'Trident' missiles. These were built to carry 20 solid fuel R-39/STURGEON, each with ten warheads. The technical specification was confirmed in December 1972, and first boat, *TK-208*, entered service in December 1981; the missiles became operational at the very end of the Gorshkov era, in 1984.[20]

As was the case with Western navies, there was a tension between general purpose naval forces and strategic naval forces. As we have seen, the production run of Pr. 671/YANKEE-DELTA reached 70 boats, and this programme placed a substantial burden on the budget of the Soviet Navy and its shipyard capacity. The trough of *general purpose* naval expenditure, according to CIA estimates, was 1970–74, when it went down to about 11 billion rubles per annum (1982 prices). This corresponded to the peak of expenditure of the strategic offence mission (including missile submarines and SLBMs) at about 12 billion rubles.[21]

A third general explanation for the growth of the Soviet Navy was its real and potential geo-strategic role.[22] This had more to do with a changing world and with Soviet foreign policy than with the Soviet Navy; in the 1950s, 1960s and 1970s Moscow established relations, some of them very close, with countries whose status had previously been colonial or semi-colonial. Admiral Gorshkov and the naval planners, however, were well positioned to exploit this to obtain resources. Paradoxically, Khrushchev both greatly expanded Soviet interest in the Third World in the mid-1950s

170

and advocated a fleet of submarines and missile-carrying bombers optimized for fighting a nuclear war. It is often argued that the latter view was changed by the Cuban fiasco of October 1962, when the US Navy's blockade undid the deployment of Soviet strategic missiles.[23] In fact, however, a change can be seen before this, in line with growing Soviet interest in the Third World. Khrushchev himself made a speech in May 1962 – five months *before* the Cuban crisis – when he said:

> The Americans often send squadrons of their ships to other countries and with this influence, to a significant degree, the politics of those countries. It wouldn't be a bad thing if we too had a fleet like that, which we could send to those countries where the situation is going in our favour, for example in Cuba, in African countries, etc.... It's time for us to 'wear long trousers'. We have gone through the transition period. There is now an even balance between our military strength and that of our opponent. But soon that balance will be changed in our favour, and we must become more active. And at that time a leading role will be played by our fleet.[24]

Certainly Soviet naval activities increased greatly at this time. According to one study, Soviet out-of-area ship-days increased from about 800 in 1956 to 9,100 in 1964.[25]

Under Brezhnev the range of the Soviet Union's contacts abroad were even wider, and its support for 'anti-imperialist' allies and 'wars of national liberation' continued. Especially significant was the establishment of a permanent naval command (an *eskadra* or squadron) in the Mediterranean in 1967 and the acquisition of overseas basing rights. Out-of-area ship-days soared to 53,200 in 1974, with 20,600 of these in the Mediterranean. In the 1970s there was a growth of Soviet deployments in new areas. Out-of-area ship-days in the Pacific increased from 5,900 in 1970 to 11,800 in 1980, and in the Indian Ocean from 700 to 11,800.[26] Soviet ships that entered service in the 1970s had longer range, greater habitability and more capability for power projection. A high point was the visit by the VTOL carrier *Minsk* to Angola in 1979.

On the other hand, there was relatively little investment in naval forces that were especially suitable to what might be called this 'colonial' role. General-purpose aircraft carriers capable of projecting air power, a fleet train to support them, and long-range amphibious forces only existed in pilot form. Much was made of the Pr. 1174 amphibious ship *Ivan Rogov*, but while she was, at 13,880 tons, larger than other Soviet amphibious vessels, *Rogov* was much smaller and less capable than the contemporary *Tarawa* class of 39,300 tons. The design process of Pr. 1174 was very protracted; the technical specification was issued in 1964 but *Rogov* only entered service in 1978 and only two more units of this class were built. Likewise, only one prototype long-range supply ship entered the fleet, the

24,956t Pr. 1833/*Berezina*, in 1972. She was built to a technical requirement issued in 1967, and Gorshkov was unable to get funds for a follow-on class, Pr. 11611.[27] The related difficulties of the aircraft carrier decision will be discussed below. Out-of-area ships days reached a peak of 53,200 in 1974, and did not pass that level again until 1980; in the Mediterranean there was a significant decline, from 20,200 to 16,600 in 1980.[28] This has to be put in context; the most important element was the loss of a major partner in the Middle East with the breakdown of the alliance with Egypt in the early 1970s. Crises like those of the 1967 and 1973 wars were not repeated. From 1979 Russia was drawn into another expensive Third World conflict, in Afghanistan, that had no naval dimension.

Yet another general explanation of the naval build-up is the pressure of the Soviet military-industrial complex. A general feature of Soviet development was the creation in the early 1930s of a large-scale armaments industry, something that was further accelerated by the experience of the Second World War. One outspoken critic of naval policy, the retired Admiral N. N. Amel'ko, blamed the wasteful and poorly thought-out naval procurements on the military-industrial complex:

> [A] variety of types greatly increases costs of construction and operation. The military-industrial complex, and especially the Ministry of Shipbuilding, was interested in a large quantity of newer and newer projects, because for each of these they would receive huge prizes and thousands of awards, and the top leaders of the institutions even got the title of Heroes of the Soviet Union or Heroes of Socialist Labour.[29]

According to Amel'ko, naval matters 'were worked out not by experts of the fleet, but by the industrial complex through the Central Committee of the CPSU, in which the armaments industry was looked after by a man who came from *oboronprom* (the Ministry of the Defence Industry), D. F. Ustinov.[30] Formerly the manager of a big arms factory, Dmitrii Ustinov was deputy prime minister from 1957; from 1965 to 1976 he was the CPSU Central Committee secretary responsible for the defence industry, and from 1976 until his death in 1984 minister of defence, holding the rank of marshal. Amel'ko exaggerated the situation, but we do know that in the late 1940s conflict between what the Ministry of Shipbuilding wanted to produce and what the navy wanted to procure led to considerable tension and, in the end, to industry getting its way.[31] Another recent source has mentioned the 'monopoly position' of defence contractors sometimes forcing the navy to accept inferior equipment.[32]

The final factor to consider is the role of individuals and institutions, especially that of Admiral Gorshkov. Gorshkov had an extraordinary tenure as commander-in-chief of the Soviet Navy, 29 years, from 1955 (*de facto*) to 1985. In contrast, Tirpitz was minister of marine for only 19 years (1897–1916) and Fisher was first sea lord for seven. Unlike Tirpitz and Fisher, Gorshkov had had a significant career as a combat comman-der.[33] In addition, a number of widely publicized works on seapower appeared under Gorshkov's name, making him seem like Tirpitz and Mahan rolled into one.

Gorshkov's importance as a thinker should not be exaggerated. True, he was a successful publicist of seapower, although it was not until 1972, when he had been in post for over 15 years, that a systematic series of arti-cles appeared under his name in *Moskoi sbornik*, to be followed four years later by the first edition of *The Sea Power of the State* (1976). His books were not particularly original, and he was prepared here, as elsewhere, to trim his sails on an independent strategy for the navy.[34] He was essentially the advocate of a strong navy. Perhaps the clearest statement of his objec-tives appeared in his memoirs.

> The essence of the conception of a balanced fleet is that we have in our navy, aside from submarines and powerful maritime strike and ASW aviation, major surface ships in order to escort our submarines through narrows, straits and [enemy ASW] positions. Therefore we consider as well-balanced a fleet which, by virtue of its content and equipment, is able to carry out tasks both in a war involving missiles and nuclear weapons and in a war that does not involve these weapons, and also to secure interests of the state at sea in peace time.[35]

This was not consistent with his early acceptance of the Khrushchev cuts; more important, successfully achieving all these objectives implied a competition with the West which the Soviet economic system could not sustain.

Gorshkov was not a lone voice calling for a great Soviet fleet. The Soviet government undertook two major warship construction programmes before Gorshkov, one in the late 1930s and the other from the late 1940s. Kuznetsov had been even more of a 'navalist' than Gorshkov. Khrushchev maintained that he had wanted 110–130 billion rubles over the ten years of the abortive 1956–65 programme: 11–13 billion a year.[36] This was at a time when the annual defence budget – for *all* branches of the armed forces – was officially 9.7 billion rubles.

Gorshkov was an important Kremlin bureaucrat, and Robert Herrick has wittily compared him with J. Edgar Hoover.[37] This is a useful analogy, but one that must be taken with a grain of salt, as there were a number of 'Hoovers' in this period of Soviet history, and especially under Brezhnev when 'stability of cadres' was a keynote. It is true that the turnover of ministers of defence was higher (five during Gorshkov's tenure), but a number of other general administrators held posts for decades under Brezhnev; Ustinov had a central role in the armaments industry from 1941 to his death in 1984, and E. P. Slavskii was head of the armaments-related Ministry of Medium Machine-Building from 1957 to 1986. Gorshkov also stayed in post precisely because he did *not* make waves. Kuznetsov was sacked twice (in 1947 and 1955) for pushing the navy's case too hard. Gorshkov was explicit about this in his memoirs: '[I] well remembered G. K. Zhukov's warning about the complications of work in Moscow, and indeed his own fate and that of N. G. Kuznetsov were an object lesson for me'.[38] Gorshkov was much more of a diplomat. He had no obvious problems working with Khrushchev and cultivated relations with Zhukov, despite the latter's advocacy of naval cuts; in contrast, Zhukov and Admiral Kuznetsov had been personally very antagonistic. Gorshkov accepted the abandonment of the 1956–65 programme and, as we will see below, accepted delays in the aircraft carrier programme. Although he had been a protégé of Kuznetsov the bitter events of 1955–56 left a lasting personal legacy between the two men.

On the other hand, Gorshkov's long period in post was – for better or worse – one which gave him influence. The fact that he had been appointed under Khrushchev did not make it difficult to have good relations with Khrushchev's successors; after all, Brezhnev himself was a protégé Khrushchev. Links with Brezhnev were indeed critical to Gorshkov's career. Unlike Khrushchev, Brezhnev had some experience of the fleet before becoming the national leader in 1964. In addition to wartime experience on a coastal front (where he probably had contact with Gorshkov) he was chief commissar of the navy briefly in 1953, and from February 1956 to July 1960 he was Central Committee secretary responsible for the defence programme in general and missiles in particular. Gorshkov had had good working relations with Brezhnev in this capacity and, for Brezhnev, Gorshkov represented a pair of safe hands with which to entrust naval affairs once he became party leader in 1964. Gorshkov was in fact well situated in a network of useful relations, having good personal links with Brezhnev's first two ministers of defence, Marshal Malinovskii and Marshal Grechko; he had served with the latter during the war.[39]

Other actors wanted a significant Soviet Navy, although not necessarily a 'balanced' or 'oceanic' one. Ustinov and the military-industrial complex have already been mentioned. Khrushchev and Brezhnev, who were the dominant arbiters of policy in 1955–64 and 1964–82 respectively, wanted the USSR to play on the world stage. A central role in overall military policy, including naval policy, was played by the ministers of defence, Marshals Zhukov (1953–57), Malinovskii (1957–67) and Grechko (1967–76), all senior army commanders, and by Ustinov (1976–84), who came, as we have seen, from the military-industrial complex.[40] Grechko was especially important for the navy, backing the VTOL carriers and overriding the General Staff's 1967 objection to a Mediterranean squadron. The decision to proceed with the giant Pr. 949/OSCAR and Pr. 941/TYPHOON submarines and the Pr. 1144/*Kirov* nuclear cruiser all date from the early Grechko years (1969–72). According to Gorshkov, the decision to hold the famous 'Okean' manoeuvres in 1970 came from Grechko rather than himself.[41]

Interestingly enough, however, there is evidence that many analysts' image of a well-thought-out and integrated Soviet defence policy is at least partly a misconception. Admiral Amel'ko, as the naval representative on the General Staff from 1978 to 1988, was in a position to know. Zhukov, Malinovskii and Grechko, he recalled, left the navy to sort out its own affairs (presumably once global defence resources had been divided up); as for Ustinov, he treated the General Staff as a chancellery: 'he never asked the advice of the General Staff'. Talking about what he regarded as the wasteful expenditure on the aircraft carriers and the Pr. 941/TYPHOON missile submarines Amel'ko said that '[t]here was no state strategic concept [and] no understanding whatever of military affairs'.[42] The institution that did play a major part in the development of naval procurement was the Main Staff of the Navy (*Glavnyi shtab VMF*), as a recent account had indicated:

> In the Soviet period there were a series of ten-year [shipbuilding] programmes. They were all thoroughly worked out by the Main Staff together with the defence sectors of industry and the planning organs. It was the case that state and party organs and above all the senior leaders of the state [*pervye litsa v gosudarstve*] always played a key role and much depended on a well-based programme and on the ability clearly to argue a case to particular government and party organs.[43]

Gorshkov did not have a radical conception of technology or operations It would not be appropriate, for example, to compare Kuznestov and Gorshkov with the leaders of the German Navy, Raeder and Dönitz, one the advocate of the surface ships, the other of submarines. Gorshkov's training and early command posts had been traditional. He had the same view of the fleet that Kuznetsov had. His first flag command – at age 31 – was the cruiser 'brigade' of the pre-war Black Sea Fleet. (Where there is a sharp contrast is with Gorshkov's 1985 successor, Admiral Chernavin, nearly all of whose experience had been as a submariner.) Many of the technological developments thought of as dating from the Gorshkov era actually preceded it or came from outside the navy. For example, anti-shipping missiles (ASMs) were developed well before Gorshkov was appointed. They were one of a handful of key weapons technologies identified at national leadership level in the late 1940s, an astute decision given the West's naval supremacy; the model was the Luftwaffe's Henschel Hs 293. The development of what became the MiG KS (*Kometa*, KENNEL) anti-ship cruise missile began in 1947; the weapon was tested and deployed in small numbers in 1952,[44] carried by the piston-engined Tupolev Tu-4K bomber (the famous B-29 copy). Ship-launched surface-to-surface missiles (SSMs) also originated in the Kuznetsov years. A ship-launched version of *Kometa* called 'Strela' (Arrow) was trialled on the new *Sverdlov* class cruiser *Admiral Nakhimov* in the Black Sea in January 1956.[45] In 1956, after his dismissal, Admiral Kuznetsov wrote a long letter to the Communist Party Presidium (Politboro) in his own defence, in which he stressed this development.[46] The first operational SSM, the rocket-powered KSShch/SCRUBBER, was test launched early in 1957, but had originally been developed in 1948–53 as an air-launched weapon. The nuclear submarines and submarine-launched strategic ballistic missile originated before Gorshkov's tenure of office, and indeed outside the direct control of the navy.[47] As we have seen, the Pr. 627/NOVEMBER class nuclear submarine was conceived originally in 1952 – without direct naval involvement – to carry a strategic nuclear torpedo. In the end more reliance was placed on missiles. The programme to adapt the army's R-11/SCUD ballistic missile for naval service dated from January 1954, and it was test launched from a surfaced submarine in September 1955. The successful P-5/SHADDOCK cruise missile began development in the second half of that year.[48]

The decision to embark on the construction of the *Eagle* project, a super carrier capable of operating large and high-performance conventional aircraft, serves as a finale to this discussion. The decision was one of the most difficult of the post-war period.[49] Although officially denied at the highest level, the navy wanted such ships. Khrushchev was critical of large surface ships and a draft design for a 'floating fighter base' was not supported. However the anticipated threat from *Polaris* led him to authorize in December 1958 the first major Russian aircraft-carrying ships, the ASW helicopter carriers of the Pr. 1123/*Moskva* class. The design made sense as a platform for helicopters and a long-range ASW missile, but the third (stretched) ship of the class was broken up on her building slip in 1969.[50]

There was still some discussion within the shipbuilding industry in the late 1960s about a light conventional carrier. Soviet secrecy and lack of enthusiasm in high quarters had the extraordinary result that the appropriate team had to base their design around the operating characteristics not of Soviet but of American aircraft, the F-111 and the Grumman S-2 Tracker.[51] Nothing came of this light carrier, but a top-level decision was made on a new aircraft-carrying ship. In the place of the third *Moskva* was laid down a vessel twice her size, indeed the largest warship thus far designed in the USSR, the 36,000 ton *Kiev* (Pr. 1143). Her technical specification was approved in October 1968, and she was laid down in July 1970. As already noted, the support of the new minister of defence, Marshal Grechko, was important.[52] The *Kiev* class carried eight launchers for a powerful new anti-ship missile, and a larger helicopter complement than the *Moskvas*, but the ships' striking feature was their fixed-wing aircraft. The new ship design was based largely on the development of a sub-sonic VTOL jet 'light attack plane' (*legkii shturmovik*) by the Yakovlev design bureau. The aircraft, the Yak-36M (later Yak-38), was not specifically designed for the navy, but Ustinov became an advocate of its use by the navy.[53] Only one building slip in the Nosenko Shipyard (Nikolaev South) on the Black Sea was devoted to the *Kievs*, so it took nearly two decades to get the whole class into service, *Kiev* in 1975, *Minsk* in 1978, *Novorossiisk* in 1982, and *Baku/Gorshkov* (to a modified design) in 1987.

The navy wanted something altogether bigger alongside the *Kiev* class in the 1971–80 shipbuilding plan. The Nevskoe Design Bureau (*PKB*) put forward in 1972 Pr. 1160, which was an 80,000-ton nuclear-powered carrier on about the same scale as the contemporary *Nimitz*. This ship would have carried a conventional air group of 70–80 aircraft, and the proposal evidently had the support of B. E. Butoma, the minister of the shipbuilding industry. Unfortunately for the navy, Ustinov, the key figure in the military-industrial complex, was for both compromise and postponement of a decision. The projected solution agreed in September 1973 (coincidentally at the time of the Yom Kippur War) was to deploy a supersonic VTOL aircraft, the Yak-141, on a third *Kiev*, and to build a 72,000-ton nuclear-powered carrier, Pr. 1153, in place of the fourth *Kiev*. Then, in 1976, both Marshal Grechko and Butoma died. Ustinov replaced Grechko as minister of defence, and he favoured the less ambitious VTOL variant. Gorshkov on his own was unable to sustain the project; 'I did not get involved in open polemics', he admitted.[54]

The navy did get its carrier – the *Eagle* design – but only *after* the fourth *Kiev*. *Riga* was laid down in September 1982 (and almost immediately renamed *Leonid Brezhnev*; she is now the *Kuznetsov*). Despite this fifth ship's designation as Pr. 1143.5, she was much more than a scaled-up Pr. 1143/*Kiev*, and could operate a version of the standard Soviet Air Force heavy supersonic fighter, the Sukhoi Su-27. Nevertheless the design involved serious compromises compared with the proposed Pr. 1160 or Pr. 1153. Pr. 1143.5 displaced only 67,500 tons and lacked the nuclear power and steam catapults of the larger designs (she was fitted with a 'ski jump' to assist aircraft takeoff). The USSR only began a full-sized nuclear-powered carrier (the 75,000 ton Pr. 1143.7) in November 1988, once *Riga/Kuznetsov*'s sister ship (*Variag*) had been launched and – significantly – after the death of Ustinov and the departure of the cautious Marshal N. V. Ogarkov from the General Staff.[55] Gorshkov had been able to approve the technical specification in December 1984 but the carrier, named *Ul'ianovsk*, was fated to be broken up for scrap, 20 per cent complete, in an independent Ukraine.

The carrier decision was one of many, but it shows some of the problems faced by the Soviet effort, the limited resources available and the competing pressures. Like other procurement decisions it was influenced by a range of factors. In the 1960s and 1970s the USSR was involved in a series of confrontations where the ability to project seapower was important. Nevertheless, the element of competition and prestige was significant, as Admiral Amel'ko noted:

> The special features [of military doctrine in the later Brezhnev years] were not to fall behind the Western armies and therefore we expanded our armed forces in all directions. To overtake even the US Navy. That's why aircraft carriers were built. Not because we needed them, but because they had them.[56]

Between 1946 and 1991 the USSR built 394 major surface warships and 664 submarines.[57] In the same period the Soviet Navy acquired over 1,800 fixed-wing combat aircraft and 1,050 helicopters.[58] The navy's nuclear stockpile at the end of the period was estimated to consist of 4,050 warheads for SLBMs and 5,730 'non-strategic' warheads.[59] The rise of Soviet seapower, which led to so much apprehension in the West, can now be viewed from a better perspective. This development had a range of causes and was less of a rational process than it seemed at the time. The Soviet Navy had to compete for resources with four other services, and within a military establishment that was dominated by the army. The same range of factors that made naval power attractive to Moscow pulled policy in different directions: the Soviet Navy was a base for strategic nuclear forces *and* a tool for gaining influence in the developing world, it was a force for effectively defending the Russian coast *and* part of a competition for prestige. The party–state structure was prepared to commit a high proportion of GNP to defence, but it was not capable of rationally assessing threats or determining force structures. Gorshkov's long tenure probably put the navy in a good position to compete for resources, but an even bigger role was played by the activities of the 'likely opponent' and by a changing world.

The Russian drive for seapower was, as it turned out, doomed to fail. Happily, and unlike the case of Germany and Japan, this did not result from the loss of a major war. Russia did not come close to effectively challenging Western maritime supremacy, but even the limited achievements were undone because the Soviet system collapsed. Although there is a curious coincidence between Russian naval build-ups and systemic crises – 1905, 1917, 1941, 1991 come to mind – it would be misleading to think that Gorshkov's oceanic navy was a central part of the crisis that led to the fall of communism. Naval expenditure was perhaps no more than 13 per cent of Soviet defence expenditure in the period 1970–84.[60] However, what happened in the former USSR brings home the point that naval power is based on economic power. The Soviet Navy fits into the notion of 'imperial overstretch' that Paul Kennedy put forward in *The Rise and Fall of the Great Powers*.[61] Although the naval build-up was not the most important of the military expenditures which prevented the Soviet economy from modernizing and the USSR from surviving, it was certainly a significant factor.

NOTES

1. There is much new information of technical developments in post-Soviet publications of which the most outstanding is V. P. Kuzin and V. I. Nikol'skii, *Voenno-morskoi flot SSSR: 1945–1991: Istoriia sozdaniia poslevoennogo voennogo-morskogo flota SSSR i vozmozhnyi oblik flota Rossii* (The Navy of the USSR: 1945–1991: The History of the Creation of the Post-War Soviet Navy and the Possible Shape of the Russian Fleet), St Petersburg, Istoricheskoe Morskoe Obshchestvo, 1996. The more narrow topic of ship design is covered by I. D. Spasskii, *et al.*, eds, *Istoriia otechestvennogo sudostroeniia* (History of the Fatherland's Shipbuilding), vol. V, *Sudostroenie v poslevoennoi period, 1946–1991 gg.* (Shipbuilding in the Post-War Period, 1946–1991), St Petersburg, Sudostroenie, 1996. See also S. G. Pavlov, *Voennye korabli SSSR i Rossii: 1945–1995 g.* (Warships of Russia and the USSR: 1945–1995), Iakutsk, n.p., vol. III, 1995. On missiles there is A. Shirokorad, *Rakety nad morem: Raketnaia tekhnika otechestvennogo voenno-morskogo flota* (Missiles over the Sea: Missile Technology in the Fatherland's Navy) (published as a special number of the journal *Tekhnika i vooruzheniie* (Technology and Armaments), 1997, nos 11–12). Much useful information is also available in the Russian Navy's professional journal *Morskoi Sbornik* (Naval Digest) and in the technical journals *Sudostroenie* (Shipbuilding), *Aviatsiia i kosmonavtika* (Aviation and Space Travel), *Tekhnika i vooruzheniie*, and *Gangut*. Much new information is also available in English in the long entry by Norman Friedman on the Russian Navy in Robert Gardiner, ed., *Conway's All the World's Fighting Ships: 1947–1995*, London, Conway Maritime Press, 1995.
2. Especially useful are the recently published memoirs of three commanders-in-chief of the Soviet Navy: N. G. Kuznetsov, *Krutye povoroty: iz zapisok admirala* (Abrupt Turns. The Notes of an Admiral), Moscow, Molodaia gvardiia, 1995; S. G. Gorshkov, *Vo flotskom stroiu: voennye memuary* (In Naval Service: War Memoirs), St Petersburg, Logos, 1996; Vladimir Chernavin, *Atomnyi podvodnyi ...: flot i sud'be Rossii: razmyshleniia posle shtormov i pokhodov* (Atomic, Submarine ...: The Navy and Russia's Fate: Reflections after Storms and Cruises), Moscow, Andreevskii flag, 1997.
3. Kuzin and Nikol'skii, *Voenno-Morskogo flota SSSR*, pp. 26–7; Spasskii, *Istoriia*, vol. V, pp. 6–10; Nikolai Simonov, *Voenno-promyshlennyi kompleks SSSR v 1920–1950-e gody: tempy ekonomicheskogo rosta, struktura, organizatsiia proizvodstva i upravlenie* (The Military-Industrial Complex of the USSR in the 1920–1950 Period: The Pace of Its Economic Growth, Its Structure, Its Organisation of Production, and Its Administration), Moscow, Rosspen, 1996, pp. 297–8; E. Shitikov, 'Stalin i voennoe korablestroenie' (Stalin and Naval Shipbuilding), *Morskoi sbornik*, no. 12, 1993, pp. 58–61; V. Iu. Gribovskii, 'Pervaia poslevoennaia korablestroitel'naia programma VMF SSSR (1946–1955 gody)' (The First Post-war Ship Building Programme of the Soviet Navy (1946–1955)), *Gangut*, vol. 12, 1997.

4. A. B. Morin, *Legkie kreisera tipa "Chapaev' and tipa 'Sverdlov"* (Light Cruisers of the 'Chapaev' Class and the 'Sverdlov' Class), St Petersburg, n.p., 1997.
5. This article will use the offical Russian designation, rather than simply the NATO code-name (like 'WHISKEY' or 'ZULU') assigned at a time when the offical designation was secret. Soviet warship classes each had a 'Project' (*proekt*) number, by which they were officially referred to and which became known in the West in the 1990s. The NATO codename is also given here, in small capitals (Pr. 941/TYPHOON); if a class was known by the lead ship's actual name, that will be given in italics (Pr. 1143/*Kiev*).
6. The immediate cause of Kuznetsov's disgrace was the accidental loss of the old battleship *Novorossiisk* in Sevastopol harbour. He was also in poor health, having suffered a heart attack in May 1955.
7. The CIA estimate was that the Soviet Navy took up as much as 29 per cent of defence spending in the period 1951–59, compared with 19.3 per cent in 1960–69, and 13.0 per cent in 1970–74. Going beyond the general reliability of the CIA figures, comparisons are confused by a rapidly growing CIA category, 'Other', comprising spending on research and development, intelligence and communications. For what it is worth, naval expenditure was estimated as 29 per cent *higher* than Soviet expenditure on ground forces in 1951–59, 34 per cent higher in 1960–69, but 23 per cent *lower* in 1970–74 (Noel E. Firth and James H. Noren, *Soviet Defense Spending: A History of CIA Estimates, 1950–1990*, College Station, TX: Texas A&M Press, 1998, p. 112).
8. From Amelko's 'Afterword' in Kuznetsov, *Krutye pouoroty*, p. 249.
9. The Pr. 633/ROMEO (improved WHISKEY) class of medium diesel submarine was to have had 560 units (Kuzin and Nikol'skii, *Voenno-morskoi SSSR*, p. 87). The first Pr. 633 submarine entered service in December 1959, but only 21 further units followed it.
10. Fragmentary archival evidence of the 1959–65 plan indicated that it combined traditional mass and advanced technology, with the astonishing total of 421 nuclear submarines (Simonov, *Voenno-promyshlennyi kompleks SSSR*, pp. 299–300). Simonov produces a table based on a 'draft plan for naval shipbuilding for 1959–1965' from the State Archive of the Economy (*RGAE*). This is not dated. It includes 553 submarines (421 nuclear, 132 diesel) and 152 large surface ships, including 12 light cruisers. Submarines made up 55 per cent of the total shipbuilding allocation of 55.8 billion rubles (1962 prices); the unit cost of diesel submarines was to have been greater than that of nuclear submarines (62 million rubles versus 53 million). These production figures for nuclear submarines were consistent with the naval reactor production target, which was to reach 134 units a year by 1968. In actual fact, Russia produced in this period only 8 Pr. 658/701/HOTEL, 34 Pr. 659/675/ECHO (to 1967), and 13 Pr. 627/NOVEMBER, some 55 boats, but these were to twin-reactor designs. Gorshkov mentions a naval conference in 1958 where Khrushchev proposed the construction of 180 nuclear boats of various types (Gorshkov, *Vo flotskom stroiu*, p. 175).
11. Kuzin and Nikol'skii, *Voenno-morskoi flot SSSR*, 480.
12. Gorshkov, *V flotskom stroiu*, pp. 180–1.
13. Kuzin and Nikol'skii, *Voenno-morskoi flot SSSR*, p. 464. For a well-informed discussion of this see Stephen J. Zaloga, 'Tupolev Tu-22 "Blinder" and Tu-22M "Backfire"', *World Air Power Journal*, vol. 33 (Summer) 1998, pp. 56–103.
14. For a list of disposals see S. G. Pavlov, *Voennye korabli Rossii, 1997–1998: Spravochnik* (Russian Warships, 1997–1998: Handbook), Iakutsk, n.p., vol. 5, 1997, pp. 136–47.

15. This point was made in a seminal article by M. K. MccGwire, 'The Background to Russian Naval Policy', *Brassey's Annual*, 1968, pp. 141–58.
16. In addition to Kuzin and Nikol'skii, *Voenno-morskoi flot SSSR*, see the discussion of airborne ASW hardware in Anatolii Artem'ev, 'Okhotniki za submarinami' (Submarine Hunters), *Aviatsiia i kosmonavtika*, vol. 18, no. 7, 1996, pp. 3–18.
17. A remarkable new source on this subject is P. L. Podvig, ed., *Strategicheskoe iadernoe vooruzhenie Rossii* (Russian Strategic Nuclear Armament), Moscow, IzdAT, 1998, which includes extensive treatment of sea-based systems. The development of early nuclear strategic forces is well covered in Steven J. Zaloga, *Target America: The Soviet Union and the Strategic Arms Race, 1945–1964*, Novato CA, Presidio, 1993.
18. Podvig, *Strategicheskoe*, pp. 204–5. A smaller 533 mm T-5 nuclear torpedo, designed to be fired from a standard torpedo tube, was tested in September 1955.
19. V. V. Gagin, *Sovetskie atomnye podvodnye lodki* (Soviet Nuclear Submarines), Voronezh, Poligraf, 1995, pp. 11.
20. Podvig, *Strategicheskoe*, pp. 264–5, 285–7; Gorshkov, *Vo flotskom stroiu*, pp. 265–6.
21. Firth and Noren, *Soviet Defense Spending*, pp. 107, 111.
22. The standard work on this is Bradford Dismukes and James McConnell, *Soviet Naval Diplomacy*, New York, Pergamon Press, 1979.
23. See, for example, G. Kostev, 'Karibskii krizis glazami ochevidtsev' (The Caribbean Crisis through the Eyes of Participants), *Morskoi sbornik*, no. 11, 1994, pp. 12–15. Rear Admiral Kostev noted that the problems apparent in 1962 made Marshal Grechko pay more attention to the problems of the navy when he became minister of defence (in 1967) than his predecessors, Zhukov and Malinovskii, had.
24. Simonov, *Voenno-promyshlennyi kompleks SSSR*, p. 299. In contrast, at a 1955 naval conference Khrushchev pitched into one captain who had argued for building cruisers and aircraft carriers: 'What are you planning to do, then, are you planning to sail to America and fight there?' (L. Tomashevskii, 'Glavnyi korablestroitel' (k 85 letiiu admirala P. G. Kotova)', *Morskoi sbornik*, no. 1, 1996, p. 31).
25. Bruce W. Watson, *Red Navy at Sea: Soviet Naval Operations on the High Seas, 1956–1980*, Boulder, CO, Westview, 1982, p. 183.
26. Ibid., p. 183.
27. Kuzin and Nikol'skii, *Voenno-morskoi flot SSSR*, pp. 248–250, 269.
28. Watson, *Red Navy at Sea*, p. 183.
29. N. Amel'ko, 'Problemy stroitel'stva voenno-morskogo flota Rossii' (Problems of the Development of the Russian Navy), *Morskoi sbornik*, no. 4, 1994, p. 6. See also his similar comments in his 'Afterword' to Kuznetsov's memoirs (*Krutye povoroty*, p. 249). Amel'ko who emerged as critic of naval policy under Gorbachev, had held a range of important positions. Born in 1914, he had been commander-in-chief of the Pacific Fleet in 1962–69, deputy commander-in-chief of the navy (under Gorshkov) in 1969–78, and deputy chief (navy) of the General Staff in 1978–88. He won the Lenin Prize for chairing a commission that developed a satellite targeting system for cruise missiles (N. N. Amel'ko interview, May 1992); for the background to this interview see Stephen White, Olga Kryshtanovskaia, Igor Kukolev, Evan Mawdsley and Pavel Saldin, 'Interviewing the Soviet Elite', *Russian Review*, vol. 55, no. 2, April, 1996, pp. 309–16.
30. Kuznetsov, *Krutye povoroty*, p. 249.
31. See S. A. Zonin, *Admiral L. M. Galler: Zhizn' i flotovodcheskaia deiatel'nost* (Life and Activities as a Naval Commander), Moscow, Voennoe izdatel'stvo,

1991, p. 384, where it is speculated that the political fall of Admiral Kuznetsov and Admiral Galler in 1947 may have had something to do with this conflict with Nosenko, the minister of the shipbuilding industry.

32. B. Rodionov, 'Tsentral'nye organy upravleniia v otechestvennom flote' (Central Organs of Administration in the Fatherland's Fleet), *Morskoi sbornik*, no. 6, 1998, p. 86.

33. In addition to Gorshkov's memoirs see the article by his successor, Admiral of Fleet Chernavin on the eightieth anniversary of Gorshkov's birth, 'Ego zhizn' – vernost' dolgu i flotu' (His Life was One of Devotion to Duty and the Fleet), *Moskoi sbornik*, no. 3, 1990, pp. 85–9, and Jürgen Rohwer, 'Das Ende der Ära Gorchkow', *Marine-Rundschau*, vol. 83, no. 2, 1986, pp. 88–97.

34. N. S. Gorshkov, 'Voenno-morskie floty v voinakh i mirnoe vremia', *Moskoi sbornik*, nos. 2–6, 1972, 8–12, no. 2, 1973; N. S. Gorshkov, *Morskaia moshch' gosudarstva*, Moscow, Voenizdat, 1976; N. S. Gorshkov, *Morskaia moshch' gosudarstva*, 2nd edn, Moscow, Voenizdat, 1979. Gorshkov himself admitted that he had much help in his writing, notably from Admirals K. A. Stalbo and N. P. V'iunenko, and Colonel A. P. Anokhin (*Vo flotskom stroiu*, pp. 196–8).

35. Gorshkov, *Vo flotskom stroiu*, 1996, p. 238.

36. N. S. Khrushchev, 'Memuary', *Voprosy istorii*, no. 2, 1995, p. 81.

37. Robert W. Herrick, 'Roles and Missions of the Soviet Navy: Historical Evolution, Current Priorities, and Future Prospects', in James L. George, ed., *The Soviet and Other Communist Navies: The View from the Mid-1980s*, Annapolis, MD, Naval Institute Press, 1986, p. 34.

38. Gorshkov, *Vo flotskom stroiu*, pp. 163, 173.

39. Ibid., pp. 162, 172. An early link between Gorshkov and Brezhnev has been suggested by the latter's biographer. Brezhnev was a senior commissar among Soviet forces defending the Kuban (the northeast Black Sea coast) in 1942–43 when Gorshkov commanded local naval units there (Roi Medvedev, *Lichnost' i epokha: Politicheskii portret L. I. Brezhneva* (The Personality and the Era: A Political Portrait of L. I. Brezhnev), Moscow, Novosti, 1991, kn. 1, p. 46). Curiously there is no reference to Brezhnev in the wartime part of Gorshkov's memoirs; it would not be implausible to suggest that after Brezhnev's death in 1982 and subsequent criticism of him Gorshkov was attempting to distance himself from the deceased leader. Curiously, too, the dedication at the start of the Gorshkov's memoirs states that he never enjoyed anyone's patronage (*protektsiia*).

40. The leading study of the military politics of this period does not include Gorshkov among eight 'key personalities' (Dale R. Herspring, *The Soviet High Command, 1967–1989: Personalities and Politics*, Princeton, NJ, Princeton University Press, 1990).

41. Gorshkov, *Vo flotskom stroiu*, pp. 250, 341–2. Admiral Amel'ko rated Malinovskii ('extremely intelligent') more highly than Grechko as a minister of defence (N. Amel'ko interview, p. 15).

42. Kuznetsov, *Krutye povoroty*, p. 249; Amel'ko interview, p. 17.

43. B. Rodionov, 'Tsentral'nye organy upravleniia v otechestvennom flote' (Central Organs of Administration in the Fatherland's Fleet), *Morskoi sbornik*, no. 5, 1998, p. 82. Significantly, this quotation makes no reference to the armed forces General Staff. On the planning organs of the navy see: Khmel'nov, 'Mozg voenno-morskogo flota' (The Brain of the Navy), *Morskoi sbornik*, no. 1, 1997, pp. 3–9, and Rodionov, 'Tsentral'nye organy', *Morskoi sbornik*, no. 4, 1998, pp. 80–93, no. 5, 79–82, and no. 6, pp. 83–7. The key leaders of the Main Staff in the Gorshkov era were Admirals F. V. Zozulia (1958–64), N. D. Sergeev (1964–77), G. M. Egorov (1977–81) and V. N. Chernavin (1981–85).

44. Bill Gunston and Yefim Gordon, *MiG Aircraft since 1937*, London, Putnam,

1998, pp. 266–9; Kuzin and Nikol'skii, *Voenno-morskoi flot SSSR*, 336; *Aviatsiia i kosmonavtika*, 1996.

45. Shirokorad, *Rakety*, pp. 16–17; Morin, *Legkie kreisera*, pp. 55–63.
46. 'Narkom voenno-morskogo flota N. G. Kuznetsov', *Voenno-istoricheskii arkhiv*, vol. 1 (1997), p. 69.
47. N. M. Lazarev, *Pervye sovetskie atomnye podvodnye lodki: U istokov atomnogo voennogo korablestroeniia. Trudnosti i uspekhi. Liudi. Sobytiia. Fakty* (The First Soviet Nuclear-powered Submarines: The Origins of Nuclear Warships. Difficulties and Successes. People, Events, Facts), 2nd edn, Moscow, Paleia, 1997.
48. Shirokorad, *Rakety*, pp. 2, 31.
49. The discussion of the carrier decision is based largely on the following recent articles: A. B. Morin, 'Korabel'naia aviatsiia i avianesushchie korabli otechestvennogo flota' (Shipboard Aviation and Aircraft-Carrying Ships of the Fatherland's Navy), in *Kryl'ia nad Morem*, Moscow, 1992 (*Mir aviatsii*, no. 6, 1994), pp. 35–52; A. B. Morin, 'Tiazhelyi avianesushchii kreiser (The Heavy Aircraft-Carrying Cruiser) "Admiral Flota Sovetskogo Soiuza Kuznetsov"', *Gangut*, no. 11, 1996, pp. 3–34; Kuzin and Nikol'skii, *Voenno-morskoi flot SSSR*, pp. 96–106; Spasskii, *et al.*, *Istoriia*, pp. 312–28; Mikhail Nikol'skii, 'Razvitie avianostsev posle votroi mirovoi voine' (The Development of Aircraft Carriers after the Second World War), *Tekhnika i vooruzhenie*, no. 5–6, 1998, pp. 10–17. Arkadii Morin, the best authority, was a senior naval architect in the Nevskoe Design Bureau (formerly TsKB-17) and was directly involved in both the 'Sverdlov' and the carrier projects.
50. Kuzin and Nikol'skii, *Voenno-morskoi flot SSSR*, pp. 96–7; Pavlov, *1945–1995*, p. 66.
51. Morin, '*Kuznetsov*', p. 17.
52. Gorshkov, *Vo flotskom stroiu*, p. 245
53. Iu. Lunev, 'Vertikalka (Jump Jet)', in *Kryl'ia nad Morem* (Wings over the Sea), Moscow, n.p., 1992 (*Mir aviatsii*, no. 6, 1994), pp. 16–25; Efim Gordon, 'Samolet vertikal'nogo vzleta i posadki Iak-38' (The Yak-38 Vertical Takeoff and Landing Aircraft), *Aviatsiia i kosmonavtika*, 1995, vol. 8 (June), pp. 3–17; Gorshkov, *Vo flotskom stroiu*, p. 246. In the end the navy acquired 231 Yak-38s (Kuzin and Nikol'skii, *Voenno-morskoi flot SSSR*, p. 469).
54. Morin, 'Tiazhelyi avianesushchii kreiser', p. 18; Gorshkov, *Vo flotskom stroiu*, pp. 246, 264–5.
55. Nikol'skii, 'Razvitie', p. 15.
56. Amel'ko interview, p. 18.
57. Kuzin and Nikol'skii, *Voenno-morskoi flot SSSR*, pp. 27, 32, 40. The surface ship figures include frigates (SKR) and larger warships; there was also a large number of smaller warships and auxiliaries.
58. Ibid., p. 469. The Soviet Navy also acquired 500 fixed-wing transport aircraft. The figure excludes about 2,000 jet fighters and 1,100 medium bombers acquired to operate from land bases in the first post-war decade.
59. Thomas B. Cochran *et al.*, *Soviet Nuclear Weapons: Nuclear Weapons Databook*, vol. IV, New York, Harper & Row, 1989, pp. 28, 36–7. This was the figure for the 1988, when the total Soviet warhead stockpile was estimated as 33,000, including some 11,800 warheads for 'non-strategic' ground and air forces. Naval 'non-strategic' nuclear warheads were estimated to consist of 2,200 air-to-surface missiles, 1,270 naval 'attack aviation' bombs, 400 naval cruise missiles, 575 torpedoes, 425 ASW missiles, 400 depth bombs, 260 naval surface-to-air missiles, 100 6 inch guns of the 'Sverdlovs', 100 coastal missiles and an unknown number mines.

60. Firth and Noren, *Soviet Defense Spending*, p. 112. Another indication of the relative weight of the navy in the Soviet defence establishment is personnel. In 1955 Zhukov reported that of 4,638,000 personnel in the armed forces 747,000 (16.1 per cent) were in the navy, compared with 2,321,000 in ground forces, 732,000 in the air force and 499,000 in the air defence force (PVO) ('Sokrashchenie Vooruzhennykh Sil SSSR v seredine 50-kh godov' 'The Reduction of the Armed Forces of the USSR in the mid-1950s', *Voennye arkhivy rossii*, vol. 1, 1993, p. 280). The CIA estimated for mid-1988 that of 4,350,000 personnel in the armed forces proper 435,000 (10 per cent) were in the navy, compared with 1,610,000 in ground forces, 480,000 in the air force, 545,000 in the PVO and 315,000 in the strategic rocket force (Firth and Noren, *Soviet Defense Spending*, p. 211).
61. Paul Kennedy, *The Rise and Fall of the Great Powers: Economic Change and Military Conflict from 1500 to 2000*, London, Fontana, 1988, pp. xvi, 496–504, 554–7.

11

The Royal Navy, 1945–90

Eric Grove

The initial Cold War planning assumption adopted by the post-1945 Attlee government was that hot war was unlikely before 1957.[1] In the meantime the emphasis would be on air and sea forces sufficient to act as a deterrent to hot war and as a foundation for fighting the Cold War at a political level. The top defence priority was the creation of a nuclear bomber force for strategic offence to deter in peace and defend in wartime. Carrier-based nuclear bombers were considered, only to be dismissed on grounds of both practicability and cost. This also had the beneficial side effect of preventing the kinds of inter-service battles that dominated the post-war American scene. Indeed, next in line in defence priorities was a fleet based on carrier and anti-submarine forces to maintain sea communications in war and exert both presence and more limited military and constabulary force in peace. After much controversy a well-named 'Revised Restricted Fleet' plan was adopted in 1949. This envisaged a peacetime active fleet of two fleet carriers, three light fleet carriers (with a Naval Aviation strength of 250 aircraft), 13 cruisers, 60 destroyers and frigates, 20 submarines and 36 mine-countermeasures vessels. Even when the international situation deteriorated seriously in 1950 with the outbreak of the Korean War and the Attlee government began to re-arm beyond its means, the active fleet corresponded to this plan. At its peak in 1952–53 the active fleet's 123 major combat units comprised five carriers, 12 cruisers, 67 destroyers and frigates and 39 submarines (the maintenance of twice the number of submarines in active service is noteworthy).

It would not have been so bad for the Admiralty if naval technology had not being undergoing a major revolution at this time. It is not too much of an exaggeration to say that the new types of aircraft had made obsolete or obsolescent both the fleet's carriers and its ship-borne air defences, while new fast battery drive submarines required new surface escorts and sensors, not to mention a new submarine fleet trained in the novel art of submarine versus submarine warfare.[2]

Even the final generation of piston-engined aircraft could not be operated by the Royal Navy's wartime carriers. There were two fleet and four large light fleet carriers (designed to operate these larger types) left under construction after the round of wartime cancellations: *Eagle* at Harland and Wolff and *Ark Royal* at Cammell Laird; *Hermes* at Vickers at Barrow, *Albion* at Swans, and *Bulwark* and *Centaur*, both at Harland and Wolff. All of these could operate the first generation of jets with little modification. All but one were completed by the mid-1950s and replaced older ships that had soldiered on with Sea Furies, Fireflies, Seafires and (in the operational fleet carrier) Firebrands and Sea Hornets. The wartime-built carriers had proved adequate for limited war – the *Commonwealth* light fleet carrier on station in Korea proving a disproportionately large contributor to the support of the UN forces ashore – but they needed replacement if carriers were going to contribute adequately to fighting the air battle in the Mediterranean (the main expected war role of the fleet carriers) or supporting convoys in the Atlantic (the role of the light fleets).

The chief problem was the fleet carrier situation. With only two new hulls on their way it was hoped that at least some of the armoured hangar carriers of the *Illustrious* type could be converted to operate the latest jets to meet the full wartime requirement of six of these ships (two in full commission, one training and three at up to three-months' notice in reserve). HMS *Victorious* was taken in hand at Portsmouth dockyard in 1950 but the work proved long and expensive in both material and labour and the ship did not recommission until 1958. When she did recommission with her large 984 radar, the outward and visible sign of the first modern computerized fighter direction system based around the Comprehensive Display System (CDS) and operating Scimitar swept-wing fighters from a fully angled flight deck, she was an enormous leap in capability but the decision had long since been taken to make her the only such conversion of the old fleet carriers.[3] All the rest had been sold for scrap by 1956 – *Indomitable*, the last to serve as a fully operational carrier, being decommissioned in October 1953.

Even work on *Victorious* had virtually been cancelled. Successive and increasingly 'radical' defence reviews were undertaken by the Churchill government to cut back the Attlee programme that was unaffordable in industrial as well as in financial terms. Part of this review process were the major reconsideration of the carrier programme in 1953–54 and the attempt to reduce it to, effectively, a light carrier force reduced in size and un-modernized with an emphasis on anti-submarine warfare and only limited anti-air warfare capability. Such would be sufficient for the 'broken-backed war' concepts being used by the navy to justify its existence in the nuclear age. But the role of the carrier had changed significantly two years before with the creation of NATO's Atlantic Command and its Striking Fleet of carriers. There were strong arguments for a major British contribution to this force with at least some carriers capable of operating the latest jet fighter – and later nuclear strike – aircraft. Without such ships there would be no UK voice in the operation of NATO's major single concentration of naval power in the intense opening phase of any future hot war. This argument eventually carried the day and although the Admiralty could not maintain its full planned strength in fleet carriers, it at least retained three, *Eagle, Ark Royal* and *Victorious*, with five light fleet carriers, *Albion, Bulwark, Centaur, Hermes* and *Warrior*, the latter being the only one of the older light fleet to be partially modernized. Development of a new long-range carrier strike aircraft, the NA39, later the *Buccaneer*, was also confirmed.

A major opponent of the carrier in the Radical Review had been the minister of supply, Duncan Sandys, and the Admiralty feared the worst when Macmillan made him minister of defence with greatly increased powers in 1957 to carry out a *truly* radical review. The Admiralty was lucky in that the Suez Crisis, as well as precipitating this unwelcome development, had also demonstrated the utility both of carrier air in limited conflict ('warm' war as it was referred to at about this time) and of the potential of helicopter flying from the unmodernized light fleet carriers, Korea veterans *Ocean* and *Theseus*, for amphibious landings. The first sea lord, the politically astute and devious Lord Louis Mountbatten, used every weapon in his not inconsiderable bureaucratic armoury to safeguard the carrier as the centrepiece of his fleet. There were other arguments powerfully used: first, the negative Alliance impact of large-scale naval cuts and, second, a feeling shared by everyone, including Sandys, that some capacity for anti-submarine warfare was required by an island nation that might not be destroyed totally in the opening phases of a war. But it was by emphasizing the limited war role east of Suez that Mountbatten was able to save the strike carrier. Only *Warrior* was deleted, sold, ironically enough, to Argentina. *Bulwark* and later *Albion* were converted to commando carriers, while the remainder were kept as strike carriers, *Hermes* being completed by Vickers and *Eagle* being converted at Devonport dockyard. *Hermes* had the same fit as *Victorious* with 984/CDS while *Eagle* had the more advanced digital 984/ADA combination. From 1961, strike carriers began fully to live up to their name when they took to sea the first navalized Red Beard nuclear bombs for use by their Scimitar (and later Sea Vixen) fighter bombers.

The story of enhanced capability but reduced numbers was the same in the escort force. The problem was a very serious one in the early post-war years. The existing frigates (variously built in the war years as sloops, corvettes and frigates) had insufficient speed and inadequate weapons and sonars to deal with the latest submarines. Despite the recent move to fully dual-purpose 4.5 inch guns in the latest destroyers and the advent of proximity fuses and better fire control, modern aircraft were a formidable threat, especially at the ranges from which they could now attack with stand-off missiles. Even current construction was obsolescent. The urgent requirement for new high-speed ASW frigates was satisfied by converting fleet destroyers of wartime build to ASW ships: 23 ships received the full conversion and 10 a more limited rebuild. They seemed much less powerful after they had shed their visually striking anti-surface armament of guns and torpedoes but they were transformed as ASW assets, the Type 15 full conversions especially. With their 170/174 sonar suite combined with Mk 10 Limbo 1,000-yard-range mortars, operated from a modern operations room, they were formidable opponents for any new generation high-speed conventional submarines based on the German Type XXI. The work was done both in the Royal Dockyards and in private yards such as Stephen and Yarrow.

The full conversions were also built to allow operation in heavy weathers, a clear lesson of the Battle of the Atlantic. The new frigate designs also had hull forms that reflected the exacting requirements of escort operations in the Atlantic. The standard hull was built with both steam turbine power, as, for example, the Type 12, for ASW duties with a weapons fit similar to the Type 15s, and with diesels for AAW escort, some as Type 41 AA ships with four long-range 4.5-inch dual-purpose guns (the armament of wartime destroyers) and others, Type 61s, for aircraft direction with sophisticated radars and larger operations rooms. These latter ships symbolized the results of the post-war revolution, being designed not so much to fight themselves but to direct more effective weapons platforms at a distance. The late 1950s' reviews led to this programme being altered to concentrate on an enhanced version of the ASW ship with improved aircraft control characteristics and sonars a little more capable against SSNs. This was the new 'General Purpose' *Leander* class, constructed throughout the 1960s and into the 1970s. By this time, these 'first-rate' frigates had ceased to be primarily convoy escorts for a hot war: they were now seen first and foremost as fleet assets for limited war forces. Similarly, the second-rate frigate ceased to be an ASW ship capable of cheaper and more rapid production (the 12 specialized Type 14 *Blackwood* class built by Thornycroft, White, Yarrow, Stephen and Swan Hunter in the 1950s were eventually used as fishery protection vessels). The new second-rate ships were built self-consciously as latter-day colonial gunboats, the seven general purpose 'sloops' laid down in 1958–60 and completed as Type 81 frigates named after old *Tribal* class destroyers. Building of all these general purpose frigates was spread around the maximum number of suitable yards, 13 concerns being involved in constructing the first 16 *Leanders* and each Type 81 being built by a single yard.

The long-range guided missile Seaslug was expected to give some long-range anti-air protection to the fleet or convoys, but it was a large and cumbersome device. Originally intended for a slow convoy escort vessel and then for a new generation of cruisers, these proved far too expensive and instead a fleet escort corresponding to the American 'DLG' was built around the new missile. Destroyers had been getting bigger anyway; the 3,600-ton *Darings* of wartime design completed in 1952–54 were run as cruisers and rated for a time as '*Daring* Class Ships', having defeated the contemporary ship classification system. An attempt to develop a still larger 5-inch gun armed 'cruiser-destroyer' stretched rapid-fire gun design beyond the practical limit and proved abortive. Eventually new fleet escorts were built around Seaslug. At over 6,000 tons the ships were the size of the smaller light cruisers of old but to ease their political path they were rated 'guided missile destroyers'. The first four County Class DLGs were laid down at Cammell Laird, John Brown, Swans and Harland and Wolff in 1959–60. Fitting them with 984/CDS would have meant they could have carried no armament other than missiles and an ASW helicopter but limited war requirements dictated they carry guns – four 4.5-inch weapons comparable to an existing destroyer armament. They were thus fitted with advanced Digital Plot Transmission (DPT) data links to receive the carrier's computer synthesized air picture on their reduced Guided Missile Destroyer Display Systems. The Counties were the first ships in the world to have such links – which have since become both commonplace and essential in modern major surface combatants.[4]

These DLGs effectively replaced the older cruisers. The survivors from the Second World War were regarded as the platforms *par excellence* for Cold War duties, being able to provide an imposing presence, transport troops over short to medium distances and bombard the shore with their heavy guns – a capability much used in the early 1950s off Korea and Malaya. Although the existence of Soviet cruisers meant the ships' main armament had a hot war role too, fleet work required improved AA potential. This was only fitted to the last three ships left over from the wartime programmes, *Tiger*, *Lion* and *Blake*, all completed on the Clyde in 1959–60. Their fully automatic 6-inch and 3-inch guns could put up an extraordinary weight of fire, over 100 rounds per minute. Plans to refit other ships similarly were, however, abandoned. Aircraft took over their anti-cruiser role and commando carriers were more attractive and flexible ways of using a cruiser-sized ship's company. So, the number of cruisers dwindled, the last wartime ships being decommissioned in the early 1960s. But the commissioning of the DLGs – four more were built with ADAWS computerized action information organization in the late 1960s, two by Fairfields and two on the Tyne – maintained an operational fleet of about half a dozen larger surface combatants throughout the decade.

The largest surface combatants of all, the battleships, had all gone by 1960. Their manpower demands were just too enormous for the operational return. The four *King George V* class were decommissioned to reserve in 1949–50 under the Revised Restricted Fleet plans and the latest and best battleship, *Vanguard*, was used as a royal yacht. She did see some

189

limited active service in the Mediterranean but became a training ship in 1949. She was notionally reactivated as Home Fleet flagship by the Churchill government in 1951, although her main guns were kept at extended readiness to allow her to operate with a reduced complement. Plans to reactivate her fully in 1955 were affected by the Radical Review and she went into reserve after refit. The KGVs were victims of the Sandys' review and *Vanguard* followed soon after, as the Reserve Fleet was converted into a much slimmed down operational reserve under the Way Ahead Review that did much to shield the active fleet from the Sandys' knife.

The role of the battleship as a covering force for forces exercising and exploiting command of the sea was taken over by a fundamentally new type of submarine, the SSN, powered by a nuclear reactor. The advent of the nuclear submarine did much to negate the ASW advances of the 1950s. The first nuclear submarine, USS *Nautilus*, literally ran rings round Royal Navy forces in the first exercises with her in the mid-1950s. The only answer to the SSN (other than a nuclear depth bomb, and these did not appear in RN service until 1971) was another SSN and Mountbatten put his personal weight behind a British programme. Thanks to Mountbatten's mendacity (he had promised Admiral Rickover that the latter would interview British nuclear submarine captains as he did American[5]), an American reactor was procured to power the first British boat, HMS *Dreadnought*, laid down at Vickers in 1959 and commissioned in 1963, a year after the first SSN with a British designed reactor had been laid down alongside in Barrow. Meanwhile, construction continued of fast battery submarines to a very quiet *Porpoise* design. Completed between 1958 and 1961 by Vickers, Cammell Laird and Scotts, the eight original boats were followed by 13 improved *Oberons*, two of which were built in Chatham dockyard. Although there were problems fitting them with effective weapons, these were true 'Hunter Killer' SSKs, with their own kind as their primary targets. Some 27 A and T class submarines had been modernized in the 1950s with streamlining and improved batteries to give them a performance comparable with the latest boats. The active flotilla of over 30 or more operational modern or modernized SSKs could in the early 1960s deploy three home-based squadrons and four overseas divisions at Malta, Singapore, Sydney (NSW) and Halifax (Nova Scotia). The latter two divisions substituted for the lack of submarines of the local Commonwealth navy.

A major priority in the early days of the Cold War had been mine countermeasures. A clearly remembered lesson of the chaos created by German-influence mines in the early days of the last war, combined with a known propensity of the Russians for mine warfare, advised a major MCM programme. The Revised Restricted Fleet had called for a wartime force of 61 ocean minesweepers and no less than 250 coastal and inshore MCM vessels. Wartime *Algerine* class units were retained for the former requirement

190

and a new replacement projected, but doubts about the ability of such large ships to cope with the latest threat led to the concept being abandoned, although some of the *Algerines* were retained for a time as coastal escorts with modernized ASW armament. The focus of the post-war MCM flotilla was on smaller craft The rearmament programme boosted plans for no less than 170 coastals and 150 inshore vessels but these were cut back steadily in the Radical Review and, in the end, 118 coastals and 104 inshore vessels were built. The original plan to give them names based on colours and insect or bird names mercifully having been abandoned, the coastals became the 'Ton' class and the inshores 'Hams' and 'Leys'. It had been intended to build 'mine location' (that is, minehunting) versions of both coastal and inshore types but the failure of the intended sonar for the coastals led to all being completed as sweepers. Eleven of the smaller vessels, the 'Leys', were minehunters, their 179 sonar being able to cope with inshore conditions. The Tons proved to be particularly useful general purpose patrol vessels as well as being effective in their designed role.

A coastal capability that did not survive the 1950s was the fast attack craft. In the immediate post-war years there was a wartime (and peace-time intelligence gathering) role for these vessels around the shores of mainland Europe. Korean rearmament had led to renewed interest but by 1957 German rearmament reduced this requirement and Coastal Forces had to be sacrificed to Duncan Sandys to maintain more important capabilities. HMS *Hornet*, the headquarters at Gosport was closed. Most of the 11 boats running were paid off and only a handful were retained for fishery protection and training duties.

On the whole, however, the attempt to maintain a balanced fleet by emphasizing the limited war role east of Suez was a triumphant success. Its victory was marked in the last Statement on the Naval Estimates to be issued as a separate document in 1962. Basking in the glow of the highly successful deterrent landing in Kuwait the previous year, which had been spearheaded by the Royal Navy's first LPH, HMS *Bulwark*, it justified the current shape of the Royal Navy purely in terms of an amphibious land-ing. The older concepts of both striking fleet and broken-backed war had been finally abandoned:

> In peace-time the ships of the Royal Navy are stationed all over the world. But when danger threatens they can be quickly assembled to take their place with the Army and Royal Air Force in combined operations to meet the threat. Every ship has her part to play. The commando ships and assault ships put ashore the spearhead of the landing forces with their guns, tanks and vehicles. The aircraft carriers provide reconnaissance and tactical strike ahead of the landing; air defence of the seaborne force; and close support of the troops ashore – especially when this cannot be done either adequately or at all by

land based aircraft. Cruisers and escorts reinforce the air and anti-submarine cover, direct our aircraft and give warning of the enemy's and use their guns for bombardment if required. Submarines provide additional protection against hostile submarines and carry our reconnaissance and minelaying. The minesweepers clear a way to the land.[6]

The sole emphasis on amphibious warfare was a complete change of tack from the naval view in the first post-war decade that forces designed to exercise command of the sea should be sacrificed to those designed to gain it. The weaknesses of the amphibious posture that resulted were shown only too dramatically at Suez in the time taken to mobilize an amphibious task force. Mountbatten, as both first sea lord and chief of defence staff, was a strong supporter of a much improved amphibious capability that lay at the heart of the emphasis on the limited war options that he was using as the foundation of his new naval case. First came the two carrier conversions into commando carriers (LPHs), next the ordering of two amphibious transport docks (LPDs), one from Harland and Wolff and one from John Brown, and finally the replacement of the old tank landing ships by new civilian-manned landing ships logistic (LSLs) built by Hawthorn Leslie (3), Stephen (2) and Fairfield (1).[7]

By the time these ships came into service, however, in the middle to late 1960s, the east of Suez concept was no longer offering the assured role for a balanced fleet that had seemed so secure in the opening years of the decade. There were three interconnected factors in this: (a) the requirement prematurely to go for the Polaris ballistic missile system as the only option to maintain a strategic nuclear capability following the American abandonment of the Skybolt air-launched ballistic missile; (b) Britain's failure to gain admission to the EEC which destroyed previous hopes for rapid growth in the economy to sustain high defence budgets and avoid difficult decisions; and (c) the Royal Air Force's successful attempt to assert a monopoly of the limited war air power role as the basis of its continued institutional existence.

The Admiralty entered the 1960s with high hopes of a programme for replacement of all five strike carriers with new high-performance fighters and strike aircraft *and* the construction of a new generation of helicopter-carrying guided missile escort cruisers to provide platforms for large ASW helicopters. East of Suez provided the key rationale for the carriers. If it were abandoned, as the Admiralty explained to the minister of defence at a major briefing in 1961, an increased number of cruisers would suffice.[8] The possibility of British withdrawal from fixed bases was turned to advantage to argue the carrier case, and the Admiralty used the enthusiasm of the Ministry of Defence for a joint STOV/L fighter, the P1154, to argue the case for a joint (RN/RAF) carrier-based air arm planned around this type; plans for a Buccaneer replacement had to be dropped. The Admiralty envisaged joint air groups of naval and RAF versions of the type using both conventional and STOV/L forms of operation. The RAF countered by arguing the virtues of long-range strike aircraft based on a chain of island bases and small STOV/L support ships to give forward operating platforms for their P1154s. Even at this early stage, it was a planning assumption that there would be no major amphibious operations without the support of allies. The advantages of the carrier were clearly accepted by many in the defence establishment but the RAF and the Treasury were implacable foes. Only by saying (on advice that the aircraft would never be successfully developed) that it would accept the simpler RAF P1154 was the government persuaded to authorize a 50,000 ton CVA01 in 1963. This was the maximum size compatible with existing dock infrastructure. It took two meetings of full Cabinet for even this to be agreed. The new ship, for which the name *Queen Elizabeth* was chosen secretly, was to be a replacement for *Ark Royal* and *Victorious*, nothing more. *Eagle* and *Hermes* would be retained to provide a three-carrier force. The Admiralty thought they had got a foot in the door and planned to call CVA02 'Duke of Edinburgh' when the time came, but they were to be sadly disabused of these high hopes.[9]

The Admiralty had shown interest in Polaris from the time that the missile proved practicable but in-house doubts, from Mountbatten downwards, about the whole doctrine of the independent deterrent, coupled with fear of costs and the RAF's reaction to an attempt to take over the strategic role, advised treading cautiously. The navy contented itself with contingency planning for an eventual replacement of the V-bomber–Skybolt combination. These plans assisted in the smooth creation of the Polaris programme when the Nassau Agreement at the end of 1962 led to the need to procure both Polaris A3 missiles and five, later reduced to four, SSBNs to carry them. The Polaris programme was not unproblematic, however. It was used as the excuse de Gaulle needed to veto British EEC entry. Despite the favourable joint funding arrangements, the opportunity costs of the programme were also serious, not only in occupying available SSN building berths at both Vickers and Cammell Laird (constructing the 'R' class submarines prevented the laying down of further *Valiant* class boats in 1964 and 1965), but also in consuming a significant proportion of the navy's most skilled personnel. Most important, however, was the effect on the Air Ministry, which saw the very survival of the Royal Air Force threatened if it did not destroy the carrier and naval air programmes.

The creation of a unified Ministry of Defence in 1964 and its absorption of the Admiralty into the new organization should have been good news for the navy in that it could argue for a maritime foundation for joint strategy (hence the RAF's real fears). Mountbatten was still chief of defence staff but his influence seems to have been on the wane (there was no leak of the Mountbatten-inspired name for the new carrier that might have made cancellation a little more awkward) and did not make up for the loss of the faithful and powerful civilian Admiralty Secretariat that had assisted, crucially, in allowing the navy to weather the storms of the 1950s. The new institutional structure provided the framework for the next round of the carrier controversy when the new Labour government initiated a defence review to limit the growth in the defence budget. The RAF put forward a superficially impressive case for the Island Plan to the new self-consciously reformist secretary of state, Denis Healey, and he was convinced by it. When the results of the review were announced in early 1966 a major feature was the cancellation of CVAO1. However, although the 'no more opposed landings' planning assumption was now publicized, it was still expected to remain east of Suez until the 1970s. A carrier force would therefore still be useful until then and HMS *Ark Royal* was reprieved to receive limited modernization, to allow three carriers to run on for about another decade.

Nevertheless, CVAO1 cancellation was a dreadful blow to the service. The centrepiece of the fleet for the previous 20 years was doomed to extinction. In fact, there had been dissension already in naval planning circles as to the advisability of continuing what was perhaps an over-emphasis on large carriers. The cancellation of the *Queen Elizabeth* allowed some of these critics to come to the top, notably Sir Varyl Begg, who replaced Sir David Luce who had resigned as first sea lord in protest. Begg created a Future Fleet Working Party which used sophisticated planning tools to map out an affordable future within the government's new expenditure ceiling. This fleet would have the capability both to provide sustenance for whatever east of Suez role the government was planning (a steadily diminishing one) and to provide conventional options for NATO closer to home. Since the early 1960s the Naval Staff, although rejecting previously accepted ideas close to the heart of the NATO's Atlantic Command (and previous British Naval Staffs), such as the Striking Fleet and broken-backed war, had been working on the naval implications of the 'shield forces' (later 'flexible response') ideas originating from SACEUR. The future fleet might well have to operate conventionally in European and Atlantic waters as well as in the Gulf or off South East Asia. The Working Party recommended the building of larger numbers of smaller Sea Dart missile-armed destroyers (DDGs) rather than the larger DLGs of the past. The follow-on class of later ships, the Type 82s (themselves an attempt at some limitation in expense – if not in displacement), were cancelled after one unit, HMS *Bristol*, built by Swans and replaced by a frigate-sized Type 42 DDG, the first of which, HMS *Sheffield*, was laid down at Vickers' yard in Barrow in 1970. A new general purpose frigate was also recommended and this eventually turned out as the attractive Type 21 design used to replace the old Type 41 and 61 ships and commissioned between 1974 and 1978. Although designed by Vosper, most, five out of eight, were built by Yarrow, a yard that also built half the final batch of *Leanders*, completed between 1968 and 1973.

The Working Party favoured continued construction of SSNs, a new improved class of which, the *Swiftsures*, replaced the *Valiants* in 1969. No more conventional submarines were to be built, at least for the time being. It also recommended the maximum utilization of helicopters in surface ships. The *Leander* and *Tribal* classes had introduced small Wasp helicopters as torpedo (and potential nuclear depth bomb) delivery vehicles and they were now to be used more for surface search and missile attack also (the sinking of the Israeli destroyer *Eilath* by Egyptian missile boats in 1967 dramatically confirmed this requirement). Development of a radar-equipped follow-on small ship helicopter, the Lynx, began as part of the Wilson government's Anglo-French initiatives.

It was the requirement for platforms for the large Sea King helicopters which led to serious controversy. The planned helicopter-carrying escort cruisers remained in the programme (indeed *Blake* and *Tiger* were taken in hand for conversion to provide interim examples). The Working Party argued that the new build command cruisers should be in effect small carriers, carrying the operational 'Harrier' variant of the P1127 development aircraft for the P1154 as well as large helicopters for ASW and airborne early warning (AEW). This would provide vital organic air cover where the RAF could not reach. This caused an explosion at the top and the end of the career of the Working Party's chairman, the very able first ACNS(P), Rear Admiral J. H. Adams, but the idea had been planted for future reference.

The decision to withdraw from east of Suez by 1971 was eventually taken at the beginning of 1968 in the aftermath of devaluation. Although this meant an earlier than expected end to the carrier force, the adoption the previous year of Flexible Response allowed the existing and planned fleet to continue with remarkably few problems. The amphibious ships could just as well be used on the northern and southern flanks of NATO as they had been covering the withdrawal from Aden or countering Sukarno around Malaysia. Operations in the Atlantic against the growing Soviet Navy required submarines and surface escorts. And from 1968, with the departure of the champions of the anti-carrier party (notably the replacement of Sir Varyl Begg by Sir Michael LeFanu and Sir Edward Ashmore replacing Sir Peter Hill-Norton as VCNS), the design of the command cruiser began to evolve towards an aircraft carrier. A design of almost 20,000 tons was chosen in 1970 for the so-called 'Through Deck Command Cruiser' (TDCC). The through deck made sense in helicopter operational terms but it could, when the time was right and RAF opposition to organic naval air had diminished, do much more.

The election of the Heath government in 1970 did little to affect the continuity of naval policy. The withdrawal from east of Suez was upheld with only a few cosmetic changes. HMS *Ark Royal*, fresh from her rebuild got a reprieve but she remained the only aircraft carrier, *Eagle* being placed in storage on schedule as a source of spares and *Hermes* being converted to an LPH to replace *Albion*. The first of the new TDCCs was ordered from Vickers in April 1973 but the economic problems of the government, coupled with continued RAF hostility, delayed an order for the newly designed Sea Harrier. These economic difficulties led eventually to the crisis of 1974 and the return of Harold Wilson to Downing Street. In an apparent defence review to save hundreds of millions of pounds the navy's proportion of the budget actually increased. The new government was interested primarily in defence as a source of domestic jobs but this could be manipulated by Defence Secretary Mason to justify major new naval construction.

As a result, the defence industries remained busy both throughout the life of the Wilson government, and that of its successor led by the more actively pro-navy Jim Callaghan. The second production line for SSNs at Cammell Laird had been abandoned after *Conqueror*'s completion in 1971 as a result both of the 1967 devaluation crisis and dissatisfaction with the product, but Barrow built four more S class SSNs commissioned between 1974 and 1979 and a last one was laid down in 1977 (to commission in 1981). Two of a follow-on 'T' class were on order by the time the Labour government fell. Type 42 construction went ahead at Vickers, Cammell Laird, Vospers and Swans with a total of 14 units being constructed, the last four, ordered in 1978–79, to a lengthened design.

The *Leander* class were modernized into a 'Batch 1' with Ikara ASW missiles or a 'Batch 2' with Exocet anti-ship missiles and a programme of completely rebuilding the final Batch 3 ships with not only Exocet but the advanced Sea Wolf point defence SAM was begun. A new first-rate ASW frigate appeared in 1979 in the shape of the Type 22, one of which had been laid down at Yarrows every year from 1975. This was a large and expensive 4,000 tonner and the programme came close to cancellation after the first four. It was decided, however, to continue the programme with a lengthened Batch 2 design to carry new and very powerful US 'Outboard' long-range passive electronic surveillance and code-breaking equipment. The willingness of the Americans to provide this equipment to the British was an interesting index of the depth of the 'Special Relationship' in its naval and intelligence dimensions. The first Batch 2 Type 22, HMS *Boxer* was ordered from Yarrow yard in April 1979, one of the last acts of the Callaghan administration. By the time she was commissioned, at the beginning of 1984, three more were under construction at the same yard.

Most important of all, however, were carrier developments. In 1975, Sea Harriers were finally ordered for the TDCC, HMS *Invincible*, the chief of air staff having been persuaded not to oppose the measure. By this stage the RAF wanted to use the naval order as a vehicle to develop a new Harrier airframe but the Admiralty, understandably suspicious of RAF good faith, was worried that the latter were just trying to undermine and delay the programme by increasing its expense and complexity.[10] The Sea Harrier was to be based on the existing airframe. It was also announced that two more through deck cruisers were to be ordered, both, this time, from Swans. The second *Illustrious* was given a 'carrier' name and the name of the third, ordered at the end of 1978, *Ark Royal*, made it even more obvious what kind of ships these were. On commissioning in 1980, *Invincible* was rated an ASW support aircraft carrier, CVS, later altered to CVSG to mark the retention of Sea Dart, a kind of evolutionary throwback to the ship's cruiser origins.

To act as interim CVSs, the LPHs were modified for this role, both *Hermes* and *Bulwark* serving with Sea Harrier and Sea King air groups. The former received the same 'ski-jump' fitted to the bows of the *Invincibles* to optimize the performance of her Sea Harrier aircraft. Effectively, Britain never ceased to be a carrier power, despite the decommissioning of the old *Ark Royal* at the end of 1978.

Despite its pro-defence rhetoric, the Thatcher government was potentially disastrous for the Royal Navy. First, it altered the balance of defence spending by increasing the pay of personnel. This was necessary to staunch an outward flow of manpower but it forced economies elsewhere. Next, it decided to replace Polaris with the improved but expensive Trident system, the expenditure for which would fall on the naval component of the budget. And, finally, with a programme that clearly could not be fitted into the planned financial allocations, its second defence minister, John Nott, began a rigorous defence review that firmly placed the UK maritime contribution in the Atlantic fourth in priority, behind the maintenance of the nuclear deterrent, the defence of the UK and the land and air contribution on the European mainland. The navy did not help itself by its failure to develop a coherent strategic and operational doctrine for its contribution to NATO's deterrent posture. Therefore, Mr Nott made cuts on the basis of what sized fleet could be supported by a reduced infrastructure, Chatham dockyard being slated for closure and Portsmouth for reductions. The emphasis would be on submarines, both nuclear and conventionally powered. The frigate and destroyer force was to be reduced from 58 units to 42 active and eight reserve ships. The *Leander* modernization programme would cease and an austere Type 23 frigate brought into production to replace the Type 22s. Sea Dart would not be improved and Type 42 modernization cancelled. The LPDs were to be scrapped and the carrier force reduced to two. *Illustrious* would replace *Hermes* and *Ark Royal* would replace *Invincible*, which was to be sold to Australia. Keith Speed, the junior navy minister, was sacked when he made his opposition to the naval cuts public. He was the last minister to have specifically naval responsibilities.

Changes were soon made in these controversial plans. The LPDs were saved by a combination of American pressure and revision of the Trident programme. But it was a minor cut, that of the Ice Patrol Ship *Endurance* which helped stimulate the invasion of the Falklands, that allowed Sir Henry Leach to demonstrate the continued relevance and capabilities of the 'Eastlant Navy' far from its primarily intended area of operation. All of its elements were used to recover the islands; SSNs provided cover from major units of the Argentine fleet; Sea Harriers from *Hermes* and *Invincible* inflicted decisive attrition on Argentine land-based air power; escorts protected the amphibious forces from air and submarine attack; amphibious assets carried troops and landed them. Mrs Thatcher suddenly became very pro-navy, the service that had saved her political skin, but one must not over-state the results. The destroyer/frigate force was returned to 55 (of which about 42 were in service at any one time) until 1984 although it was to fall again to 50 thereafter, all notionally in service (although late 1980s Defence White Papers usually only listed about 42 as actually active). *Invincible*'s sale was cancelled although only two CVSGs were to be kept in service at any one time. The new *Ark Royal* replaced *Hermes*.

The Type 22 programme was given a new lease of life by the Falklands War, two more 'Batch 2' ships being built by Swans to replace the lost DDGs *Sheffield* and *Coventry*, and four more heavily armed 'Batch 3s' being completed in the late 1980s, one by Yarrow, one by Cammell Laird and one by Swan Hunter. The Type 23 was also redesigned into a more general purpose frigate rather than just a platform for the towed array sonar. The first, HMS *Norfolk*, was laid down at Yarrow in 1985.

It was not only the Falklands War that helped the Royal Navy in the 1980s. The development of a more coherent doctrine for fighting in the Atlantic beneath the nuclear threshold helped make it easier to justify remaining force levels. NATO's forward maritime strategy gave the British the command of the Anti-Submarine Striking Force that would lead the US carriers through the Greenland–Iceland–UK gap to their Norwegian bastions.[11] British submarines would, like their US counterparts, penetrate Soviet SSBN operating areas to tie down Soviet assets in defensive operations.

There was also a new emphasis on 'out of area' operations, something the Naval Staff had never ignored even in the NATO-oriented 1970s. Even the Nott review had spoken of the need to operate globally. The war between Iraq and Iran provided a requirement for escort operations and an opportunity to demonstrate the Royal Navy's facility at MCM. The latter assets had benefited from being included in Mr Nott's first and second priorities and the 1980s saw the completion by Vosper and Yarrow of 13 *Hunt* class combined mine hunter-sweepers and the commissioning of 12 Richards-built (seven at Lowestoft and five at Great Yarmouth) *River* class minesweepers to clear the continental shelf seabed off Britain's submarine bases of advanced rising ASW mines. A new cheaper class of single role minehunter was also designed, the first being launched by Vosper in 1988; three could be afforded for the price of two *Hunts*.

So the Royal Navy ended the Cold War with a better defined role than it had possessed for the previous two decades but also with sufficient flexibility to cope more than adequately with a strategic revolution. The fleet was still the strongest outside the superpowers. Total displacement of major surface combatants had stayed remarkably stable from 1960 to 1990, at around 200,000 and 300,000 respectively. Despite the demise of the last large carrier, a comprehensive set of capabilities was still deployed. This was a remarkable tribute to those who had made the 'Naval Case' in its various forms, strategic and industrial, during some trying and difficult years.

NOTES

1. This article is based in large part on the author's *Vanguard to Trident: British Naval Policy Since World War Two* (Annapolis, MD: Naval Institute Press and London: Bodley Head, 1997). Unless otherwise stated, readers are referred to this text for footnotes and further discussion.
2. For the best account of this see Norman Friedman, *The Post-War Naval Revolution* (London: Conway Maritime Press, 1986).
3. For the development of CDS and its impact see the author's 'Naval Command and Control Equipment: The Birth of the Late Twentieth Century "Revolution in Military Affairs"', in *Cold War, Hot Science: Applied Research in the UK's Defence Research Laboratories, 1945–90* (Amsterday, Netherlands: Harwood Academic Publishers, 1999), ch. 9.
4. Ibid.
5. Author's interview with Admiral Crowe (Washington, 1998).
6. Command 1629, paragraph 2.
7. For a detailed account of the development of amphibious warfare in this period see Ian Spellar, 'The Role of Amphibious Warfare in Britain 1945–64' (PhD thesis, Department of War Studies, Kings College, London, 1996).
8. For the records of this event see PRO file ADM205/192.
9. See ibid., and the author's 'Partnership Spurned, The Royal Navy's Search for a Joint Air Force East of Suez', in N. A. M. Rodger, ed., *Naval Power in the Twentieth Century* (London: Macmillan, 1996).
10. See Sir Edward Ashmore's memoirs, *The Battle and the Breeze* (Stroud, Gloucestershire: Alan Sutton, 1997) for a first-hand account of these negotiations.
11. See the author's *Battle for the Fiords: NATO's Forward Maritime Strategy in Action* (London: Ian Allan, 1990).

12

Purposes and Platforms in the US Navy, 1945–90

George W. Baer

INTRODUCTION

At the end of the Second World War, the US fleet was victorious, new, strong and strategically obsolete. It was obsolete because it had not found a method to put to strategic use the new instruments of war: the fast, high-endurance, deep-traveling submarine, jet combat aircraft, guided weapons, cruise missiles, ballistic missiles and the atomic bomb. In the hands of a determined enemy these could contest the navy's command of the sea – and put the US homeland at risk. The navy's challenge, which became urgent as the Cold War militarized, was to match these new weapons to navy needs to prepare to fight the country's most likely foes.

To prevent its victorious offensive force from becoming marginalized in the atomic age, the navy first established a mission for its heavy attack carriers as part of the policy of containment. Then, through revaluing its submarine force, it made the navy central to the other framing policy of the era: deterrence of nuclear war. Success, calculated in terms of capacity for use in a possible war with the Soviet Union, was the extent to which these innovations were strategically relevant. In 1990, when the Soviet Union – and Cold War strategy – collapsed, the navy found itself once again victorious, thoroughly modern, still based on heavy carriers and sub-marines, and again strategically obsolete.

The navy's innovators, Admirals Radford, Rickover, Burke, Raborn and Thomas Hayward, managed well because they tied their favored platforms to prevailing doctrines of offensive warfare, to the privileged strategies: nuclear attack and force projection. Less successful innovators failed because they could not carry a case for other types of forces or strategies. The sea control argument, for instance, gathered little steam. Zumwalt and others who argued for lighter, low-end, defensive platforms were defeated by the fact that an offensive threat at sea barely existed, and the assumption that the Soviets would react to US offensive strategy by withdrawing their nuclear attack submarines from the open ocean.

In discussing the Cold War decades I will look first at how the navy in the 1940s and 1950s saved its carrier fleet. It did this by justifying a sea-borne delivery system for the atomic bomb through a doctrine called attack-at-the-source: land attack as a means of sea control. This was in its origins a strategy of war-fighting, not yet part of the emerging doctrines of containment or deterrence under which it and so much other strategy was soon subsumed. In grasping an atomic mission – in creating a naval purpose for the most important weapon of the time – the navy saved its attack carriers, which were in turn its highest technological achievement. This kept the limelight on the navy's air branch, shadowing its surface and sub-surface sister communities.

Second, I will show how the development of underwater-launched missiles in the late 1950s and early 1960s, and the platforms and doctrines for their use, gave the navy a new strategic standing in the policy of deterrence. The Polaris and Poseidon programs joined advances in missile technology to the nuclear-propelled submarine by which the navy won parity with its rival, the air force, in strategic delivery systems. Then in the 1980s the navy trumped the air force with the Trident system, an accurate, submarine-launched counterforce weapon carried on a platform more secure than an air force silo and less vulnerable than a land-based bomber.

Third, I will argue that the favored nuclear-strike capabilities came at the cost of reducing the technologies, doctrines and strategies available to other naval missions and needs. Force modernization suffered, innovation was constrained and other missions, notably sea control, were limited or bypassed. In the 1970s the navy sought to overcome this deformation and regain capabilities of sea control and intervention based on a newly designed mix of ships and missions, the ships of a high/low force structure.

Finally, with its deterrence mission secured by Trident II, I will note how the maritime strategy of the 1980s re-established mission flexibility and pulled together a high-end, bravura offensive strategy that the navy could conduct with only slight reference to its competitor – the air force. The doctrine of this maritime strategy returned offensive purpose to attack carriers and attack submarines, and amphibious assault to the Marine Corps. The naval services reverted to a strategy of force projection, based on the inherent mobility of naval platforms. The maritime strategy of the 1980s was an assertion of a war-fighting, offensive doctrine, supported by a force build-up, 'on-site, on-time'. It remained, however, a naval strategy, and was not integrated into the national military strategy, where the fear was that mobility – the navy's great virtue – might lead to horizontal escalation and to an expanded, protracted kind of war.

None the less, by the end of the Cold War the navy had become immensely strong, well supplied, technologically advanced and operationally robust. Its strategy was based on a familiar and comfortable force, centered on the attack carrier and the submarine, with which it had fought the previous war. It is proof of the navy's successful adaptation of its dominant platforms that their numbers remained almost constant throughout the 40 years of the Cold War. And yet, the navy's role after 1990 was poorly stated. Despite the astounding amount of power and technological sophistication it deployed afloat, the US Navy, in 1990 as in 1945, was strategically unfocused.[1]

THE TIME OF THE CARRIER, 1945–60

An Atomic Offensive

In 1945 the navy's problem was this: if it could not deliver atomic bombs against Soviet targets on land, it could not claim a strategic rationale for the attack carriers on which the navy based its way-of-war. To be sure, the navy might have deduced a sea-control mission to guard Atlantic shipping against an improved force of Soviet submarines. But that was defensive, part of a conventional utility as a patrol and transport service, routine jobs for lesser ships. To a navy leadership of offensive-minded carrier aviators, that meant marginalization. To save the attack carriers, to put them in a forward offensive role, to break the US Air Force's monopoly of atomic bombing, the navy's leaders had to establish a rationale for sea-launched atomic-loaded attacks against targets ashore.

This was done by connecting attacks against land targets to the navy's primary defensive mission of sea control. As in the previous world wars, the optimum Anti-Submarine Warfare (ASW) strategy was to destroy enemy submarines in their ports. To secure platforms for this attack, carrier air would have to strike inland also, against the bases of Soviet anti-ship bombers. This strategy, the navy said, was connected in turn to shaping a particular type atomic war: a phased and protracted war favored by maritime powers. With sea control and carrier mobility, the US could determine the tempo of operations and put the ocean spaces to its advantage. Navy precision strikes, counter-force bombing (that is, against military targets) would support a phased land campaign, leading to a victory that would be more meaningful, more moral even, than one derived from the inaccurate, urban/industrial targeting of air force-driven strategic planning. If a Soviet attack could not be stopped, troopships could extract US forces and return them for an eventual counterattack, another D-Day invasion – a maritime strategy based on sea-control.

For this the navy needed permission for strategic land-attacks, platforms large enough to carry atomic bombs and larger, and consequently heavier, aircraft. That meant bigger carriers.

202

The service at once reconfigured its first carrier-launched heavy-attack bomber, the AJ-1 Savage, to carry deep inland the 10,000 lb MK III Fat Man. Simultaneously, the navy began studies for a long-range bomber twice as heavy and for a new class of flush-decked, all-weather super-carriers able to operate in rough North Atlantic waters. In 1947, the Chief of naval operations (CNO) approved plans for such a carrier, 1,000 feet at the waterline with a beam of 125 feet. In 1948 Congress authorized its construction.

Opposed, of course, were the air force and the army. This was a time of ruthless downsizing and mercantilist competition for budget share. Money given to one service was taken from that available to the others. Institutions for joint coordination in peacetime were still in their infancy. Also, compromises made on air-atomic roles were vaguely worded, adding to the urgency of each service to protect its claims.

Yet, there had been Congressional authorization for a super-carrier and in April 1949 its keel was laid. Five days later the secretary of defense canceled its construction. In scuttling navy hopes, he was supported by the army and air force chiefs of staff who argued that existing national war plans and the B-36 made the navy's air-atomic strategy superfluous. Furthermore they believed that smaller carrier classes should serve the navy's sea control mission, and that a forward-deployed super-carrier would be vulnerable to Soviet maritime defenses.[2] The air force (and national strategy) took the Soviet atomic explosion of 1949 as validation for deep-strike, short-war, counter-value intercontinental bombing.

Carriers for Intervention and Support

It was a shock to aviators to see the carriers' now jet-powered, air-atomic mission challenged by new delivery systems, long-range land-based bombers and missiles. To expand (and preserve) the utility of its carrier force the navy adapted its attack aircraft to missions of intervention and to tactical support operations, directly supporting the policy of containment. Using carriers for intervention strikes enabled the navy to keep the platforms at the core of the fleet even after their air-atomic mission was over.

Two years after it was canceled, construction on the super-carrier began again. The *Forrestal* was the child of a huge militarization, product of the changed strategic environment, of Soviet and Chinese military resurgence and of the heating-up of the Cold War. In NSC-68 the US declared re-armament to be imperative, while the Korean War showed the value of the carrier. Air-combat sorties demonstrated the support navy air could give in limited wars. Sea forces had a place in the atomic age after all. Ships took the amphibious force to Inchon to unhinge the North Koreans. Ships hauled the supplies and extracted troops in danger. At Hungnam,

193 ships removed 193,000 people, 350,000 tons of cargo and 17,500 vehicles. Amphibious operations, notably Inchon, showed the relevance of fleet marines. In 1951 the JCS ended the navy's air-atomic frustration by giving it a partial victory: doctrinal authority not for a deep 'strategic' role, but for carrier-launched atomic 'attack at the source' and for striking land targets in battlefield flank support up to 600 miles from the launching ship. The navy at once established a list of land targets: 98 Soviet naval bases and 287 airfields.

Highlighting this revival, new general-purpose super-carriers, the *Forrestal* class, were designed to use jet aircraft for both limited air-atomic attack and strikes in support of limited interventions. Heavy aircraft became lighter (the A-4 Skyhawk) and dual-purpose, designed to carry smaller atomic weapons as well as for close combat support. Carrier air shifted, as Norman Friedman wrote, 'from strategic strikes by small numbers of heavy bombers to tactical air strikes by much larger air groups of smaller aircraft'.[3] Major design innovations in this period – angled deck, steam catapult, mirror landing system (all British inventions), and safer fuel – permitted the launching and landing of jet aircraft.[4]

Interdiction, tactical support and presence gave carrier air a broad role in the policy of containment. For containment (as opposed to nuclear deterrence) was a peripheral strategy, sustained around the edges of a land empire. So containment interventions were often maritime, and it was the navy, its carriers, its regional fleets, its Fleet Marine Force, that carried the flag. Between 1946 and 1960 the navy and marines responded to 60 political emergencies. The appearance of ships and amphibious forces off Haiti, Turkey, Greece, Trieste, Lebanon, Italy, Israel, Norway, Taiwan, Quemoy, Panama, Indo-China, Suez, Indonesia, Venezuela and, of course, action in Korea and Cuba reminds us of the reach and influence of naval forward presence in those years, years that established the spheres of influence of the Cold War.[5] It was this utility, this reach, this flexibility, that kept up the carrier levels. After 1950 the navy regained its carrier strength, and the number of heavy attack carriers remained roughly constant at around 14 for the rest of the Cold War.[6] Underway replenishment operations acted as a force-multiplier. The navy's great system of logistical supply at sea remained its key to expanding maritime capabilities.[7]

By 1960, then, the navy could claim success in maintaining its carrier force. Attack carriers, technical marvels, were still at the fleet's fighting core. But, after a decade of adaptation the navy was not where its leaders wanted it to be. The surface force was shrinking. The Defense Reorganization Act of 1958 took operation command of naval combat forces and control of the navy's force structure from the CNO and gave it to the secretary of defense. In 1962 the secretary of defense took the attack carriers out of the hair-triggered strategic-alert force of the SIOP.

That decision reflected the administration's questioning of the strategic value of the hugely expensive ships. The cost of nuclear-power carriers threatened to unbalance the fleet. Secretary of Defense McNamara who, after *Enterprise* was commissioned in 1961 halted follow-on designs for a second nuclear-propelled carrier, overrode navy assertions of their endurance and versatility. The first of the subsequent *Nimitz* class was not laid down until 1968 and not commissioned until 1975. McNamara questioned carriers' value. They were not being used for sea control. There were no Soviet carriers to oppose. Attack-at-the-source had become too risky. The deterrent role of carriers was being outpaced by the strategic missile programs. In the early 1960s strategic attack-carrier doctrine as it was formed in the war and developed in the late 1940s and early 1950s was at a dead end.

On the other hand, deletion from the short-fused strategic-alert force, had, the VCNO said, 'removed a restraint on CVA operations and restored flexibility for conventional missions while retaining a nuclear capability against non-time-sensitive targets and tactical targets'.[8] In the 1960s two more fossil-fuel carriers were commissioned, and the workhorse of attack-air became the A-6 Intruder, a high-subsonic, all-weather, low-level performer with a 1,000 mile range. Freed for more movement, carriers regained the mobility that was their hall-mark, the ability to approach a target area from any direction, for intervention and for complicating Soviet air defenses – and on this mobility, the central feature of flexible response, their contribution to the strategic force was continued until the mid-1970s.[9]

Meanwhile, to the fore of naval and national strategies came a renewed call for sea control and the advent of sea-launched IRBMs. The submarine and the missile, not carrier air, became the center of Navy attention going into the 1960s. The most costly of these, and strategically the most important, was *Polaris*.

STRATEGIC STRIKE REVIVED, 1960–80

Polaris

The development of nuclear propulsion by Rickover and the concurrent development of an undersea-launched IRBM under Raborn and Burke were by far the most important technical achievements of the Cold War US Navy. They formed a system that has been called 'possibly the most revolutionary development in weapons technology in the twentieth century'.[10]

With nuclear propulsion Rickover aimed at what he called a 'new navy'. With Polaris the Navy regained a central strategic role. Nuclear propulsion transformed the length of time submarines and carriers could stay at sea, as well as their sustained speed. The marriage of nuclear submarines to a reliable atomic and, after 1954, nuclear (hydrogen)-tipped ballistic missile created the most secure, and the most credible, weapon supporting the policy of deterrence.

As in any process of technical innovation, the skill and drive of managers was paramount. Rickover's vision, political and bureaucratic skill, and ruthless control of all design and construction are legendary. The way he shepherded his program through Congressional committees and around opponents within his own service, and the way he used the support of private contractors, while retaining and increasing his tsar-like authority, is a story of major managerial achievement.[11] 'Never has a naval engineering project of such complexity been accomplished in so short a time.'[12]

Rickover's first priority was the nuclear submarine, a true submarine of enormous undersea endurance. The keel of the 320-foot *Nautilus* was laid in 1952; three years later she was 'under way on nuclear power'. Shipbuilding and technical successes, however, were not the same as defining use or establishing purpose. Those were matters of further political and military decisions.

And what of the technical situation? In this case, as with the carrier, we see a conjunction of innovations that were part of the navy's embrace of atomic strategy. Already the navy had developed an atomic-capable sea-launched cruise missile, the pre-set, jet-powered, 550-mile Regulus I, and was looking forward to a 1,000-mile supersonic Regulus II. To carry these, the navy was planning to convert – or build – diesel submarines (as indeed they did). By the early 1960s five Regulus-bearing strike submarines (one nuclear-powered) were available for patrol, playing minor parts in the strategy of nuclear deterrence. Large nuclear-propelled submarines were vastly improved platforms, and Polaris a vastly more powerful weapon. But there was reasoned opposition to connecting nuclear submarines and the nuclear ballistic missile into a single delivery system. Many navy leaders wanted to use the speedy and silent nuclear-powered boats as sea-control weapons, for torpedo attack and intelligence gathering, and they cautioned delay until development of both missile and platform was further advanced.

Disputes over how to employ nuclear-powered submarines were part of the rapidly changing technological and strategic environments. A decision was needed for one to prevail, and that choice was to be made by Arleigh Burke who, in his six-year tenure as CNO (August 1955–August 1961), made a lasting impression on the Cold War navy.

Taking advantage of the transforming technologies of the transistor, digital computation, miniaturization, inertial guidance, solid propellants for ship-board launch, underwater launchers and smaller and lighter nuclear warheads, Raborn, with Burke's aggressive support, drove the Polaris program. He matched weapon to platform, while Rickover oversaw the submarines' nuclear-propulsion system.

Together, nuclear vessel and nuclear weapon were combined as a navy project in a single fleet ballistic missile system. This became the navy's main contribution to the national strategy of deterrence, and hence to the national way of (non-)war. At the end of 1960 *George Washington* was deployed on strategic patrol, carrying a full load of 16 Polaris A-1s, solid fueled, with a range of 1,200 miles, long enough to hit Moscow from many places in the sea. That missile was retired in 1965, and followed by the second generation, Polaris A-2, with a 1,500-mile range and much greater reliability. The A-3 model, in the fleet in 1964, ranged 2,500 miles and carried a payload of three warheads having a force of 200 kilotons. The Polaris A-3, as we will note later, was a counter-city weapon, its warheads shotgunned to the target. To carry these came a new class of submarines. The *Ethan Allen* class, commissioned in 1961, was designed from keel up to hold any of three types of Polaris missiles. Its five boats were the first of the future fleet of ballistic missile submarines.

The Polaris system worked. The program was one of the great technical and managerial successes of navy history. Complex inventions were brought to life. Graham Spinardi called it a success of 'heterogeneous engineering', an organizational triumph in a dense intellectual, social and fiscal environment.[13] Harvey Sapolsky wrote 'there were many technologies involved in the Polaris system and many technologies had to be advanced. Perhaps the real achievement was advancing them all at the same time.'[14] Raborn and Rickover were both outsiders to the submarine community and had to overcome internal opposition. They had very different styles of management and they ran the missile and propulsion projects in very different ways. Their successes demonstrate that 'there is no single path to technological innovation'.[15]

Polaris, however, was developed at the expense of other navy programs. The navy had hoped at first that Polaris would be funded as a national project, outside the navy budget. It was not, and the price of autonomy of the fleet ballistic missile program, mainly the cost of the submarine platform for carrying and launching, dug deeply into the navy's budget. Top technical personnel were assigned to Polaris. To pay for this, other programs were canceled, among them the cruise missile program centered on Regulus II which was facing problems of development and operation. Submarines had to surface to fire it, its accuracy was poor and its fuel dangerous. Admiral Zumwalt said that killing the Regulus program was 'the single worst decision about weapons [the Navy] made during my years of service' and blamed the heavy-carrier enthusiasts for their hostility to cruise missiles.[16] It is debatable, on grounds of strategic effectiveness, whether some of the cancelations actually (or potentially) reduced strategic and operational alternatives, or whether they were poor designs with no future, and were wisely canceled. Also canceled was a jet-powered bomber that could land on the sea, and plans for a nuclear-powered airplane, an ecological nightmare with radioactive exhaust and limited payload because of its heavy reactor shield. Nuclear propulsion of warships, however, surged. By 1980, 25 years after *Nautilus*, the navy operated, and Rickover's reactors propeled, the growing offensive force of ballistic-missile submarines and the new *Nimitz* class of heavy attack carriers. Meanwhile, ship maintenance fell behind, development of other weapons lagged, attack submarines, cruisers, blimps, fast-deployment logistic ships, transport aircraft, all had less because of the strategic value set on Polaris. 'It was the popularity of Polaris and not the Navy that accounts for the Navy department's steady claim on the defense budget in the years between Korea and Vietnam.'[17]

What Polaris did was put a navy system into the forefront of national strategy. That had been the clear purpose of the navy's command. Burke, Rickover and Raborn knew full well that, in Sapolsky's words, 'the choice among weapons projects is the choice among defense strategies'.[18] It is therefore worth noting the nature of this strategic value, for Polaris served a fundamentally different strategy than had the strike carriers or cruise missiles of the previous decade.

Those other navy forces were, and remained, counter-force. They were for military targets, for sea control, for targets of naval opportunity, a way-of-war meant to be different in kind from the counter-value city-busting strategy of the air force and the SIOP. Introducing the fleet ballistic missile, the navy joined the air force strategy. Polaris was less vulnerable but less accurate than land-based missiles, strong but not accurate enough to destroy hardened military targets. So its targets were, and had to be, centers of population and areas of large concentration – cities and industry – not armies or air bases.

To favor Polaris, Burke redirected strategic discussion. He introduced the concept of 'finite deterrence', based, as Polaris, on a mobile, concealed, second-strike retaliatory missile force, not able to hit military targets but strong enough to establish deterrence value, and hidden and invulnerable enough for controlled response. On these terms of retaliatory deterrence the fleet ballistic missile was justified and placed in the national strategy.

HIGH/LOW FORCE MIX, THE 1970S

Admiral Elmo R. Zumwalt (CNO 1970–74) sought to reconstitute the 'low' end of the fleet. He did not ignore the 'high' end. He led a successful campaign for the fourth nuclear-powered super-carrier and strongly supported the F-14 Tomcat fighter (633 of which were built), and the Trident submarine and missile program to replace Polaris and its successor Poseidon. But Zumwalt saw that the ships at the 'low' end of the fleet, ships for missions of sea control and intervention, were being

208

retired and had to be replaced. He decided that the international environment permitted him to risk current readiness to prepare for a more dangerous future. Despite growing Soviet naval strength, an aggressive Soviet naval doctrine, improved Soviet stand-off bomber defenses, and increases in sea-denial attack submarines and global-ranging missile-carrying SSBNs, the 1970s were a period of relative calm in US political relations with the Soviet Union. In this warmer atmosphere Zumwalt gambled that he could afford a preparedness gap during which he could modernize the low end of the fleet for the sea control contest that the Soviet build-up portended.

The most successful of his low-end ship-building initiatives was a new frigate for ASW and AAW escort, the *Oliver Hazard Perry* class, of which some 55 were built. A subsequent navy secretary called it 'one of the most successful ship-building programs in the navy's post-war history'.[19] The goal of most of the other 22 of Zumwalt's reforms was to design lower-valued combatants for varied sea control missions.[20] These included improved ship-based helicopter operations and better mine, missile, gun and surveillance systems. Some had a strong future. Cruise missiles returned with the Harpoon anti-ship missile which became a major defensive protection against Soviet surface-ship attack and gave surface ships a strike role in fleet-on-fleet sea control engagements. Tomahawk was both an anti-ship missile and a land-attack cruise missile. Amphibious assault ships (LHA-*Tarawa* class) supported an offensive capability for land attack. Captor mines, although not fully developed, permitted extended ASW barriers.

Zumwalt's management of innovation also suffered some low-end setbacks when he failed to establish the strategic utility of his proposals. He limited himself to mission statements and plans for weapons that were deeply opposed by many within the navy itself. Most of Zumwalt's reforms did not last beyond his term of office. His ideas for a mini-carrier sea control ship, for V/stol aircraft, for an air-cushioned surface effect ship and for hydrofoils, were not so much before their time as outside it. They were not integrated into regnant doctrine, and Zumwalt had neither the institutional authority nor external motivation (such as a strong Soviet sea-power threat) to overcome opposition. There were other problems, it should be noted. Some innovations remained technically precarious. For instance, officers complained that the *Perry* class frigates, the FFGs, had dangerously thin aluminum hulls, limited fire control and communications, and power-plant problems that were the result of choosing quantity over quality. Zumwalt would disagree, but he had not managed to match innovation to doctrine, or platforms to strategy.

It would have been hard to do so. Zumwalt had to deduce the navy's war-fighting needs within a foreign policy context that had no central place for the navy. The foreign policies of President Richard Nixon and

President Jimmy Carter stressed deterrence, détente and disarmament. Carter encouraged an air–ground defense in Europe. If those failed, what was envisioned was a short nuclear war in which there would be no need for offensive seapower, protection of shipping or overseas intervention. To be sure, the Nixon Doctrine seemed to encourage continued maritime strength to support states on the periphery, but this was not its main theme. So, without much policy guidance, Zumwalt responded to what he saw, which was the intra-navy need to shore up a diminished force of both ships and men to prepare for competition at sea. He did not offer a broader perspective by which to prioritize his platform proposals. His deductive approach did not make it emphatically clear how sea control and power projection, defense and offense, were important to the nation in the 1970s.

Within the service, furthermore, Zumwalt was opposed by differing views on naval strategy and by contrary judgments on technology. High-value advocates, carrier admirals and submariners, whose community dominance Zumwalt sought to reduce, argued that the low-value combatants were strategically inadequate platforms for the many, adaptable missions the navy required of its carrier force. Proposed for protective sea control, they lacked offensive punch should the United States engage in a limited nuclear or a serious but non-nuclear shooting war. Smaller in size, endurance and force, they could not compete with heavy forces in such a conflict, delivering neither sea control nor force and fire against the land. The low-end force, opponents said, was defensive when the US needed an offensive navy to overcome a defensive Soviet maritime strategy. 'It's a Third World-oriented strategy', said a subsequent air-minded CNO. 'It's what I call the "convoy syndrome".'[21]

The navy did not resolve this controversy by a strategic consensus. In 1975, the navy's 200th anniversary, the active fleet was smaller than that of 1939. Draw-downs had hollowed the force, restricting operations. Post-Vietnam, penury and manpower discouragement beset the service. By the end of the 1970s it seemed the navy had lost its course. To be sure, it was often called upon for crisis response. In the period of the drifting and confused 1970s, the navy and marine corps were called for 33 crisis-response missions, with strike carriers deployed on over 70 per cent of those occasions. During the Cold War, from 1946 to 1990, navy and marine corps forces played a role in at least 207 US responses to international incidents, exclusive of the combat action in the Korean and Vietnam wars. This number of crisis-management operations does not include humanitarian missions such as disaster relief or medical-ship port calls, intelligence or law enforcement operations or diplomatic assistance.[22]

RETURN TO OFFENSIVE POWER PROJECTION, THE 1980s

Both nature of focus and priority of force structures changed in the 1980s. It was a decade that brought remarkable revivals of naval strength and the doctrine of offensive war at sea.

Offensive sea control was the result of a new assessment of how to contend with the Soviet Navy. The US Navy contrived a strategy to shape Soviet strategy by forcing it into bastion defense, not oceanic interdiction. Relying on a vast intelligence network of underwater sensors, spies and submarine surveillance, the navy concluded that in a general war the primary Soviet naval mission would be to protect its ballistic-missile submarines and its capital ships, held in reserve near home waters.[23] That meant that, if the US Navy could mount a threat to them, the Soviets would have to withdraw their attack submarines from oceanic sea-denial patrols in order to protect this strategic reserve. If the threat were credible, it would give the Soviets a major reason to avoid war, and hence be a most important deterrent.

This planning was presented as the offensive, war-fighting maritime strategy of the 1980s. If, using their great mobility, flexibility and surprise, US and Nato forces could overcome Soviet maritime defenses they could put at risk the enemy's strategic reserve, the backbone of any hope the Soviets could win a general war. The navy had returned to attack-at-the-source, and that source was now in part at sea. High-value targets could be destroyed without hitting Soviet centers of population. And with many Soviet sea-control submarines withdrawn from the open ocean, and with improved and extended ASW controlling the remaining diesels, the seas would remain open so the United States could wage amphibious campaigns on the flanks of a land war. The United States, from its maritime position, would, with its naval forces, seize the strategic initiative.

The framers of this strategy were the carrier admirals who had rejected both the defensiveness of the 1970s and Zumwalt's low-end gunboat-and-escort force. Only heavy units could force the northern seas and destroy the enemy's naval forces.[24] Furthermore, strike carriers and battleship-led surface action groups existed, whereas the proposed lighter ships had not been built. In the 1980s the navy's leadership imposed internal agreement on an offensive strategy, and the appropriation for another *Nimitz*-class carrier ended the high–low debate. Direct offensive action was based not on the immoral threat of mutual assured annihilation, but on the premise that, with the air–land battle strategy of the army and the air force, the United States could shape and win a general war. Not since Mahan had the navy presented in peacetime such a comprehensive theory of victory.

In the rising tide of 1980s remilitarization, the navy, under John Lehman, returned carrier air, attack submarines and amphibious-assault fleet marine forces to the center of its planning: 600 ships, four combat fleets, 15 heavy-carrier battle groups, four battleship surface-action groups, 100 attack submarines – an increase of 120 combatants above the force level of 1980. Nato partners would pick up V/Stol carriers, diesel-electric submarines and minesweepers. The US Navy had, and would stay with, the high-performance, big-ticket platforms. Those were current assets, and alone could execute an immediate offensive.

The navy increasingly imbued its platforms with sophisticated computer and communications systems, and internal wirings for navigation and fire control, tying the fleet together around its intelligence and command controls. These were the fleet foundations of today's information RMAs. As a battle group advanced, for example, the Aegis Air Defense System was to provide an impenetrable screen of radar-targeted fire against Soviet missile and air stand-off defenses. At the end of the decade, a new combatant, the missile-bearing, Aegis-directed *Arleigh Burke* destroyer topped the surface shield. Technology improved the ranges, accuracy and impact of cruise missiles, and this enabled the navy more easily to concentrate its fire while dispersing its shooting platforms. The ships of the mobile shooting fleet readied fire from ocean locations of their own choosing against Soviet defensive networks at sea and ashore. And for flank attack, for littoral warfare, the marine corps developed a multi-purpose amphibious assault ship with V/stol carrier capability, of the sort that had been a gleam in Zumwalt's reforming eye the decade before.

With the disappearance of the Soviet enemy and the danger of general war, the ambitious, offensive, top-heavy maritime strategy died at the end of the 1980s. One system that had changed its character, and remained in force after the end of the Cold War, was the fleet ballistic missile. As we saw, Polaris and Poseidon were, from the 1950s, largely countervalue weapons, part of a strategy of retaliatory deterrence, of assured destruction. Improvements in accuracy and yield by the 1980s permitted strategists to rethink the purpose of these underwater-launched missiles. They remained the most secure instrument of the country's nuclear strategy. SLBMs could now destroy hardened military targets, such as missile silos, something that would have been impossible for the earlier generations. This counter-force capability, and hence potential first-strike capacity (hitherto the province of the air force), was embodied in the Trident II submarine-and-missile system. Adopted by the national planners, Trident II was a shift away from the role of the fleet ballistic missile as a last resort, soft-target, retaliatory deterrent. This fitted the offensive mood of the 1980s. It also corresponded to the deterrence mission of navy strategy, part of the counter-force potential of the SSBNs at sea, illustrating once again how service doctrines and strategies are created, and changed and justified, by technological opportunity, and vice versa.[25]

CONCLUSION, 1990s

Apart from the SSBN force still valued for deterrence, the navy after the Cold War was again at a loss. Then, in a remarkable burst of initiative and innovation, so different from the confusion, shrillness and desperate competitiveness of the previous post-war period, the navy smoothly recast its inherent values of flexibility, versatility and mobility into missions of influence and intervention. These supported the post-war policies of protecting and promoting a global system of free trade based upon enlarging political liberties. This time the US Navy and Marine Corps came up with their own definition of roles and missions. *From the Sea* was published in 1992, and other statements followed, fitting existing surface, air and fleet marine assets to forward presence and intervention ashore. At present the strategic and technological renewal of the US naval services, the utility of their platforms and the definition of their purposes, are to be assessed by the degree of success with which they support foreign policy by putting forces and fires against land targets, 'Forward ... from the Sea'.[26]

NOTES

I thank Frank Uhlig, Jr, whose critical comments on my writing and generous sharing of his knowledge of the navy helped me greatly.

1. For further on these subjects, see George W. Baer, *One Hundred Years of Sea Power: The U.S. Navy, 1890–1990* (Stanford, CA: Stanford University Press, 1994). For two astute overviews of the period, see David Alan Rosenberg, 'American Strategy in the Era of the Third World War: An Inquiry into the Structure and Process of General War at Sea, 1945–1990', in N. A. M. Rodger, ed., *Naval Power in the Twentieth Century* (London: Macmillan, 1996), pp. 242–54, and, Colin S. Gray, 'Sea Power for Containment: The U.S. Navy in the Cold War', in Keith Nelson and Elizabeth Jane Errington, eds, *Navies and Global Defense: Theories and Strategy* (Wesport, CT: Praeger, 1995), pp. 181–207. Also recommended are the chapters in R. W. King, ed., *Naval Engineering and American Sea Power* (Baltimore, MD: Nautical & Aviation Publishing Company of America, 1989).

2. For conclusions on the contentious (and on the part of navy aviators insubordinate) testimony before the House Committee on Armed Services in 1949, see Philip S. Meilinger, 'The Admirals' Revolt of 1949: Lessons for Today', *Parameters* (September 1989), pp. 81–99, and Jeffrey G. Barlow, *The Revolt of the Admirals: The Fight for Naval Aviation, 1945–1950* (Washington, DC: Naval Historical Center, 1994).

3. Norman Friedman, *U.S. Aircraft Carriers: An Illustrated Design History* (Annapolis, MD: Naval Institute Press, 1983), p. 256.

4. David Steigman, 'Aircraft Carriers', in Robert Gardiner, ed., *Navies in the Nuclear Age: Warships since 1945* (Annapolis, MD: Naval Institute Press, 1993), pp. 14–37, and Friedman, *U.S. Aircraft Carriers*, ch. 12.

5. See Adam B. Siegel, *The Use of Naval Forces in the Post-War Era: U.S. Navy*

and U.S. Marine Corps Crisis Response Activity, 1946–1990 (Alexandria: Center for Naval Analyses, 1991).

6. Michael M. McCrea, Karen N. Domabyl, Alexander F. Parker, *The Offensive Navy Since World War II: How Big and Why* (Alexandria: Center for Naval Analyses, 1989), and, for full statistics, Roy A. Grossnick, *United States Naval Aviation, 1910–1995* (Washington, DC: Naval Historical Center, 1997), pp. 421–45.

7. See Thomas Wildernberg, *Gray Steel and Black Oil: Fast Tankers and Replenishment at Sea in the U.S. Navy, 1912–1995* (Annapolis, MD: Naval Institute Press, 1996).

8. Admiral H. Rivero, cited in Floyd D. Kennedy, Jr, 'David Lamar McDonald, 1 August 1963–1 August 1967', in Robert William Love, Jr, *The Chiefs of Naval Operations* (Annapolis, MD: Naval Institute Press, 1980), p. 344.

9. With their ability to complicate Soviet air defense, attack carriers remained part of the US strategic force until 1976. Norman Friedman, *The Postwar Naval Revolution* (Annapolis, MD: Naval Institute Press, 1986), p. 20.

10. James M. Roherty, *Decisions of Robert S. McNamara: A Study of the Role of the Secretary of Defense* (Coral Gables, FL: University of Miami Press, 1970), p. 122.

11. And one not without critics on the technical side: for one design and construction criticism, see Harold C. Hemond, 'The Flip Side of Rickover', *Proceedings* (July 1989), pp. 42–7. A strong defense, with a pointed sub-title, is Francis Duncan, *Rickover and the Nuclear Navy: The Discipline of Technology* (Annapolis, MD: Naval Institute Press, 1990).

12. Willis C. Barnes, 'Korea and Vietnam', in King, ed., *Naval Engineering and American Seapower*, p. 178.

13. Graham Spinardi, *From Polaris to Trident: The Development of the US Fleet Ballistic Missile Technology* (Cambridge: Cambridge University Press, 1994), chs. 3, 9.

14. Harvey Sapolsky, 'Technological Innovators: Admirals Raborn and Rickover', in Arnold R. Shapack, ed., *The Navy in an Age of Change and Crisis: Some Challenges and Responses of the Twentieth Century* (Annapolis, MD: USNA, 1973), p. 26.

15. Richard G. Hewlett and Francis Duncan, *Nuclear Navy, 1946–1962* (Chicago, IL: University of Chicago Press, 1974), p. 391.

16. Elmo R. Zumwalt, Jr, *On Watch: A Memoir* (New York: Quadrangle, 1976), p. 81.

17. Harvey M. Sapolsky, *Polaris System Development: Bureaucratic and Programmatic Success in Government* (Cambridge, MA: Harvard University Press, 1972), p. 172.

18. Ibid., p. 237.

19. John F. Lehman, Jr, *Command of the Sea* (New York: Scribners, 1988), p. 392, cited in Jeffrey I. Sands, *On His Watch: Admiral Zumwalt's Efforts to Institutionalize Strategic Change* (Alexandria: Center for Naval Analyses, 1993), p. 108.

20. These are helpfully complied by Jeffrey Sands, *On His Watch*, pp. 93–109.

21. Admiral Thomas B. Hayward, 'Remarks', *Wings of Gold*, 7, 2 (Summer 1982), p. 59. A mid-sized carrier alternative was advocated in 1978 by later Navy Secretary John Lehman, with Zumwalt's approval, to bridge the high–low gap. John Lehman, *Aircraft Carriers: The Real Choices* (Beverly Hills, CA: Sage for CSIS, 1978).

22. Siegel, *The Use of Naval Forces in the Post-War Era*, and Adam B. Siegel, *The US Experience in Forcible Entry, Sustained Land Operations, and Sustained*

Land Combat since World War II (Alexandria: Center for Naval Analyses, 1995).

23. An early analysis of the defensive nature of Soviet naval strategy was presented in 1968 by Robert W. Herrick, *Soviet Naval Strategy: Fifty Years of Theory and Practice* (Annapolis, MD: USNI, 1968). The CIA's 1982 National Intelligence Estimate, *Soviet Naval Strategy and Programs Through the 1990s*, gave as a 'key judgment' that in the Soviet strategy for war 'the primary initial tasks of the Navy remain: To deploy and provide protection for ballistic missile submarines in preparation for and conduct of strategic and theater nuclear strikes [and] To defend the USSR and its allies from strikes by enemy ballistic missile submarines and aircraft carriers'. To this end, 'virtually all of the Northern and Pacific Fleets' available major surface combatants and combat aircraft and some three-quarters of their available attack submarines would be initially committed to operations in these [home and surrounding] waters'. How this was developed into 'the Maritime Strategy' is related in John B. Hattendorf, *The Evolution of the U.S. Navy's Maritime Strategy, 1977–1986* (Newport, VA: Naval War College, 1989).

24. There is a useful discussion of how the navy proposed to do this in Norman Friedman, 'The Maritime Strategy and the Design of the U.S. Fleet', *Comparative Strategy*, 6, 4 (1987), pp. 415–35.

25. Graham Spinardi, 'Why the US Navy Went for Hard-Target Counterforce in Trident II (And Why It Didn't Get There Sooner)', *International Security*, 15, 2 (Fall 1990), pp. 147–90, and, Spinardi, *From Polaris to Trident*.

26. See George Baer, 'Alfred Thayer Mahan and the Utility of US Naval Forces Today', forthcoming, pp. 14–18.

PART IV

PREPARING FOR THE NEXT WAR

13

The Royal Navy in a New World, 1990–2020

Geoffrey Till

The dramatic changes that have affected the world since the end of the Cold War have affected its navies too. This chapter will consider whether such changes constitute a 'Revolution in Maritime Affairs' and how such a revolution might affect the role, importance, structure and function of the Royal Navy up to 2020.

TECHNOLOGICAL CHANGE AND THE REVOLUTION IN MARITIME AFFAIRS

The notion of there being a 'Revolution in Maritime Affairs' derives of course from the debate that there is a much wider 'Revolution in Military Affairs' (RAM) by which navies and maritime air forces are being affected. Although the term and the concept are Soviet in origin, the debate has been dominated by American writers, who have tended, perhaps not surprisingly, to focus their gaze on the influence of technology in general and of information technology in particular.

One of the most 'revolutionary' aspects of the situation, indeed, is the extent to which military developments are being led by civilian industrial and business technology.[1] It now seems much less to be the case that war, or preparation for war, is the mother of invention. Navies are much more likely to be affected by external technological developments over which they have no control than they have been before. They are floating on a fast-running current of technology and steering; they are not directing it.

This technological change affects platforms, fleets and the environment in which navies operate. Starting with the effects on platforms, changes to their shape, propulsion systems, sensors and weapons of the platforms are very well documented, the subject of lively debate and often remarkable in themselves. They are leading to the production of warship classes like the US Navy's evidently revolutionary DD-21 surface combatant.[2] But, around the world, navies are acquiring advanced warships, submarines and aircraft that are faster, more manoeuvrable, leaner-manned and fitted with significantly better sensors and weapons capable of precise engagement. Their shape and appearance are also fast evolving partly in order to increase their stealthiness and partly, as in the case of the Trimaran and SWATH ships being considered by the Royal Navy, for more hydrodynamic efficiency.

Even more radical than this, however, is the notion of the 'system of systems' outlined by Admiral Owens in his seminal *Proceedings* article of 1995,[3] which is fast revolutionizing attitudes to squadrons, fleets and other such aggregations of maritime power. It seems that information technology can now link together ships, submarines and aircraft so tightly that it hardly makes sense to think of the efficiency of the individual unit anymore. This networking hugely increases the flexibility and efficiency of the group. Space-based and other command, control, communications, computers, intelligence, surveillance and reconnaissance assets (which now are mysteriously referred to by the *cognoscenti* as C4ISR) can provide 'total situational awareness' for all units; everyone can see everyone else's tactical picture and can operate each others' sensors and weapons. At least potentially, sea-based units can 'co-operatively engage' with aircraft and land forces and with the equivalent forces of other nations, and can bring their collective power to bear ashore much more efficiently than ever they could before.

But perhaps still more radical, though much less remarked by maritime strategists and policy-makers, is the impact of technology on the environment in which navies operate. At the highest level, technology has induced the developing impact of global warming. The increasingly serious potential consequences of this have focused attention on the world ocean which is seen often as a barometer of the health of the planet and the stabilizer of its climate. For example, human disease pathogens leaking into the sea through sewage systems are apparently killing three-quarters of the coral reefs off the Florida Keys and are likely to affect shellfish, fish and swimmers. According to Professor James Porter of the University of Georgia at Athens:

> These are the little cries and whispers which when you look at the ocean carefully, and really think about what is going on, begin to affront you with the dangers that lie ahead ... Things are folding on top of each other at a rate that we are unable to keep up with.[4]

But the ocean is more than a passive indicator of the harm that we all, rich and poor alike, are doing to our own futures; it helps determine that level of harm by changing sea levels, currents and weather patterns. It is likely to increase the need for systems designed to explore, monitor and protect all aspects of the ocean environment.

We know remarkably little about the ocean, especially about its depths and bottom topography. We may be moving into an era when sailors' attitudes to the environment in which they operate will be transformed. The deep sea bed, instead of being dark, mysterious and frightening, something to be avoided at all costs, may become a familiar area to be exploited for its scientific interest and its commercial and strategic value. The Soviet Navy, with its huge associated oceanographic fleet and its development of the bastion strategy under the canopy of the Arctic ice was something of a pioneer in this regard. But now the expanding efforts of the US Navy's Hydrographic Service strongly suggests that navies are likely to be involved in the accumulation and exploitation of knowledge of the ocean and will certainly play a part in its protection. Knowledge, after all, is power.

The world ocean is also increasingly valued for its resources in oil, gas, fish, minerals and perhaps ultimately for its enormous energy potential – all technology related issues. Such concerns have resulted in the long and difficult process of negotiating, agreeing and ratifying the UN Convention on the Law of the Sea which has transformed the way we think of the sea. Now the extent of the open ocean has been drastically reduced, and many littoral states have vast new areas over which they will need to exercise their jurisdiction, if it is to be effectively recognized by other people. Most of the world's navies are preoccupied by the requirement to protect national interests within the 200 mile Exclusive Economic Zone. To do this properly, coastal navies are becoming noticeably less coastal. This tendency is particularly marked where jurisdictions are disputed, as they are for example around the South China Sea.

To summarize so far, modern technology has affected maritime purposes and maritime conduct in a variety of ways. Despite its advocates, and despite those who point to the analogy of pocket calculators and computers which have become cheaper in real terms, the sensors, weapons and platforms of modern navies have become progressively more expensive. Over the past half century the unit cost of most types of military equipment has risen about 10 per cent per year.[5] In consequence, financial resources available for defence being considered finite, most of the world's navies have fewer platforms than previously, although each is a good deal more individually capable and is usually significantly larger. Such shrinkage has been particularly noticeable among the erstwhile antagonists of the Cold War, but rather less so with the navies of the Gulf and the Pacific Rim, at least until the onset of the economic crisis of the mid-to-late 1990s.

Technological developments appear to enable modern navies to project maritime power ashore with much more assurance than before. Maritime power projection can now be confidently extended several hundreds of miles behind the shore line. But that same technology appears to be blurring the lines of demarcation between sea, space, air and land power in a way which both mandates and facilitates closer cooperation between the services. The issue of whether new maritime technology helps or hinders cooperation between different national contingents remains controversial.

Observers most impressed by developments in IT tend to argue that with gateway systems, modern technology can link up the C4ISR systems of different navies much more easily than was possible before. Sceptics, on the other hand, argue that IT widens rather than narrows the gap between the great and the small. Americans appear to predominate in the first group, their allies in the second. It is probably too early to tell who is right.

At the same time, operations within the world's littoral areas makes maritime forces more vulnerable than they were because even countries in the developing world have access to the civilian technology which underpins so many military developments. Area denial weapons ranging from mines, through modern coastal submarines and fighter/attack aircraft to theatre ballistic missiles, are increasingly commonplace. Interestingly, for the first time, *Jane's Fighting Ships* has now started to include land-based anti-ship missiles in its coverage, indirect evidence of the fact that navies around the world are having to devote thought to how they respond to such threats. Even interest in defence against theatre ballistic missile attack is far from being a preserve of the US Navy.[6]

All this, at least at first glance, certainly seems sufficient to warrant the description of another phenomenon dear to the hearts of former sovietologists, 'a military-technical revolution', a period of unusually rapid technological advance in the military sphere. But even here, something of a divide can be seen between platform-dominated traditionalists who stress the prospect, and the need, for incremental adaptation on the one hand and information-oriented modernists, on the other, who think that something much more fundamental is in progress. This is not such an arcane and academic (in the worst sense of that word) issue as it may seem. Navies have to decide their strategy for investment in new platforms, sensors and weapons. If they conclude that the world is at the beginning of rapid and fundamental technological change, it may make sense for them to wait a while until the dust settles. If, on the other hand, they foresee no more than steady and general development they may decide to invest and build now before further price rises take the systems out of reach.[7]

Sceptics make the persuasive point that Vietnam shows that modern technology does not win wars on its own and argue that the effects of modern technology even in the Gulf War were often overdrawn. The Coalition's obvious advantages in the C4ISR dimension notwithstanding, there were few if any successes in the hunt for Iraqi Scuds, defensive Patriot missiles were much less effective than was thought at the time, and Battle Damage Assessment suggested that the strategic effects of the cruise missile/air bombardment of Iraq had been exaggerated.

Moreover, this is not the first time that there have been dramatic periods of technological change. Krepenevich[8] identifies ten in Europe since the sixteenth century, some of them purely naval. Previous experience suggests that the advantages conferred by being decisively ahead in key military technologies often prove quite fleeting as the adversary either catches up, or finds an appropriate response. In many cases, that response may itself be technological (for example, answering the threat of the U-boat with ASDIC or Sonar). But, as in the Vietnam war, where the Viet Cong and the North Vietnamese Army found many very low-technology or tactical or political answers to US air superiority, the response may be quite asymmetrical, hardly technological at all, in fact.[9] Thus, in 1993, Akbar Torkar, the Iranian minister of defence spoke for many when he remarked:

> Can our air force for example take on the Americans, or our navy take on the American navy? If we put all of our country's budget into such a war we could have just burned our money. The way to go about dealing with such a threat requires a different solution entirely.[10]

Moreover, such periods of dramatic technological change only seem to become truly revolutionary when the technological impulse is reinforced or directed by other social and political changes. For a start, whether such technological potentialities are fully or sensibly exploited is dependent on the political or strategic judgement of the decision-makers: 'More than anything else, it is perceptions of future contingencies and likely enemies that determines whether, and when, there is full exploitation of the advantages offered by the military revolution.'[11]

All this suggests that there is significant danger in being seduced by advanced technology. In some ways, navies may be facing a repeat of the situation that afflicted the Royal Navy in the period before the First World War where there was a damaging division of opinion between the *matériel* school who believed that technology provided all the answers, and the historical school who argued that experience showed that it did not.

OPERATIONAL CHANGE AND THE REVOLUTION IN MARITIME AFFAIRS

The notion that there is much more to a revolution in military affairs (RMA) than mere technology, however advanced it may be, is reinforced by those who focus on the world scene more generally. Thus Lawrence Freedman: 'The future development of the military art will be more the result of the changed structure of international politics than of advances in military technology.'[12]

Globalization is one of the remarked-upon characteristics of this change to the international scene. If humankind is indeed embarked upon a process of economic and social convergence likely to increase the susceptibility of all nations to what happens elsewhere, then Britain is sure to be affected more and first. As we were reminded in the *Strategic Defence Review* (*SDR*), exports form a higher proportion of GDP in Britain than they do in the United States, Japan, Germany and France and the British invest proportionately more abroad than do any of their major competitors. Nor are such effects merely to be found in the economic sphere: 90 per cent of the heroin on British streets comes from Afghanistan, a country whose disorder prevents control of the drugs trade at source and which therefore threatens the British way of life. Such vulnerabilities help explain why the British feel it so important to be 'a force for good in the world'.[13]

The apparent increase in non-military threats to British security suggests that substantial changes in the way we think of the use of military force may be afoot. The end of the Cold War, it is argued, may not signify merely the end of the latest round of endless conflict among great powers; instead, it may foreshadow the end, at least for the time being, of the whole idea of warfare between great powers. Especially in the nuclear age, the costs of such war are too high and the rewards, even of victory, are too low. War, it is said, is no longer the paying proposition that it might once have been.[14]

Clearly, it is important not to exaggerate the hypothesis. The end of major war will not necessarily prove permanent. Prudent military policymakers might well conclude that they still need to take precautions against its possible reappearance. Nor does the end of major war between the great powers imply the end of conflict. A glance at today's newspapers shows the disappearance of neither war between minor powers, nor one-sided conflicts between great powers and small ones, nor, still less, of intra-state conflicts and wars of one sort or another. The great powers at least appear to be moving into an era of wars of choice, rather than wars of necessity.[15] Where they lead, optimists may argue, others might follow – in due time.

The implications of this, if true, could well be described as revolutionary. Taken with the necessarily uncontrollable and unpredictable consequences of a world in which so many variables in the equation are quite unfamiliar, the whole notion of 'strategy' itself seems to be under threat. Strategy, after all, is supposed to be a conceptual framework that enables us not only to understand past campaigns but to conduct present ones and prepare for coming campaigns as well. In the last analysis, strategy is about shaping the future and seeking to determine outcomes. At the moment, this seems a more than usually presumptuous aspiration. Of course, diplomats and their military servants must continue to do their best to mould their environment, but probably in a less confident spirit and in a more incremental, more tactical, way than they did in the past.

More solidly, the form that strategy takes is likely to be different too, since its basic and most familiar concepts have been derived, at least in the West, from the study of great powers at war with each other. With very few exceptions, Westerners have rarely tried to draw out the lessons of even their own conflicts with minor powers, say in the nineteenth century.[16] Easterners may have much to teach us here since their concepts derive from more modest entities – the armies of princes and warlords in the case of Sun Tsu, and of individual swordsmen in the case of Musashi. It is no coincidence that Sun Tsu and the Eastern way in warfare (with its emphasis on the limitation of means, aspirations and the victor's costs) has become so fashionable in recent years.

At the very least, such uncertainties require policy-makers to rethink their approach to maritime strategy. This is not new, of course. Rear-Admiral Herbert Richmond, reflecting on the effects of the sudden disappearance of a familiar adversary nearly 20 years ago, made the point very well:

> Accuracy of thought is particularly necessary now, when we have no immediate, concrete problem. For many years, twenty perhaps – we have had one. We have seen Germany rising like a giant, and our problem was comparatively clear – no problems are wholly clear. But, now, the policy of the world is unsettled – everything is vague, we appear to have nothing settled to work to, nothing corresponding in clearness to the German menace.[17]

Substitute the Soviet Union for Germany, and Richmond could have been talking about the 1990s.

NAVAL RESPONSES

Around the world, navies have responded to this challenge with the development of serious conceptual thinking and in the creation of impressive sets of doctrinal conclusions. Of course, this was particularly difficult for the pragmatic British, for as Oscar Wilde reminds us, '"doctrine" … [is] … a word full of terror to the British mind'.[18] This healthy scepticism was reinforced by the sailor's notion that the nature of the medium precluded doctrinal approaches. 'Sea power is and must remain inherently flexible, so the argument goes, and does not lend itself to the application of rigid rules of conduct that … doctrine would entail.' It is noteworthy, then, that the British, of all people, have been in the vanguard of the development of a maritime doctrine. Their scepticism, moreover, has played an important role in stressing the health warning that should accompany every book on doctrine, namely, that it is likely to prove ephemeral in some or all respects, and that 'It is authoritative but requires judgement in application'.[19] Thus doctrine should not degenerate into dogma. This world-wide process, perhaps in some sense the equivalent of the intellectual surge that produced Mahan, Corbett, Richmond and other naval thinkers in the periods just before and just after the First World War, is likely to have a number of important consequences for the maritime future.

First, doctrine is a great force multiplier, enabling the best use to be made of limited means. Second, it encourages comparative analysis of the doctrine of the other services and of other nations in a manner that facilitates cooperation with armies and air forces and with the military services of friends and allies in joint and combined operations. Third, it encourages the notion that thinking about maritime purposes and procedures in a time of turmoil is a front-line task, not something to be conducted by consenting adults in private. All of these consequences are likely to make maritime forces more professional, more useful, more cost-effective – better able to cope with a confusing world.

And what have been the conclusions drawn from this current and very welcome outburst of naval creativity? In broad terms it a concept of operations along the lines of Figure 13.1. Navies around the world have drawn perhaps five broad and interrelated conclusions from all this.

Keeping the edge. First, navies usually seem to feel that is important to retain the technological edge, even when the tasks in question are of a humdrum and routine character in an environment where the operational risks are low. For the politicians, this traditional military preference for

Figure 13.1

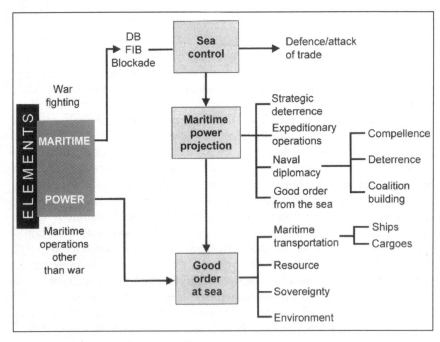

erring on the side of safety is reinforced by their dislike of incurring casualties, especially in messy situations around the world (Somalia, Bosnia, Kosovo) where vital national interests are not involved, but where the news media are. The argument that 'only forces equipped and trained for war-fighting will have the range of specific capabilities – as well as the deterrent effect – to be effective across the full range of peace support and humanitarian operations', is made repeatedly in the SDR.[20]

Assuming control. The world's major navies generally acknowledge a shift from winning command *at* sea, to exploiting it *from* the sea. For Western navies, this is a natural conclusion to draw from the substantial reduction in the naval power of their erstwhile opponent, the Soviet Union. It has led to the claim that 'naval' strategy (as represented by a Mahanian struggle for sea control) has been replaced by a Corbettian 'maritime strategy', in which the focus is on projecting military power ashore. Few would go so far as to argue that naval strategy is 'dead',[21] but certainly for Western navies, it seems to be ailing at the moment. None the less, the reappearance of a major naval adversary would quickly revive it. Moreover, it does not seem to follow that having control of great chunks of the world ocean necessarily means controlling the littorals. Finally, the world's smaller navies may be able to mount asymmetric challenges to the larger ones, and may eye each other in distinctly 'traditional' sea control terms.

An expeditionary future? Third, among the greater navies, there is the near universal view that future maritime warfare is likely to be expeditionary in nature, conducted in the world's littorals rather than the open ocean, at some distance from the homeland, and fought in the company of other services and other nations, with limited means, limited aims and probably limited expectations. For the time being, the future looks expeditionary.

Looking to the moat. Fourth, there is general acceptance that maritime responsibilities have grown, and are likely to grow still further. Thanks to the UN Convention on the Law of the Sea, littoral states now have much bigger areas over which they need to exercise their jurisdiction. This is no accident; changes in the law of the sea derive from the manifest increase in the importance of the sea, relative to the land. In this respect, the general responsibilities of the maritime agencies (navies included) appear to be growing.

Maritime operations other than war. Finally, there appears to be something of a move away from the large-scale and highly intense activities that characterize major war and towards the diverse gaggle of activities sometimes lumped together under the umbrella term of 'Maritime Operations Other Than War', and which now seem so much more appropriate to the task of managing the turmoil of the post-Cold War world.

IMPLICATIONS FOR THE ROYAL NAVY, 1990–2020

It seems safe to predict that this revolution in maritime affairs will have some important consequences for the Royal Navy. These will be discussed under three headings:

- Gaining and exploiting sea control;
- Maritime power projection;
- Good order at sea.

Gaining and Exploiting Sea Control

The current fashion is to argue that 'naval strategy' (by which is meant naval operations conducted largely at sea by navies against other navies) is 'dead', and that strategy must now be maritime, involving all the services and directed against the shore. To some extent, the titles of successive doctrinal formulations from the US Navy nicely illustrate the point with their transition from power 'At Sea', to power 'From the Sea'.

None the less, the Royal Navy when contemplating its future would surely be wise to enter significant caveats against too enthusiastic an espousal of this as a novel and revolutionary concept, however fashionable it might be. The idea that seapower is at its most effective when it influences the outcome of events on land is, for a start, far from new; it was Corbett's *leitmotif* after all, but he was certainly clear about the importance of command of the sea. Moreover, although the forces of good probably do command the seas that they would need to cross to get to their more distant theatres of operation, it is far from clear that they can be so confident in the difficult and complex littoral battlespace that await them. Especially in an age when even small and generally weak states have access to modern technology (modern coastal submarines, sophisticated mines, ground-launched missiles, modern attack aircraft and so on), littoral operations are manifestly not a soft option for great navies more familiar with the open ocean, as the varying fates of the British casualties in the Falklands campaign, the USS *Stark* and the USS *Tripoli* should remind us. Moreover, the theoretical threat posed by a couple of obsolete *Foxtrots* in Libya to coalition shipping *en route* to the Gulf in 1990–91, needed to be taken very seriously indeed, not least because of the effect that some accidental success by grossly inferior forces could have had on world public opinion.

Finally, the putative sailing of elements of the Russian Black Sea Fleet during the early stages of Operation Allied Force and the continued flexing of muscles exhibited by the Chinese Navy should perhaps be seen as timely reminders that the permanence of automatic and effectively uncontested Western sea control is something that may need to be kept under constant review.[22]

Maritime Power Projection

Since, in the period under review, the British intention is to maintain the Trident force, its conduct of the Royal Navy's erstwhile 'Strategic Deterrence' role will continue. But as we are told in the *SDR*, it will be reduced in size (to 200 warheads), detargeted and put at lower stages of readiness (days rather than hours). The expectation that it will also be less threatened is held to justify a small reduction in mine-countermeasure forces. The sub-strategic mission of the Trident force is mentioned several times, but not discussed. The recent round of Indian and Pakistani nuclear tests would appear to suggest that the era of nuclear deterrence is far from over, irrespective of the end of the Cold War.

We have seen already signs of the developing interest of the US and other navies in theatre anti-missile defence of various kinds. The firing of a North Korean missile over Japan in August 1999 has certainly focused attention on such a requirement in the Far East. The arguments for such a capability, however costly and complex it is likely to be, may be particularly persuasive for navies like the Royal Navy which are likely to be involved in distant operations in potentially hostile waters.

Expeditionary operations

The capacity to mount and sustain expeditionary operations is the Royal Navy's obvious growth area, although the *SDR* does not use this term. 'In future', we are told, 'littoral operations and force projection, for which maritime forces are well suited, will be our primary focus.'[23] This shift in focus to such 'highly demanding' activities has led to a focus on littoral operations, and, in turn, a new shape to the fleet. Open-ocean ASW is now deemed less important (hence small reductions in the DD/FF force and in the number of attack submarines). But other areas seem likely to do better.

The most obvious beneficiary of this is Britain's amphibious capacity which will include HMS *Ocean*, two new LSLs and two new LPDs in the shape of HMS *Bulwark* and HMS *Albion*. The first sea lord claims that this will be 'a truly impressive capability',[24] and it will certainly reinforce the perception that Britain is the European leader in this area. But the enormous gap between this aspiration and the much greater potential of the US Marine Corps raises again the fundamental question of whether Britain can hope to keep up with the techniques and expertise of the United States. Should Britain seek to emulate US developments, within the confines of its own limited resources, or should it seek to plough its own furrow, seeking distinctive answers to smaller-scale problems? Perhaps *Operation Haven* should be regarded more as the template for the Royal Marines than *Desert Storm*.

At first glance, a rather similar problem might seem to apply to the development of carrier aviation – that other main beneficiary of the Royal Navy's historic shift from ASW to expeditionary operations. 'The emphasis is now on increased offensive airpower, and an ability to operate the largest possible range of aircraft in the widest possible range of roles.'[25] Hence the Navy's Sea Harrier FA-2 force is to be merged with the RAF's GR7s into Joint Force 2000 and there is to be more coordination between its commando helicopters and equivalent forces in the army and RAF. More distantly, two substantial new carriers are to be commissioned 'from around 2012',[26] with a complement of capable modern aircraft very possibly of the JSF type. This is a particularly interesting development in that it does seem to represent a coincidence of view with the United States – a point nicely suggested by the current interest in the Anglo-American JSF aircraft. No doubt the intention is to make this imaginative exercise in 'jointery' a good deal more harmonious than it was in the 1920s and 1930s when it was foisted on the navy in the unhappy guise of 'Dual Control'!

The submarine force is to be enhanced in this area as well with all the *Trafalgar* class being fitted with Tomahawk land attack missiles, 'thereby extending our ability to apply pressure in times of tension and our power to influence events up to 1000 miles inland'.[27] Here the only question is what such a comparatively modest SLBM force could be expected to achieve against a determined adversary if used in isolation; no doubt the real expectation is that such a force is only likely to be used in conjunction with the United States and possibly with a view to being able to influence US policy as well as to contribute to the desired effect on the adversary.

These major new capabilities are constructively supported by the less thoroughly discussed maritime requirement for extra sea lift (four more Ro-Ros to add to the two already in train), for new survey ships, for better medical capacities (a new 200 bed primary casualty receiving ship), for the capacity to respond to the probable lack of port infrastructure in the expected area of operations, and, above all, perhaps in the development of 'jointery' in all its forms:

> By 2015, the Review expects further major change in methods of warfare. Operations will no longer be characterised as land, sea or air. There will instead be a single battlespace in which land, maritime and air forces will be directed, targeted and supplemented by a new generation of intelligence, surveillance, information and communications systems offering a step change in military capability.[28]

The creation of the Joint Rapid Reaction Force, an organized pool of forces from all three services considered appropriate for short-notice distant and expeditionary operations, illustrates well the revived interest in 'jointery' and, although it may be politically incorrect to make such a point these days, the centrality of naval power to such operations is unlikely to do the Royal Navy any institutional harm.

In fact, however, there is little that is new in all this. In many ways, the Royal Navy appears likely to revert to its experience of previous eras (most obviously the eighteenth and nineteenth centuries) when general deterrence, force projection and the conduct of a whole variety of expeditionary operations were the main preoccupations of the exponents of the 'British Way in Warfare'.[29] But this is less of a change than might appear on the surface, for even at the height of the Cold War there were very many such operations (Korea, Suez, the Falklands campaigns being only the most obvious). What seems likely to happen, in fact, is more a shift of emphasis than a radical and revolutionary change. Nor, moreover, is it obvious that this shift is permanent. It may be dangerous to conclude that the British would be immune to the sort of public doubts that the bombing of US marines in Beirut or the barbaric treatment of US helicopter pilots in Mogadishu prompted, were they to suffer some such expeditionary disaster.

What is novel, however, is the dilemma of whether in this form of activity to stay as closely alongside the Americans as resources permit or whether closer links should be formed with the other Europeans. For, as the *SDR* tells us: 'Wherever possible, European governments should harmonise the requirements of their Armed Forces and pursue co-operative solutions. This not only avoids unnecessary duplication of development and production costs but makes sound operational sense.'[30]

Maritime diplomacy
At a time when coercion from the sea is being practised against Serbia and Iraq, there can hardly be any doubt of its continuance as a requirement of Britain's maritime forces for the foreseeable future, unless something happens that gives Britain a sudden dislike of a policy of 'punching above its weight'. Britain's readiness to do so is in large measure a function of its historic vulnerability to external influences and partly to its general perception of past success in this role.

But the focus in the *SDR* is on the friendly version of defence diplomacy which is characterized as having the forces, 'to dispel hostility, build and maintain trust and assist in the development of democratically accountable armed forces, thereby making a significant contribution to conflict prevention and resolution'.[31] It comes in a variety of forms. Joint exercises, staff college exchanges, visits to other ports and participating in maritime meetings across the world have all proved effective ways of establishing the importance of national perspectives and interests. Sometimes visits by big ships seem to do the trick. One Foreign Office official in Norway reported in 1919, 'I have been credibly informed ... that the arrival of HMS battlecruiser *New Zealand* ... created a profound impression in Bergen, especially among the working classes and the socialists'.[32] Sometimes small ships seem better suited to the task – a point apparently very well made by the visit of a group of MCMVs to Kuwait and elsewhere in the Gulf in 1998. Small ships may sometimes seem more appropriate for the task of coalition-building with small nations.[33]

As to the particular targets of this maritime diplomacy, the Royal Navy through much of last century has always paid particular attention to the requirement to influence US behaviour in directions favourable to British interests, and this will no doubt continue in this century. No doubt, though, it will be balanced by the need to improve coordination with the navies of continental Europe with whom Britain has more and more in common. Indeed something of a process of 'creeping integration' appears to be taking place, such that in the more distant future the Royal Navy may increasingly be seen as a component of a European Navy.[34] Much more immediately, however, the *SDR* gives emphasis to the conduct of defence diplomacy in East/Central Europe, the Mediterranean and the Gulf as particular arenas and the navy will certainly be important for all three areas. In practice, though, this is a global requirement. In some cases the British will continue to respond to urgent need (West Africa and the Caribbean) and in some cases to perceived future importance (the Asia-Pacific).

The only thing new about this diverse activity in fact is the name given to it. As James Cable continues to show us, the Royal Navy has been in the business of influencing the behaviour of foreigners in peacetime for many generations.[35] Equally, the fact that sailors are sometimes concerned about the operational consequences of such diplomatic activities is not new either. Thus the concern of *Invincible*'s captain that a posting in the eastern Mediterranean 'did give rise to the potential for erosion of the operational capability of my joint air group'.[36] Maritime diplomacy, whether it takes this form, or the form of continuing visits to the JSCSC, is not a cost-free exercise, but for the foreseeable future it is likely to be a cost-effective one.

Before leaving the matter of maritime diplomacy it is worth making the point that using navies in this way *is* a matter of strategy. We should remember Liddell Hart's useful definition that 'Strategy is the art of employing military force to achieve the ends of national policy'.[37] This is a variant of strategy which aims at meeting national objectives and moulding the international environment in desired directions by influencing the behaviour of friends, rather than enemies. The more powerful your friends are, the more important it may be to participate in such activities.

Good Order at Sea

With the ratification of UN Convention on Law of the Sea, the security of their EEZ is the major preoccupation of most of the world's navies. The bigger navies are also concerned with good order on the high seas, and perhaps in the EEZs of other nations. Good order at sea breaks down into four areas of concern:

Securing maritime transportation
Britain's security and prosperity will continue to depend on sea trade. Although sea trade is likely to expand considerably over the next 30 years, possibly tripling in fact, it faces many threats and challenges. Naval forces and coastguards provide the necessary response in peacetime by a series of tasks designed to control threats associated first with shipping and second with cargoes.

Shipping. In European waters there appears to be little manifest need to reducing the risk of *intentional harm* being done to shipping through foreign attack, terrorist attack or piracy. Elsewhere, however, this is much less true, and the British may need to consider whether they should or could become involved in it.

There is also the risk of *unintentional harm* being done to international shipping through its inadvertent involvement in other peoples' wars. The so-called 'Tanker War' during the first Gulf War between Iraq and Iran is the most obvious example of this. Concerns have been expressed that the same might happen in the critical South China Sea should the complex dispute over the Spratly islands degenerate into armed conflict. The Taiwan Straits crisis implied similar such threats. Nor should the more mundane prospect of shipping accidents in busy but unregulated seas and straits be forgotten. In European waters, as elsewhere, there is a continuing trend for the increasing regulation of sea traffic for safety and environmental reasons.

Cargoes. It may, however, be a question of controlling the maritime transportation of cargoes that threaten national, regional or global security. This might take the form of violations of UN-sponsored sanctions restrictions, destabilizing arms trafficking, or the transport of hazardous (nuclear) cargoes. Here the issue may be the extent to which the Royal Navy becomes regulated, rather than its regulating role. More obviously, cargoes may be illegal or prejudicial to the prosperity of the state. Controlling the smuggling of untaxed cargoes is an obvious means of protecting state revenues. The organized smuggling of illegal drugs and immigrants also threatens domestic order and is becoming common.

Securing marine resources
The world commercial fishing catch has more than quadrupled since 1950. The demand for edible fish produce is likely to rise from 80 million tons now to 115 million tons by 2015, as the population increases. Already, most world fishing grounds are under severe pressure, and many local fishing communities around the world are threatened by the advent of highly

mechanized distant-water fishing fleets from elsewhere. Over the last three years, there have been ten fishing crises in which lethal force has been used and people killed. Although in none of the areas for which the Royal Navy is responsible are such levels of confrontation likely to be reached, there are still some tricky differences of national opinion around, for example, the Falklands.

None the less, the regulation of the fishing industry remains an issue, even where jurisdiction is not in dispute, since the sustainability of European fishing grounds requires protection and regulation. This calls for supervision of fishing grounds against illegal fishing both by British and foreign fishermen. This is largely a constabulary matter, calling for wide levels of coverage and inspection but low levels of physical force. The Scottish Fishery Protection Agency in fact has decided recently that no naval support is needed for this at all.

Much the same can be said about concern for the security of oil and gas resources at sea. One-third of the world's petroleum reserves are at sea, and these are likely to be of increasing commercial interest as land sources become depleted. Moreover, exploitation of these resources is steadily being conducted in deeper and deeper waters, currently reaching 10,000 feet in some cases. Oil and gas resources will also need to be defended against all manner of intentional and unintentional harm.

Maritime sovereignty

All this becomes much more difficult when the waters in question are disputed. UNCLOS does not in itself resolve these disputes, it provides a set of parameters by which such disputes need to be interpreted and put into effect, with the agreement of all parties concerned. Generally, this is not a major problem in European waters, and force is unlikely to play much part in the eventual resolution of outstanding disputes. The one exception to this is the dispute in the Aegean between Greece and Turkey, which has serious implications for Cyprus, NATO's command structure and general efficiency, and potentially, if things deteriorate, for maritime security in an area where the British have traditionally regarded themselves as significant players.

Protecting the marine environment

It is now frequently said that poor countries and rich countries, the industrial world and the developing world, the great and the small, are all co-operating in different ways to destroy the marine environment they share. In 1998, the UN Year of the Ocean and its associated reports and exhibitions, drew world attention the extent to which the marine environment is under threat. This is especially true in the littoral area and is likely to get worse as world population increases. Our prosperity, even our health, perhaps even our existence, depends on getting marine pollution under control.

234

In consequence, increasing recognition is now given to the need to regulate activities at sea, and activities on land which pollute the sea. This is as true of European waters as of anywhere else. This impulse is taking the form of a growing body of national and international regulation which naval and coastguard forces will increasingly need to monitor and enforce. First and foremost, the pressure will be on the Royal Navy to demonstrate that it is not, in itself, a source of pollution and this requirement is likely to grow ever greater. Thereafter, the Navy may well become involved in attempts to help police the polluters.

This, however, may be seen as taking the navy well away from its main military preoccupations – into areas for which it was not designed and for which other, cheaper, alternatives exist – and could be said to reduce its capacity to achieve its main purposes. None the less, it may well happen. In rather the same way, the Royal Navy's increasing requirement to conform to ever more stringent social legislation (both national and European) is already becoming a major preoccupation which will certainly have an impact on its fighting efficiency.

The maritime requirements of good order
Coping with the diverse requirements of good order, the maritime forces (by which is implied more than just the Royal Navy) will probably need a fleet mix containing minor combatants and even simple patrol craft, as well as major sophisticated warships. Experience around the world suggests that good order requires specialist craft to deal with the particular problems of the littoral. Even the US Navy found itself outwitted by the so-called 'go-fast' boats used by drugs smugglers in the Caribbean, the semi-submersibles and the 25 foot cigarette boats. Simply using conventional naval high seas forces against this kind of threat will often not work, whatever the adverts say. Around the world, there is also an increasing emphasis on partnership between naval and usually cheaper and often more politically acceptable civilian maritime forces, and Britain is not immune to this.

Such forces have an obvious need for higher levels of cooperation with the other services and with the forces of friendly nations since this mandates good command, control, communications and intelligence facilities to ensure that data can be shared among all participating units.

CONCLUSION

All this will clearly have a major impact on the size and shape of the Royal Navy to the year 2020. Whether it will survive and prosper will depend in large measure on its leaders not being seduced into an exclusive focus on high seas and high-intensity tasks, while none the less preserving that crucial capacity, on being alert to the need for inter-agency work as part of a national and regional oceans policy, and on being prepared for a loss of naval independence to other international groupings and to the other services. The Royal Navy has entered an era of radical change, but there are encouraging signs that it is well aware of this fact and is thinking seriously about its consequences.

NOTES

The views expressed in this article should not be taken necessarily to reflect official opinion in any way.

1. Admiral J. Paul Reason, *Sailing New Seas* (Newport, RI: Center for Naval Warfare Studies, Newport Paper, no. 13, 1998), p. 13.
2. Scott Truver, 'Surface Revolution: DD 21 Redefines the Destroyer', *Jane's Navy International* (July/August 1998).
3. Admiral William J. Owens, 'The Emerging System of Systems', *Proceedings of the USNIP*, vol. 121, no. 5 (1995).
4. 'Coral Reef Eaten Up by Effluent Plagues', *Guardian*, 25 January 1999.
5. C. V. Betts, 'Developments in Warship Design and Engineering', *Proceedings of the Institution of Mechanical Engineers*, vol. 210 (1996).
6. For Dutch interest in TBMD, see 'TBM Defence Maturing', *International Defence Review*, 1 (1998).
7. See 'Is There a Revolution in Military Affairs', *Strategic Survey* (1995–96) (London: International Institute for Strategic Studies, 1996), pp. 19–40.
8. Andrew F. Krepenevich, 'Cavalry to Computer: The Pattern of Military Revolution', *National Interest*, no. 37 (Fall 1994).
9. Ibid.
10. Interview with Akbar Torkan, London *Financial Times*, 8 February 1993.
11. Krepinevich, 'Cavalry to Computer'.
12. Lawrence Freedman, 'The Changing Focus of Strategy and War', *Survival* (Winter 1998/99).
13. *Strategic Defence Review* (London: The Stationery Office, 1998), p. 7. Hereafter *SDR*.
14. For useful discussions of all these points see all the articles under 'The Future of Strategy and War', *Survival* (Winter 1998/99).
15. Lawrence Freedman, *The Revolution in Strategic Affairs* (Oxford: Oxford University Press for the IISS, Adelphi 318, 1998), p. 34.
16. One exception to this was Major-General Sir Charles Callwell, *Small Wars: Their Principles and Practice* (London: HMSO, 1896).
17. Rear-Admiral Herbert Richmond, Autumn 1920, RN War College, Greenwich, Richmond MSS, NMM/RIC/10/4. I am indebted to Joe Moretz for this reference.
18. See the contributions by Admiral J. McAnnally in G. Sloan *et al.* (eds), *Doctrine and Military Effectiveness* (Exeter: University of Exeter, Strategic Policy Studies Group, 1997).
19. UK Doctrine for Joint and Combined Operations, 0207-b.
20. *SDR*, p. 21, Supporting Essays 2–4 and 6–4 para 14.
21. Jan Breemer, 'Naval Strategy is Dead', *Proceedings of the USNIP*, vol. 120, no. 2 (February 1994).

22. 'Russians Ready to Sail', *Sunday Telegraph*, 4 April 1999.
23. *SDR*, p. 22.
24. *SDR*, Fact Sheets, 'A Message from the First Sea Lord'.
25. *SDR*, SE 6–7.
26. *SDR*, p. 29.
27. *SDR*, 'A Message from the First Sea Lord'.
28. *SDR*, p. 55.
29. Brigadier Robert Fry, MBE, 'End of the Continental Century', *Journal of RUSI* (June 1998).
30. *SDR*, p. 44.
31. *SDR*, Supporting Essays, no. 4, p. 41.
32. Confidential Monthly Intelligence Report, no. 15, 15 July 1920, NMM RIC/4/1. I am indebted to Joe Moretz for this reference.
33. Broadsheet 98 (London: MOD, 1998), p. 88.
34. Gert de Nooy (ed), *The Role of European Naval Forces After the Cold War* (The Hague: Kluwer Law International, 1996).
35. See most recently, James Cable, *The Political Influence of Naval Force in History* (London: Macmillan, 1998).
36. Captain T. Burnett-Nugent, 'HMS Invincible and Operation Bolton – A Modern Capability for a Modern Crisis', *Journal of RUSI* (August 1998).
37. B. H. Liddell Hart, *Strategy? The Indirect Approach* (London: Faber and Faber, 1967), p. 335.

14

The Transformation of the US Navy

Norman Friedman

Surely the most striking development in the US Navy, from the late 1970s on, was the change in the status of its surface combatant ships, from escorts to capital ships. From the middle of the Second World War through to the late 1970s, these ships were primarily escorts for the only effective offensive ships, the carriers. In that role they changed enormously, guns being exchanged for missiles and grease-pencil plots for computers. However, in a fundamental sense they did not change at all. Even the advent of the Harpoon anti-ship missile made little difference. In an important sense it was a longer-range equivalent to the guns and torpedoes of the past.

The key point was that carrier aircraft greatly outranged anything a surface ship could fire. A second point, very nearly as important, was that apart from shore bombardment, no surface combatant could inflict much damage on targets on land. It seemed that surface ships were inevitably secondary to the carriers. As the US carrier force shrank, that limited capability came to have more and more strategic significance. First, the US Navy could handle very few crises simultaneously. In the 1970s, with a total of 12 carriers, the navy could keep only four forward-deployed at any one time: usually two in the Mediterranean and two in the Far East. The situation was somewhat eased by permanently basing carriers abroad (most prominently at Yokosuka), but numbers could never be sufficient.

The navy did have much larger numbers of surface combatants, but in the early 1970s it seemed unlikely that, without a carrier, they could survive mass attacks by Soviet long-range bombers carrying stand-off missiles. They could not, then, operate independently. The development of the Aegis anti-air warfare system seemed to solve this particular problem, but it did not provide surface combatants with anything remotely like the offensive firepower of carriers.

In the 1970s, with too many commitments and too few carriers to meet them, the US Navy considered building what it called a strike cruiser, a nuclear-powered surface combatant armed with Aegis. In theory, a strike cruiser could operate alone, providing naval presence in a medium-threat area and thus freeing carrier battle groups for more dangerous areas. In fact, to be effective, a ship on a presence mission ought to present a real threat to those ashore. The best the strike cruiser could do was a single, lightweight 8 inch gun. This problem was symbolized by a proposed strike cruiser variant provided with a short-angled flight deck, from which STOVL aircraft could have flown. They provided the offensive punch the ship otherwise lacked. The ship would have made do with relatively few aircraft because, in a moderate-threat situation, Aegis would have made up for the absence of defending fighters and their radar aircraft. In fact, the combination was so expensive that this strike cruiser was never built, either as a nuclear surface combatant or as a small aircraft carrier.

The situation a quarter-century later is radically different. The US government often calls upon US surface combatants to attack very distant land targets – during 1998, in Afghanistan, Iraq and the Sudan, and during early 1999 in Kosovo as well. All US cruisers and missile destroyers function, in effect, as strike cruisers, albeit without the nuclear powerplant that would have made the strike cruiser of the 1970s truly autonomous.

SOMETHING REMARKABLE HAPPENED

It was the combination of a new kind of missile, Tomahawk, with space assets for both surveillance and communication. The new missile could hit targets 1,000 miles away. The space assets extended a ship's horizon to the point where that range was worthwhile. The combination did not make a surface combatant into an aircraft carrier, but it did transform the fleet in a way that is only now becoming evident.

Tomahawk was conceived of as a nuclear-armed cruise missile. At first it was valued because many kinds of ships could carry it and it could be widely dispersed. The Soviet capacity to attack the US fleet depended on an ability to keep track of major targets. It was widely believed, within the US Navy of the 1970s, that the Soviets could barely track the forward-deployed carriers and major amphibious ships, a total of perhaps ten or fewer ships.[1] Because Tomahawk imposed a nuclear threat, they would feel obliged to track any ship carrying it, so that the threat could be neutralized at the outbreak of a war. Thus simply placing Tomahawk aboard many US surface combatants would require them to track at least ten times as many platforms, and thus indirectly would dramatically reduce a growing threat to the most important offensive ships, the aircraft carriers. Initially, surface combatants carried their Tomahawks in very visible armored box launchers above decks, so the Soviets were forcibly reminded of which ships they had to fear.[2]

The nuclear-armed land-attack Tomahawk made it possible for the US

Navy to counter the Soviets' main naval tactic. In the 1970s the Soviets espoused the concept of the 'battle for the first salvo', in which they would seize sea supremacy by making a coordinated attack on all major forward-deployed US warships at the outbreak of a war. In the Okean 1970 exercise they had, it seemed, demonstrated an ability to coordinate attacks on a global scale. That was necessary, since the first attack on one US ship would open the war and quite possibly lead to counterattacks by all other US ships. If all were hit simultaneously, that danger would be obviated.

One way to reduce the danger of an initial Soviet strike would be to replace valuable forward-deployed carriers with less vulnerable surface combatants. Around 1974 an official US Navy study showed, for example, that although a missile hit might easily destroy a carrier (by penetrating to her magazines, which were above water), a battleship (which could be recommissioned from reserve) would be very difficult to sink. Recommissioning the battleships, and forward deploying them instead of carriers, would place the Soviets in an untenable position. They would have to waste their first salvoes on these ships – which would be difficult to sink in any case – and in doing so would lay themselves open to counterattack by fully alerted carriers (which would start the war outside the range of any Soviet first missile strike).[3]

The problem was that, as in the case of the abortive strike cruiser, there was no particular reason for the Soviets to have to deal with the battleships. They did not pose a threat to anything the Soviets really needed; attacking them would merely have ruined Soviet naval plans. Once Tomahawk was available the situation changed radically. Now a battleship armed with Tomahawks really did present a direct threat to Soviet interests. It had to be dealt with. Conversely, it could be used to project power. When the Reagan Administration came into office in 1981, it badly needed some way of increasing US naval effectiveness. In large part that meant some way of dispersing US naval power. The administration decided to buy more carriers, but that would take time. As an interim measure, it recommissioned the four existing *Iowa* class battleships, arming them with Tomahawk missiles. Each now became the centerpiece of a surface action group, at least one ship of which provided air defense in the form of the Aegis system. To some extent the surface action group equated to the strike cruiser concept of the previous decade, except that now it had the requisite punch. The battleship added the tactical punch of her guns.

Early deployments of Tomahawk coincided roughly with the US Navy's decision to abandon trainable missile launchers in favor of vertical launchers. Initially, the great virtues of the vertical launcher were its rapid firing rate and its reliability.[4] The vertical launcher could accommodate a wide variety of weapons, limited mainly by the dimensions of the launch cell. The key US decision was to make the cells long enough to accommodate Tomahawk missiles. Thus, when Aegis cruisers and destroyers were armed with vertical launchers, they were automatically given some Tomahawk capability. How much of that capacity they could realize depended of course on the extent to which they could control the weapons.

One advantage of the vertical launcher was that there was no easy way for an observer to identify what kind of missiles it accommodated. Alternatively, one might say that a ship equipped with it could easily shift from anti-air duty to strategic attack duty; or that it would normally have mixed responsibility. At the very least, a ship armed with nuclear Tomahawks offered just the sort of threat the Soviets felt bound to counter, and thus was an excellent way to saturate their ship-tracking and ship-attack capabilities.

As the Tomahawk missile was developed during the 1970s, it became obvious that it had a wider potential. One version was designed for land attack using non-nuclear warheads. Although it was far more expensive, per pound of explosive delivered, than carrier-based aircraft, it was also much stealthier. It could, for example, destroy air defenses and thus make carrier aircraft far more effective. Perhaps more importantly, non-nuclear Tomahawks could deliver precise attacks on targets even in very bad weather conditions, in which aircraft could not deliver laser-guided bombs.

These missiles are responsible for the current state of US surface combatants. They are the ones first used during the Gulf War in 1991, and later in Bosnia, in Afghanistan, in the Sudan and most recently in Kosovo. In an important sense, a ship armed with these weapons is a capital ship in the sense that a carrier is a capital ship – something that could not be said of a surface combatant any time after about 1943–44.

The other non-nuclear version of Tomahawk was an anti-ship missile, capable of attacking at a range of 250 nautical miles – far beyond a ship's sensor horizon. Although this missile is no longer in service, it was extremely significant. Because its range so exceeded the sensor range of the ship firing it, anti-ship Tomahawk was viable only if the surface ship could receive its targeting data from some other source. There had to be some way to extend its horizon.

Whatever way was chosen had to be inexpensive, because anti-ship attack was a very low priority for the US Navy. Strikes against land targets were far more important.[5] By the early 1970s, the US Navy was already trying to track Soviet missile-carrying warships, at the least to provide its own carrier battle groups with warning that they might be attacked. It was developing a passive radar satellite system, White Cloud, to provide some indication of the positions of these ships. This effort can probably be dated back to the emergence of a powerful Soviet fleet in the Mediterranean after the 1967 Middle East War. For example, in 1968 the US government pressed its NATO allies to form a special intelligence center to monitor Soviet warships in the Mediterranean. Prior to this, the main Soviet threats to US and other Western warships were submarines and missile-carrying bombers (mainly 'Badgers'). After 1967, and particularly after the sinking of the Israeli destroyer *Eilat* that autumn, the US Navy took the threat of surface-launched missiles much more seriously.[6]

There was a considerable difference between the sort of information a carrier group needed and the sort a missile-shooter needed. Unlike a surface missile-shooter, a carrier had organic means of collecting information. Cued by the intelligence system, the carrier could send out search aircraft to locate Soviet missile ships that would subsequently be attacked. From the point of view of the status of surface ships in ship-to-ship combat, that was a profound difference. Because she had this organic search capability, a carrier greatly outreached any surface combatant ship.

Conversely, any development that provided surface ships with reach comparable with that of carriers would profoundly change the balance of maritime power. That is, it used to be said that a capital ship could be sunk only by another capital ship. In that sense the carrier's capital ship status was a function of her long reach, due not only to the range of her strike aircraft but also to the range of her search aircraft. Strike without search was relatively worthless. That is why, when the Royal Navy lost its large-deck carriers after 1974, its greatest problem was not to develop a Soviet-style long-range anti-ship missile, but rather to replace the search capability lost with the airborne early warning aircraft – which were also sea search aircraft – of the big carriers.

Similarly, the Soviets' greatest efforts were concentrated not on the mechanics of their missiles, but rather on ocean reconnaissance. In the early 1960s the Soviets began to deploy surface ships, beginning with the *Kynda* (Project 58) class, carrying long-range anti-ship missiles. They became truly effective only when they were accompanied by long-range radar aircraft ('Bear D,' which the Soviets designated Tu-95Ts) which could extend their radar horizons sufficiently to bring ship targets into view.[7]

In the US case, the origins of an anti-ship missile can be traced, not to the surface ship but to the submarine community. In 1968, in connection with a design review of what became the *Los Angeles* class, US submarine officers called for development of a stand-off weapon which they called STAM.[8] It was to be partly a non-nuclear equivalent of the Subroc anti-submarine stand-off missile then in service, and partly an anti-ship weapon to overcome expected improvements in Soviet anti-submarine warfare. Given recent developments in the Mediterranean, the submariners presumably expected an increased emphasis on anti-ship attacks, and they wanted to be able to strike from outside the range of Soviet defenses.

STAM would have had a range of perhaps 30 miles, within the submarine's sensor range. By 1971 this idea had been transmuted. If the submarine had a much longer range missile, she could outrange the Soviet anti-ship missiles. The idea that a submarine should escort US carriers (to

242

deal with Soviet nuclear submarines) had already been accepted, and indeed was a major rationale for the new *Los Angeles* class. If the same submarine were armed with long-range anti-ship missiles, she could also deal with the new threat of surface missile shooters.[9]

However, to do that, the submarine would need not only a missile but also some way of detecting the enemy ships far beyond her sensor horizon. The new intelligence system designed to track the Soviet surface fleet would solve the problem. If it was precise enough, then it might provide not merely an indication of where the threats were, but actual targeting data. A second satellite system might provide such data to the submarine.

By 1971, then, the submariners were proposing a new supersonic anti-ship cruise missile (for which a new submarine would be needed) and a satellite transmission system for targeting data, which they called SSIXS, the Submarine Information Exchange System. All of these elements went together. The submarine would receive only a quick report that a target was in a particular place at a particular time. If the missile were fast enough, it could arrive there before the target had moved very far. Supersonic long-range performance in turn demanded a big new submarine, and that helped generate support for the overall concept.[10]

The chief of naval operations, Admiral Elmo Zumwalt, Jr, saw no point in the big submarine. In 1972 two smaller cruise missiles, Harpoon and what became Tomahawk, were already under development. Zumwalt made them the basis for submarine-launched anti-ship missiles. An encapsulated Harpoon would become the interim weapon. The longer-term weapon would be an anti-ship version of the Tomahawk already scheduled for submarine installation, using Harpoon guidance technology. Since both weapons could fit the existing 21 inch torpedo tube, no new submarine was needed.

Since it was already planned to put Tomahawk on board surface warships, Zumwalt's decision automatically gave the surface fleet a long-range anti-ship weapon which, incidentally, had much the same range as the Soviet weapons already in service. At a stroke, Soviet superiority in surface anti-ship missiles had been eliminated, at least potentially.

What was needed was a way of targeting the missile. It was no longer enough simply to flash the submarine the location of a specific target. The missile would take about half an hour to get to the target area, and during that time the target might move a considerable distance (15 miles at 30 knots). If the missile spent a long time searching the area around the last target location, it would surely be shot down.

The solution developed was ingenious. The US Navy was already collecting data on the movements of the Soviet fleet. If a specific Soviet ship was detected several times in sequence, that roughly defined its path. Its position could be projected ahead, assuming that it did not take evasive action. Since the information would come from a variety of sources, nearly all of them passive, it was unlikely that any specific ship would know that it was under surveillance, let alone due for attack. Evasive action would, therefore, be unlikely.

A picture of Soviet fleet movements could be transmitted to the fleet for use in targeting long-range anti-ship missiles. No new sensor would be used; instead, data from existing ones would be correlated at shore data fusion centers (which were already being built up simply to support the carriers). Each shooter would need considerable information, which only a satellite channel could carry. Fortunately the navy was already developing a satellite communication system easily adapted to exactly such a purpose.

As a result, when anti-ship Tomahawks entered service in the early 1980s, the US Navy suddenly acquired an effective long-range surface ship anti-ship capability. Its surface ships became capital ships, in a way they had not been since the middle of the Second World War.

The transformation of the surface ships was one facet of a larger transformation of the navy, a change which can be seen in other navies as well. Conventionally, we imagine a navy as a collection of ships and supporting aircraft. If the shore assets of the navy are considered at all, they are lumped together as bases and industrial assets. Thus it is common to associate the global reach of the Royal Navy with its global network of bases (often reduced to the level of 'coaling stations'). The quick rise of the US Navy from 1938 onwards is clearly attributable in large part to its industrial base, which survived the industrial disasters of the Great Depression.

There is, however, something more, which is only slowly emerging. In both world wars, naval intelligence had a very important operational element. It functioned as a kind of sensor, sometimes giving information only slightly time-late. We typically differentiate intelligence from the physical plant of a navy; we think of it in terms of rooms of experts poring over messages and, perhaps, a plot of ship positions. However, the Second World War system also involved numerous radio direction-finding sites ashore, not to mention radio intercept stations.

Sensors external to the fleet became far more important post-war. Examples include SOSUS, the vast undersea sensor system operated first by the United States and then in part by NATO; the post-war HF/DF nets; White Cloud and other satellite systems; and the Relocatable Over-the-Horizon Radar (ROTHR) developed by the United States. From an organizational perspective, many of these sensors feed intelligence groups. However, from a strategic one, they are fleet sensors. Their product is generally fused into a picture of shipping movements – which is fed to deployed ships for their operational use.

All of this may seem abstruse. After all, the US Navy never fired anti-ship Tomahawks at anyone, and now that missile has gone. However, the supporting sensor structure is very much alive. While Tomahawk was being developed, it became obvious that successful use demanded a picture not only of the targets' movements, but also of surrounding shipping. Otherwise the very few missiles fired might well be wasted on the wrong targets.[11]

As the system ultimately developed, the world shipping picture was assembled at a fleet command center (FCC) ashore and transmitted, via satellite, to ships with computers capable of assembling the data. Initially they were special machines (USQ-81) associated with Tomahawk and with a tactical fleet command center (TFCC) aboard carriers. However, in the early 1980s commercial computer technology was improving very rapidly, and it was soon clear that relatively inexpensive machines could be installed on board all US surface warships. The initial system was called JOTS.[12] It was approved for service in June 1990.

Ship-tracking is important for many roles other than for Tomahawk shooting. For example, ships blockading a wide area of sea need cueing if they are to intercept merchant ships passing through. Without that cueing, the ships must be spaced very closely, and a huge force is needed. JOTS provided the necessary cues. It was essentially software running on a standard commercial computer, so it was easy to reproduce and to distribute. It was the key to the successful blockade of Iraq.

The success of the blockade in turn proved that the concept embodied in the anti-ship Tomahawk was workable. In contrast to the Soviets, the US Navy took existing sensors and integrated them using the powerful computers American industry provided – which the Soviets lacked. The result was a reasonably comprehensive picture of Soviet naval operations, assembled without warning any Soviet ship that it was under surveillance.

The basic idea, that a surface ship derived much of her effectiveness from outside sensors whose data were assembled at a shore station, developed into current ideas of Net-Centric Warfare, where the surface ship's connectivity – her continuous access to satellite-borne information – and her firepower are her key assets.[13]

NOTES

The opinions in this paper are the author's own, and do not necessarily represent those of the US Navy or of any other organization with which he has been associated.

1. There was some real evidence. In the 1970s, Soviet destroyers ('tattletales') often trailed US attack carriers. Their role was to identify the high-value target within a formation, so that missiles would not be wasted on, for example, escorts – a role necessitated when the US Navy installed blip-enhancers on its destroyers, so that Soviet radars could not necessarily distinguish them from carriers. Often it was possible for a carrier to escape her tattletale, and there was clear evidence that the Soviets were trying frantically to regain contact. Had their tracking systems been adequate, escape would have been impossible.

2. It is sometimes suggested that the box launchers were chosen specifically so that ships carrying the new missile would clearly show their new offensive capability, hence would be more effective in the presence role. However, in the early 1980s the US Navy did not yet have any other launcher capable of firing the missile. The vertical launcher was not yet available.

3. Soviet striking range at the time, in the mid-1970s, seemed to be limited by two factors. First, the attacking platforms would be cued either by reconnaissance aircraft or by land-based HF/DF systems; in either case they were unlikely to offer sufficient information for strikes more than about 1,000 miles from the Soviet coast. Second, few of the strike systems themselves – bombers, surface ships and submarines – could operate reliably very far from the Soviet Union. By the late 1970s, with the advent of Soviet ocean reconnaissance satellites, the situation was rather different.

4. The last major trainable launcher, Mark 26, fired about one missile per second, and that was at least matched by the new vertical launcher. Mark 26, however, was subject to water damage. In a vertical launcher the main moving parts were the doors over the launch cells; if one jammed, another could be selected and its cell used. Similarly, if a missile in a cell proved defective, another could easily be fired. In a trainable launcher, that sort of failure generally required that the missile be pushed overboard and a new one brought up from the magazine, a time-consuming procedure. Also, a vertical system accommodates more missiles in its volume than a trainable one does in a similar volume, because the trainable launcher needs space for its machinery. Vertical launchers also offer considerable flexibility in overall ship arrangement, a point nicely illustrated by the Canadian and Dutch practice of locating launch cells along the side of the superstructure, in the 'City' and 'M' classes. Many navies have now abandoned trainable launchers. In the US case, the last ships to have trainable (rail) launchers for their primary armament were the first group of Aegis cruisers. Among the consequences is that these ships, unlike all other Aegis ships, cannot carry Tomahawk missiles.

5. Indeed, in the 1990s anti-ship Tomahawks were withdrawn from service specifically so that they could be converted for land attack.

6. Note, however, that US Navy programs for countermeasures to these weapons, such as the Sea Sparrow (BPDMS) program, predate the *Eilat* sinking. These programs did receive considerably more priority after the sinking.

7. In the Soviet system, as it came into service in 1965, the naval command center ashore would cue both ship and bomber, based on initial intelligence (typically, using an HF/DF net). The bomber would transmit its radar picture down to the ship, which would aim the missiles on that basis. To avoid tipping off the target, the Bears would do their radar reconnaissance some hours before the planned missile strike. On the basis of these observed Soviet tactics, the word in the US Navy was 'Bears in the morning, missiles in the afternoon'. The next step, which became operational in the 1970s, was a system of passive and active radar satellites. The basic architecture, in which all information was collated ashore, and in which a platform was cued to attack a specific target, remained.

8. The new submarine design having excited considerable controversy, an *ad hoc* panel was formed to review it. A second panel reviewed weapons to be carried on board the next-generation submarine, *circa* 1975.

9. For the origin of this advanced cruise missile (ACM) or Submarine Tactical Anti-Ship Weapons System (STAWS) see Kenneth P. Werrell, *The Evolution of the Cruise Missile* (Maxwell Air Force Base, AL: Air University Press, 1985), p. 151. Werrell does not mention STAM. He dates the ACM concept to April 1971, when the FY72 budget was being prepared, and notes that in January 1972 the

secretary of defense ordered a strategic cruise missile (SCM) developed using supplemental FY72 funds. The Navy formally chose the torpedo-tube option in November 1972.

10. Admiral Hyman Rickover, who commanded the Naval Reactors branch of the Naval Sea Systems Command (NAVSEA), particularly supported the overall concept, some said because it required a new reactor he already had under development (a single reactor capable of powering a cruiser, to replace the two re-actors previously used for that purpose). Conversely, one might see in the new submarine a direct extension of the submarine escort idea embodied in the *Los Angeles* class that Rickover had championed. A cynic within NAVSEA later remarked that Rickover had rejected any possibility of using a smaller anti-ship missile because it could have been accommodated on board an existing sub-marine; he really liked the idea of being forced to a larger hull (private communication to the author, 1993).

11. This point emerged from studies of Soviet tactics; it became clear that the Soviets took considerable pains to distinguish the high-value target from surrounding ships (hence, among other things, the use of 'tattletales'). The present author was involved in these studies, at the US Naval War College, in the mid-1970s.

12. The Joint Operational Tactical System – but, to wags, the Jerry O. Tuttle System, after its creator, Admiral Tuttle, who eventually headed the Space and Electronic Warfare Systems Command.

13. For more details of space-based systems and their implications, see the author's forthcoming *Space and Seapower: Navies in the Missile Age* (London: Chatham Press, 2001) and his *Naval Institute Guide to World Naval Weapons Systems* (Annapolis, MD: Naval Institute Press, 1991–92 and 1997–98 editions).

15

Technology, Shipbuilding and Future Combat beyond 2020

David Andrews

Anyone trying to predict the future some 30 years hence is verging on the foolish: to guess whether the US, supported by its Western allies, remains the one global superpower, given the size of China and India, or to predict the world's economic and ecological health, which governs the foreign and defence policy imperatives, is hardly what one would expect of a warship designer and acquisition manager. Such speculation is best left to historians such as Paul Kennedy[1] and Francis Fukuyama.[2] Instead, what this chapter will do is give a glimpse into some possible technological solutions, but it assumes an awful lot of 'ifs'.

The first thing to say about the shape of navies in the third and fourth decades of the twenty-first century is that it remains highly likely that the general shape of any fleet, as well as the types of vessels it comprises, will be set in the two preceding decades. If one realizes how long it takes to develop and widely deploy a major new system, such as the US Aegis Air Defence System or the T23 frigates passive towed sonar array suite, then, clearly, there will be new sensors and weapons that will come into service in this time. To get some feel for the wide scope of technological possibilities, one might inspect the September 1994, 150th anniversary edition of *Scientific American*.[3] Interestingly it begins with 'The Uncertainties of Technological Innovation' then looks at these main areas:

- information technologies
- transportation
- medicine
- machines, materials and manufacture
- energy and environment
- living with new technologies

All one can be certain about is that, to some degree, development in all these areas will have an impact on the technology deployed by navies in the second quarter of the next century. However, choosing the most likely developments is a highly speculative pastime. Rather than review any possible developments for their potential applicability, it might be more useful to look at overall naval technology and consider the range of possible naval vessels that might be deployed. After that we can conclude with a brief consideration of the manufacturing possibilities for this disparate range of vehicles and consider the nature of the design process likely to be required to provide for some of these possible future fleets.

ISSUES FOR FUTURE WARSHIPS

It is probably sensible to start with the mono-hull which, despite all the exotic design concepts to follow, remains the most likely configuration for most ships, and possibly most warships, in the time-frame of this chapter. However, it is likely that within the role assigned to any ship, given the technologies of its weapons, sensors, propulsion, ship systems and hull, it will be noticeably different. Some reasonably predictable developments are those in weapons directed energy, in sensors using sophisticated electronics and remote autonomous and intelligent vehicles, in totally electric propulsion and ship services powered with electronic controls and in the use of 'intelligent composites' for the hull. All that may seem radical enough until one focuses on the shape of future warships, beyond the mono-hull, even if that shape might itself be considerably different to today's most stealthy concepts, such as Vosper Thornycroft's SeaWraith.[4]

Before future ship shapes are considered it is worth being reminded that, thanks to the end of the Cold War, there is something that can be called the new defence Nexus.[5] That is, the successful end of the Cold War has led and will probably continue to lead to a reduction in defence expenditure. The other side of this Nexus is that the role required of these fewer naval forces is less clearly defined, and so we need more capable, more adaptable ships fulfilling the Pax America 'from the Sea'[6] concept. In giving priority to power projection in brown or littoral waters naval warfare has placed its emphasis on the amphibious role, with the rest of the naval forces (including submarines) in support. This has radically redefined the US Navy's role. For the other significant NATO navies this reorientation of the world's remaining superpower will have an inevitable knock-on effect. Given that the operational justification of any new class of warship is derived from its concept of operations, such a radically new emphasis will mean that future warships are likely to be different not just technically, but in their operational capabilities.

It is perhaps too early, a mere few years into the new geopolitical environment, to predict exactly how future warships will be configured. While it is likely that increased emphasis will be given to those formerly 'Cinderella' arms of navies, such as amphibiosity and mine counter-measures, it is perhaps harder to say how those workhorses of navies, the frigates and destroyers, will change. The only thing that seems clear is that the old certainties of a well-defined threat and highly tuned weapon suites will be less of a prime justification for a new class of warship. The hall-mark of the frigate/destroyer has been its flexible role. It is likely that in the future this flexibility will be required to an even greater degree to meet the much more diffuse threat posed by potentially hostile forces attempt-ing to resist 'Coalition Forces' exercising power projection from the sea.

Just when navies appear to need more flexible and adaptable warships able to contend with almost any threat, from the simplest level of peace-keeping to major regional power confrontations, they are faced with the ratcheting down of the resources available for such procurement. The reduced aspirations of all NATO governments has led to ongoing reduc-tions in the defence forces' order of battle.[7] This is symptomatic of a water-shed in defence procurement, which even before the collapse of the Warsaw Pact was showing signs of overheating. Philip Pugh[8] showed starkly that defence equipment in general, including warships, has been escalating in cost at a greater rate (7 per cent per annum) than the growth in GNP. Warships were rapidly becoming unaffordable even when there was still some consensus that a single major threat needed to be countered. Thus, in the procurement of warships we have a classic Scylla and Charybdis situation of a more demanding and complex requirement as well as greatly reduced resources. This situation is the overriding issue in current defence procurement, and provides an unprecedented stimulus for achieving the most effective design solutions, taking into consideration budget con-straints, well into the twenty-first century.

The above has led naturally to two classic approaches being attempted to keep down warship costs. First there is SLEPing – Ship Life Extension, practised most noticeably by the US Navy which, through major upgrades at the end of their massive aircraft carriers' normal life, has doubled their life span to some 60 years. This clearly suggests that there will be several of the current US Navy's carriers still afloat in 2040. Whether this applies to other less expensive naval vessels depends to a certain degree on some of the design issues discussed later in the chapter. The second approach to cost reduction also has a typically ugly acronym: STUFT – Ships Taken Up From Trade. STUFT vessels were prominent during the Falklands War of 1982, in the guise of the large number of merchant ships converted, to a limited extent, to provide the Royal Navy with troop and stores trans-ports. But the term can be used also more routinely to provide a quick (and dirty) way to get auxiliary vessels into naval service, such as the aviation training ship RFA *Argus*. Whether this approach could be adopted for the roles of mainstream warships, such as those undertaken by frigates and destroyers, depends on technology, appropriate standards and the configuration of future merchant vessels.

This leads on to a review of possible future merchant ships, some of which have configurations which will be considered as possible naval vessels while others pose interesting broader options for future naval technology. The examples of future merchant vessels are suggested from illustrations in a publication which is now 16 years old and, although published by a major European marine equipment company, was written by four East German academics.[9]

The first examples given by Schönknecht *et al.* are of submersible tankers, one of which is an ice-breaker. Next, the reference shows a series of unconventional hull types, namely a catamaran cruise liner and three very large ferries adopting high speed concepts, the hydrofoil, the air surface effect ship (SES) and the air cushion vehicle (ACV). The latter example suggests strongly that this vehicle could be seen as a highly attractive means for projecting military forces on to a sea shore. Rather more radical is the ekranoplane or wing in ground effect machine that operates close to the sea–air interface limit. The reference also includes several examples of SWATHs (small waterplane twin-hulled vessels), a container ship, a ferry and even a suspended box structure arrangement for passenger ride. Finally, in the examples in this interesting view of the future there are two floating and potentially mobile islands that also could have clear military applications in maritime power projection. These examples have been highlighted partly to make the point that the diminishing defence technology base is likely to draw on commercial developments, that is, COTS (commercial off the shelf) solutions, partly to introduce some of the possible future ship configurations and partly, despite their age, because they are excellent illustrations that stimulate visions of possible future solutions.

RADICALLY NEW HULL FORMS

It is worth looking more closely at some of these unconventional hull types. Several of those mentioned in Schönknecht *et al.* address in particular the issue of ships going at speeds much greater than 30 knots.[10] To do so in a conventional mono-hull requires an enormous increase in propulsive power. Even if such an increase could be more readily provided in the future, it is more intelligent to change the configuration. Thus the ship designer can avoid relying solely on buoyancy and having to continue to push the hull through the water–air interface. Instead, the hydrofoil, the ACV and, largely, the SES lift the hull out of the water at speed. This can best be seen by comparing the forms of lift in the sustension diagram (Figure 15.1) where the non-displacement forms (the ACV and the hydrofoil) are the configurations exploiting each of the lift mechanisms, while the SES, the HYSWAS (hydrofoil small water plane single hull) and the O'Neill form exploit more than one lift mechanism. The latter are not the only possible hybrids, but so far they seem the most attractive. This is because, as the East German academics speculated, the partial use of buoyancy reduces the installed power necessary to get pure cushion lift or hydrodynamic lift for vessels of ocean-going size.

In Figure 15.1 the top (buoyancy) end of the sustension triangle shows several other displacement forms in addition to the mono-hull. Now most of these variants on the buoyancy form have been adopted to improve either speed, as in the case of the wave piercing catamaran, or seakeeping, as in the case of the SWATH.

The small water plane area twin-hull (SWATH) vessel, such as the US Navy's USS *Victorious*, has also been called a semi-submerged catamaran.

Figure 15.1: Sustension diagram.

It is best for sea-keeping with relatively deeply submerged hulls so that the surface piercing 'legs' or struts then support the box structure well above the wave surface (Figure 15.2). The small waterplane of the struts means the vessel is also relatively insensitive to wave action and thus it can maintain speed in waves better than an equivalent mono-hull. Perhaps a more twenty-first century vision of the SWATH concept is provided by the US Navy Black programme's *Sea Shadow*, a SWATH designed for stealth, so much so that its existence was unknown until the US Navy revealed it after several years' operating at night from San Diego Naval Base.[11] It is also worth saying that for larger ships, such as the amphibious warfare vessels at well over 10,000 tonnes displacement, there is no perceived advantage in departing from the mono-hull, as their bulky payload means their size brings the sea-keeping performance directly.

Considerably more information has become available in recent years on the wing in ground, ekranoplane or Caspian Sea Monster, the Soviet equivalent Black programme to *Sea Shadow*. Whether this technically viable means of transporting sizeable loads at some 200 km/hr will prove to be economically viable, depends on whether the additional price per tonne load per mile or kilometre is justifiable. A similar argument will determine whether the Japanese 57 tonne prototype *Hyswas* is selected for their techno super liner proposal.[12] But should either of these concepts prove commercially viable, then one can see the former as a ready means of power projection at speed and the latter as a possible high-speed deep-ocean escort, able to ride out rough weather at cruise speeds, when not partially foil borne.

This chapter has concentrated so far on surface and above ships despite the two submarine or submersible visions mentioned earlier. It is clear already that any new class of naval submarine likely to be in service in the second quarter of the twenty-first century will have a quite different operational role from the traditional nuclear submarine (SSN). Ideas on multi-role capabilities such as Special Forces insertion, forward communication bases and subsurface land attack imply quite different configurations. When this is combined with technological possibilities such as air independent propulsion (other than nuclear), autonomous underwater vehicles operating from submarines as mother ship, far greater

Figure 15.2: SWATH characteristics.

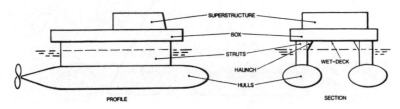

automation, new means of weapons discharge and smarter structural materials, one can see that naval submarines may be quite different. Both Houley's[13] vision of a mission-adaptable submarine and a slightly less radical but more realizable AIP submarine study, produced at University College London,[14] provide some indications. The latter is illustrated by a computer-aided representation, an issue covered at the end of the paper.

Finally, on future warships it is appropriate to say something about a possible warship configuration in which I have personally been closely involved for the last decade, and one that is now showing distinct signs of coming to fruition, ahead of all the radical ideas just reviewed. This point is made deliberately as it highlights the fact that an idea that did not figure in Schönknecht *et al.* in 1983 or even in the NATO advanced vehicles group's study in 1990[15] is now the front runner as the alternative to the ubiquitous mono-hull for the Royal Navy's Future Surface Combatant – that concept is the Trimaran[16] (see Figure 15.3).

If the current 1,100 tonne trimaran demonstrator being built by Vosper Thornycroft for the MOD's Defence Evaluation and Research Agency, Research Vessel *Triton*, is successful in her sea trials commencing late next year, then there is a real possibility that the Royal Navy's main class of frigates from early in the second decade of the new millennium will be of

Figure 15.3: Trimaran design study for the future surface combatant. (Courtesy of the Ministry of Defence.)

trimaran configuration. Thus, in the subsequent two decades this may well be the pattern for many warships of this size. Why do I say that, when this hull configuration was not conceived by naval architects until just under a decade ago?

Well, strange as it may seem, it took an ocean racing yacht designer, Nigel Irens, to apply this quite ancient principle, of small outriggers attached to a fine central hull, to the first power-boat trimaran. This was so successful that Irens approached my predecessor at UCL, Doug Pattison, to see if it could be extended to fast ferries, competing with the highly successful wave-piercing catamarans. As a warship naval architect, he then applied the configuration to a 5,000-tonne frigate study quite expecting to find a drawback since it seemed incredible that no one had thought of it previously. Well, nearly ten years later, with some 20-odd design studies ranging from 200 to almost 40,000 tonnes, from frigates to aircraft carriers and cruise liners, we are continuing to find some genuine benefits in the configuration.

Why is this so? It is worth repeating a view expressed in a series of papers[17] on trimarans, that the configuration is not that radical in its technology compared with, say, SES or hydrofoils. These configurations seem to require design development and construction approaches more akin to the aerospace industry and with commensurate costs. Rather, the trimaran is a conventional but slender mono-hull with two small side hulls (1/20th of the main hull's displacement). What these side hulls give the naval architect is the ability to deal with stability (keeping the ship upright) separately from producing a really slender main hull, thereby minimizing resistance at speed. This then implies less installed engine power and hopefully results in a cheaper ship for the same capability.

Beyond this first advantage in this form there are further potential benefits from, particularly, the cross-structure in the central portion of the ship which connects the three hulls together. The traditional frigate-sized warship suffers from having inadequate beam both on the upper deck and the main through deck near midships. All the main weapons, sensors and operational and working compartments are best located centrally and this is just not possible in a long narrow form. Considering the likely requirements for warships in the future suggests, for several reasons, the need for highly adaptable ships. First, the roles that are likely to be demanded for these ships will be more diffuse than those required of NATO naval vessels designed for the era of the Cold War major power block confrontation. Expeditionary warfare will be much more variable and less predictable, requiring role adaptable or changeable outfits in warships. Technology is likely to march ahead as rapidly and diversely as the initial summary of the anniversary edition of *Scientific American* suggests.[18] This means future warships must be configured for technology insertion both late in build and through life without extensive redesign and costly rebuilding. If, as seems only too likely, there will be fewer and fewer warships, then each one will have to be highly adaptable and able to be used as continually as possible without the current long down times for maintenance and for updating of military capability. Again, the trimaran, unlike the more highly tuned other advanced hull configurations or indeed our ubiquitous mono-hull, seems tailor-made to this unpredictable future.

FUTURE WARSHIP MANUFACTURE AND DESIGN

Having concentrated on some dramatic crystal-ball gazing with regard to the shape and nature of future warships it is appropriate to consider briefly how those future ships might be produced. This is best done by showing something of the way in which this major construction and assembly process is already being approached. The largest single building in Europe, is the Devonshire Dock Hall at VSEL's Barrow shipyard. This was built for assembling Trident submarines but is now being used to assemble large (1,000 tonne) units of major naval vessels. These assemblies are themselves made up of modules as Figure 15.4 shows for VSEL's build sequence for the Royal Navy's new Assault Ship (LPD(R)). This approach, unlike the traditional steelwork, launch and outfit sequence enables as much work as possible to be done on the modules when it is easily accessed and is considerably less demanding in time and labour resources. This approach also opens up the significant possibility of manufacturing modules and

Figure 15.4: Build sequence for HMS *Albion* construction at Marconi Naval Systems Barrow Shipyard. (Courtesy of VSEL, now BAE Systems.)

even construction units elsewhere – provided they can be transported to the final assembly facility. Perhaps this could even occur in other countries, where possibly the power plant or the accommodation modules might be being manufactured.

Currently, there is one major constraint requiring the construction units to be welded together earlier than desirable. This arises from the need for the main electrical power cables and, to a lesser degree, the extensive electronic data highway to be run throughout the ship. It seem highly likely, well before the second quarter of the twenty-first century, that this little local technical difficulty will have been solved and with it will come a major change to the way very complex ships, typified by the modern naval vessel, are manufactured, and this could mean the classical shipyard will then be a thing of the past.

Part of the engine for this revolution will be the already extensive computerization of the construction process; not just in the fabrication of steel structures and production of pipework but also in the use of CAD information to outfit the modules and assemblies. This leads on directly to the further change process that is already under way in using the power of modern computer-aided design systems, pioneered by the automotive and aerospace industries, to produce Integrated Product Models (IPM). By the end of the detailed design process, these computer descriptions will produce a detailed three-dimensional representation of the ship that will foster significant improvements in the production process. This approach has been called the Virtual Shipyard[19] as the computerized representation of the ship can be interrogated to work out how it can be most conveniently broken down into readily manufactured modules which are then most efficiently assembled into the whole ship. This approach relies on not just the predictable growth in computer hardware and software but also the moves already under way to ensure common standards in computer data that will enable not just distributed manufacture and assembly but also distributed design. This is just one element of the increasing trend towards Concurrent Engineering[20] which aims to ensure that future complex engineering artifacts are designed concurrently for production and through-life supportability. This is a step change, since until recently performance and procurement affordability have had to be the limit of design intent.

The final topic in this overview of the likely future of warship design is the design process itself. It is worth remembering that the design process required to produce a warship is immensely complex – and well caught in Graham's statement: 'It is understandable that today's warships are the most complex, diverse and highly integrated of any engineering system.'[21] It is also important to realize in talking of warship design and the various options already discussed that there are in this diverse and complex artifact, a mass of issues to be considered both in the choice of the overall

Table 15.1

Aspects to be Considered in the Choice of Warship Hull Form

Speed, power and endurance
Space and layout
Structural design and weight
Stability
Manoeuvrability
Noise, radar and magnetic signature
Weapon placement and effectiveness
Construction costs and build time
Through life costs

configuration and then subsequently in the detail below that. Table 15.1 lists typically the major issues to be considered in the choice of a warship's hull form. Whether this list will still be relevant and comprehensive enough for future warships is somewhat speculative and it would be surprising if there were not some new entrants to this list.

In this summary review it is not possible to do real justice to the topic of ship design. Andrews 'Comprehensive Methodology for the Design of Ships', published by the Royal Society last year,[22] provides further justification of the above assertion by Graham. Second, it is worth emphasizing that not all warship design is the same; it ranges from simple evolutionary design following largely on previous practice to, at the advanced vehicle end of the design spectrum, a design process typical of the aerospace industry where several full-scale prototypes are produced well before tooling for manufacture commences. Aside from this extreme, warships, like civil engineering construction, are typified by the lack of a prototype owing to the small production run and sheer scale of the individual product. Now in the time-frame this chapter addresses this could subtly change because of CAD advances. Thus a product model could be considered a virtual prototype, but only if all the performance characteristics, including the ability of the operators in the ship, could be simulated in the computer model.

However, the goal of Concurrent Engineering for future ship design cannot be achieved solely by massive investment in integrating computer standards and using the computer technology to handle the vast amount of data required to define a warship properly. To achieve real Concurrent Engineering requires some creativity if one is not to reproduce current solutions with just detailed engineering improvements. If the initial or preliminary design stages are considered to be the most crucial in determining the future ship, then massive integrated product models are too detailed and rigid to enable the exploitation required to both explore the requirement and sensibly explore the solution space. For the next new warship this front-end process is summarized in Figure 15.5, which marries the elucidation of the requirement with the material options through systems engineering. System engineering addresses all the cross-discipline and system capabilities (such as reliability, maintainability, human factors, producibility and supportability) through life, that is, Concurrent Engineering. It is considered that this can only be achieved through an initial synthesis approach which is fully integrated in creatively exploring the configurational possibilities right from the beginning, as Figure 15.6 shows.[23]

This emphasis on synthesis through configuration is now being achieved in the UK Ministry of Defence, again, because of advances in computer graphics. The MOD has developed a building block approach to initial synthesis which enables the designer to explore better many of the capabilities that really matter in achieving the requirement, or at least in exploring the options, which previous synthesis models were not able to do. This approach was first used on submarine concept work[24] and is now being extended to surface vessels, including SWATHs and Trimarans. Figure 15.7 shows the logic of this SURFCON system prototyped at UCL.[25] Coupled with the powerful data bases now being used to undertake requirements engineering, this approach enables future warship requirements definition and option exploration to be far more effective

Figure 15.5: Current design process for future surface combatant. (Courtesy of Ministry of Defence.)

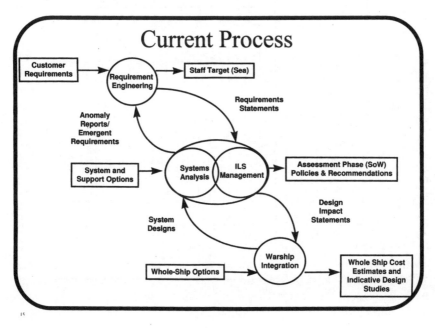

Figure 15.6: Design synthesis as key to ship design.

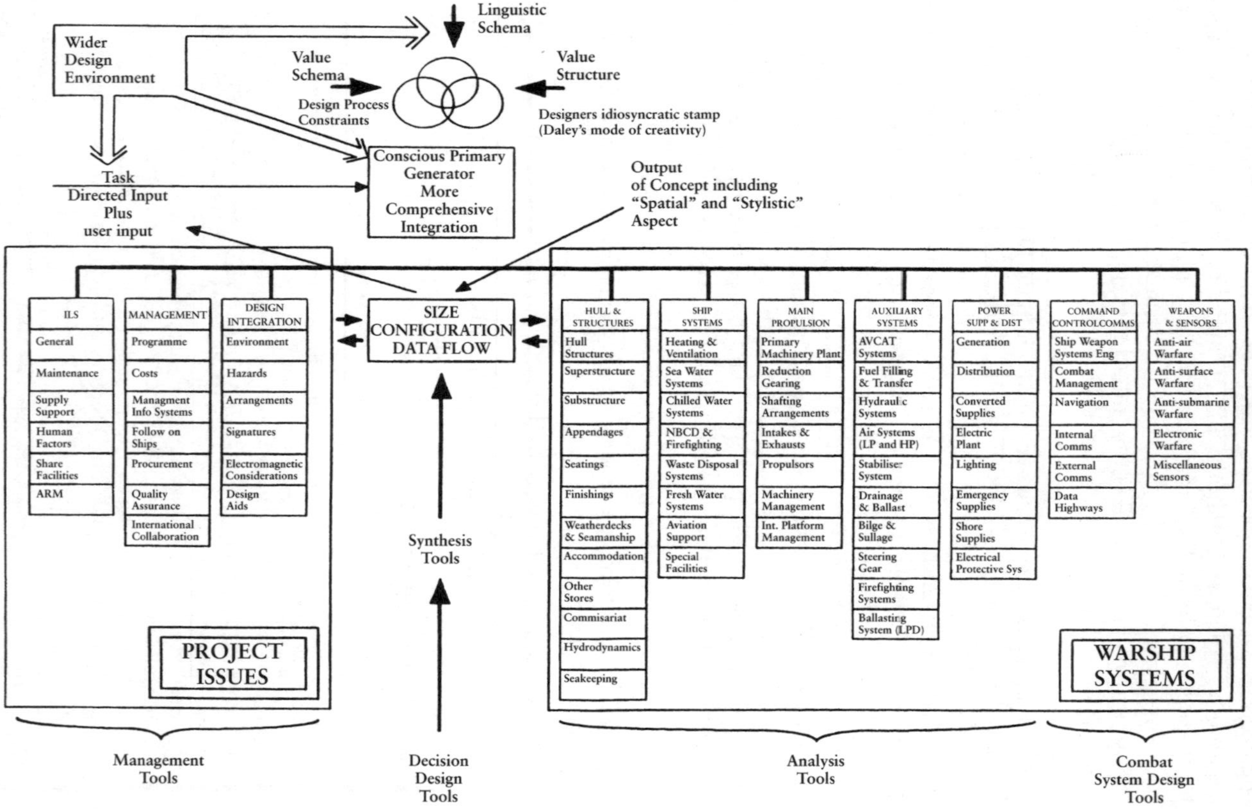

Wider Design Environment

Task Directed Input Plus user input

Linguistic Schema

Value Schema

Value Structure

Designers idiosyncratic stamp (Daley's mode of creativity)

Design Process Constraints

Conscious Primary Generator More Comprehensive Integration

Output of Concept including "Spatial" and "Stylistic" Aspect

SIZE CONFIGURATION DATA FLOW

Synthesis Tools

Decision Design Tools

Analysis Tools

Combat System Design Tools

Management Tools

WARSHIP SYSTEMS

HULL & STRUCTURES	SHIP SYSTEMS	MAIN PROPULSION	AUXILIARY SYSTEMS	POWER SUPP & DIST	COMMAND CONTROL COMMS	WEAPONS & SENSORS
Hull Structures	Heating & Ventilation	Primary Machinery Plant	AVCAT Systems	Generation	Ship Weapon Systems Eng	Anti-air Warfare
Superstructure	Sea Water Systems	Reduction Gearing	Fuel Filling & Transfer	Distribution	Combat Management	Anti-surface Warfare
Substructure	Chilled Water Systems	Shafting Arrangements	Hydraulic Systems	Converted Supplies	Navigation	Anti-submarine Warfare
Appendages	NBCD & Firefighting	Intakes & Exhausts	Air Systems (LP and HP)	Electric Plant	Internal Comms	Electronic Warfare
Seatings	Waste Disposal Systems	Propulsors	Stabiliser System	Lighting	External Comms	Miscellaneous Sensors
Finishings	Fresh Water Systems	Machinery Management	Drainage & Ballast	Emergency Supplies	Data Highways	
Weatherdecks & Seamanship	Aviation Support	Int. Platform Management	Bilge & Sullage	Shore Supplies		
Accommodation	Special Facilities		Steering Gear	Electrical Protective Sys		
Other Stores			Firefighting Systems			
Commisariat			Ballasting System (LPD)			
Hydrodynamics						
Seakeeping						

PROJECT ISSUES

ILS	MANAGEMENT	DESIGN INTEGRATION
General	Programme	Environment
Maintenance	Costs	Hazards
Supply Support	Management Info Systems	Arrangements
Human Factors	Follow on Ships	Signatures
Share Facilities	Procurement	Electromagnetic Considerations
ARM	Quality Assurance	Design Aids
	International Collaboration	

Figure 15.7: Building-block design methodology applied to surface ships.

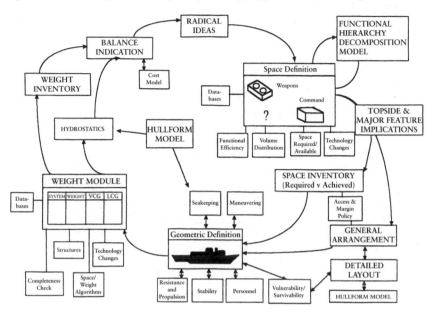

than in the past. Whether it will produce better warships – whatever is considered to be the basis for that assessment (perhaps virtual battlespaces, where we can test out our virtual warships) – may remain more an issue of organizational behaviour. And that is likely to be less amenable to engineering, even with computer, and best left by engineers, such as myself, to historians, given Sam Goldwyn's rejoiner: 'I never ever make predictions, especially about the future.'

NOTES

1. P. Kennedy, *Preparing for the Twenty-First Century* (London: HarperCollins, 1993).
2. F. Fukyama, *The End of History and the Last Man* (New York: The Free Press, 1992).
3. *Scientific American*, 150th anniversary edn (September 1994).
4. B. W. Spilman, 'Sea Wraith', IMDEX '97, vol. II (Greenwich October 1997).
5. D. J. Andrews and D. L. Kirkpatrick, 'Design Related Issues in Defence Procurement', Conference on Directing and Managing Cost Effective Design (Royal Aeronautical Society, 1998).
6. F. Kelso, 'From the Sea: Preparing the Naval Service for the 21st Century', *US Naval Institute Proceedings* (November 1992).
7. D. J. Andrews, 'Current Issues in Warship Procurement', International Naval Engineering Conference, Plymouth, Institute of Marine Engineers (June 1994).
8. P. G. Pugh, 'The Procurement Nexus', *Defence Economics*, vol. 14, no. 2 (1993).

9. R. Schönknecht *et al.*, 'Ships and Shipping of Tomorrow' (MacGregor Publications, 1983).
10. Ibid.
11. P. A. Chatterton and R. G. Paquette, 'The Sea Shadow', *US Naval Engineers Journal* (May 1994).
12. J. R. Meyer, 'Hybrid Ships: Variations On A Theme', *US Naval Institute Proceedings* (August 1995).
13. W. P. Houley, '2015', *US Naval Institute Proceedings* (October 1993).
14. D. J. Andrews *et al.*, 'SUBCON – A New Approach to Submarine Concept Design', Warships '96 Submarines 5 RINA (June 1996).
15. D. R. Lavis *et al.*, 'The Promise of Advanced Naval Vehicles for NATO', *Marine Technology*, vol. 27, no. 2 (March 1990).
16. D. J. Andrews and J. W. Zhang, 'Considerations in the Design of a Trimaran Frigate', International Symposium, High Speed Vessels, RINA (November 1995).
17. J. W. Zhang and D. J. Andrews, 'Manoeuvrability Performance of a Trimaran Ship', RINA International Symposium, Ship Motions and Manoeuvrability (February 1998); D. J. Andrews and J. A. Baylis, 'The Trimaran Ship – A Potential New Form for Aircraft Carrier Ships', RINA Warship '97 Symposium, 'Air Power at Sea', London (June 1997).
18. *Scientific American*, 150th anniversary edn (September 1994).
19. B. F. Tibbits and R. G. Keane, 'Making Design Everybody's Job', *US Naval Engineers Journal* (May 1995).
20. B. Butler, 'Design for the Future, New Technology to Transform the Design Engineer', Royal Acadamy of Engineering and the Royal Society, London (12 October 1995).
21. C. Graham in P. J. Gates and S. C. Rusling, 'The Impact of Weapons Electronics on Surface Warship Design', *Transactions of the Royal Institution of Naval Architects* (1992).
22. D. J. Andrews, 'A Comprehensive Methodology for the Design of Ships (and Other Complex Systems)', *Transactions of the Royal Society* (January 1998).
23. Ibid.
24. Andrews *et al.*, 'SUBCON'.
25. D. J. Andrews and C. A. Dicks, 'The Building Block Design Methodology Applied to Advanced Naval Ship Design', International Marine Design Conference '97, Newcastle (June 1997).

Notes on Contributors

David Andrews is currently Director Frigates and Mine Countermeasures in the Ministry of Defence Procurement Executive. Previously, he had been, for five years, Professor of Naval Architecture at University College, London. He has also served as the Royal Navy's Head of Preliminary Design in the Future Projects Directorate, where he was responsible for studies into future submarines and surface ships.

George W. Baer is Chairman of the Department of Strategy and Policy and holds the Alfred Thayer Mahan Chair in Maritime Strategy at the US Naval War College. His most recent book is *One Hundred Years of Sea Power: The US Navy, 1890–1990* (1996), which received the Theodore and Franklin D. Roosevelt Naval History Prize. His is currently writing on the 'utility of force'.

Michael Epkenhans works at the Otto-Von-Bismarck Stiftung at Friedrichsruh in Germany. He has published widely on numerous aspects of Imperial German naval history, including the acclaimed work *Die wilhelminische Flotterüstung 1908–1914. Weltmachtstreben, industrieller Fortschritt, sociale integration* (1991).

David Evans received his undergraduate and doctoral degrees from Stanford University. A member of the History faculty of the University of Richmond, Virginia, he was concurrently associate dean of faculty at the same institution for the last five years of his life. Though a specialist in the institutions of the Japanese navy in the late nineteenth and early twentieth centuries, his initial contribution to the field of naval history was his editorship, in 1986, of a new edition of Raymond O'Connor's *The Japanese Navy in World War II*. He not only updated that work, but added five new essays, two of which he translated himself. He was also co-author (with Mark Peattie) of the award-winning study, *Kaigun: Strategy,*

Tactics, and Technology in the Imperial Japanese Navy, 1887–1941. He was revising the article included in this volume when he died in June 1999 after a six-month struggle with cancer.

Norman Friedman is a defence analyst who has lectured at the Naval War College, the Naval Postgraduate School, the Air War College, and the Royal United Services Institute, among other places. He has published numerous articles and 21 books, the most recent being *Naval Institute Guide World Naval Systems* (1997–98).

Eric Grove is Senior Lecturer at the University of Hull, where he is also Deputy Director of the Centre for Strategic Studies. He has published extensively on different aspects of maritime strategy, naval history and sea power. Recent publications include: *Vanguard to Trident: British Naval Policy since 1945* (1987), *The Future of Sea Power* (1990) and *Maritime Strategy and European Security* (1990).

Paul Halpern has been a member of the History Department of Florida State University since 1965. He is author of *The Mediterranean Naval Situation, 1908–1914* and *The Naval War in the Mediterranean, 1914–1918: A Naval History of World War One.* He is currently working on a study of the naval situation in the Mediterranean in the inter-war period.

Nicholas Lambert received his doctorate from Oxford University in 1992, and has since held an Olin-postdoctoral fellowship at Yale University, a Hartley visiting fellowship at Southampton University and a Charter fellowship at Wolfson College, Oxford. He has published a number of major articles and two books: *Australia's Naval Inheritance: Imperial Maritime Strategy and the Australia Station 1880–1909* (1999) and *Sir John Fisher's Naval Revolution* (1999). He also edited *The Submarine Service, 1900–1918* for the Naval Records Society (2001).

Evan Mawdsley is a reader in history at the University of Glasgow. Among his interests are Russian military history. He has published *The Russian Revolution and the Baltic Fleet* and *The Russian Civil War*. He is currently writing a history of the Russo-German war of 1941–45.

Phillips P. O'Brien is currently a lecturer in modern history at the University of Glasgow. In 1998 he published *British and American Naval Power: Politics and Policy, 1900–1936*. He has also written about Winston Churchill and the United Stated Navy. Current research topics include the influence of party politics on American foreign policy between 1900 and 1941.

Mark R. Peattie is currently a senior research fellow at the Hoover Institution at Stanford University. He has also taught at the Pennsylvania State University, UCLA, and the University of Massachusetts in Boston. Recently he co-authored *Kaigun, Strategy, Tactics and Technology in the Imperial Japanese Navy* (1997). His current research interests include Japanese imperial history.

Werner Rahn recently retired as head of the Militärgeschichtliches Forschungsamt in Potsdam and now lives in Berlin. He is author of numerous works on naval history, including *Reichsmarine and Landesverteidigung 1919–1928* (1976), and he co-edited *The Global War*, Volume VI of *Germany and the Second World War*, which appeared in an English edition in 2001. He has also edited the *Kriegstagebuch der Seekriegsleitung 1939–1945. Teil A* (1988–97).

Brian R. Sullivan is an independent scholar who has previously taught at Yale University and the US Naval War College. He specialises in modern Italian naval and military history and contemporary American defence issues. He is co-author of a biography of Margherita Sarfatti, Mussolini's closest adviser, *Il Duce's Other Woman* (1993). He is now writing a study of the theory and practice of space power.

Jon Sumida is a professor of history at the University of Maryland at College Park. He has written extensively on the subject of technological change and naval power in the early twentieth century. He has edited a collection of Arthur H. Pollen's papers and in 1993 published *In Defence of Naval Supremacy: Finance, Technology and British Naval Policy 1889–1914*.

Geoffrey Till is the Dean of Academic Studies at the Joint Service Command and Staff College, UK, where he is also Head of the Defence Studies Department. He is also Visiting Professor in Maritime Studies at King's College, London. He has authored or edited many books including *Sea-Power: Theory and Practice* (1994) and *Maritime Strategy and the Nuclear Age* (1984). He is General Series Editor of the Cass Series on Naval Policy and History.

Index